INNOVATIONS IN LEADERSHIP COACHING

Research and Practice

Fielding University Press is an imprint of Fielding Graduate University. Its objective is to advance the research and scholarship of Fielding faculty, students, alumni and associated scholars around the world, using a variety of publishing platforms. For more information, please contact Fielding University Press, attn. Jean-Pierre Isbouts, 2020 De la Vina Street, Santa Barbara, CA 93105. Email: jisbouts@fielding. edu. On the web: www.fielding.edu/universitypress.

Library of Congress Cataloging-in-Publication data
Innovations in Coaching Research and Practice by Terry H. Hildebrandt, Francine Campone, Kathy Norwood, and Erek J. Ostrowski (Eds.)
1. Social Sciences-Executive Coaching

INNOVATIONS IN LEADERSHIP COACHING
Research and Practice

EDITED BY

TERRY H. HILDEBRANDT, PHD, MCC, MCEC
FRANCINE CAMPONE, EDD, MCC
KATHY NORWOOD EDD, PCC
EREK J. OSTROWSKI, PHD, PCC

FIELDING UNIVERSITY PRESS

KATRINA S. ROGERS
PRESIDENT, FIELDING GRADUATE UNIVERSITY

MONIQUE L. SNOWDEN
PROVOST, FIELDING GRADUATE UNIVERSITY

BARBARA MINK
CHAIR, SCHOOL OF LEADERSHIP STUDIES

TERRY HILDEBRANDT
PROGRAM DIRECTOR, EVIDENCE BASED COACHING

JEAN-PIERRE ISBOUTS
EDITOR, FIELDING UNIVERSITY PRESS

Innovations in Leadership Coaching

Contributors

Lilian Abrams

Mary Jo Asmus

Asma Batool

Valerie Malhotra Bentz

Jacqueline Binkert

Mary Ann Burke

Francine Campone

Ann L. Clancy

Lynn Harrison

Terry H. Hildebrandt

Charles M. Jones

Jim Knickerbocker

James Marlatt

Kate McAlpine

Kimcee McAnally

Carol-Anne Minski

Annabelle Nelson

João Noronha

Kathy Norwood

Erek J. Ostrowski

Lee Palmer

Penny Potter

Kristin E. Robertson

Kristen Truman-Allen

Leni Wildflower

Alex Eunkyeong Yu

Diane P. Zimmerman

TABLE OF CONTENTS

CONCLUSION

CHAPTER 1

INTRODUCTION

Terry Hildebrandt, PhD, MCC, MCEC
Fielding Graduate University

We are proud to present in this monograph a collection of authors offering thought leadership and research in the growing field of coaching. Practicing coaches, researchers, coach educators, students, and scholars will all find value in these pages as we offer new theories and methodologies to drive the field of coaching forward with research to ground our practices and theories. This brief introduction provides a roadmap for the reader to understand how to best navigate this book as you explore these innovations in coaching research and practice.

Theory Matters in Coaching Practice and Research

Fielding Graduate University has been educating and training coach scholar-practitioners in Evidence Based Coaching (EBC) since 2006. Our philosophy of coaching is based on four pillars: (1) the coach's use of self, (2) knowledge of the client, (3) theories and models, and (4) skills of the coach (Hildebrandt, 2019). While almost all coach training programs include developing coaching skills, evidence based coaching is distinguished by the focus on key theories derived from the root disciplines of coaching including (but not limited to) humanistic psychology, adult development, neuroscience, leadership, anthropology, social psychology, sociology, and organizational theory. Fielding defines EBC as coaching that applies grounded knowledge and theory to skilled coaching, which is a basis for informed decision making in coaching practice. Our vision at Fielding is to cultivate coaches who are grounded in evidence and who practice with personal and professional mastery. Our goal in this monograph is to continue to build a theoretical and practical foundation for masterful coaching.

Kurt Lewin, the grandfather of organizational development, is often quoted as saying, "nothing is as practical as a good theory" (Lewin, 1945, p. 129). In this volume, the authors present new theories and models and their applications in coaching. The included research studies add to a growing body of evidence that provides grounding to coaching practice. Our hope is that the theories and research outlined in this book will inform your own practice of coaching.

Intended Audience

This volume is intended for practicing coaches, researchers, coach educators, and students of coach training programs. Researchers will enjoy reading about current studies using both qualitative and quantitative research methodologies applied in multiple coaching contexts, including corporate, nonprofit, and education for both individuals and groups. Coach practitioners will appreciate innovations in coaching theory and methodology that have immediate practical application with their clients. Coach educators will find fresh perspectives and new reading material to include in their training programs. Students will gain a deeper appreciation of the theories underpinning evidence based coaching, which serve as lenses through which we work with clients as evidence based coaches and scholar-practitioners.

Overview of the Five Parts in the Volume

This volume is organized in five parts:

• Part I: Transcending the Ordinary: Learning from Coaching's Ancestors,

• Part II: Coaching for Leadership,

• Part III: Embodiment in Coaching,

• Part IV: Beyond the Individual: Social Processes in Coaching,

• Part V: Insights into Coach Education and Development,

and a concluding chapter.

In Part I, Wildflower provides an overview of the "ancestors" of coaching whose theories and practices have informed coaching from its beginnings. She provides insight into the root concepts that have informed the coaching movement and discipline including cognitive therapy, analytical psychology, humanistic psychology, human motivation, and adult development. Wildflower sets the historical and theoretical foundation for evidence based coaching.

Part II consists of five chapters including research, theories, and models that inform coaching with leaders and executives. Minski begins with her research on coaching leaders for peak performance, which reveals five theory based strategies for enhancing self-efficacy and provides a new coaching model for positive goal accomplishment. Zimmerman describes the importance of "locus of control" when working with clients to get them to accept responsibility for their actions. She also describes how this practice builds efficacy in the client and how practice-based knowledge increases the efficacy of the coach. Knickerbocker and Jones describe a new approach to coaching clients in emotional intelligence using the five step TENOR method, based on their theory of emotions in driving performance. Harrison provides specific coaching approaches to address abrasive

12

leadership behavior based on a recent phenomenological study and her experience working with executive clients. Batool integrates principles and research in neuroscience and mindfulness and applies them to coaching leaders in VUCA (Volatility, Uncertainty, Complexity and Ambiguity) environments. Together these five chapters shed light on the importance of theory and research informing leadership and executive coaching.

Part III includes four chapters focused on a variety of theories, research, and techniques that enable transformational change with coaching clients. In their chapter, Clancy and Binkert examine how theory influences who coaches are, thereby influencing how they coach, based on their own lived experience and related evidence based coaching research. Nelson, Noronha, Palmer, and Truman-Allen offer four methods for transformational coaching, including metaphors and somatic resonance, metaphors and movement, life story coaching, and archetypal imagery. Yu presents the results of a qualitative study of executive coaches of how they experience and create intersubjectivity with their clients, based in phenomenology and neuroscience. Marlatt and Bentz apply the theories and methods of somatics and phenomenology to create embodied awareness in transformative coaching.

Part IV includes four chapters focused on coaching in an organizational or group context. Ostrowski discusses his research findings on group coaching as a setting for learning and change, connections to related theory and research, and implications for working with groups. Robertson demonstrates how leadership coaches can act as catalysts for organizational culture transformation. McAlpine describes a research study of how coaching was used as an intervention in a construction company to build more inclusive cultures. Burke combines her research and theory to drive more equity in Pre-K to 12th grade culture through the practices of transformational, educational coaching.

Part V includes three chapters covering research and applied theory for developing coaches. Norwood continues the conversation started by Burke on driving equity in schools by sharing her research findings and their implications for using coaching to detect and mitigate hegemonic and non-hegemonic barriers to coaching in schools. Potter shares her research on the transformative experiences of becoming a coach and proposes a coaching dialectics model that can be used by organizations to develop coaching leaders and coaching cultures. McAnally, Abrams, Asmus, and Hildebrandt provide an update on the current status of coaching supervision and its adoption and value, based on their recent global survey. They also discuss implications for the future of coaching supervision for continuing professional development of coaches.

Campone provides a final integrative, concluding chapter with "Coaching in Wonderland," where she summarizes key themes from the monograph and implications for coaching practice, research, and education.

About the Author
Terry H. Hildebrandt, PhD, MCC, MCEC is a certified executive coach, organization development consultant, coach educator, coach supervisor, and author. He is the founder and CEO of Terry Hildebrandt and Associates, LLC and has served as the Director of the Evidence Based Coaching ACTP program at Fielding Graduate University. Prior to starting his own business in 2008, Terry worked at HP for 22 years in management and engineering roles. He is an expert in the principles of evidence based coaching, using the best existing theoretical and researched knowledge in combination with his

personal coaching skills and client knowledge to deliver effective coaching. Terry is a Master Certified Coach (MCC) with the International Coaching Federation (ICF), a certified Master Corporate Executive Coach (MCEC) with the MEECO Leadership Institute, and a member of the Association of Corporate Executive Coaches (ACEC). He is also a Certified Coaching Supervisor from the Goldvarg Consulting Group, Inc. Terry earned his PhD in Human and Organizational Systems from Fielding Graduate University. He can be reached at terry@terryhildebrandt.com.

References

Lewin, K. (1945). The Research Center for Group Dynamics at Massachusetts Institute of Technology. Sociometry, 8(2), 126-136. doi:10.2307/2785233

Hildebrandt, T. H. (2019). Four pillars of skillful evidence based coaching. https://www.fielding.edu/blog-post/four-pillars-of-skillful-evidence-based-coaching/

CHAPTER 2

TRANSCENDING THE ORDINARY: LEARNING FROM COACHING'S ANCESTORS

Leni Wildflower, PhD, PCC
Fielding Graduate University

Abstract

One of coaching's ancestors is Gallwey's *Inner Game* concept, which applied spiritual techniques to competitive sports and then to executive development. Cognitive therapy is another. But we should also acknowledge the psychoanalytic tradition. Although Freud's aims, assumptions and methods were radically different from those of coaching, he was a pioneer in exploring unconscious motivation and recognizing the value of listening. Followers challenged or reworked his approach; Jung shifted the focus from sexuality and trauma towards tasks in adult life, Reich recognized the somatic dimension of wellbeing, Perls introduced Gestalt. The humanists too were reacting to the Freudian tradition; Rogers established client-centered therapy, Maslow explored peak experiences and identified the need to be self-actualizing. Viktor Frankl survived Auschwitz to develop his own therapeutic method, based on the need for people to find purpose and meaning in their lives. There is still much to be learned from these predecessors, as well as from fresh discoveries in related disciplines.

Keywords: Adult development, client-centered therapy, Gestalt, knowledge-based coaching, peak experience, MBTI, midlife, necessary task, ontological coaching, search for meaning, self-actualization, self-transcendence, unconditional positive regard, unconscious motivation.

Introduction: Coaching's necessary conditions

Coaching as we know it came into existence, as an identified practice, in the last decades of the twentieth century. Anyone who has experienced the power of skillful coaching to clarify issues, unblock obstacles and motivate one to move forward in work or life may wonder why it took so long. Conceptually, coaching isn't complicated. It isn't dependent on technology. In practical terms it requires nothing more elaborate than two human beings in conversation.

While coaching may seem simple enough in theory, however, it is difficult in practice. It demands of the coach considerable self-discipline and insight to listen and probe respectfully without giving instruction or offering advice or passing judgement. The human impulse to express attitude, either shutting down another person's story with disapproval, or being drawn empathetically into sharing one's own concerns, experiences and feelings, has to be overcome. This is neither easy nor instinctive.

It also seems likely, in retrospect, that significant cultural shifts were necessary for coaching to develop. Coaching demands an absence of hierarchy so that coach and client can meet as equals. In the United States, Europe, and elsewhere, the twentieth century was marked by unprecedented challenges to traditional hierarchies, of gender, class, race, age, and sexual orientation. In earlier times, for most people the need to know one's place in any social or professional context was deeply engrained.

More significantly, coaching assumes that clients have a degree of autonomy; that they are able to make choices, to discover preferences and act on them, to at least have some influence on the trajectory of their lives. Coaching would have struggled to find a role at a time when professional employment was impossible for women, career options for men were extremely limited and almost entirely determined by class, and midlife transitions from one kind of occupation to another were rare. Even where choices were possible, major life decisions, such as who to marry or what occupation to train for, were typically taken irrevocably in early adulthood or before. As for the Third Age, the problem of how to transition in later life from full-time career employment into other productive and fulfilling activities was not a concern when life expectancy was relatively short. For many people in prosperous Western societies, the twentieth century opened up previously unimagined possibilities.

Zen and the Inner Game

Among other developments, the later decades of the twentieth century saw a particular mingling of Eastern and Western thought. One version of the origin of coaching is that it sprung from the kinds of exploration of the human psyche that were occurring in the USA in the 1960s and '70s among people who were studying Eastern spiritual practices.

One ground-breaking product of this time was Timothy Gallwey's *The Inner Game of Tennis*. Gallwey was a professional tennis player and coach who was applying to his tennis coaching approaches he had learned in yoga and meditation. In place of more familiar instruction on technique, Gallwey recommends "letting go of judgment" (Gallwey, 1986. p. 25) and developing "nonjudgmental awareness" (p. 38). Clearing the mind of doubts and strivings and other distractions, he says, players should focus only on "the here and now" (p. 125), increasing "awareness of what actually is" (p. 2).

Acknowledging what he has learned from Zen Buddhism, he attributes all the mental upsets experienced by players to "attachment" (p. 124):

> *Abandon* is a good word to describe what happens to a tennis player when he feels he has nothing to lose. He stops caring about the outcome and plays all out. This is the true meaning of detachment... It is caring, yet not caring; it is effortless effort... It happens when one lets go of attachment to the results of one's actions and allows the increased energy to

18

come to bear on the action itself. In the language of karma yoga, this is called action without attachment to the fruits of action, and ironically when the state is achieved the results are the best possible. (p. 124)

The concept of the "Inner Game" could obviously be applied to other sports: what works on the tennis court would work on the golf course. Less predictably it turned out to have an impact in c-suite offices, as business executives began to take an interest in fresh approaches to improving their performance, and in other contexts where individuals were wrestling with life choices and dilemmas.

Ideas relating to mindfulness have now entered the mainstream, but in 1974 this short, elegantly written book was a revelation to many readers. It was part of a wider movement. Warner Erhard, for example, had begun his own more aggressive repackaging of Eastern spiritual ideas with his first Erhard Seminars Training (EST) session in 1971. Worldly success and Christianity had long mingled in the Protestant work ethic, which presents hard work, self-discipline and righteous living as the conditions for material prosperity. But this harnessing of Eastern spirituality for the purposes of worldly achievement was new. Though clearly inspired by spiritual ideas, the promises of EST and the Inner Game were a long way from the Tibetan Buddhist project of liberating oneself from the Wheel of Life. They answered a desire to engage more effectively with the world and with greater success.

What's in a name?

It was not inevitable that this new activity would come to be called *coaching*. The name has its drawbacks; many people outside the coaching world still associate the word with that mixture of instruction, exhortation, and encouragement that more traditional sports coaching is thought to consist of. But these associations have also allowed coaching to gain access and acceptance. What we are doing, that label seems to say, is thoroughly practical; it is not to encourage introspection for its own sake or to heal psychological wounds, but to improve outcomes.

Certainly, it has been important for coaching to distinguish itself from psychotherapy in order to establish its own separate identity. There has also been a tendency, in arguing for its role in the workplace and its benefits for successful people, to overemphasize what coaching is not: not a treatment for mental instability, nor an opportunity to work through childhood traumas. But the division between coaching and therapy should not be overstated. Although the image of the bearded analyst with his couch lives on in the popular imagination (see *New Yorker* cartoons on this theme, for example), therapy and counselling in the real world take many forms. Some forms are significantly forward-looking, solution-focused and collaborative, some use agreed term-limits to help steer the process towards measurable results.

Keeping it cognitive

When Aaron Beck was writing *Cognitive Therapy and the Emotional Disorders* in the 1970s he found it appropriate to put his ideas in the context of what were still at that time the two dominant ways of thinking about the mind in America: Freudian psychoanalysis and behavioral psychology. For practitioners of classical psychoanalysis, he writes, "the patient's own explanations are regarded as spurious rationalizations, his coping mechanisms as defenses. Consequently, his conscious ideas, his reasoning and judgements, his practical solutions to problems are not taken at face value; they are treated as stepping-stones to deeper, concealed components of the mind" (Beck, 1979, p. 8). Meanwhile, behavior therapists have their own, completely different reason for disregarding the patient's thoughts. Attempting to emulate the precision of the physical sciences, they reject the patient's personal insights and reflections, since the only valid data is "behavior that could be directly observed by an independent outsider" (p. 8).

In contrast with both of these schools of thought, Beck emphasizes the importance of "genuine collaboration between therapist and patient" (p. 220):

It is useful to conceive of the patient-therapist relationship as a joint effort. It is not the therapist's function to try to reform the patient; rather, his role is working with the patient against 'it,' the patient's problem. Placing the emphasis on solving problems, rather than his presumed defects or bad habits, helps the patient to examine his difficulties with more detachment and makes him less prone to experience shame, a sense of inferiority and defensiveness. (p. 221)

Beck identifies some distinct practical advantages of the cognitive approach. First, since the therapeutic work centers on issues that are within the patient's awareness, the patient is able to understand and take part in the process of identifying and defining them: "Therapist and patient actively collaborate to work out the formulation that 'feels right' to the patient and discard the ill-fitting formulations" (p. 317). As Beck reminds us, this contrasts significantly with classical psychoanalysis, in which "the patient's rejection of an interpretation is regarded as a sign of 'resistance'" (p. 317). Furthermore, the formulations agreed with the cognitive therapist "may be continually tested, rejected, or refined by the patient in his experiences outside therapy" (p. 317), and so patients are additionally empowered to take control of their own development. For these reasons, the cognitive approach speeds things up. "In many cases," he says, "short-term, structured cognitive therapy may take only ten to twenty sessions" (p. 317).

Cognitive therapy, as Beck defined it, is much closer to coaching than it is to traditional psychotherapy. First, therapists must pay clients the respect of taking them literally and of trusting them to be the most reliable witnesses of their own experience. Second, clients must be fully engaged in the process of identifying their issues and are free, both during and between sessions, to redefine what they consider they should be working on. Third, the work can be conducted during a program of negotiated and relatively brief duration.

21

The talking cure

With Beck's work in mind, it might seem unnecessary or even inappropriate for coaches to acknowledge a debt to Sigmund Freud. In practice, Freudian psychoanalysis and coaching have hardly anything in common. Freud developed his techniques while treating patients suffering from a condition that was identified then as "hysteria" (Storr, 1989, p. 17). Analysis as he conceived it was open-ended and could last for years. In its classic form, a patient might be "expected to attend for treatment about five or six times a week" (Brown, 1987, p. 33). It depended on a power imbalance between an analyst acting as a blank screen and a patient incapable of self-help. The focus was overwhelmingly on past and inner life, with attention paid to dreams and early memories. If applied in a coaching engagement, the assumptions and strategies of analysis would violate most of coaching's essential principles.

Nevertheless, Freud is important for a number of reasons. First, his great innovation as a practitioner was to invite his patients to talk and to listen without judgment. "Patients were asked to relax on a couch and say whatever came into their minds, however absurd, unpleasant or obscene it might appear by everyday standards" (Brown, 1987, p. 17). In attending to neurological problems, he had previously experimented with cocaine and, in collaboration with colleagues, hypnosis. This decision to set aside drugs and other interventions in favor of listening represented a radical break with previous practice.

Second, while there is much to be rejected in Freud's theories, he is responsible for a whole cluster of insights about unconscious motivation and the extent to which we play out patterns of behavior laid down in early life (Wildflower, 2013, pp. 51-52). The focus of coaching is on present circumstances, thinking and behavior and on assisting the client to shape and realize future possibilities, but it cannot be an entirely cognitive and forward-looking process. A coach who, while challenging the client to move forward, is afraid to follow them into areas of emotional distress or acknowledge the importance of an early experience is likely to shut down opportunities for learning and growth. In any context, human beings bring their emotional baggage with them, and the person at work cannot be separated from who they are in their private or family life.

The third reason to acknowledge Freud is that so many innovations that have more clearly influenced coaching were made by therapists and psychologists who were closely associated with Freud, had Freudian training, or were reacting against Freudian methods.

The stages of life

Carl Jung began defining his ideas in distinction from Freud's early in their working relationship. He disagreed with Freud's contention that sexuality and childhood experience always lie at the root of neurosis. In a lecture delivered in 1916, he spoke about the need to pay attention to the current task facing the patient. The word task in this context suggests a transitional challenge that must be faced in shifting from one phase of life to another. He argues that the neurotic patient differs from the rest of humanity only in finding such tasks particularly difficult, but that resistance to change is universal:

> I no longer seek the cause of a neurosis in the past, but in the present. I ask, what is the necessary task which the patient will not accomplish?... You may ask why the neurotic has a special tendency not to accomplish his necessary tasks. Here let me point out that no living creature adjusts itself easily and smoothly to new conditions. The law of inertia is valid everywhere. (Jung, 1967a, para 569-570)

Jung was interested in how humans continue to develop through their adult lives. In his work on what he called the "stages of life" he focused on the question: "Why does man, in obvious contrast to the animal world, have problems?" (Jung, 1933, p. 97). In Jung's view, a problem occurs when "an external limitation becomes an inner obstacle;

23

when one impulse opposes itself to another" (p. 99). At midlife, the third of four stages after childhood and youth, which begins, by Jung's definition, between the ages of 35 and 40 (p. 104), it begins to become apparent that "the achievements which society rewards are won at the cost of a diminution of personality" (Jung, 1967b, para 772). We achieve outward success only by burying parts of ourselves.

Removing the mask

Jung's own midlife crisis occurred with the publication of his Psychology of the Unconscious in 1912 when he was 37. The book contained ideas that Freud rejected. In the following year, they met for the last time. Along with some of Freud's essential teachings, Jung left behind the analyst's couch and began to sit facing his patients. He had come to believe that "the real therapy only begins when the patient sees that it is no longer father and mother who are standing in his way, but himself" (Stevens, 1994, p. 131). He considered that the therapist must meet the patient as a partner in the process; that he must "emerge from his anonymity and give an account of himself, just as he must expect his patients to do" (p. 131). Remembering this break, Jung reported a period of "disorientation" (Jung, 1965, p. 170). He found it necessary to develop a new attitude towards his patients:

> I resolved for the present not to bring any theoretical premises to bear upon them, but to wait and see what they would tell of their own accord. My aim became to leave things to chance. The result was that patients would spontaneously report their dreams and fantasies to me and I would merely ask, 'What occurs to you in connection with that?' or 'How do you mean that, where does it come from, what do you think about it?' The interpretations seemed to follow of their own accord from the patients' replies and associations. (Jung, 1965, p. 170)

In encountering the client face-to-face, in respecting their

24

perception of where the problem lay, in focusing on current issues as they were experiencing them, in meeting the client with humility rather than armed with his own theoretical agenda, and in allowing them as autonomous adults to set the agenda, Jung anticipated much of what we would now recognize as coaching.

Gifts differing

This spirit of openness to human complexity lies at the heart of Jung's work on psychological types. Far from wanting to slot people into neat pigeonholes, he was inclined to celebrate the variety of human nature. After years of clinical practice, he wrote, "one is struck by the enormous diversity of human individual cases" whose lives and characters "can be squeezed into the straitjacket of a diagnosis only by force" (Jung, 1983, p. 139).

In the late 1920s, two remarkable American women began to take a keen interest in Jung's theories of personality. Isabel Briggs Myers and her mother Katherine Cook Briggs wanted to use these ideas "to help ordinary, healthy, normal people understand that it is all right to be unique individuals, often quite unlike those around them" (Myers, 1995, p. xii). The Second World War, which drew large numbers of women into the industrial workforce, most of them for the first time, gave fresh impetus to this project. With no formal education in psychology, Myers and Briggs acquired the knowledge they needed to devise a personality test that would help women identify what kind of job might suit them. This became the Myers-Briggs Type Indicator. There are many psychometric instruments, but MBTI remains one of the sturdiest.

Listening to the body

Jung was the first and most prominent psychotherapist to distance himself from Freud. Other dissidents from Freudian orthodoxy followed. Wilhelm Reich trained with Freud in Vienna. In the 1920s he began teaching sex education in Berlin and in the 1930s published books promoting sexual liberation. Meanwhile, through his work as an analyst both in private practice and in public clinics, he became acutely aware of the impoverished circumstances of some of his patients. This was a factor in their mental health that his colleagues refused to acknowledge. He joined the communist party, where he came up against an opposing but equally unyielding orthodoxy. For his fellows Marxists, genuine neuroses, as opposed to imagined ones, could only be symptoms of poverty; there was no personal problem, in their view, that could not be cured by an improvement in material conditions. Attempting to combine these two theoretical frameworks, he was expelled from both the International Psychoanalytic Association and the German Communist Party (Anderson, 2004, p. 92).

Through his partner Elsa Lindenburg, who was a choreographer and dance therapist, Reich came into contact with Elsa Gindler, a pioneer of somatic bodywork. Reich began to focus on the idea that strong emotions that are unexpressed become trapped in the body and that emotional growth cannot be achieved unless there is a physical component to the work. The mechanism whereby emotions become trapped Reich saw in militaristic terms:

> The character structure of modern man, who reproduces a six-thousand-year-old patriarchal authoritarian culture, is typified by characterological armouring against his inner nature and against the social misery which surrounds him... Man has alienated himself from, and has grown hostile toward, life. (Reich, 1993, p. 7)

This image of an authoritarian patriarchal culture that arms its members against feeling inevitably evokes an image of the Nazis, who were not only abhorrent to Reich but directly threatened his life and the lives of his family and many friends and colleagues. But Reich's ideas still have a deep resonance today, and the ambition to liberate people from rigid thinking that keeps them alienated from themselves and others has a relevance that goes beyond the politics of his own time.

Alexander Lowen built on Reich's work to develop a form of therapy that paid equal attention to the psyche and the body. Reich also influenced Fernando Flores and Julio Olalla, two Chilean exiles and survivors of the Pinochet regime, who went on to found ontological coaching, which challenges the concept of the mind-body split and finds the essence of what it is to be human at the intersection of language, emotions and physiology (Seiler, 2003).

The search for wholeness

Fritz Perls, another German émigré, maverick thinker, and renegade from Freudianism, was meanwhile searching for his own way to liberate the human spirit in its wholeness. Having left Berlin for South Africa, where he joined the South African Army as a psychiatrist, Perls settled in New York. In 1952, Perls and his wife Laura formed the New York Institute for Gestalt Therapy.

His own therapeutic manner was idiosyncratic and aggressive. He said that his aim was "not to achieve a breakthrough; rather, it was to achieve a break-in, a sudden invasion of one's privacy, a re-established contact with lost and deadened feelings" (Anderson, 2004, p. 97). He made free use of role play, inviting participants to put dream figures, significant others or aspects of their own personalities in an empty chair and confront them (Rowan, 1993, p. 100). It is tempting to see in this the influence of experimental theatre. Fritz's contemporary and fellow Berliner Bertolt Brecht had been shaking up drama in a similarly confrontational way, having characters break through the "fourth wall" to prevent the audience from settling comfortably into a state of passive enjoyment and, instead, challenging them directly with questions.

Perls' confrontational style has fallen out of favor. But Gestalt therapy flourishes and its ideas have had influence beyond the therapeutic setting. It rests on two key principles. First, everyone is part of a complicated web of relationships; it is possible to understand ourselves only in the context of our relation to others. Second, to be

27

effective, therapy should concentrate on what is happening in the present moment. Instead of interpreting and analyzing past events, or reflecting on feelings experienced elsewhere, the process should focus on what people are doing, thinking and feeling right now, so that the drama of the individual's responses to others can be explored dynamically.

Putting the client at the center

The personal lives of these German Jewish émigrés, Wilhelm Reich and Fritz and Laura Perls, were at times intensely dramatic and characterized by danger and upheaval. Their ideas and practices challenged the conventions of the time, intellectually, politically and morally. For Reich, even the escape to America did not secure his physical safety. Imprisoned in the 1950s for investigating the therapeutic benefits of orgasm with the aid of equipment not approved by the Food and Drug Administration, he died of heart failure during a two-year sentence (Wildflower, 2013). For Wilhelm Reich and Fritz Perls, the revolutionary spirit of their thinking went hand in hand with a kind of self-belief that at times looked very much like arrogance and a lack of caution that bordered on recklessness.

On a personal level, the contrast with Carl Rogers could not be greater. The qualities that come through in Rogers' writing include personal humility and experimental caution. Paradoxically, these qualities led him as a therapist towards radical positions, such as treating the client as an equal and only following approaches that, in his experience, actually worked. A dutiful, bookish child from a devoutly religious farming family, he first went to agricultural college before transferring to Union Theological Seminary to train for the ministry. He switched to psychology when he realized that his beliefs were mutable and would continue to develop: "I could not work in a field where I would be required to believe in some specified religious doctrine" (Rogers, 2004, p. 8). As it turned out, this conscientious reluctance to follow any established dogma applied to therapy as well as religion.

In 1951, twenty years after he had received his PhD in clinical psychology, and on the basis of rigorous research, Rogers laid out his approach in *Client-Centered Therapy*. He emphasizes in the introductory chapter that there is nothing fixed about the methods the book describes. Those working in this field, he writes, "are working with dynamic concepts which they are constantly revising in the light of continuing clinical experience and in the light of research findings" (Rogers, 2015, p. 6). Rogers is mistrustful of methods: "In our experience," he writes, "the counsellor who tries to use a 'method' is doomed to be unsuccessful unless this method is genuinely in line with his own attitudes" (p. 19).

The challenge of positive regard

This is true even of the essential principles that lie at the heart of Rogers' approach. It is well known that in client-centered therapy, the therapist should view the client with unconditional positive regard. But for Rogers this is an ideal to work towards, not a technique that one can simply apply. In a later article, he reflects on the challenging nature of this ideal. First he states his "overall hypothesis" in a single sentence: "If I can provide a certain type of relationship, the other person will discover within himself the capacity to use that relationship for growth and change and personal development will occur" (Rogers, 2004, p. 33). The first requirement, he says, is to be "genuine" in the relationship, rather than "presenting an outward façade of one attitude, while actually holding another attitude at a deeper or unconscious level" (p. 33). He must express his actual feelings. "I have found this to be true even when the attitudes I feel are not attitudes with which I am pleased, or attitudes which seem conducive to a good relationship. It seems extremely important to be real" (p. 33). It is clear that, even for Rogers, the state of positive regard, is not always possible, or not always fully achieved, though it is undoubtedly a state worth reaching for:

I find that the more acceptance and liking I feel towards this individual, the more I will be creating a relationship which he can use. By acceptance I mean a warm regard for him as a person of unconditional self-worth—of value no matter what his condition, his behavior, his feelings... This acceptance of each fluctuating aspect of this other person makes it for him a relationship of warmth and safety, and the safety of being liked and prized as a person seems a highly important element in a helping relationship. (p. 34)

Belief in the capacity for change is a crucial element in this process, the aim being "the development of creative, adaptive, autonomous persons" (p. 38). In this respect, the therapeutic relationship was, for Rogers, "only a special instance of interpersonal relationships in general" (p. 39). While studying theology, he had been introduced to the existentialist philosopher Martin Buber, author of I and Thou. Buber remained a strong influence. In a lecture delivered in 1958, Rogers said:

Martin Buber... has a phrase, "confirming the other," which has had meaning for me. He says 'Confirming means... accepting the whole potentiality of the other....' If I accept the other person as something fixed, already diagnosed and classified, already shaped by his past, then I am doing my part to confirm this limited hypothesis. If I accept him as a process of becoming, then I am doing what I can to confirm or make real his potentialities. (p. 55)

The self-actualizing impulse

Rogers and the other humanistic psychologists had high ambitions for what therapy could achieve. Significantly, Rogers speaks of "clients" rather than "patients." Therapy is no longer just about repairing damage: it promises a fuller life. In the opening sentence of *Toward a Psychology of Being*, Abraham Maslow speaks of "a new conception of human sickness and of human health" that he finds "thrilling" and "full of wonderful possibilities" (Maslow, 1968, p. 3). Maslow was passionate about the need to respect the unique experience of the individual. Anticipating Beck, he criticized the tendency among therapists to rush to diagnose and, when the patient rejects the diagnosis, to pathologize as "resistance" what is in fact a "legitimate self-protective reaction" to being categorized (p. 129).

Maslow is perhaps best known for his five-stage hierarchy of needs, starting with the basic physiological needs for food, shelter and sleep, and rising through needs such as safety and stability, love and belongingness, and achievement and reputation, towards personal growth and fulfilment. He saw these five stages as a progression. At the same time he insisted that progress for any individual is not necessarily linear and the drive toward self-actualization, the highest of the five stages, is universal: the innate aim for all of us is to become self-actualizing. Of those who have achieved this condition, Maslow writes:

> The determinants which govern them are now primarily inner ones, rather than social or environmental. They are the laws of their own inner nature, their potentialities and capacities, their talents, their latent resources, their creative impulses, their needs to know themselves and to become more and more integrated and unified, more and more aware of what they really are, of what they really want, of what their call or vocation or fate is to be. Since they depend less on other people, they are less ambivalent about them, less anxious and less hostile, less needful of their praise and affection. They are less anxious of honors, prestige and rewards. (p. 35)

In Maslow's view, our inner nature is "good or neutral rather than bad.... If it is permitted to guide our life, we grow healthful, fruitful and happy." Denying or suppressing this inner nature leads to sickness; and it is all too easily suppressed, being "weak and delicate and subtle and easily overcome by habit, cultural pressure and wrong attitudes towards it." Nevertheless, "though denied, it persists underground, forever pressing for actualization" (p. 4). Maslow sees a connection between this natural yearning to become more fully and freely oneself and the spiritual impulse.

He conducted research into peak experiences, asking people about their "happiest moments, ecstatic moments, moments of rapture, perhaps from being in love, or from listening to music or suddenly 'being hit' by a book or a painting, or from some great creative moment" (p. 71). He considered that anyone might have had such moments, not only those who might be called self-actualizing. He noted that such experiences did not necessarily have any usefulness or survival value in a Darwinian sense and that they had therefore been relatively neglected in Western thought. He found that in such states, "perception can be relatively ego-transcending, self-forgetful, egoless. It can be unmotivated, impersonal, desireless, unselfish, not needing, detached" (pp. 78-79).

Light out of darkness

Toward a Psychology of Being became a key text at the Esalen Institute, the spiritual home of the human potential movement during the 1960s. It was "one of those books that goes around changing people's lives... It was talked about, passed along from person to person, cherished, read, and remembered" (Anderson, 2004, p. 66). Esalen, on the coast of Northern California, with its encounter groups and experimental seminars, could be seen as emblematic of a certain kind of freedom and privilege. Similarly, Maslow's exploration of peak experiences might be considered a product of a post-scarcity society, where enough people have the leisure to reflect on higher concerns than the need for food and shelter.

But out of the darkest circumstances imaginable, Viktor Frankl had felt the same impulse towards transcendence. In Vienna in 1942, Frankl and his wife were taken by the Nazis and put in the concentration camp at Theresienstadt. His wife died in Bergen-Belsen. Frankl survived Auschwitz and Dachau. In *Man's Search for Meaning*, he records extraordinary moments of hope, arising from the bleakest conditions. On one occasion he has been put to work digging a trench. Everything is grey – the sky, the snow, the faces of his fellow inmates, the rags they wear. In his mind, he is talking to his absent wife, searching for the meaning of his suffering:

> In a last violent protest against the hopelessness of imminent death, I sensed my spirit piercing through the enveloping gloom. I felt it transcend the hopeless, meaningless world, and from somewhere I heard a victorious 'Yes' in answer to my question of the existence of an ultimate purpose. (Frankl, 2004, p. 51)

Out of such experiences as these, Frankl developed his own system of therapy. His account of this in *Man's Search for Meaning* embraces the concept of self-actualization, but with a significant shift of emphasis. "The true meaning of life," Frankl writes, "is to be discovered in the world rather within man or his own psyche" (p. 115). Meaning is discovered in giving oneself to a cause or in loving another person.

> What is called self-actualization is not an attainable aim at all, for the simple reason that the more one would strive for it, the more he would miss it. In other words, self-actualization is possible only as a side-effect of self-transcendence. (p. 115)

In Frankl's view, "mental health is based on a certain degree of tension, the tension between what one has already achieved and what one still ought to accomplish, or the gap between what one is and what one should become." The search for "equilibrium" is misguided. What we actually need "is not a tensionless state but rather the striving and struggling for a worthwhile goal, a freely chosen task" (p. 110).

Conclusion: Implications for coaching

Coaching has established its own distinct purpose and identify. Much has been done in recent decades to formulate the essential principles of the practice and to identify what works in a coaching engagement. It is important to remember, however, that many of these principles have been derived and modified from other fields, and there is still much to be learned from thinkers in the psychotherapeutic tradition.

Of course, coaches are not in the diagnostic business. Far from wanting to label our clients, we are rightly cautious about overlaying, even in the most casual way, the client's account of their experience with our own words and metaphors. Yet, frameworks can be helpful. Clients can find it reassuring to see that their private struggles fit into a larger pattern, to discover that different kinds of tasks might be appropriate to different life stages, to consider that the dissatisfaction they are experiencing with their career reflects a basic drive towards self-actualization, or that their search for meaning, together with the state of tension this puts them in, is part of the human condition. Change and the desire for change are often accompanied by feelings of anxiety or stress. Coaches can help clients normalize unpleasant or difficult experiences by putting them in a wider perspective.

There are other concepts that have been readily embraced by the coaching community. The importance of viewing our clients with unconditional positive regard, for example, is widely recognized. It is helpful, then, for coaches to read what Carl Rogers has to say about this and to know that even for a deeply empathetic and instinctively skillful practitioner, positive regard is not always possible, and that faking it is not an option. We are right to work towards achieving this, but we should forgive ourselves when we fall short. The same is true of any ideal behavior.

It is hard to overlook that most of the key figures mentioned in this chapter are men. It seems likely that female practitioners have played not only equal but leading roles in the development of coaching in recent decades. This history is also dominated by European and American thinkers. As an increasingly global activity, coaching is even now being enriched by other kinds of diversity.

Above all, coaching, like any vital human endeavor, is dynamic. Looking back, we can identify the mistakes of our predecessors. There is no doubt that, in the future, some of our own certainties will be modified or even discarded. We should remain open to fresh insights and new findings, including those from other disciplines. Challenged by cultural developments and shifting needs, we must continue to question how we can most effectively serve the interests of our clients.

About the Author

With a PhD from Fielding, Leni Wildflower developed Fielding's Evidence Based Coaching program, which she directed from 2004 to 2009. A thought leader on coaching, she has worked extensively within corporations and other organizations and with private clients in the US, UK, Europe, China and Latin America, offering her own ICF-accredited program, Knowledge Based Coaching in the Workplace. With Dian Brennan, she co-edited *The Handbook of Knowledge Based Coaching* (John Wiley 2011). She is the author of *The Hidden History of Coaching* (McGraw-Hill 2013). Leni lives in London with her husband, Joe Treasure.

References

Anderson, W.T. (2004). *The Upstart Spring.* Lincoln, NE: iUniverse.

Beck, A.T. (1979). *Cognitive Therapy and the Emotional Disorders.* Madison, CN: Meridian.

Brown, J.A.C. (1987). *Freud and the Post-Freudians.* Harmondsworth, UK: Penguin Books.

Frankl, V.E. (2004). *Man's Search for Meaning.* London, UK: Random House.

Gallwey, T.W. (1986). *The Inner Game of Tennis.* London, UK: Pan Books.

Jung, C.G. (1933). *Modern Man in Search of a Soul*. London, UK: Kegan Paul.

Jung, C.G. (1965). *Memories, Dreams, Reflections*. New York, NY: Vintage Books.

Jung, C.G. (1967a). "Psychoanalysis and Neurosis" in *Collected Works*, Vol 4. Princeton, NJ: Princeton University Press.

Jung, C.G. (1967b). "The Stages of Life" in *Collected Works*, Vol 8. Princeton, NJ: Princeton University Press.

Jung, C.G. (1983). *The Essential Jung*. Ed. Storr, A. London, UK: Fontana Press.

Maslow, A.H. (1968). *Toward a Psychology of Being*. New York, NY: Van Nostrand Reinhold.

Myers, I.B. (1995). *Gifts Differing*. Palo Alto, CA: Davies-Black Publishing.

Reich, W. (1993). *The Function of the Orgasm*. Channel Islands, UK: The Guernsey Press.

Rogers, C.R. (2004). *On Becoming a Person*. London, UK: Constable.

Rogers, C.R. (2015). *Client-Centered Therapy*. London, UK: Robinson.

Rowan, J. (1993). *The Transpersonal: Spirituality in Psychotherapy and Counselling*. London, UK: Routledge.

Seiler, A. (2003). *Coaching to the Human Soul*. Melbourne, Australia: Newfield Australia.

Stevens, A. (1994). *Jung: A Very Short Introduction*. Oxford, UK. Oxford University Press.

Storr, A. (1989). *Freud: A Very Short Introduction*. Oxford, UK: Oxford University Press.

Wildflower, L. (2013). *The Hidden History of Coaching*. Maidenhead, UK: Open University Press.

CHAPTER 3

COACHING LEADERS FOR PEAK PERFORMANCE

Carol-Anne Minski, PhD, MBA

Abstract

Executive coaching has been proposed as an intervention that helps executives improve performance to achieve the goals of the organization. Research on social cognitive theory and goal-setting theory provides evidence that self-efficacy is a key causal variable in performance (Locke, Frederick, Lee, & Bobko, 1984). Self-efficacy is the belief that one has the personal capabilities and resources to meet the demands of a specific task and situation. This research paper examines the strategies used by executive coaches to enhance their clients' self-efficacy.

The five theory-based strategies for enhancing self-efficacy uncovered by this research strengthen the case for an evidence-based approach to coaching. These strategies include adaptive leadership, appreciative inquiry, social cognitive theory, adult learning theory, and change theory. This paper provides a coaching model that coaches may utilize to enhance leader's self-efficacy for positive goal accomplishment.

Keywords: Executive coaching, goal-setting, self-efficacy, social cognitive theory, appreciative inquiry, adaptive leadership, adult learning, change theory, coaching models.

Introduction

Coaches help leaders move from uncertainty to a creative, strategic sense of goal-setting. Executive coaches seek to comprehend leadership concepts and practices, as well as understand the special challenges that leaders face. Goal-setting is a proven practical managerial tool (Latham, 2004), and coaches that understand the fundamental theories and best coaching practices will be better prepared to help their clients set and achieve goals. Leaders with higher self-efficacy will set higher goals and find better strategies to attain their goals (Locke & Latham, 1990).

Despite the work that has been done to clarify the subject of coaching over the last 25 years, what happens in coaching engagements remains somewhat of a mystery. Executive coaching has been linked to increases in self-efficacy (Baron & Morin, 2010). However, are there consistent self-efficacy enhancing patterns that coaches utilize in goal-setting sessions with executive clients? And if so, are there underlying theories that coaches can utilize in their practice? Regarding the processes that executive coaches use to increase self-efficacy, very little is known about the variables that influence its effectiveness. This self-efficacy variable may provide a deeper understanding of how to overcome obstacles to goal-setting.

The following research report discloses coaching strategies for building leaders' self-efficacy to achieve positive goal accomplishment. The coaching community that participated in this study was the International Coach Federation (ICF) community of North America (including the United States and Canada). According to the International Coach Federation (ICF) guidelines, competency in planning and goal-setting is defined as the ability to develop and maintain an effective coaching plan with the client (ICF, 2012).

The foundation for this research is that executive coaching positively affects self-efficacy so that leaders can improve performance, accomplish their goals, and enhance organizational change. The purpose of this research was to describe and document executive coaches' strategies for building self-efficacy to achieve positive goal accomplishment.

Conceptual model

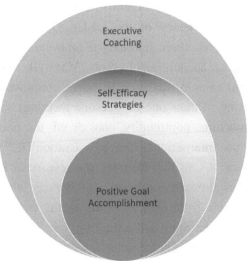

2014 Dr. Carol-Anne Minski

This conceptual model portrays the inter-relationships of executive coaching on self-efficacy and goal-setting in order to produce positive accomplishments for the leader. The model is based on social cognitive theory. Based on the view that self-efficacy is one of the most important factors impacting human performance (Bandura, 1982), Grant (2006) suggested that increased self-efficacy should be a natural consequence of effective coaching. "Coaching is a goal-oriented solution focused process in which the coach works with the client to help identify and construct possible solutions, delineate a range of goals and options, then facilitate the development and enactment of action plans to achieve their goals" (Grant, 2006, p. 156). The interventions taken by the executive coach will potentially increase the self-efficacy of the leader, which in turn increases goal accomplishment.

Methodology

A qualitative study is the method of choice when rich descriptions of phenomena are desired (Sandelowski, 2000). This research study was designed to ascertain how executive coaches utilize interventions to enhance the self-efficacy of the leader. Qualitative descriptive studies offer a comprehensive summary of an event in everyday terms and seek an accurate accounting of events (Maxwell, 1992).

A purposeful sample was used to select executive coaches that utilize goal-setting in their one-on-one-one meetings with executive clients. The coaching community considered for participation in this study was the International Coach Federation (ICF) community of North America. As an ICF member, the researcher had access to executive coaches through meetings, conferences, newsletters, and professional contacts from over 25 years in the coaching field and through related work. Snowball sampling was utilized by asking coaches who may know other coaches interested in participation to forward the recruiting letter.

The initial criteria for inclusion in the study included:

1. The executive coach considers himself/herself an external business coach and receives compensation for coaching services.

2. The coach resides primarily in North America and coaches primarily in English.

3. The coach works with leaders/executives in a one-on-one coaching relationship either in person or by telephone. (Group coaching or training does not usually provide in-depth meeting with client needed to capture the rich detail needed for this analysis.)

This research study utilized a semi-structured interview method via telephone. Twenty-four executive coaches volunteered, and four internal coaches were eliminated. The sample comprised eleven females and nine males. All of the coaches held coaching certifications, and seven had achieved doctoral level education. The number of years of executive coaching experience ranged from two years to 35 years.

The main focus of the interview was to ask participants to describe the specific coaching that takes place during goal-setting with executive clients.

Thematic analysis was the method for identifying, analyzing and reporting patterns (themes) within data. The analytic process involved a progression from description to interpretation in order to attempt to theorize the significance of the patterns and their broader meanings and implications (Patton, 2003). Here is where the data begin to shed light on the specific self-efficacy enhancing strategies that coaches use. The researcher examined the data, comparing them for similarities and differences, using ATLAS.ti. This is a qualitative data analysis tool that helps arrange, reassemble, and manage large bodies of textual, graphical, audio, and video data.

Two tools in ATLAS.ti helped with this process. One was the coding log, and another was the ATLAS.ti network view that allows one to explore the data visually. The focal point for this analysis was to discover the ways coaches enhance self-efficacy. There is a progression from strategies that coaches use in general to specific strategies that are utilized when the coach is attentive to enhancing the client's self-efficacy.

Descriptive Findings
Goal-Setting

The barriers to goal-setting as described by the executive coaches in this research include behavior change, emotional intelligence, personality style, lack of goal clarity, and lack of belief in self. These coaches use a skillful blend of core strategies to overcome barriers to goal achievement: asking powerful questions, deep listening, assigning homework, brainstorming, and challenging assumptions. These strategies exhibit the core coaching competencies as defined by the International Coach Federation (ICF, 2012).

When asked about goal-setting models, the coaches note most clients are aware of the how-to part of goal-setting and admit that

41

some variation of the SMART goal model is utilized in their practice. SMART goals are: Specific, Measurable, Achievable, Realistic, and Time-bound. Coaches emphasized that the most important part of the goal-setting process is clarification of the goal. Coaches were asked, "What are the key steps that you think are important when in a goal-setting session with your client?"

Key steps include:
- Clarify the meaning and wording of the goal.
- Confirm accountability and ownership.
- Set action steps and milestones.
- Look at future state.
- Have a written record of commitment.
- Check on the environment /organizational goals.

Self-Efficacy

The coach participants in this study were asked, "How has self-efficacy played a part in your goal-setting sessions with your clients?"

Coaches view self-efficacy as important to goal achievement:

"Ultimately the whole process, not only goal-setting, but goal-achieving is about self-efficacy. It is the process of self-efficacy in building capacity to do that. It's almost like self-efficacy is the definition of goal-setting and achievement, not only the setting but the achievement of those goals." (Coach One)

"Well I think it's really critical. I think sometimes clients set goals because it's something that they want, but they don't necessarily believe that they can do it." (Coach Four)

Coaches see high self-efficacy as beneficial to achieving significant goals in the workplace:

"There are those who are a little bit more pessimistic and some of the work that I do has to do with that. And then there are others who are more optimistic and have a real learning mindset." (Coach Six)

"I definitely think if a client comes with a high efficacy, then they are—how can I say that?—just the growth that they are able to attain and the goals they are able to achieve seems to be more significant in the workplace."(Coach Five)

Strategies for Enhancing Self-Efficacy

The next section of findings moves from the general coaching strategies to the specific strategies used to enhance self-efficacy. Here is where the data begin to shed light on the specific self-efficacy enhancing strategies that the coaches use. "The 'keyness' of a theme is not necessarily dependent on quantifiable measures, but rather on whether it captures something important in relation to the overall research question" (Braun & Clarke, 2006).

The five core strategies that executive coaches say they utilize to enhance self-efficacy in order to develop positive goal accomplishment are:

- Gaining perspective (Adaptive Leadership)
- Reviewing past success (Social Cognitive Theory)
- Social experiments (Adult Learning)
- Acknowledging skills and competencies (Appreciative Inquiry)
- Change Models (Immunity to Change, Intentional Change)

Adaptive Leadership

Coaches in this study noted that their clients gain perspective through uncovering assumptions, changing frame of reference, and reflective thinking. The strategy of gaining perspective helps the client develop capacity for critical reflection on what is happening while remaining objective. A frame of reference is composed of a habit of mind (set of assumptions) and the resulting point of view. The coaches constantly challenged their client's frame of reference by looking at supervisory roles, by checking negative self-talk, and by asking the leader how they might reframe negative self-talk in a helpful way. Frame of reference is a "meaning perspective," the structure of assumptions and expectations through which we filter sense impressions (Mezirow, 2000, p. 16).

The coach participants described gaining perspective in a variety of ways:

"We check out assumptions, what other perspectives might there be on this?" (Coach Three)

"So often in the life story, there are many opportunities to reframe how successful they have been at doing a number of things that they haven't really considered that they've done because they haven't framed it properly." (Coach Fifteen)

Heifetz and Linsky (2002) use the metaphor of a dance floor where the leader gets up on the balcony to see what is really happening by separating from the situation. Getting on the balcony allows the leader the freedom to look objectively at his or her role.

"Ronald Heifetz's work with adaptive leadership and Heifetz's idea of getting up on the balcony to be able to see the floor from a vantage point and getting perspective. Kegan and Lahey would be another. Again, you can see that the paradigm is getting perspective on the stuff that might have a hold of you." (Coach Eight)

Social Cognitive Theory

According to Bandura, perceived self-efficacy arises from a variety of sources as follows:

Personal accomplishments (mastery experience), observation of

44

others like oneself succeeding (vicarious experience and modeling), verbal or social persuasion (including coaching), and physiological state (Bandura, 1997). Reviewing past accomplishments reflects on past times as a way of building self-efficacy. The specific strategy of reviewing past success (mastery) was discussed often by the coaches. Social persuasion underlines positive feedback used in social cognitive theory. The coaches elicit past successful experiences to provide evidence that the client has been successful in the past. Some coaches mentioned using somatic techniques or helping the client with stress or relaxation, however this was not verbalized as being connected by the coaches to self-efficacy. The word modeling was not mentioned in this research, although obtaining vicarious experience may be implicit when the coach recommends that the client find a mentor.

The coaches helped clients look at history to point out what worked in the past and point out success:

"Just by asking the question of what's worked for you, and what have you already tried, or tell me about a time when you were successful doing this, enables them to reflect on those times of self-efficacy and things that have worked." (Coach One)

"Give them potential evidence of how they have been successful in the past. Or if they haven't been, help them find transferable situations in which they have had success." (Coach Four)

Adult Learning Theory

Executive coaches discussed their uses of adult learning theory in several ways. The executive coaches cited social experiments as ways to enhance self-efficacy. A social experiment in this study involved trying a new behavior, or changing a behavior to observe the reactions of others. The use of social experiments by the coaches falls into the category of experiential learning. Kolb (1984) asserted that adults learn by doing, so experiential learning involves a direct encounter with what is happening in the present and adapting to the situation as it unfolds. Four elements are involved: a concrete experience, reflective observation, understanding the principles that affect the action, and active experimentation.

The Kolb experiential learning model can often guide the coaching process (Leary-Joyce & Wildflower, 2011).

Coaches described social experiments as on-going:

"We get back together the next time and see if the social experiment worked and repeat this until we can come to a solution." (Coach One)

"Would you be open to doing an exercise for the next two weeks? I would share what the exercise I think might work and I'll say to them, do you think this might work for you?" (Coach Nine)

The executive coaches in this study noted that they utilize adult learning theory, and adults learn when they want to, or in some cases, when they need to think about changing behavior. One coach noted "If it is going to stick, it does when the individual really wants it to happen."

Knowles' (1998) adult learning theory can be stated with six assumptions related to the motivation of adult learning:
1. The need to know. Adults need to know the reason for learning something. Learning must be relevant and goal oriented.
2. The learner's self-concept. Adults have formed a self-concept, prefer to be self-directed and in control of their learning. Adults need to be seen by others as being capable of self-direction.
3. The role of the learner's experience. Prior experience of the learner provides a rich resource for learning.
4. Readiness to learn. Adults are most interested in learning with

immediate relevance to their work/life.

5. Orientation to learning. Adult learning is problem-centered rather than content-centered.

6. Motivation. Adults respond better to internal versus external motivation.

Appreciative Inquiry

In this research, all the executive coaches use the art of questioning to point out client's success, acknowledge skills and competencies, and to provide sources of positive feedback.

Coaches described how they encourage the client by acknowledging what is working.

"I help them see where it's working for them. And reinforce that." (Coach Nineteen)

"I bring up in their own mind skills, abilities and competencies that they already have but just may not be thinking about at the moment." (Coach One)

"And the terms they're using to describe it are sort of neutral, but what I am hearing is, Oh, my goodness! That's amazing! Shouldn't you have some more energy around this event? It went well and I'm happy for you." (Coach Seven)

Appreciative inquiry is noted as a way of bringing up the client's strength areas and self-efficacy:

"I'm just struck at how often people don't know their own strengths. They seem to be keenly aware of their weaknesses and shortcomings. So, I like to do a lot of appreciative inquiry and point it out in the moment if possible, when somebody is demonstrating strength so that they become more self-efficacious. To build their belief that they can do it. Well, the tried and true strategy again from the playbook of appreciative inquiry is to ask them to cite times when they have done something similar to it in the past with success." (Coach Six)

Coaches emphasized the importance of celebrating strengths and success. Appreciative inquiry (Cooperrider, Whitney, & Stavros, 2008) intersects with all the above-mentioned theories through its underlying questions that provide an acknowledgement of skills, review of past successes, positive feedback, reframing, and reflective thinking.

Change Models

Coach participants in this research were articulate in using the theoretical based frameworks for interpreting change. The two major change models described most often by the coaches include Intentional Change Theory and the Immunity to Change Model.

Intentional Change Theory (ICT). In this current research, many coaches talked about future state, future vision, and learning plans that lead to the future state. The coaches that described using the ICT model spoke about helping the client identify their ideal self. According to the Boyatzis and Akrivou (2006) model, the ideal self is composed of three major components: an image of a desired future, hope (self-efficacy and optimism), and a comprehensive sense of one's core identity (past strengths, traits, and other enduring dispositions).

Intentional Change Theory (Boyatzis, 2006) describes five steps for producing change, and most of the coaches included at least four of the steps in their descriptions of ways to help their clients. These five steps from ICT (Boyatzis, 2006) involve: (1) the ideal self and a personal vision; (2) the real self and its comparison to the ideal self, resulting in an assessment of one's strengths and weaknesses, in a sense a personal balance sheet; (3) a learning agenda and plan; (4) experimentation and practice with the new behavior, thoughts, feelings, or perceptions; and

(5) trusting, or resonant relationships that enable a person to experience and process each discovery in the process.

The ideal self, optimism and self-efficacy are seen as the main determinants and generators of hope, and therefore, key determinants of the ideal self. Efficacy and optimism research provided insights on the nature and the difficulty of goals selected and the mechanisms through which the ideal self becomes a motivational force within the self, guiding the individual on goals selection (Boyatzis & Akrivou, 2006).

"Intentional Change Theory starts with helping people to identify their ideal self, and that includes their deepest aspirations for the work and the life that they wish to have." (Coach Ten)

Immunity to Change Model. Executive coaches talked about helping their client gain perspective or gain self-awareness through revealing competing commitments. The executive coaches talked about underling emotions, and the assumptions that underlie their client's commitments.

"I would say that if I were to boil down some of the bigger obstacles that it's owing to a story that the leader is telling himself. So, I really like to use the Immunity to Change coaching model when it seems like the assumptions are really holding the person back. So, I have found that that has been a very, very useful coaching protocol." (Coach Six)

The Immunity to Change Model (Kegan and Lahey, 1994) lays the groundwork for understanding change-resistance by helping the client uncover "competing commitments" and adult meaning making. Kegan and Lahey (1994) present a practical method, called the immunity map, intended to help leaders overcome an immunity to change. Even as they hold a sincere commitment to change, many people are unwittingly applying productive energy toward a hidden competing commitment.

The resulting dynamic equilibrium stalls the effort in what looks like resistance but is in fact a kind of personal immunity to change. Kegan and Lahey (2009) further distinguish between our increased understanding of the need for change and the lack of understanding as to what prevents it. The immunity to change model involves three adult meaning systems: the socialized mind, the self-authoring mind, and the self-transforming mind. The coaching process involves a map consisting of a four-column worksheet.

In their book, *Immunity to Change, How to Overcome it, and Unlock Potential in Yourself and Your Organization*, the authors note that even though we want to accomplish the goal if we are not sure what we can do, we will not act on it. Self-efficacy, including having a notion of what we can do to accomplish our desired change, is a factor (Kegan & Lahey, 2009).

"I would say, "Well, why do you want to do it now? Why is it important for you to change this behavior or develop this skill now? Why is it important?" (Coach Nine)

"The next step really is to also consider who can help them because really for behavior change to be sustainable, you really can't go it alone. So, I encourage them to think about who can be on their support team, who might be already modeling that behavior or embodying whatever the goal is focused around." (Coach Nineteen)

Conclusions

This research provides evidence that coaching strengthens self-efficacy. The results of this investigation highlighted the theory-based strategies that coaches use to enhance self-efficacy and positive goal achievement. The coaches in this investigation described complementary strategies that play a role in developing positive goal accomplishment for their clients: adaptive leadership, adult learning, social cognitive theory, appreciative inquiry, and change models.

This investigation strengthens the case for an evidence-based approach to coaching and provides a link to self-efficacy literature (Baron & Morin, 2010; Moen & Allgood, 2009). The executive coaches in this research use a skillful blend of core strategies to overcome barriers to goal achievement: asking powerful questions, deep listening, assigning homework, brainstorming, and challenging assumptions. This study confirmed the importance of ICF core coaching skills and centers the positioning of those skills within the goal-setting framework.

Model of theory-based strategies

Dr. Carol-Anne Minski

This research highlighted evidence-based strategies that coaches use to enhance self-efficacy and positive goal achievement. The executive coach participants in this study described five main theory-based strategies: gaining perspective (adaptive leadership), reviewing past success (social cognitive theory), acknowledging skills and accomplishments (appreciative inquiry), social experiments (adult learning), and change models (intentional change and immunity to change).

Executive coaches that utilize adaptive leadership strategies will build their client's self-efficacy by helping their clients gain perspective. Coaches in this study noted that their clients gain perspective through uncovering assumptions, changing frame of reference, and reflective thinking. The strategy of gaining perspective helps the client develop capacity for critical reflection on what is happening while remaining objective. For this strategy of gaining perspective, terms like adaptive leadership and adaptive change are used interchangeably. Heifetz and Linsky (2002) describe adaptive leadership in terms of gaining perspective with a view from the balcony. Kegan and Lahey (2009) describe adaptive change in terms of thinking about the competing commitments and the assumptions that underlie these commitments.

The coaching applications for social cognitive theory include reviewing past success (mastery experiences), observation of others similar to oneself succeeding (vicarious experience), verbal persuasion (positive feedback), and physiological state (relaxation, bio-feedback). Reviewing past successes helps clients start from a place of success, positive feedback helps the client confirm competencies. Appreciative inquiry offers the opportunity to celebrate strengths and successes and build self-efficacy for positive goal accomplishment. The coaching applications for appreciative inquiry involve guiding the client in discovering and remembering best self, and finding clarity and hope in the desired future (Binkert, 2011). The coaches in this research guided learning through social experiments and recognized the client as the self-directed learner. Coaches worked with clients to set learning goals, milestones, and action steps. Appreciative inquiry intersects with all of the above-mentioned theories through its underlying questions that provide an acknowledgement of skills, review of past successes, positive feedback, reframing, and reflective thinking

Executive coaches that utilize adult learning theory build self-efficacy by providing their clients with ongoing opportunity for practice and reflection. Adult learning theory encompasses a variety of associated theories such as transformative learning, reflective practice, learning styles, leaning goals, and experiential learning. Adults learn when they are ready to learn and there is an immediate relevance to their life or work. Research on adult learning suggests that deeper levels of learning (Mezirow, 1991) occur when there are sufficient opportunities for reflection and experimentation.

Findings from this research place self-efficacy at the threshold of change. Two change models described by the executive coaches in this study are the immunity to change model and intentional change theory. The relationship of change and self-efficacy are supported by the research on change models. Kegan and Lahey (1994) lay the groundwork for understanding change-resistance by helping the client uncover "competing commitments" and adult meaning making. Kegan and Lahey (2009, p. 211) note that "feeling it in the gut" is a vital source for the motivation for change; yet without self-efficacy, or if we are not sure we "can do" it, we do not act on it. Similarly in the Boyatzis and Akrivou (2006) model of the ideal self, optimism and self-efficacy are seen as the main determinants and generators of hope and motivation. Intentional change theory (Boyatzis, 2006) offers a change process involving a series of discoveries that function to produce change at the individual level.

Adaptive leadership strategies will build self-efficacy by helping clients gain perspective. Executive coaches that utilize appreciative inquiry and social cognitive theory provide executive clients with the opportunity to build self-efficacy. Adult learning theory builds self-efficacy by providing clients with ongoing opportunity for practice and reflection. Coaches that utilize change models such as immunity to change model and intentional change theory will assist their clients in positive goal achievement.

Recommendations for Future Research

A next step in this research might be to utilize a quantitative study with a larger sample of coaches to learn how many executive coaches are employing theory-based strategies. This study protocol could be repeated for coaching practices other than executive coaches, such as career coaches. A follow-up study with coach-client pairs is recommended to track the progress of the client's goal accomplishment. Coach-client pairs would be invited to participate in a longitudinal study that provided a pre-and post- assessment. The study described in this paper invites the question of whether or not the client views the coaching strategies as meaningful or effective. Future qualitative research studies might explore the client's perspective to ask what strategies are seen as effective or ineffective and why.

Implications for the Coaching Profession

Coaches that continuously adapt new strategies and learn what works best for their clients will build their own confidence, credibility, and contribute to the coaching profession. By reflecting on the strategies described in this paper, coaches may look inward to see how their own self-efficacy is influencing their coaching practice. Coaches' own perception of self-efficacy will impact their performance. As coaches become more competent, they will be able to shift away from self-doubt to become reflective practitioners and build their own self-efficacy. This in turn will build confidence as coaches become life-long learners in the process of building their coaching practice.

Coaches will now have a firmer understanding of how the combination of these evidence-based strategies can influence self-efficacy to accelerate positive goal accomplishment. Coaching can positively affect self-efficacy so that leaders can accomplish their goals to enhance organizational change. The biggest opportunity for coaches right now is to communicate the benefits of coaching to their clients by establishing credible data that coaching increases leaders' goal accomplishment (which in turn increases the bottom line).

Coach training schools that provide strategies and tools consistently aligned with theory will provide the best practices in executive coaching. Grant (2006) used the term "evidence-based" to differentiate professional coaching explicitly grounded in theoretical knowledge from the personal development genre. Highlighting theory-based strategies in the ICF accreditation process would strengthen coaching, not only in executive coaching practices, it will strengthen professional development for all coaches.

About the Author

Dr. Carol-Anne Minski is founder and president of CMA Leadership Consultants. Dr. Minski designs training and coaching programs for Fortune 500 companies and non-profits. Dr. Minski teaches Professional Development courses and coaches MBA students at Lehigh University. She is a certified career consultant for Lee Hecht Harrison. Her areas of expertise include coaching, career development, leadership development, adult learning, organizational development, and change management.

Dr. Minski provided strategic business management and directed team-based corporate environments at McNeil Consumer Products Company, and Rhone Poulenc Rorer Pharmaceuticals. Dr. Minski is director of the Mentor and Internship Programs for BWNICE (Business Women Networking for Charity and Education). She has an MBA from Thomas Jefferson University (formally Philadelphia University), an MA in Counseling Psychology from Arcadia University, and a PhD in Human and Organizational Systems from Fielding Graduate University. She served on the Board of Directors for Greater Valley Forge Human Resource Association and is listed in Who's Who of Women Executives.

References

Bandura, A. (1982). Self-efficacy mechanism in human agency. *American Psychologist*, 37, 122-147.

Bandura, A. (1986). *Social foundations of thought and action: A social cognitive theory*. Englewood Cliffs, NJ: Prentice Hall.

Bandura, A. (1991). Social cognitive theory of self-regulation. *Organizational Behavior and Human Decision Processes*, 50, 248-287.

Bandura, A. (1997). *Self-efficacy: The exercise of control*. New York, NY: W.H. Freeman and Company.

Bandura, A. (2012). On the functional properties of perceived self-efficacy revisited. *Journal of Management*, 38(9), 9-44.

Bandura, A., & Cervone, D. (1983). Self-evaluative and self-efficacy mechanisms governing the motivational effects of goal systems. *Journal of Personality and Social Psychology*, 45, 1017-1028.

Baron, L., & Morin, L. (2009). The coach-coachee relationship in executive coaching: A field study. *Human Resource Development Quarterly*, 20(1), 85- 106.

Baron, L., & Morin, L. (2010). The impact of executive coaching on self-efficacy related to management soft-skills. *Leadership & Organizational Development Journal*, 31(18-38).

Binkert, J., & Clancy, A. L. (2011). *Appreciative inquiry*. San Francisco, CA: Jossey-Bass.

Boyatzis, R. E. (2006). An overview of intentional change from a complexity perspective. *Journal of Management Development*, 25(7), 697-623.

Boyatzis, R. E., & Akrivou, K. (2006). The ideal self as a driver of change. *Journal of Management Development, 25(7)*, 624-642.

Braun, V., & Clarke, V. (2006). Using thematic analysis in Psychology. *Qualitative Research in Psychology*, 3(77), 77-101.

Cooperrider, D., Whitney, D., & Stavros, J. (2008). *Appreciative Inquiry handbook for leaders of change*. San Francisco, CA: Berrett-Koehler.

Creswell, J. W. (Ed.). (2006). *Research design: Qualitative, quantitative, and mixed methods approaches* (3rd ed.). Thousand Oaks, CA: Sage.

Gibbs, G. R. (2007). Analyzing qualitiative data. In U. Flick (Ed.), *The Sage Qualitiatve Research Kit*. London: Sage.

Grant, A. M. (2006). An integrative goal focused approach to executive coaching. In D. Stober & A. Grant (Eds.), *Evidence based coaching handbook: Putting best practices to work for your clients* (pp. 153-187). Hoboken, NJ: John Wiley & Sons, Inc.

Grant, A. M., & Cavanagh, M. J. (2007). Evidence-based coaching: Flourishing or languishing? *Australian Psychologist* 42(4), 239-254.

Grant, A. M., Curtayne, L., & Burton, G. (2009). Executive coaching enhances goal attainment, resilience and workplace well-being: A randomized controlled study. *Journal of Positive Psychology*, 4(5), 396-407.

Grant, A. M., & Zackson, R. (2004). Executive, Workplace and Life Coaching: Findings from a Large-Scale Survey of International Coach Federation Members. *International Journal of Evidence Based Coaching and Mentoring*, 2(3), 1-15.

Heifetz, R. A., & Linsky, M. (2002). *Leadership on the line: Staying alive through the dangers of leading*. Boston, MA: Harvard Business School Press.

ICF. (2012). ICF Credentialing and Accreditation Newsletter. Retrieved November 12, 2012, from http://www.coachfederation.org/icfcredentials/

Kegan, R., & Lahey, L. L. (1994). *In over our heads: the mental demands of modern life*. Cambridge, MA: Harvard University Press.

Kegan, R., & Lahey, L. L. (2001). The real reason people won't change. *Harvard Business Review, November 2001*.

Kegan, R., & Lahey, L. L. (2009). *Immunity to change: how to overcome it and unlock potential in yourself and your organization*. Boston, MA: Harvard Business Press.

Knowles, M. S., Holton E. F., & Swanson, R. A. (Ed.). (1998). *The adult learner*. Houston, TX: Gulf Publishing Company.

Kolb, A. Y., & Kolb, D. A. (2005). Learning styles and learning spaces: Enhancing experiential learning in higher education. *Academy of Management Learning & Education*, 4(2), 193-212.

Kolb, D. A. (1984). *Experiential learning: Experience as the source of learning and development*. Englewood Cliffs, NJ: Prentice-Hall.

Latham, G. P. (2004). The motivational benefits of goal-setting. *Academy of Management Executive*, 18(4), 126-129.

Leary-Joyce, & Wildflower, L. (2011). Theories of adult learning. In L. Wildflower & D. Brennan (Eds.), *The handbook of knowledge-based coaching: From theory to practice*. San Francisco, CA: Jossey-Bass.

Locke, E. A., Frederick, E., Lee, C., & Bobko, P. (1984). Effect of self-efficacy, goals, and task strategies on task performance. *Journal of Applied Psychology*, 69(2), 241-251.

Locke, E. A., & Latham, G. (1990). *A theory of goal setting and task performance*. Englewood Cliffs, NJ: Prentice Hall.

Locke, E. A., & Latham, G. (2002). Building a practically useful theory of goal setting and task motivation. *American Psychologist*, 57(9), 705-717.

Locke, E. A., Shaw, K. N., Saari, L. M., & Latham, G. P. (1981). Goal setting and task performance: 1969-1980. *Psychological Bulletin*, 90, 125-152.

Maxwell, J. A. (1992). Understanding and validity in qualitative research. *Harvard Educational Review*, 62, 279-299.

Maxwell, J. A. (2002). *Qualitative Research Design: An Interactive Approach* (Vol. 41). Thousand Oaks, CA: Sage Publications.

McCormick, M. (2001). Self-Efficacy and leadership effectiveness: Applying social cognitive theory to leadership. *Journal of Leadership Studies*, 8(22), 22-34.

Mezirow, J. (1991). *Transformative dimensions of adult learning*. San Francisco, CA: Jossey-Bass.

Mezirow, J. (2000). *Learning as transformation: A critical perspective*. San Francisco,

CA: Jossey-Bass.

Moen, F., & Allgood, E. (2009). Coaching and the effect on self-efficacy. *Organizational Development Journal*, 27(4), 69-82.

Paglis, L. L., & Green, S. G. (2002). Leadership self-efficacy and managers' motivation for leading change. *Journal of Organizational Behavior,* 23(2), 215- 235.

Patton, M. Q. (2003). *Qualitative Research & Evaluation Methods*. Thousand Oaks, CA: Sage Publications Inc.

Richards, L. (2009). *Handling Qualitative Data*. Thousand Oaks, CA: Sage Publications.

Ryan, G. W., & Bernard, H. R. (2003). Techniques to identify themes. *Field Methods,* 15(1), 85-109.

Sandelowski, M. (2000). Focus on research methods: Whatever happened to qualitative description? *Research in Nursing & Health*, 23, 334-340.

Strauss, A., & Corbin, J. (1998). *Basics of Qualitative Research*. Thousand Oaks, CA: Sage Publications.

Wildflower, L., & Brennan, D. (2011). *The handbook of knowledge-based coaching: From theory to practice.* San Francisco, CA: Jossey-Bass.

CHAPTER 4

COACHING FOR EFFICACY—A FOCUS ON THE DEVELOPMENT OF AN INTERNAL LOCUS OF CONTROL

Diane P. Zimmerman, PhD
Retired Superintendent of Schools

Abstract

The social cognitive theory of Alfred Bandura (1986) and the research conducted by Rotter (1975) on locus of control highlight the importance of building efficacy in helping relationships. While considered key concepts in the social sciences, these terms have not often been used to describe coaching relationships. For coaching to be efficacious, the client must accept responsibility for his or her own actions. Stated another way, the client must assume an internal locus of control. Hence a coach must be constantly vigilant to shift the locus of control to the client. Part I focuses on how shifting the locus of control within the coaching relationship helps to build efficacy in the client. In Part II describes how practice-based knowledge increases the efficacy of the coach. By applying observation-based knowledge, the coach extends practices into theory.

Key words: Efficacy, locus of control, coaching, observation-based knowledge, evidence-based knowledge, dialogue, conversation.

Part I: Establishing professional efficacy as an essential goal for coaching

A primary goal in coaching is the ability to foster high-quality performance. At the heart of high-quality performance is each person's belief in his or her own competence—personal efficacy. Efficacious professionals are tenacious about making a difference and seek out opportunities to learn from experience; they find coaches and mentors that support the drive for internal control.

Experienced coaches learn how to trust an inner compass that measures the delicate balance between guiding and supporting. Yet, not all coaches understand this intricate balance. Some coaches stick to a program and are at a loss when the client does not make recommended changes. Most coaching programs are organized around a set of assumptions. Many assume a focus on professional standards. Some provide scripted guides for the coach to follow, or workbooks for the client to use in planning for or reflecting upon a session. Some coaching programs, especially in the professions, assume knowledge expertise in the coach. What isn't clearly defined in most programs is how to shift the locus of control towards the client. Some clients, those already efficacious, will do so on their own; those less confident need something more. What is it?

My coaching colleagues and I have found that by applying the concepts of efficacy and locus of control, coaches can refine interactions with clients. These concepts add a practice-based theoretical framework, which can be overlaid on any coaching model. The desired outcome is to shift the locus of control to the client to develop efficacy. Bandura's (1986) social cognitive theory provides a useful lens from which to begin learning about how agency impacts success. Bandura found those with agency take an active role in self-development and self-renewal. His theory of self-efficacy posits that the more internal control one exercises over events, the more efficacious he or she becomes. In other words, the stronger the perceived self-efficacy, the higher the goals and the firmer the commitment to follow through— two important outcomes of coaching. While Bandura is considered one of the most often cited social scientists of the 20th century, his work does not often find its way into coaching research or practice.

Another useful term, locus of control, was first described by Rotter

(1975). Locus of control refers to personal tendencies to believe that control either resides internally within the self or externally in others or a situation. Most recently, other thought leaders, namely Dweck (2006) and Pink (2009), have argued that placing too much emphasis on external criteria robs the client of the opportunity to make internal modifications.

In Figure 1 the tensions between external and internal locus of control are diagramed. When the coach assumes the mantel of an expert, the coach focuses on giving information and becomes directive. The locus of control is with the coach, not the client. When the coach uses skills of mediation to facilitate the conversation, the focus turns inward on the client's own inner resources producing higher efficacy.

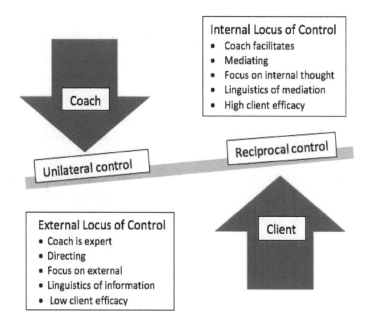

Figure 1 (Zimmerman, 2020)

In a recent book, *9 Professional Conversations to Change our Schools* (2018), my colleague Sommers and I created a dashboard of coaching options based on the degree of locus of control given to the client. We identified nine different frameworks from which to coach and organized these conversations in sequence on a dashboard from high client locus of control to low client locus of control. This type of analysis can and should be extended to other coaching models, not just the nine identified by us. By comparing and contrasting how locus of control is managed within various models, we gain a deeper understanding about the inter relationships of various coaching models. We build a more robust knowledge base.

Figure 2 orients the reader with high locus of control coaching models featured on the left, and lower locus of control models to the right. For our purposes here it is not important to know details of the specific coaching programs. What is important was that we could sequence them based on coach/client locus of control. To the left of the dashboard, the coaching conversations focus on the client's internal agendas. In these conversations the coach serves as a facilitator, and the client engages in reflective practice and develops his or her own measures of success. The coach's language mediates client thinking. To the right of the arch, the coaching conversations move towards a directive framework utilizing external data to judge performance.

Effective coaches need to know how to navigate between client-centered issues and the external needs of an organization. As school leaders, Sommers and I had both found the need to use directive coaching. What became clear as we explored the shifting locus of control was that meaningful data about performance can point the way, but it is still up to the client to take on the change. In other words, effective coaches are always striving towards conversations that return the control to the client: those to the left of the arc. Novice coaches, who do not know how to observe for client locus of control, sometimes mistakenly think the client simply needs more coaching. What we

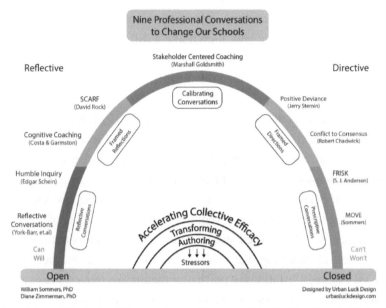

Figure 2 from: *9 Professional Conversations to Change our Schools: A Dashboard of Options,* by W. A. Sommers & D. P. Zimmerman, 2018, Thousand Oaks, CA: Corwin. Copyright (2018) by Corwin. Reprinted with permission.

found in our practice was that more coaching did not work when the client was not willing to take control of the change. For example, when working with a teacher who used sarcasm, I could provide the data and make suggested changes, but once I had outlined a course of action, it was up to the client to take responsibility for changing behavior.

Finally, the book *9 Professional Conversations to Change our Schools* suggests that coaching models should not be siloed each with its own prescriptions, but rather used together to create a common understanding for what makes coaching more effective. As expert coaches, we do not subscribe to one coaching model, but rather to a set of behaviors that work because we can observe visible manifestations such as evidence of locus of control in the coaching moment.

Part II: Becoming an efficacious coach

By definition efficacious individuals have a strong internal sense of control—they know how they make a difference in the world. Not only do clients need to be efficacious, so do coaches. Coaches need to be able to articulate how they make a difference and know when they are successful.

Over 40 years of coaching my colleagues—Costa and Garmston—and I have refined our capacities to observe efficacy relationships. Not only did we pull from the research base, we also informed our practices through a process of observation, which I argue is a subset of evidence-based practice. This entailed calibrating success as the coaching process unfolds; it required close observation of the client responses. What emerged was a deep internal understanding of the craftwork of coaching. Keen observers of coaching interactions can see visible manifestations of particular meditative moves. For example, some questions can gently challenge assumptions and cause the client to shift thinking, which is also paired with a shift in body position. This can be validated by asking the client to identify the value of the question.

Before proceeding, I need to make distinctions about how knowledge is acquired in the helping professions. Cochran-Smith and Lytle (1999) created a tripartite interpretation of knowledge by distinguishing between knowledge for-in-of practice. I apply their interpretation when considering evidence-based practices and identify three types of knowledge necessary for high-level performance. First, coaches must constantly work from a framework of knowledge that has been accepted by the profession as best practices. This level of knowledge as noted in Part I guides the "what" and "why" of professional action and informs choice. Second, coaches must put this knowledge to work and to further refine their repertoire. In particular, coaches test out the theories by applying the knowledge frameworks. They dig deeper to better understand the observational nuances that inform this work. This knowledge is often called "craft knowledge."

And finally, the journey to efficacy requires that coaches become more conscious and aware of how specific practices make a difference. Efficacious professionals do not accept research practices at face value, they question the expert and validate understandings. They become the interpreter and agent leading to knowledge creation; they seek out visible manifestations as evidence of effectiveness. For example, in his work on dialogue, David Bohm (1990) posited that the suspension of judgment opened deep listening. He could verify this by observing that when judgments were suspended, participants stopped defending positions and instead slowed down and began to inquire about each other's understanding. The change was palpable.

Practice Based Coaching Knowledge

In each of the next three sections I describe how observational knowledge produced professional efficacy. I owe credit to this form of learning to colleagues Costa and Garmston (2002), who invited a cadre to probe more deeply into the coaching model they had developed. This model is known to the educational world as Cognitive Coaching. Next, I describe three important coaching moves that produce visible manifestations, which validate our coaching efficacy and greatly accelerate our ability to teach others. These observations are applicable across other coaching models as well.

Seeking emergent meanings through listening: While most coaching programs list listening as a core competency, the ability to listen is more often than not assumed. As noted above we found wisdom from David Bohm (1990), who made a distinction between discussion and dialogue. In dialogue the listener must set aside internal chatter to be fully present for the other. When this happens, the listener attends to the other and slows down, and in response the client slows down. This slowing down is observable, and I might add, can be measured.

When teaching coaching, I instruct a set of overt skills that make the coach an accountable listener (Sommers & Zimmerman,

2018). Accountable listeners understand that they are of service to a client and that listening is a gift to be given. They learn to apply the linguistics of listening: paraphrasing, pausing, and inquiring, to expand understanding:

• Confirming paraphrases communicate the emergent understandings of the coach.

• Thoughtful pauses slow down the conversation, so both have time to think.

• An ethic of inquiry requires the judicious use of questions to probe more deeply into understandings. It also puts the emphasis on the emergent understandings, not on scripted questions.

Each of these three linguistic behaviors are overt; they can be observed and measured. In addition, they produce a response that is observable in that the conversation slows down, the client elaborates more, and the questions elicit deep thinking.

Over my 40 plus years of working with these concepts, I found that those who were the least effective listeners were resistant to using the linguistics of listening, namely paraphrasing and pausing. One leader arrogantly stated, "Why do I need to paraphrase if I understand what has been said." This statement makes an important distinction about efficacy. There is a huge difference between coaches that declare they are good listeners and those who know how to slow down the conversation and linger in the emergent messages to better inquire. Being accountable means that listening is overt and of service to the client, not the coach. The best complement is when a client says, "Our conversation made me think about my problems differently."

Finding new understandings through States of Mind: In our book *Cognitive Capital* (2014) Costa, Garmston and I made a distinction between the language of information (directive conversations) and the language of mediation (reciprocal conversations). Using a grounded theory approach, we developed the States of Mind (Costa & Garmston, 2002) by categorizing the linguistic patterns of our clients' limiting beliefs. By shifting these limiting beliefs to positive cognitive resources, or States of Mind as we labeled them, we mediated the clients' sense of efficacy. The five enabling outcomes are: efficacy, consciousness, flexibility, craftsmanship, and interdependence (Costa & Garmston, 2002). The inherent meaning in each of these States of Mind carries implicit goals and presuppositions that signal positive, proactive intentions. Taken together and applied in coaching, they create a virtual cycle of success and efficacious behavior (Zimmerman, Roussin, Garmston, 2019).

As we listened to our client's language through the filter of these States of Mind, we could now listen for limiting beliefs. When we attended to these limitations, we found that we could invite a shift in the thinking. These are outlined in Table 1 along with descriptions of client/coach language and thinking patterns.

Cognitive Resources	Client's Limiting Belief	Client's Limiting Language	Coach's Response Pattern	Coach's Mediation
Efficacy	Placing blame outside of personal control	"The program is the problem....."	Accept the view, and the probe for where client has control.	"While the program limits you, what is it you can do to.....?"
Consciousness	Seems unaware that there are other solutions	"There is nothing I can do to...."	Empathize and query for times when the statement was not true	"You are feeling out of solutions today. Has there ever been a time when..."
Flexibility	Options seem limited	"This group will never ....."	Accept situation and query about what else	"It does seem futile, what else might you consider....?
Craftsmanship	Seems vague about intentions. Does not seem to attend to details.	"I hope to involve everyone,....."	Identify an intention and then probe for more specificity.	"So you intend to involve everyone, how specifically do you plan to do this?"
Interdependence	Sees self as the only one who can do the work	"I feel so alone, no one else seems to care about...."	Empathize and inquire about other times when they were worked with others	"You feel alone, and yet you want to work with others. When has there been a time when your work with others made a difference?"

Table 1

An interesting observation made when working with these thinking outcomes was that we could not rush the process. If we did not slow down and practice the linguistics of listening to show empathy, the client would often reject our invitation to shift thinking. When we slowed down, really listened, and paraphrased, the client gladly accepted the invitation to think differently. We found that our clients wanted solutions, but they also wanted empathy and to be validated. Once again, the paraphrase was invaluable in communicating that we accepted the situation without judgment. The acceptance of an inquiry to delve deeper into a problem by the client was a tangible measure of our moment by moment success. If the inquiry was not accepted, the coach knew to back up and empathize before probing further.

Observing the shift in thinking

Like with other coaching programs, as cognitive coaches we started with a set of assumptions and a script of goal focused questions. Initially, because we were coaching teachers, we engaged in coaching rounds in which we pre-conferenced and post-conferenced based on data from an observation. It was in the post-conference that we began to linger and found that our scripts, while they gave our conversation shape, did not always produce the thinking we wanted. As we studied successful inquiries, we began to see a response pattern that was overt. As our skills at inquiry improved, we could almost always predict that at some point our client would shift his or her position, and in the shifting make a cognitive shift—a move towards enhanced understanding. This was validated by feedback from our clients. They often reported that they had changed their thinking, combined ideas, or that they wanted to think about a question over time.

As we studied this phenomenon, we found that when we practiced with each other, we could feel the shift in our own minds; an aha moment that was palpable. The shift was so visible in the client that we named it "the cognitive shift" and it has become essential practice-based skill that we taught in our courses. (A video example of this shift in thinking can be seen at https://www.thinkingcollaborative.com/video-12/)

Implications for the profession

This paper argues for a more robust understanding of evidence-based practices. Coaching as an applied science lends itself to both theoretical and practice-based knowledge. Indeed, the combination of these multiple ways of knowing is essential to build coaching efficacy. As is evident from this article, my colleagues and I applied theory and spent years refining the little moments in coaching in order to quantify visible manifestations of efficacious relationships.

I also suggest that the field of coaching is uniquely poised to develop a more robust understanding of evidence-based coaching. I point out how certain theoretical concepts add to the knowledge base and provide practical applications for coaches. I further refine coaching efficacy to include ways that coaches become more efficacious in their practices by developing craft knowledge and by finding overt ways to measure success. Efficacy requires action in real time and requires a consciousness that can be articulated or demonstrated to others.

In conclusion, I call for coaches to join me in creating collective efficacy, the ability of a group of professionals to make a difference. I once again draw wisdom from the States of Mind, for they define professional efficacy. As coaches we need to:

• Accept responsibility for identifying visual manifestations (evidence) of positive outcomes (efficacy)

• Become more aware of gaps in our knowledge (consciousness)

• Have multiple pathways to reach solutions and to observe success (flexibility)

• Pay attention to details that matter especially in the moment of coaching (craftsmanship)

• Work with others to build professional knowledge (interdependence)

About the Author

Diane P. Zimmerman, PhD, lives in Suisun Valley, California on a sixty-acre ranch with her husband Rich and their two dogs. She retired as superintendent of schools after a thirty-six year career in education. During her tenure as a teacher and administrator, she perfected her skills in the art of the conversation, dialogue, coaching, conflict management, and leadership development. In retirement, she has reinvented herself as an author and consultant, focusing specifically on investing in human capital.

Zimmerman has coauthored five books on leadership. She draws from a rich repertoire of practice-based knowledge that makes her teaching and writing about leadership authoritative, accessible, and practical. In 1998, Zimmerman received a PhD in Organizational Development from the Fielding Graduate University. She obtained her B.A. in English from UC Davis, an administrative credential from Sacramento State University, and a M.A. in communicative disorders from the University of Pacific. As a lifelong learner she codesigned a learning organization, the Learning Omnivores, that travels to experts' home territories to spend a day probing the depths of their knowledge.

References

Bandura, A. (1986). *Social foundations of thought and action: A social cognitive theory.* Englewood Cliffs, N.J.: Prentice-Hall.

Bohm, D. (1990). *On dialogue.* (David Bohm seminars). Ojai, CA: Bob Wilkins.

Bandura, A. (1993). Perceived self-efficacy in cognitive development and functioning. *Educational Psychologist, 28,* 117-148.

Cochran-Smith, M. & Lytle, S. (1999). Relationships of knowledge and practice: Teacher learning communities. *Review of Research in Education, 24,* 249-305.

Costa, A. L. & Garmston, R. J. (2002). *Cognitive coaching: A foundation for renaissance schools* (2nd ed.). Norwood, MA: Christopher-Gordon.

Costa, A.L. & Garmston, R.J. (2015). *Cognitive coaching: Developing self-directed leaders and learners* (3rd ed.) Lanham, MD: Rowman & Littlefield.

Costa, A.L., Garmston, R.J., & Zimmerman, D.P. (2014). *Cognitive capital: Investing in teacher quality.* New York: Teachers College Press.

Dweck, C. (2006). *Mindset: The new psychology of success.* New York: Random House.

Pink, D. (2009). Drive: *The surprising truth about what motivates us.* New York: Wiley.

Rotter, J. B. (1975). Some problems and misconceptions related to the construct of internal versus external control of reinforcement. *Journal of Consulting and Clinical Psychology, 43,* 56-67. Downloaded at https://psycnet.apa.org/

record/1975-11748-001

Schein, E. (2013). *Humble inquiry: The art of asking instead of telling.* San Francisco, CA: Berrett-Koehler.

Sommers, W. A. & Zimmerman, D.P. (2018). *9 professional conversations to change our schools: A dashboard of options.* Thousand Oaks, CA: Corwin.

Zimmerman, D.P., Roussin, J. L., & Garmston, R.J. (2019). *Transforming teams: Cultivating collaborative cultures.* Thousand Oaks, CA: Corwin.

CHAPTER 5
A NEW APPROACH TO COACHING CLIENTS IN EMOTIONAL INTELLIGENCE

Jim Knickerbocker, PhD and Charles M. Jones

Abstract

While emotional intelligence is widely accepted in academic and coaching realms as an important component of success, there have been few interventions that significantly increase it. We contend this is because current ideas about emotion do not go far enough to explain the root cause of emotions, nor sufficiently empower clients to resolve them. We propose new hypotheses that state: 1) Emotions are not caused by evaluations of life conditions, but rather by evaluations of need fulfillment; 2) Emotions do not drive reactive behavior; maladaptive assumptions and tactics drive reactive behavior; 3) Emotions do not impair rational decision making; working against emotions leads to irrational decisions. Based on these hypotheses, we developed a five-step method to help clients better resolve distressing emotions. Over the past five years, we and our colleagues have taught this method to over 200 coaching and 600 training clients, the vast majority of whom reported improvements in their performance.

Keywords: Emotional intelligence, TENOR, stress management, self-awareness, self-management, social awareness, relationship management, emotional literacy, leadership development, decision making, accountability, engagement, amygdala hijack, Social and Emotional Learning (SEL).

Review of the Literature

Coaches routinely encounter clients who are not working with their emotions productively, to the point that it is a barrier to their work performance and relationships, or an obstacle to achieving important goals. Gottman and DeClaire (1997) noted, "researchers have found that even more than IQ, your emotional awareness and abilities to handle feelings will determine your success and happiness in all walks of life." In addition, a meta-analysis with data from over 10,000 participants (O'Boyle Jr., et al., 2011) found that emotional intelligence has a significant impact on job performance.

The field of emotional intelligence has provided useful frameworks for discussing emotions (Goleman, 1995; Mayer, 2004), accumulated evidence for the importance of emotional intelligence, developed numerous assessments for measuring it, and offered suggestions that coaches might use to support clients in working more productively with their emotions.

However, while we agree that there is value in many existing emotional intelligence frameworks and techniques, we also believe that the current state of the art falls short of what is needed to effectively coach clients in emotional distress. For example, while we have been able to help clients struggling with volatility to use breathing techniques and mindfulness to reduce the number and intensity of their outbursts, the results have been short of a cure. Likewise, while we've been able to help clients use reframing techniques to better manage their anxiety, the results tend to be short-lived. This has led us to conclude that while current approaches can help clients manage distressing emotions, they fall short of *resolving* distressing emotions because they do not address the root cause of the emotions.

In this chapter, we will critique some conventional ideas about emotion and offer a new theory. As far as application to coaching practice, we will describe gaps in current practice and present a new method which we've found helpful in fundamentally shifting how clients relate to their emotions in ways that significantly improve their performance.

Our Critique of Conventional Hypotheses about Emotion

In this section, we critique some commonly accepted ideas about emotion underlying the current practice of emotional intelligence, highlighting three hypotheses that are at odds with observations we've made of real-life experience.

Conventional Hypothesis #1: Emotions are caused by one's evaluations of life conditions.

This hypothesis is evident in such commonly heard statements as: "He is so frustrating to work with!" or "You made me proud today!" or "That just ruined my day."

One of the most common challenges faced by coaches is a client asserting that their problem is due entirely to the behaviors of other people (or life conditions). Since the coach is not coaching those people (or can't control those life conditions), as long as the client persists in seeing the problem as "out there," the options for coaching are severely limited. Only by helping the client see their role in creating the situation can the coach develop sufficient leverage to help the client. Similarly, as long as clients believe their emotions are strictly the result of life conditions "out there," they are likely to identify as a powerless victim of those conditions. A common coaching maneuver is to help a client look at their current evaluations of life conditions and choose more productive assessments.

To this end, the theory of emotion that many coaches appear to employ is some version of appraisal theory. First suggested by Magda Arnold (Arnold, 1960; Mooren & van Krogten, 1993) and further developed by Richard Lazarus (Lazarus, Averill, and Opton, 1970; Lazarus, 1991), the central tenet of appraisal theory is that emotions are elicited according to an individual's subjective interpretation or evaluation of important events or situations. While this theory of emotional causation tells the coach what they are looking for (the appraisal that is generating the client's emotion), it provides no guidance on how to sort through the many thoughts in the client's mind to identify and verify the specific appraisal that is responsible for the client's present emotion. It's as if the coach is looking for the proverbial "needle in the haystack" when they aren't even sure what the needle looks like.

In an attempt to address this inadequacy, several researchers have sought to identify the criteria that individuals use to arrive at the appraisal that generates a given emotion. For example, Smith and Kirby (2009) found experimental support for the idea that the more important the situation, the more intense the emotional response. They also found support for the idea that the more confident the individual was about their ability to cope with this situation, the more positive their affect and vice-versa. While these criteria may be worth considering, the guidance they provide falls short of what coaches would need in practice (i.e., "appraisal X generates emotion Y") to accurately and reliably identify the appraisal that is giving rise to a particular emotion.

In the "Alternative Theory of Emotion" section below, we'll propose criteria which we and other coaches have found helpful for identifying the particular appraisal generating the client's present emotion.

Conventional Hypothesis #2: Emotions drive reactive behavior.

The hypothesis that reactive behavior (fight, flight, and freeze) is driven by strong emotions is evident in statements like: "I was so angry, I just lashed out," "I was so frustrated, I had to leave," or "I was frozen with fear." Goleman (1995) affirms this hypothesis, noting that "the emotional brain responds to an event more quickly than the thinking brain." He then famously coins the term "amygdala hijack" to refer to any kneejerk behavioral response which one later realizes was inappropriate given the situation. The implication here is that our emotions are to blame for our reactive behavior and, as such, we must learn to "manage" our emotions.

If this hypothesis regarding the causality of reactive behavior were true, it would be impossible for people to remain composed in the presence of strong emotions and this is clearly not the case. Stories abound of people who, in life-threatening situations, manage to retain their composure and lead themselves and others to safety. Likewise, history books are filled with examples of great leaders who described themselves as angry but who rarely lost their composure [1]. It's likely you've observed this ability to remain composed in the presence of strong emotions in yourself and others.

Examples of well-respected academics who challenge the conventional hypothesis include Lisa Feldman Barrett, University Distinguished Professor of Psychology at Northeastern University and Director of the Interdisciplinary Affective Science Laboratory. As Barrett (2008) noted:

> As common sense has it, emotions are triggered automatically, happen to people, and cause them to act in specific and diagnostic ways. An offense triggers anger. A death triggers sadness. A gun triggers fear [2]. As the pent-up energy of an emotion is discharged, the result is a largely inescapable set of stereotyped outputs that occur rapidly, involuntarily. People feel the heat of anger and attack, the despair of sadness and cry, or the dread of fear and freeze —or even run away. The way that emotion seems to control behavior without awareness is usually taken as proof that emotions are automatic responses to things that happen in the world over which people have little control. These commonsense assumptions are not warranted by the available empirical evidence (p.189).

Joseph E. LeDoux, Henry and Lucy Moses Professor of Science at New York University, and Director of the Emotional Brain Institute, is ironically the neuroscientist whose research inspired Daniel Goleman to coin the term "amygdala hijack." However, LeDoux (2015) pointed out that:

The conclusion that the amygdala is the brain's fear center wrongly assumes that the feelings of "fear" and the responses elicited by threats are products of the same brain system. While amygdala circuits are directly responsible for behavioral/physiological responses elicited by threats, they are not directly responsible for feelings of "fear" (para.6).

The point here is that while it is true that the amygdala drives reactive behavior, LeDoux's research indicates that the amygdala is not the part of the brain that is responsible for generating fear and other "distressing" emotions. Rather, the brain system generating our emotions and the brain system driving our reactive behavior may actually operate in parallel. So, while our reactive behavior may be accompanied by strong emotions, our reactive behavior may not be driven by these emotions and, therefore, "managing" our emotions is not likely to be an enduring solution to reactive behavior.

Conventional Hypothesis #3: Emotions impair rational decision making.

This hypothesis is evident in statements like: "There's no place for emotion in the boardroom," "Your emotions are clouding your judgment," or "We need to take the emotion out of this decision."

If emotions such as fear, anxiety, and anger were impediments to making sound decisions, great leaders would not praise these emotions as being an integral part of their decision-making process. For example, Winston Churchill, Prime Minister of the UK during WWII, described the value of fear when he said, "it is better to be frightened now than killed hereafter" (Halle, 1987). Likewise, Andy Grove, former CEO of Intel Corporation, asserted the value of anxiety when he said, "success breeds complacency. Complacency breeds failure. Only the paranoid survive" (Grove, 1996). As far as anger, Aristotle noted that "anybody can become angry—that is easy, but to be angry with the right person and to the right degree and at the right time and for the right purpose, and in the right way—that is not within everybody's power and is not easy" (Aristotle, & Freese, J. H., 1939). The point is that anger can be useful if one channels it properly.

While painful emotions may be unpleasant, they are nonetheless useful. Research has shown that painful emotions can help resolve incongruent or conflicting information (Zinchenko et al., 2015; Kanske & Kotz, 2010; 2011) as well as maintaining healthy boundaries to stay focused on important goals (Qiao-Tasserit, Corradi-Dell'Acqua, & Vuilleumier, 2017). As Bradberry, Greaves, and Lencioni (2009) advised, "the next time you feel an emotion begin to build, take notice of it immediately. Refrain from putting it into the good or bad pile and remind yourself that the feeling is there to help you understand something important" (p. 65).

Marc Brackett, professor at Yale University's Child Study Center and the founding director of the Yale Center for Emotional Intelligence, has conducted extensive research on emotions. In his most recent book, Brackett (2019) describes in detail how emotions are vital to good decision making, and that ignoring emotions that are integral to a decision creates the risk of making the wrong decision. The fact that some people blame their emotions for their poor decisions while others credit these very same emotions for their very best decisions suggests that an intermediary process must be involved.

Summary

In this section, we've provided observations that call into question the adequacy or accuracy of three common ideas about emotion underlying the current practice of emotional intelligence:

- Emotions are caused by one's evaluations of life conditions.
- Emotions drive reactive behavior.
- Emotions impair rational decision making.

In the section that follows, we'll offer a new theory of emotion that goes beyond conventional ideas in a way that may better address the root causes of distressing emotions and provide clients with better options to resolve those emotions.

Alternative Theory of Emotion
Alternative Hypothesis #1: Emotions are caused by one's evaluations of need fulfillment.

In our critique of the current hypotheses of emotional causation, we argued that the emotions that arise in response to a given event or circumstance cannot be explained exclusively in terms of evaluations of those events and circumstances. Some intermediary mechanism must determine what emotions arise in response.

Here we argue that human behavior is driven by psychological needs, and our emotions are generated in response to evaluations of whether we are (or are not) on track to fulfill these needs. Because this sentence is central to our theory, let's unpack each element carefully.

Psychological needs, as previously formulated by Maslow (1943), are "needs for" something (e.g., safety, achievement, autonomy). The problem with this formulation is that it describes an end state (such as safety) but doesn't provide operational guidance about what to do to move toward that end state (knowing that you are not safe does not tell you what actions you need to take to meet your need for safety). For this reason, we believe it is better to describe psychological needs as "needs to" (e.g., protect assets, achieve goals, assert rights), because it specifies the kind of action you need to take (e.g., protect, achieve, assert), and the specific object you're acting upon (e.g., assets, goals, rights).

The idea that emotions are caused by one's evaluations of need fulfillment was originally proposed by Rosenberg (2003) who argued that pleasurable emotions arise when needs are met, and painful emotions arise when needs are unmet. Our theory extends this notion by asserting that the subconscious generates a pleasurable emotion when the person is on track to fulfill a need but generates a painful emotion when the person is not on track to fulfill a need. The importance of this distinction is that pleasurable emotions serve the purpose of encouraging the conscious mind to "keep going," while painful emotions serves the purpose of alerting the conscious mind to "course correct" while there is still time to intervene (see diagram below). If a car's low-fuel indicator only flashes when the car's tank is completely empty, it would not be a very useful indicator. It is only useful because it flashes with sufficient lead time for the driver to refuel the car.

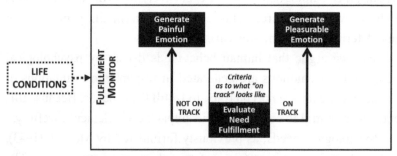

© 2019-2020, Institute for Adaptive Mastery, LLC. Used with permission.

For example, frustration signals being off-track to achieve a goal. Below are the emotion-need mappings for five common emotions:

You'll feel this painful emotion whenever you ARE NOT on track to fulfill this need:	When the following psychological need is activated:	You'll feel this pleasurable emotion whenever you ARE on track to fulfill this need:
Frustrated	Achieve Goals	Satisfied
Anxious	Mitigate Risks	Confident
Angry	Assert Rights	Empowered
Fearful	Protect Assets	Secure
Resentful	Receive Consideration	Appreciative

© 2019-2020, Institute for Adaptive Mastery, LLC. Used with permission.

This new hypothesis provides criteria sufficient for identifying the particular appraisal generating a given emotion. As such, it is an empowering extension of the conventional explanation of emotional causation (i.e., appraisal theory).

Alternative Hypothesis #2: Maladaptive assumptions and tactics drive reactive behavior.

In our critique of the current theory of reactive behavior, we noted research from the field of neuroscience that while reactive behavior may be accompanied by strong emotion, our reactive behavior is being driven by a different circuit in the brain than the circuit generating our emotion.

Here we argue that the circuit driving our reactive behavior (the bottom rectangle labeled "Behavior Machine" in the diagram below) works as follows: first, it compares the current situation to previously learned assumptions about what situations call for the activation of one or more needs, and then activates these needs (box titled "Activate Needs"). Next, it compares the current situation to previously learned tactics for fulfilling these needs and takes action (box titled "Take Action").

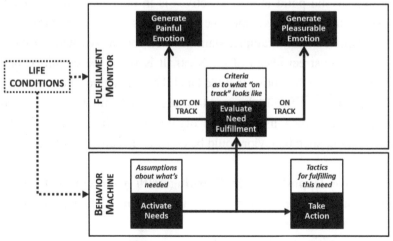

© 2019-2020, Institute for Adaptive Mastery, LLC. Used with permission.

For example, a coaching client complained to us about a colleague who had routinely taken credit for the client's ideas. We walked him through the above diagram, pointing out how this situation ("Life Conditions" in the diagram) resulted in his subconscious responding by:
• Activating a need to receive credit for his work (box labeled "Activate Needs") and
• Taking action based on the most practiced tactic he had for asserting this right (box labeled "Take Action"), which was to yell at the other person in front of his entire office: "How dare you take credit for my work?!"

There are two points we want to make here. The first is that we believe his behavior (yelling "How dare you?!") is being driven by his subconscious, but not by his feelings of anger. As such, his anger is not the root cause of his behavior. His behavior is being driven by: (1) the pre-existing assumptions that led his subconscious to conclude that this was a situation in which he needed to assert his right to receive credit for his work, and (2) the pre-existing tactic to confront his colleague with, "How dare you?!"

The second point is that "reactive" is in the eye of the beholder. Most of the time, these split-second responses from the amygdala are "adaptive"—for example, slamming on the brakes when a child runs into the street ahead of one's car. It is when these split-second responses are maladaptive that we label them "reactive." For instance, yelling, "How dare you take credit for my work?!" may be considered an appropriate response in some organizations, but in our client's organization, such behavior could be considered career limiting.

Alternative Hypothesis #3: Working with your emotions leads to rational decisions but working against your emotions leads to irrational decisions.

In our critique of the idea that emotions impair rational decision making, we pointed out that while it is true that some people blame their emotions for their irrational decisions, others credit these very same emotions for their best decisions. This suggests that there is an intermediary process between the appearance of an emotion and the making of a decision that determines the quality of the decision made. Here we propose that the essence of this intermediary process is that working with your emotions leads to rational decisions, while working against your emotions leads to irrational decisions. We further detail this intermediary process in what we call the Adaptive Performance System (APS), which is our name for a triad of cognitive subsystems (see diagram below) that are responsible for someone's performance as measured by the fulfillment of their psychological needs.

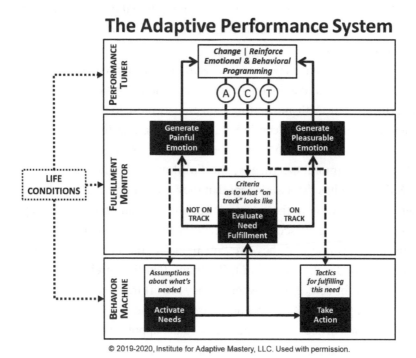

© 2019-2020, Institute for Adaptive Mastery, LLC. Used with permission.

When someone's conscious mind (represented by the top rectangle labeled "Performance Tuner" in the APS diagram above) is working with their APS, they:

• Welcome every emotion, especially the painful ones, as vital data regarding their performance. In practice, this means allowing themselves to feel and then name their emotions.

• Own the psychological need behind each of these emotions. We provide a list of emotion-need mappings to facilitate this practice.

• Examine the "ACT" (i.e., the subconscious Assumptions, Criteria, and Tactics) driving their current emotional and behavioral responses (indicated by the letters A, C, and T in the diagram).

• Change any portions of this ACT that are not serving them and reinforce any portions that are [3].

We argue that doing this will result in a rational decision and that skipping any of these steps will result in a suboptimal, if not an outright irrational, decision.

For example, let's say someone utilizing this approach is driving on a two-lane road to a doctor's appointment and they notice that they are gritting their teeth and getting dangerously close to the car in front. Allowing themselves a deep breath, they realize that they are feeling frustrated. Inquiring into their frustration, they recognize that their subconscious (more specifically, the Fulfillment Monitor box in the APS diagram) has the assessment that they are not on track to achieve their goal of getting to their doctor's appointment on time. When they inquire further, they see that the criteria that their subconscious is using to determine that they are "off-track" is the fact that they are now going under the speed limit. Realizing that this might not be the best criteria for determining whether they are off track to achieve their goal, they open the Maps app on their phone and see that their ETA to the doctor's office is 5 minutes prior to the appointment time. They then ease off the accelerator and put several car lengths between their car and the one in front. Working with their APS has led to a rational decision.

Now compare this to what might happen if this person was working against their APS. Instead of allowing themselves to feel and name their frustration, they will continue gritting their teeth and, because they are not owning the need behind their frustration, they will misattribute their unnamed emotional pain to the driver of the car directly in front of them, saying "What's wrong with this idiot! Don't they know that it's rude to drive below the speed limit?" They might then feel justified in honking their horn and tailgating the car in front of them—an irrational decision.

Summary

In this section, we've offered a new theory of emotion that we believe better explains the root cause of emotions and opens up additional options for successfully resolving these emotions. The table below summarizes the key distinctions we've made:

	Conventional Theory of Emotion	Alternative Theory of Emotion
Hypothesis #1	Emotions are caused by one's evaluations of life conditions.	Emotions are caused by one's evaluations of need fulfillment.
Hypothesis #2	Emotions drive reactive behavior.	Maladaptive assumptions and tactics drive reactive behavior.
Hypothesis #3	Emotions impair rational decision-making.	Working with your emotions leads to rational decisions but working against your emotions leads to irrational decisions.

Application of this alternative theory to coaching practice

We now describe current practice in terms of how coaches are typically advised to help their clients work more productively with their emotions, organized by these four "shoulds" corresponding to the four-quadrant emotional intelligence model popularized by Goleman (1995):

• Clients should pay attention to their emotions (Quadrant 1, Self-

Awareness).
• Clients should manage their emotions (Quadrant 2, Self-Management).
• Clients should pay attention to others' emotions (Quadrant 3, Social Awareness).
• Clients should consider others' emotions as part of managing their relationships (Quadrant 4, Relationship Management).

Quadrant 1: Self-Awareness

That clients should pay attention to their emotions is a widely accepted given in coaching; some practitioners even keep an "emotion list" ready to help clients who may struggle to name their emotions. At the academic level, there are a number of efforts to promote emotional literacy (notably at the Yale Center for Emotional Intelligence) [4]. We agree that coaches should encourage clients to build their emotional literacy, but that is not enough. First, coaches should avoid biasing clients against exploring painful emotions by referring to such emotions using pejorative terms like "negative" or "bad." Beyond that, coaches should encourage clients to see the important connection between their emotions and underlying psychological needs.

Quadrant 2: Self-Management

This quadrant suggests that we should help clients to manage their emotions. The problem is that there is a wide range of understanding of what "manage" means in practice. There is not a widely accepted definition for the term emotional regulation (Thompson, 1994), with some scholars challenging (Cole, et al., 2004) or expanding (Turliuc & Bujor, 2013) current definitions. We offer a distinction between emotional regulation approaches that are focused on avoiding emotion versus approaches focused on listening to an emotion and taking action based on that listening. The vast majority of current practice is of the first kind, in which emotionality is treated as if it is the problem, with the alleged solution to learn techniques that avoid the emotion in various ways, e.g. witnessing without reacting to the emotion, distracting oneself from the emotion, talking oneself out of feeling the emotion, or simply repressing it temporarily. While such cognitive reappraisal can be helpful in other situations, it should not be used to avoid listening to the emotion, because it delays or prevents addressing the psychological need that caused the emotion to be generated in the first place. If the check engine light on your car's dashboard began blinking, and a passenger suggested that you "fix" the problem by covering the light with a piece of duct tape, would you consider that to be a responsible solution? Ignoring the data contained in the emotion is akin to covering the check engine light with duct tape.

Some positive psychology advocates encourage clients to manage their emotions by minimizing so-called "negative emotions" and filling themselves with more "positive emotions." While there may be painful or pleasurable emotions, we believe that all emotions are positive because they contain potentially useful information that can focus the client on what really matters to them.

In other cases, clients are encouraged to manage stress and reduce reactivity by using physical approaches such as mindfulness (Lin, et al., 2016; Teper, Segal, & Inzlicht, 2013), breathing, and posture. While we agree that stress management is important, these techniques should not be used as a substitute for examining the emotions and their underlying psychological needs. As clients practice relaxation techniques, they should be encouraged to name the emotions their tension is concealing, known as "name it to tame it," as popularized by Siegel and Bryson (2011). Naming emotions aloud has been shown to decrease reactivity (Lieberman, et al., 2007) as well as self-reported stress (Lieberman, et al., 2011).

We encourage practitioners to stop attributing reactive behavior to strong emotions; instead, attribute reactive behavior to faulty subconscious programming that is within the power of the client to update. Likewise, do not dismiss painful emotions as irrational, but rather help clients see their irrational behaviors as based on misinterpreting what their emotions are trying to tell them. Teach clients that tension points to emotions they are suppressing, and that instead of blaming or dissociating from their "negative" emotions they should start befriending painful emotions as useful warning signs. By learning to listen to their emotions and their subconscious, clients will be able to make sounder decisions.

Quadrant 3: Social Awareness

The Social Awareness quadrant encourages paying attention to others' emotions, including empathy as well as political, social, and situational awareness. Research by Lopes, Salovey, and Straus (2003) noted that emotional intelligence is significantly associated with satisfaction with one's relationships and positive interactions with others. Unfortunately, in practice, social awareness can result in labeling certain people as "too emotional" or irrational and encouraging them to "get a grip" on their emotions. We argue that these emotions contain information that could contribute to building a more holistic assessment of a situation. Disregarding a group member's emotions risks ignoring the "canary in the coal mine," whose subconscious may be seeing something important that others have missed.

Quadrant 4: Relationship Management

This quadrant advocates considering others' emotions as part of managing relationships. However, this can be misinterpreted as "working around" someone else's emotions, as if their emotions are a barrier to progress. This could entail avoiding needed actions (or taking unneeded actions) in an attempt to prevent them from experiencing a particular emotion. This is both unnecessary and harmful because it keeps potentially useful information from being brought to the surface. Instead, coaches should teach clients how to identify the needs behind another person's emotions, tapping valuable information that helps them to better negotiate, collaborate, and resolve conflict.

The TENOR Method

Having offered new hypotheses, we now explain how new these hypotheses can be put into practice using a set of techniques we call the TENOR Method. TENOR is an acronym of these five steps:

T - Release Tension: Ask the client to scan their body for areas of tension, tighten muscles in each tense area while inhaling, and then release the muscle while exhaling. The client may notice new emotions arising or existing emotions getting stronger. As a result of releasing tension, the client should feel more grounded.

E - Name Emotions: Encourage the client to name aloud each emotion they are aware of, known as "name it to tame it." A sign that this step has been successfully completed is that the client should shift from being reactive to being more composed.

N - Own Needs: Using the TENOR "emotion decoder" for that emotion (which explains the psychological need behind the emotion), acknowledge that the emotion is arising because they are not on track to meet that need, not directly due to particular circumstances, events or other people. This is essential for the client to own their part in the situation, and to take responsibility for making changes. Instead of being negative, the client should feel more accountable.

O - Generate Options: Have the client reflect on their current ACT (Assumptions, Criteria, Tactics) and consider revisions to each. Assumptions about what's needed in a given situation are what activate the need. Criteria include the standards, metrics, or milestones describing what "on track" looks like. Tactics are what constitute the best course of action for fulfilling the psychological need. Once a client revises their ACT, they will typically see new options for resolving the emotion and should shift from feeling powerless to instead feeling resourceful.

R - Gut-check **R**esolutions: Before following through on the option chosen in the prior step, have the client pause for a "gut-check" in which they tap their subconscious to see if it has any concerns or if there are overlooked implementation considerations. When the client is reluctant or procrastinating, it may be a sign that their subconscious is not fully on board with the planned actions. Once this step is completed, the client should feel more committed to their plans.

Client case example

To illustrate the practice of TENOR, we describe a situation with one of Jim's coaching clients, who was the CEO of a mid-sized company. As Jim began the session, the client was in significant distress, complaining of tension and anxiety because she was due to present a balanced budget to her Board of Directors in a week. As she reported, "It's hopeless, Jim. I've tried everything I can think to try. I can't cut jobs because I will lose good staff along with the bad ones. I can't cut pay, or I will kill productivity and loyalty. I'm going to get fired."

As Jim walked her through TENOR Step T (Release Tensions), she felt physically calmer, but she was more painfully aware of her anxiety. In addition, she also noticed some resentment towards herself for allowing the situation to become so dire. Jim had her use TENOR Step E (Name Emotions) to name the emotions she was experiencing (anxiety, resentment) and TENOR Step N (Own Needs) to acknowledge that her anxiety was not directly due to external circumstances, but rather because she was not on track to mitigate the risk of losing her job.

To complete TENOR Step O (Generate Options) and ACT (Assumptions, Criteria, Tactics), Jim pointed out that she had worked the tactics aspect reasonably well, but had failed to examine the assumptions and criteria involved in her situation. Through their dialog, they surfaced these assumptions:

• assuming it is mainly about cutting costs, not increasing revenues;
• assuming all cuts are equally unpalatable to stakeholders;
• assuming I need to solve the problem on my own;
• assuming I cannot involve employees or the board in solving this problem.

She agreed that these assumptions had contributed to concluding the problem to be unsolvable. Jim next asked her to consider the criteria she is using to determine whether she is on track to fulfill her need. Jim noted that her criteria appeared to be, "I am on track to mitigate the risk (of losing my job) if I come up with a complete solution to the budget problem." She readily agreed but complained, "I don't see how that is helpful." Jim replied that a more useful criterion might be, "I am on track to mitigate the risk (of losing my job) if I come up with a process in which I facilitate the board and staff to arrive at a complete solution."

Upon further discussion, she made adjustments to her assumptions and criteria, and to her surprise, new options for tactics emerged. She created a briefing document for the board meeting that included a problem statement, a description of current approaches, a list of ideas that could be discussed, and a proposed process for working with the board and employees to explore innovative solutions.

Her board appreciated the complexity of the problem and understood why she was not able to find quick or easy solutions. During a lively and thoughtful discussion, one of the board members who was a veteran of Hewlett-Packard recalled a time in the 1970s in which employees had voluntarily agreed to take days off without pay to avoid layoffs [5]. The board and CEO agreed that if cuts were needed, they would ask their employees if they would prefer to save money through layoffs, or through pay cuts for everyone. They also engaged the employees to develop new ideas for generating revenue and cutting costs; because they fully understood what was at stake; employees were clever about coming up with ideas and energetic in implementing them. While employees were personally impacted by some of the decisions and actions, because they had been actively involved in the process, there was little negative impact on productivity, morale, or retention.

This client example shows how assumptions, criteria, and tactics are interdependent. Typically, when people consider their options, they limit their exploration to tactics that are within the "bubble" of their current assumptions and criteria. When they change their assumptions or criteria, new tactics often appear. We see this regularly in TENOR coaching sessions.

We propose that the TENOR Method offers coaches a new tool for helping their clients to improve their performance, stay engaged, and become better leaders. Performance improvement comes as clients learn to listen to their emotions for valuable performance feedback, and then quickly make adjustments to their assumptions, criteria, and tactics. Increased engagement is the result of being more grounded, composed, accountable, resourceful, and committed. Leaders who are attuned to their own emotions are more confident in their decision making. In addition, they may use the method to decode others' emotions, so they have a deeper understanding of their needs and can more successfully address them.

The TENOR™ Method

Working AGAINST Emotions	TENOR Step	Working WITH Emotions
Tense	**T** Release ensions	Grounded
Reactive	**E** Name motions	Composed
Negative	**N** Own eeds	Accountable
Powerless	**O** Generate ptions	Resourceful
Reluctant	**R** Gut Check esolutions	Committed

© 2019-2020, Institute for Adaptive Mastery, LLC. Used with permission.

Recommendations for future research

We believe that releasing tensions, naming emotions, owning needs, generating options, and gut-checking resolutions are all things we naturally do. We view TENOR as a method for unlearning the cultural conditioning that has made us—both as individuals and as a society—emotionally unintelligent. As a practical matter, we have chosen to focus our work as practitioners on coaching and training organizational leaders. However, scholarly research would be beneficial in validating the theoretical underpinnings of the TENOR Method and providing data in support of the method's process and impact. Additionally, scholarly research is needed to test and validate the need for individual emotions, e.g., that the need behind frustration is to achieve goals, etc. For more information on the alternative theory of emotion and emotional intelligence coaching method presented in this article, visit tenormethod.com.

End Notes

[1] Mahatma Gandhi and Martin Luther King, Jr. both described themselves as "intensely angry" men who considered their anger a source of wisdom and inspiration constantly pushing them forward in their quest to assert what they believed to be their rights. Mahatma Gandhi's grandson explained that Gandhi "saw anger as a good thing, as the fuel for change, but he made me understand you must get control over it" (Gandhi, 2018).

[2] Note that the preceding text is consistent with Hypothesis #1 above.

[3] For readers familiar with the work of Argyris & Schön (1978), we view our process of upgrading "Tactics" as synonymous with their concept of "Single Loop Learning" and our process of upgrading "Assumptions" and "Criteria" as synonymous with their concept of "Double Loop Learning."

[4] Consult the Yale Center for Emotional Intelligence website at http://ei.yale.edu/

[5] "Veteran employees of HP remember the days in the 1970s when

Dave and Bill asked employees — and they readily agreed — to take every other Friday off without pay to cut costs and avoid layoffs" (Lacy & Mullins, 2002).

About the Author

Jim Knickerbocker received his doctorate from Fielding Graduate University, his Master's in Management from John F. Kennedy University, and his Bachelor's in Economics cum laude from Princeton University. The Fielding scholar-practitioner model suits him well as he applies his learnings as a coach and organization development consultant to diverse settings ranging from Fortune 50 companies and government organizations to start-ups and educational non-profits. In these endeavors, his personal passion is to help people adapt to change. His information technology background provids him with a structured analytical perspective with which to examine the topic of human emotion. Charles M. Jones began the research project that led to the TENOR Theory of Emotion in 1982 while pursuing an interdisciplinary degree at the intersection of Computer Science, Cultural Anthropology and Evolutionary Psychology at the University of Michigan. After graduating with a B.S., Charles continued the research project in his spare time for the next 35 years, studying with Fernando Flores (Ontological Coaching), Richard Strozzi Heckler (Somatic Leadership) and Marshall Rosenberg (Nonviolent Communication). In parallel, Charles had successful careers as a software engineer, organizational and leadership development consultant, and a CPG entrepreneur. Jim and Charles are co-founders and owners of the Institute for Adaptive Mastery, which develops and distributes the TENOR Method.

References

Argyris, C., & Schön, D. (1978). *Organizational learning: A theory of action perspective.* Reading, Mass: Addison Wesley.

Arnold, M. B. (1960). *Emotion and personality.* New York, NY: Columbia University Press.

Aristotle, & Freese, J. H. (1939). *The "Art" of rhetoric*: With an English translation by John Henry Freese. Cambridge, Mass: Harvard University Press.

Barrett, L. F. (2008). The science of emotion: What people believe, what the evidence shows, and where to go from here. In: National Research Council, ed., *Human behavior in military contexts.* Washington, DC: The National Academies Press, pp.189-238.

Brackett, M. (2019). *Permission to feel: Unlocking the power of emotions to help our kids, ourselves, and our society thrive.* New York: Celadon Books.

Bradberry, T., Greaves, J., & Lencioni, P. (2009). *Emotional intelligence 2.0.* San Diego, CA: TalentSmart.

Cole, P. M., Martin, S. E., & Dennis, T. A. (2004). Emotion regulation as a scientific construct: Methodological challenges and directions for child development research. *Child Development,* 75(2), 317-333. https://doi.org/10.1111/j.1467-8624.2004.00673.x

Gandhi, A. (2018). *The gift of anger: And other lessons from my grandfather Mahatma Gandhi.* London: Penguin Books.

Goleman, D. (1995). *Emotional intelligence: Why it can matter more than IQ.* New York: Bantam Books.

Gottman, J. M., & DeClaire, J. (1997). *Raising an emotionally intelligent child.* New York, N.Y.: Simon & Schuster Paperbacks.

Grove, A. S. (1996). *Only the paranoid survive: How to exploit the crisis points that challenge every company and career.* New York: Currency Doubleday.

Halle, K. (1987). *The Irrepressible Churchill: Stories, sayings and impressions of Sir Winston Churchill.* London: Robson.

Jones, C. M., & Knickerbocker, J. F. (2020). *Emotional intelligence for continuous improvement: From emotional pain to performance gain using the TENOR method.* In press.

Kanske, P., & Kotz, S. A. (2010). Modulation of early conflict processing: N200 responses to emotional words in a flanker task. *Neuropsychologia,* 48, 3661-3664. https://doi.org/10.1016/j.neuropsychologia.2010.07.021

Kanske, P., & Kotz, S. A. (2011). Emotion triggers executive attention: Anterior cingulate cortex and amygdala responses to emotional words in a conflict task. *Human Brain Mapping,* 32, 198-208. https://doi.org/10.1002/hbm.21012

Lacy, S., & Mullins, R. (2002, March 12). What is the HP Way? Guiding principles at center of proxy fight. Retrieved from https://www.bizjournals.com/sanjose/stories/2002/03/18/story1.html

Lazarus, R. S., Averill, J. R, Opton, E. M. Jr. (1970). Toward a cognitive theory of emotions. *In Feelings and emotions: the Loyola symposium,* ed. M. Arnold, pp. 207-32. New York: Academic Press.

Lazarus, R. S. (1991). Progress on a cognitive-motivational-relational theory of emotion. *American Psychologist*, 46(8), 819-834.

LeDoux, J. E. (2015, August 10). The amygdala is NOT the brain's fear center. Retrieved from https://www.psychologytoday.com/us/blog/i-got-mind-tell-you/201508/the-amygdala-is-not-the-brains-fear-center

Lieberman, M. D., Eisenberger, N. I., Crockett, M. J., Tom, S. M., Pfeifer, J. H., & Way, B. M. (2007). Putting feelings into words produces therapeutic effects in the brain. *Psychological Science,* 18(5), 421–428. https://doi.org/10.1111/j.1467-9280.2007.01916.x

Lieberman, M. D., Inagaki, T. K., Tabibnia, G., & Crockett, M. J. (2011). Subjective responses to emotional stimuli during labeling, reappraisal, and distraction. *Emotion* (Washington, D.C.), 11(3), 468–480. doi:10.1037/a0023503

Lin, Y., Fisher, M. E., Roberts, S. M. M., & Moser, J. S. (2016). Deconstructing the emotion regulatory properties of mindfulness: An electrophysiological investigation. *Frontiers in Human Neuroscience*, 10, 451. https://dx.doi.org/10.3389/fnhum.2016.00451

Lopes, P. N., Salovey, P., & Straus, R. (2003). Emotional intelligence, personality, and the perceived quality of social relationships. *Personality and Individual Differences*, 35, 641-658. https://dx.doi.org/10.1016/S0191-8869(02)002428

Maslow, A.H. (1943). A theory of human motivation. *Psychological Review*, 50 (4): 370–96.

Mayer, J. D. (2004). What is emotional intelligence? UNH Personality Lab, 8. Retrieved from https://scholars.unh.edu/personality_lab/8

Mooren, J. H. M.; van Krogten, I. A. M. H. (February 1993). Contributions to the history of psychology: CXII. Magda B. Arnold revisited: 1991. *Psychological Reports*, 72 (1): 67–84. doi:10.2466/pr0.1993.72.1.67. ISSN 0033-2941.

O'Boyle Jr., E. H., Humphrey, R. H., Pollack, J. M., Hawver, T. H., & Story, P. A. (2011). The relation between emotional intelligence and job performance: A meta-analysis. *Journal of Organizational Behavior*, 32, 788-818. https://dx.doi.org/10.1002/job.714

Qiao-Tasserit, E., Corradi-Dell'Acqua, C., & Vuilleumier, P. (2017). The good, the bad, and the suffering. Transient emotional episodes modulate the neural circuits of pain and empathy. *Neuropsychologia*, 116, 99-116. https://doi.org/10.1016/j.neuropsychologia.2017.12.027

Rosenberg, M. B. (2003). *Nonviolent communication: A language of life*. Encinitas, CA: PuddleDancer Press.

Siegel, D. J., & Bryson, T. P. (2011). *The whole-brain child: 12 revolutionary strategies to nurture your child's developing mind.* New York: Delacorte Press.

Smith, Craig A., & Kirby, Leslie D. (2009). Putting appraisal in context: Toward a relational model of appraisal and emotion. *Cognition and Emotion,* 23 (7), 1352–1372.

Teper, R., Segal, Z. V., & Inzlicht, M. (2013). Inside the mindful mind: How mindfulness enhances emotion regulation through improvements in executive control. *Current Directions in Psychological Science,* 20, 1-6. https://dx.doi. org/10.1177/0963721413495869

Thompson, R. (1994). Emotion Regulation: A Theme in Search of Definition. *Monographs of the Society for Research in Child Development,* 59(2/3), 25-52. doi:10.2307/1166137.

Turliuc, Maria & Bujor, Liliana. (2013). Emotional regulation, expansion of the concept and its explanatory models. *Applied Social Sciences. Psychology, Physical Education and Social Medicine* (10): 1-4438-4524-8, (13): 978-4438-4524-3. 1. 99-106.

Zinchenko, A., Kanske, P., Obermeier, C., Schröger, E., & Kotz, S. A. (2015). Emotion and goal-directed behavior: ERP evidence on cognitive and emotional conflict. *Social Cognitive and Affective Neuroscience,* 10, 1577-1587. https:// doi.org/10.1093/scan/nsv050

CHAPTER 6

PERFECT STORM: UNDERSTANDING AND COACHING THE ABRASIVE LEADER

Lynn Harrison, PhD, MCC, MCEC
Saybrook University

Abstract

In this chapter, we explore the complex nature of abrasive leadership behavior and specific coaching approaches that can address this harmful and pervasive issue. The methods presented draw on years of experience coaching executive clients as well as results of a recent phenomenological study of organizational leaders formerly perceived to be abrasive in their workplace relationships. This examination of the "lived experience" of so-called perpetrators is largely missing in the research about workplace bullying and aggression. Understandably, most of the focus to date has been on the plight of those on the receiving end of such behavior. A systems-oriented framework was used in the study, investigating not only the dispositional factors associated with abrasive leadership, but the contextual elements, including organizational practices that can unwittingly play a role in the phenomenon. In addition, the research examined the interventions, such as executive coaching, that successfully supported changes in the leaders' behavior.

Keywords: Executive coaching, abrasive leadership, workplace bullying, systems perspective, phenomenological approach.

Introduction

How is it that managers can get away with treating employees terribly? While it may be immoral and unprofessional, organizational leaders all too often engage in behaviors that cause considerable harm to coworkers. They threaten, insult, shout at, or humiliate employees. They micromanage, overreact to problems, become impatient and condescending, withhold information, or take credit for someone else's work. As the term "abrasive" suggests, this kind of behavior wears coworkers down or, at the very least, rubs people the wrong way.

And yet, many of these leaders are regarded as high performers, as stars in their organizations. Able to deliver exceptional results, create value for shareholders, and impress clients, they are promoted to exalted positions of authority. The problem is, their elevation in the company has typically resulted from their ability to get things done, not their skill as leaders (Crawshaw, 2013). Although the organization benefits financially, significant damage is caused: the poor managerial behavior leads to job stress, employee turnover, job dissatisfaction, low morale, diminished trust, and other forms of productivity loss for organizations (Nielsen & Einarsen, 2012, 2018; Pfeffer, 2018).

The aim of the qualitative study described in this chapter was to better understand the causes of abrasive behavior. Phenomenological inquiry was used to explore the perceptions of twelve organizational leaders formerly recognized to be abrasive in their workplace relationships, a viewpoint largely missing in the current literature (Bloch, 2012; Tucker, 2019). A systems lens was applied to examine the contextual factors that might be involved. In addition to in-depth individual interviews, sources of data included observations, field notes, and published literature on the broader topic of workplace aggression. Through a process of thematic analysis, common threads in the participants' experiences were identified, including what individuals believed led to their abrasive behavior, and what helped them to change.

This investigation shed light on what Rayner and Cooper (2003) called "the black hole" (p. 47) of workplace aggression research, deepening understanding of the lived experience of those perceived to be abrasive. It also offered insight into systems-oriented approaches that can assist organizations in preventing and addressing counterproductive leadership. At an individual level, the study illuminated methodologies that coaches can use in working with such leaders.

Study Background

The journey towards better understanding the phenomenon of abrasive leadership began with my observation as an executive coach. Many of the managers deemed to be abrasive were completely unaware of the extent to which their behavior negatively impacted coworkers. What was also interesting was that these individuals were usually quite pleasant with me. Quick thinking and articulate, they came across as charming and charismatic, not at all like the ogres described by colleagues.

I also noticed that the organizational representatives who had contacted me about coaching were often uncertain about what to do. On the one hand, the abrasive manager was a high producer who delivered quality results; on the other, coworkers were requesting transfers to other departments or leaving the company altogether. The company did not want to lose the talents of the leader but did not want to see good employees go to the competition either.

It seemed that the phenomenon of abrasive leadership was a bit of a mystery. The popular and academic literature typically portrayed these individuals as unchangeable bullies, people who never should have been placed in leadership roles in the first place. Many of the books, including those published by academics, had incendiary titles like *Brutal Bosses and Their Prey* (Hornstein, 1996), *Snakes in Suits: When Psychopaths Go to Work* (Babiak & Hare, 2006), *Assholes* (James, 2012), and *Corporate Hyenas at Work!* (Marais & Herman, 1997). The focus of these publications was on methods for protecting oneself from such horrible individuals.

And yet, some abrasive managers who learned of their damaging leadership subsequently did shift their behavior, becoming more approachable and even caring. It seemed that, in certain circumstances, change was possible. However, more needed to be understood about the complex nature of the abrasive leadership phenomenon, including its distinction from tough bosses and workplace bullies.

Abrasive leadership, the phenomenon of interest in this study, was defined as a pattern of interpersonal behavior on the part of an individual charged with managerial authority that causes emotional distress in coworkers sufficient to disrupt organizational functioning (Crawshaw, 2010). Unlike the tough boss, the abrasive manager was perceived to be not just demanding, but uncaring and disrespectful of coworkers (Daniel, 2009a). Distinctive from bullying, no specific target was involved; nor was malicious intent. Like bullying, however, the leader did not act abrasively on a rare occasion; rather, it became a pattern in their leadership, ultimately with deeply harmful results.

The research project involved leaders from a broad range of industries and geographic locations who self-identified as having been formerly perceived to be abrasive. The following five common forms of abrasive behavior (Crawshaw, 2007) were used as screening criteria:

Screening Criteria for Abrasive Leadership

Overreacting	Flying off the handle; jumping to conclusions; using profanities when angered
Micromanaging	Over-supervising people; correcting or rewriting others' work
Public humiliation	Dressing down/rebuking a colleague in front of peers
Condescension	Dismissing others' ideas; using a tone that implied that others are inept; cutting people off before they have finished speaking
Issuing threats	Telling people that their jobs will be in jeopardy if they do not meet expectations

Crawshaw (2007)

Finding individuals willing to acknowledge or discuss these negative patterns was not an easy task. Most organizations do not willingly admit they have abrasive managers in their employ; nor do leaders who currently behave this way tend to recognize the problem. Hence the study participants were individuals who had successfully shifted their behavior and were courageous enough to share their experience with a researcher.

After in-depth interviews with the researcher, the leaders were sent the transcriptions to make any desired revisions. Moustaka's (1994) phenomenological method was used for analysis. The findings are presented below.

Research Questions and Findings

To investigate the phenomenon of abrasive leadership, the following primary research question was posed: How do people who engage or have in the past engaged in abrasive leadership behavior perceive and describe their experience of this phenomenon? Sub-questions included: What were the underlying causes of the pattern of behavior? To what degree were precipitating factors related to the situation, as opposed to the personal attributes of the leader? What had contributed to the eventual shift in the leaders' behavior?

Participants' descriptions of their experience. The textural and structural descriptions gathered in the interview process indicated that abrasiveness typically arose out of the leaders' frustration with trying to achieve results through others. Particularly when managers felt time-pressured or weighed down by a heavy workload, they would have difficulty controlling their feelings of anxiety, annoyance, or impatience. Sometimes the frustration would be expressed as a terse remark, a frown, or bulleted questions; at other times, it would grow into more overt anger, expressed in a raised voice, expletives, or aggressive actions, like slamming down a book or pointing a finger.

These descriptions of the abrasive experience were congruent with theories of aggression: that emotions such as anger and frustration increase the propensity for various forms of aversive behavior (C. Anderson, Anderson, & Deuser, 1996; Geen, 2001). They were also reflective of the distinction made by Buss (1961) regarding instrumental aggression and reactive aggression. Consistent with instrumental aggression, the angry response occurred when efforts to pursue a desired end were thwarted. On the other hand, as with reactive aggression, the unpremeditated response was associated with highly emotional content, directed at the perceived provocateur.

Study participants described how during a display of abrasiveness, they usually felt their anger was justified. The coworker missed a deadline, made a mistake, or let the leader down in some other way, and these failings needed to be addressed. Indeed, Felson and Tedeschi (1993) noted that aggressors "often view their own behavior as legitimate and even moralistic. Thus, beliefs about justice and equity, the assignment of blame, and the accounts that people give to excuse or justify their behavior are central" (p. 3). As one participant stated, "I have this sense that I'm justified in being frustrated."

It was usually later, when the leaders calmed down, that they became regretful about their aversive reaction, wishing they had handled things differently. One of the participants described the two-way impact of abrasive leadership, noting that the harsh reaction expressed outwardly "was even stronger on the inside." The abrasive reaction thus was associated with some dissonance, a finding noted by DeSanti (2014).

The following illustration shows the stages common in an abrasive leadership experience. An already-stressed manager becomes irritated by a situation with a colleague (a trigger). Unable to control his or her annoyance, frustration or anger increases (escalation), leading to abrasive behavior (a "fight response"). The increased state of emotional arousal is accompanied by a dip in rational thinking. Eventually, once calmness is restored, the leader has feelings of regret and begins to reflect on what took place.

Consistent with the research of Crawshaw (2005) and Jenkins, Winefield, Zapf, and Sarris (2011), participants reported that although they were usually aware that they had responded with anger or frustration, they did not register of the extent of their impact on coworkers. One leader explained that because he rarely felt threatened by other people, it was hard for him to imagine that others found him intimidating. Another person stated that she was in total disbelief when her 360-feedback report indicated that half of her employees "feared and hate[d] her."

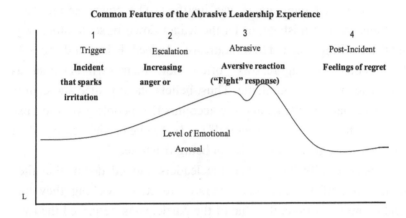

Several leaders described the Jekyll-and-Hyde nature of their abrasiveness. On most days and in certain situations, such as when meeting with a valued client or an external person, like me, they could rein in their emotional response. However, at other times, particularly when they were mentally or physically exhausted, they had difficulty restraining themselves, a finding consistent with the research of Pfeffer (2018).

Many of the participants reported that, over time, they had become beleaguered by their intense approach to work. They described working over 70 hours a week, forgoing weekends off and vacations, a pattern not uncommon among many modern managers (Pfeffer, 2018; Rayner, Hoel, and Cooper, 2002). Their stories perhaps suggest the manager-as-hero myth described by Bowles (1997), where leaders metaphorically take up the gauntlet in pursuit of the organization's goals, often putting at risk their personal wellbeing. From a systems perspective, these practices are consistent with the limits-to-growth archetype (Senge, 1990), a series of events that, in the end, generates counterproductive elements and becomes unsustainable. In the cases of some of the managers, their hard-driving ways eventually led to significant health problems, a consequence found by Pfeffer (2018).

Participants reported that the organization and their managers did little to curtail the dysfunctional pattern. Most of the leaders viewed the challenges they faced as their own responsibility to handle, even if they were suffering from the pressure. Only in three of the twelve cases in this study did their bosses intervene and suggest they get help.

Causes of abrasive behavior. The study revealed several common antecedents of abrasive leadership. One of the main findings was that the leaders started their careers as hardworking, successful individual contributors, resulting in their promotion to managerial roles. Although technically proficient at their jobs, they had little, if any, training in leadership. In some cases, they had poor role models in their organization. Several participants admitted that they did not even think about leading others; they simply did what had made them successful to date, which mainly included setting goals and doing whatever was necessary to achieve them.

Adding to the pressure was the realization that the managers were now responsible for group results, not just their own work. When employees did not produce desired outcomes, the leaders became anxious, overreactive, and controlling. As one participant said, she told herself that she just needed to "bark louder" and "keep people on a tight leash."

This kind of intense behavior often had the opposite effect to what the managers were seeking. Employees, fearful of saying or doing anything that provoked their boss's ire, would hang back, waiting for direction. They would be reluctant to raise concerns or point out any problems that might upset the leader. These observations are consistent with Edmondson's (1999) study of psychological safety in teams. The manager's volatile behavior would cause coworkers to shut down, leaving the leader with even more work to complete, not to mention a higher possibility of error.

Another common factor revealed in the study was that the abrasive leaders never received any clear, constructive feedback that they needed to change. They continued to get promoted and praised for their hard work. Often, senior leadership overlooked the poor behavior, focusing only on results. Consequently, what was initially an occasional slip in civility would become a deleterious pattern.

Part of the difficulty in bringing the problem to the leader's attention, as identified in research by Namie and Namie (2009), was that often the abrasive behavior happened behind closed doors. More junior employees were typically unwilling to raise their concerns about their boss's behavior. Further, in many companies where coworkers did speak out, the organization failed to act at all or made things worse for the complainant (Daniel, 2009b; Workplace Bullying Institute Survey, 2017). In the case of one of the study participants, an allegation of bullying behavior was put to bed when her manager, the top leader in the organization, stepped in to defend her actions.

As this suggests, the antecedents of abrasive leadership go beyond singular causes or events. Indeed, it appears that an array of forces, some beneath the surface, are at play in this complex phenomenon (Meadows, 1999). For this reason, it was important to apply a systems lens in the research, looking at the potential impact of the environment as well as dispositional factors.

Contextual and personality factors. A key finding of the study was that abrasive leadership arises out of both context and personality, a view counter to the widely-held bully-boss perspective, which squarely lays blame on "bad apples," managers with problematic personalities ((Hornstein, 1996; Marais & Herman, 1997; Namie & Namie, 2009). It also puts into question "bad barrel" explanations, which assert that a poor environment inevitably brings out the worst qualities in human beings (Sperry, 2009; Zimbardo, 2007).

Although participants identified contextual causal factors, they were quick to concede that their own personality played a part in their abrasive pattern. Consistent with Kaplan's (1991) research about expansive executives, the leaders invariably described themselves as ambitious, driven, smart, and goal oriented. In many cases, much of the stress in their role came from the high expectations they had of themselves. As one participant commented, "You want to deliver a product, but you want that product to be perfect." Such perspectives are reflective of Levinson's (1978) depiction of the prickly, perfectionistic executive with the abrasive personality, as well as Ludeman and Erlandson's (2006) hard-driving alpha leaders, for whom failing (or looking inept) is not an option.

It is worth noting that some, but certainly not all, of the participants brought to their role the experience of being mistreated or witnessing abusive behavior on the part of authority figures, at home or at work. As one person acknowledged, he had unwittingly placed himself in an environment that recreated the harsh conditions in which he had grown up. This observation corroborates the findings of Murphy (2004), whose research showed that people were often drawn to hostile workplaces, as they were familiar environments.

The leaders in the study had personal value systems that emphasized responsibility, independence, hard work, and loyalty. When asked to "take one" for the company, they did not question the request. They also held mental models of functional rationality; that is, the belief that business is about making money and getting things done efficiently (Friedman, 1970).

It is at this point in examining the antecedents of abrasive leadership that determining which elements are due to the individual and which caused by environment becomes less clear. As one of the study participants, who took an overseas career sabbatical, mused, "Are my thinking processes or those things I was taught in our North American-centric environment still something I believe in, or am I still following them because of the way that I was shaped?"

Consistent with systems theory, the contextual influences can be viewed at different levels: the societal level, the organizational level, the job level, and finally the self-system level, comprised of the leader's own view of his or her role and responsibilities. In terms of societal perspectives about business and leadership, several of the participants described perceptions of the "dog-eat-dog" nature of work, where "life is a jungle, and only the strong survive." They also pointed to the competitive, bottom-line driven, hierarchical cultures in their organizations. They said that in such task-oriented environments, managers were expected to be decisive, have all the answers, and tell others what to do. Indeed, despite commonly espoused corporate values regarding the importance of people and teamwork, it was evident that what really counted was getting the job done and making the company money. Organizational leaders were willing to turn a blind eye to how goals were achieved. As Daniel and Metcalf (2013) have argued, these kinds of societal values have contributed to the pervasive problem of dominant, aggressive leadership behavior. People learn how to "game" the system.

The leaders in the study also described working in organizational cultures that were chaotic, where change was incessant. In these settings, decision-making processes and role expectations were ill-defined. Managers competed for resources, adding to the strain in the environment, observations reflective of research showing that an absence of order and hierarchy causes workplace aggression (Roscigno, Lopez & Hodson, 2009).

At the job level, precipitating factors included pressure to deliver results, often in unrealistic timeframes and without needed equipment or materials. Consistent with Oshry's (2007) systems research, the leaders found themselves subject to demands from above and below them in the organizational hierarchy, leaving them feeling quite alone. These stresses were particularly acute in project environments, where teams needed to deliver outcomes quickly and where the competition was intense.

As mentioned previously, at the self-system level, causal factors were linked to leaders' common view that it was their responsibility to deliver results, whatever that took. Indeed, getting things done had paved their path to success and would be a go-to strategy. Particularly under pressure, leaders would choose achieving goals over building relationships. Dealing with the messiness of emotions, their own or others, seemed an impediment to progress. As one person tellingly stated, "I wish people would just leave their problems at home."

As these descriptions indicate, the phenomenon of abrasive leadership is multi-causal. It arises out of a confluence of contextual and dispositional factors, creating a "perfect storm," summarized below.

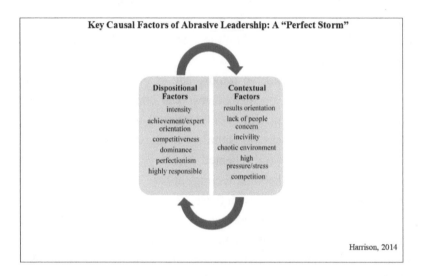

What supported shifts in behavior. One of the positive outcomes of the study was the finding that change was possible, with the right ingredients. Consistent with client readiness research (Hanna & Ritchie, 1995), these conditions included taking responsibility for past behavior and being willing to hear direct and honest evaluations of their performance. Also needed was commitment to changing and support for doing so. In all twelve cases, the leaders received help from either a coach, therapist, or both.

For many of the abrasive managers, the change began with what adult learning theorist Mezirow (2000) called a "disorienting dilemma"

(p. 22). In systems terms, they experienced "punctuated equilibrium" (Gersick, 1991), where the person's view of him- or herself is considerably altered. Learning that they were failing as leaders was a shock. One of the participants, for example, said that getting her first feedback report was "an eye-opener...a major turning point."

Participants reported that in the beginning they felt strong feelings of shame, or in some cases anger, that no one had told them about the problem sooner. They questioned whether they had what it took to lead, and whether the broken relationships could be repaired. It therefore helped if the feedback was delivered with clarity and encouragement. As one participant stated, "It didn't feel good to be told to change with a gun to your head."

The leaders described the importance of having a safe space in which they could work on themselves. The coaching or therapeutic relationship needed to provide confidentiality and support. Talking about personal issues was not familiar to these hard-driving, task-oriented individuals. Several reflected that they had long believed that they needed to be stoic, keeping feelings at bay. They were not used to talking about emotions even with those closest to them.

Consistent with intentional change theory (Boyatzis, 2006), the leaders also indicated that it was helpful to have a vision of leadership to which they could aspire. Indeed, part of the transformation included reflecting on and revising their mental models and values about leading others. For example, participants found it helpful to think about how they would ideally like to be experienced as a manager. For many, this was not something they had contemplated in the past.

Participants emphasized the need to be ready for the difficult journey ahead. Although these individuals had accomplished much in their areas of technical expertise, the "soft" skills required for leadership were unfamiliar to them. It felt awkward and humbling to not only admit they needed help and forgiveness from coworkers, but also to try new ways of communicating with them.

Part of the change involved becoming aware of one's internal reactions, so that irritation could be stopped from spiraling into anger. The leaders also needed to build capability in reading the reactions of others. Consistent with Crawshaw's (2005) research, many of the participants lacked compassionate empathy. As one person commented:

"Awareness would be one main change—just watching how I'm walking, how I'm talking. When I'm walking up to somebody, I notice, 'Are they [chuckles] looking for the exit door, or are they actually excited to see me coming towards them'?"

Achieving deep and sustained change called for new self-understanding and an acceptance of self. For example, one participant recognized that he no longer needed to carry around the chip on his shoulder that made him get angry so quickly. Another leader realized that he had been plagued by self-doubt for much of his life, leading him to try to prove his intelligence to others. One person commented on how her perfectionism thwarted her ability to accept herself: "I used to have this poisonous contempt for any mistake I made. I desperately wanted to excise, to reject, any part of me that made a mistake." She also observed that by having more self-compassion, she was able to have more compassion for others.

As part of the transformation process, many of the participants made significant lifestyle changes, such as taking yoga, doing breathwork, shifting their thinking patterns, or engaging in mindfulness practices to better manage the overall level of stress in their lives. One person emphasized the steps she had taken to have a more balanced life, without so much of her identity tied to her role at work. For some leaders, this meant starting to take regular vacations.

As this suggests, the journey to healthier patterns of leadership took perseverance and resolve. Several of the participants commented that they were proud of how much they had changed but admitted that they were "works in progress who still had their moments." Perhaps what contributed most to the managers' success in changing came from their own well-honed strengths as high achievers: they set a goal (in a new direction) and worked hard to accomplish it. This determination was reflected in the words of one of the leaders: "This is the person I want to be. Well then, it is up to me."

Implications for executive coaching

This study, which explored the phenomenon of abrasive leadership from the perspective of managers formerly perceived to be aversive in their workplace relationships, has several valuable contributions for the field of coaching. By better understanding the lived experience of the person who acts abrasively as well as the antecedents of the pattern, coaches can more effectively help bring about change.

Before describing these approaches, it should be noted that although some of the research participants attended both therapy and coaching, these individuals were mentally healthy people for whom coaching was a suitable intervention. In considering working with a toxic leader, it is important to assess whether the situation is best supported by a counselor rather than a coach. Although only a small portion of the population (10-15%) suffer from a personality disorder, it is important to direct the client organization toward the appropriate resource for the situation (Cavanagh, 2005).

Highlighted below are distinctive approaches to abrasive leadership coaching, drawn from the stories of the participants.

Coaching the person and the organization. Due to the systemic nature of the abrasive leadership phenomenon, this kind of coaching requires methodologies that address both the individual and organization. The leader's boss may need coaching on how to provide clear and specific feedback to the leader as well as guidance regarding his or her role as an internal coach. For the change to be sustained, the abrasive manager will need ongoing reinforcement—and possibly correction. The boss must set a good example and encourage healthy work practices, such as limiting hours of work and emailing after office hours.

In addition, the coaching requires good sponsorship, including enough time for change to occur. A deep-seated pattern will not shift overnight, and there will likely be slips in behavior along the way. The company needs to be prepared to invest in at least six months of coaching and to monitor the progress.

Coaching support may also be required for organization members who have been harmed by the leader's aversive behavior. Coworkers may be reluctant to trust that the manager sincerely wants to change or question whether transformation is even possible, even if the leader expresses mea culpa for past transgressions. In some cases, facilitated group meetings are valuable, where the manager undergoing the coaching and the team discuss unresolved issues. The coach can also support the manager in practices like asking for ongoing feedback or feedforward from stakeholders. The person cannot change what has already happened, but he or she can learn to do things differently going forward.

A development plan focused on leadership behavior. As described previously, study participants found that having a well-defined set of goals contributed to their transformation. A development plan, co-created with the coaching recipient, can provide clarity about what "good leadership" looks like and the kinds of behaviors associated with it. In some cases, identifying simple techniques, like counting to ten before reacting or asking questions instead of telling people what to do, can be useful in helping the client get started with new patterns. Even though these leaders were accomplished in their fields of expertise, they need to learn foundational new skills for interacting with coworkers.

Coaching inside and out. Although the coaching is often somewhat prescriptive in the beginning (including models, techniques, and rehearsal of interactions), for transformational change to occur, it must also have a developmental focus, exploring the assumptions, fears, values, and beliefs that held the pattern in place. With greater

113

awareness, the leader can then experiment with new ways of being. To do this kind of work, however, the coach must be prepared to bring personal strength, maturity, and wisdom, including a willingness to "stand in the fire" with the client.

Assessing outcomes and staying on track. Leaders who are task-oriented will benefit from tracking progress towards goals and it is especially important in these coaching engagements to conduct regular check-ins to see where improvement is perceived and where more work is required. For some leaders, assessing themselves daily is helpful to keep them focused on desired changes. Self-appraisals can be inaccurate, however; the coach should also carry out reviews with selected stakeholders, including the leader's boss.

Often, there is much to celebrate. Co-workers are relieved and grateful to their organization that the leader's behavior has changed. The company is delighted that a high performer has been salvaged and is now stronger than ever. Managers are pleased to learn that they are now viewed more positively and appreciated not only for their work output but their leadership. Sometimes (and this is the icing on the cake), these leaders not only change how they interact with others at work, but how they live their whole lives. Letting go of the need to control everything frees time and energy for other pursuits, usually things that bring much more joy and fulfillment.

Conclusions

As shown by this study, abrasive managers can shift their behavior, provided the right conditions are in place, including readiness to receive coaching, support from the company, and effective executive coaching. Of course, for broader organizational change to occur, shifts in other systemic elements are needed, including defining what healthy leadership means in the company, a willingness to hold people accountable to these norms, and providing appropriate training and development. Also required is modeling of desired behaviors at the top of the organization, providing robust feedback, and implementing reward systems based not just on results but teamwork, collaboration, and employee development. Perhaps most important, managers need to be selected not only because of their ability to deliver results, but their skill and desire to lead others. Such proactive steps which, consider both contextual and individual factors, can prevent abrasive leadership from occurring in the first place.

Areas for Future Research

As organizational life continues to be a demanding, pressure-filled environment for leaders, the focus on understanding and addressing aggression in the workplace is imperative (Leiter & Maslach, 2005; Pfeffer, 2018). Managers play a key role in setting the tone for healthy, positive work relationships and need to be supported in handling their own stress and reactivity, so they can effectively lead their teams.

An area for additional research involves the relationship between emotional intelligence and abrasive leadership. Although Ruderman, Hannam, Leslie and Steed (2003) identified self-management as a key factor in career derailment, and Crawshaw (2005) explored the dimension of empathy in abrasive leadership, more work is needed to support leadership development in these areas.

Carrying forward a systems approach, additional research is needed to understand the phenomenon of abrasive leadership in different organizational settings. For example, it would be interesting to investigate cultures that pride themselves on being humanistic and caring. In addition, in today's global economy, where many companies have employees all over the world, more learning is needed about cross-cultural differences and the impact on leadership patterns.

About the Author

Lynn Harrison, PhD, MCC, MCEC is an executive coach with 30 years of experience in management/consulting. Her background includes co-founding an international, franchised training organization, leading at the senior management level, and providing consulting services to executive leadership teams and boards. She is the Vancouver, Canada based principal of Black Tusk Leadership Inc., four-time recipient of the International Coach Federation (ICF) Prism Award.

In addition to her business leadership experience, Lynn has a PhD in Organizational Systems and an MA in Applied Behavioral Science. She is a Master Certified Coach (MCC) with the International Coaching Federation (ICF) and a certified Master Corporate Executive Coach (MCEC) with the MEECO Leadership Institute, and a member of the Association of Corporate Executive Coaches (ACEC). She is accredited as Senior Organization Development Professional and has coaching certifications in Coaching Supervision, Co-active Coaching, Ontological Coaching, Boss Whispering, and Stakeholder-Centered Coaching. Lynn is also qualified to administer a broad range of psychometric instruments. Her doctoral research focused on abrasive leaders and she has co-written a book about coaching women leaders titled, Taking the Stage: Breakthrough Stories from Women Leaders.

Lynn is the former chair of Justice Institute of B.C. and a former vice-chair on the Board of Directors for the Vancouver Chapter of the ICF.

References

Anderson, C., Anderson, K., & Deuser, W. (1996). Examining an affective aggression framework: Weapon and temperature effects on aggressive thoughts, affect, and attitudes. *Personality and Social Psychology Bulletin*, 22, 366-376.

Babiak, P., & Hare, R. (2006). *Snakes in suits: When psychopaths go to work.* New York, NY: HarperCollins.

Bloch, C. (2012). How do perpetrators experience bullying in the workplace? *International Journal Work Organization and Emotion*, 5(2), 159-177.

Bowles, M. (1997). The myth of management: Direction and failure in contemporary organizations. *Human Relations,* 50(7), 779-803.

Boyatzis, R. E. (2006). An overview of intentional change from a complexity perspective. *Journal of Management Development*, 25(7), 607-623. doi:10.1108/02621710610678445

Buss, A. H. (1961). *The psychology of aggression.* New York, NY: Wiley.

Cavanagh, M. (2005). Mental health issues and challenging clients in executive coaching. In M. Cavanagh, A.M. Grant, & Travis Kemp (Eds.), *Evidence-based coaching: Volume 1. Theory, research and practice from the behavioral sciences* (pp. 21-36). Bowen Hills, Qld, Australia: Australian Academic Press.

Crawshaw, L. (2010). Coaching abrasive leaders: Using action research to reduce suffering and increase productivity in organizations. *International Journal of Coaching in Organizations,* 29(8/1), 60-77.

Crawshaw, L. (2005). *Coaching abrasive executives: Exploring the use of empathy in constructing less destructive interpersonal management strategies* (Doctoral dissertation). Retrieved from Proquest Dissertations and Theses database. (AAT 3184798)

Crawshaw, L. (2013). Winners who become losers: Abrasive leaders. No winner ever got there without a coach: The nation's top coaching experts share their knowledge and expertise to help you win in life and business. Retrieved from http://bosswhispering.com/Winners-Who-Become-Losers-Chapter. pdf

Daniel, T. (2009a). *Tough boss or workplace bully? A grounded theory study of insights from human resource professionals* (Doctoral dissertation). Retrieved from Retrieved from Proquest Dissertations and Theses database. (AAT305169091)

Daniel, T. (2009b). *Stop bullying at work.* Alexandria, VA: Society for Human Resource Management.

Daniel, T., & Metcalf, G. (2013, July). *Taming the beast: How American corporations unwittingly conspire to make bullying a rational choice.* Paper presented at the International Society for the Systems Sciences, Haiphong, Vietnam.

DeSanti, L. (2014). *Workplace bullying, cognitive dissonance & dissonance reduction: Exploring the alleged perpetrator's experience and coping* (Doctoral dissertation). Retrieved from Dissertation Abstracts International Section A: Humanities and Social Sciences (UMI Order No. AA13638257)

Edmondson, A. (1999). Psychological safety and learning behavior in workteams. *Administrative Science Quarterly,* 44(2), 350-383.

Felson, R., & Tedeschi, J. (1993). *Aggression and violence: Social interactionist perspectives.* Washington, DC: American Psychological Association.

Friedman, M. (1970). The social responsibility of business is to increase its profits. *New York Times Magazine,* 9, 2-14.

Geen, R. G. (2001). *Human aggression.* Philadelphia, PA: Open University Press.

Gersick, C. (1991). Revolutionary change theories: A multilevel exploration of the punctuated equilibrium paradigm. *Academy of Management Review,* 16(1), 10-36.

Hanna, F.J., & Ritchie, M.H. (1995) Seeking the active ingredients of psychotherapeutic change: Within and outside the context of therapy. *Professional Psychology: Research and Practice,* 26, 176-183.

Harrison, L. (2014). Perfect storm: Exploring the phenomenon of abrasive leadership. Doctoral Dissertation, Saybrook University. Retrieved from http://upload. etdadmin.com/etdadmin/files/47/287499_pdf_280524_11495BAA-F8BC-11E3-848F-5C41EF8616FA.pdf

Heacox, N., & Sorenson, R. (2005). Organizational frustration and aggressive behaviors. *Journal of Emotional Abuse,* 4, 95-118.

Hornstein, H. A. (1996). *Brutal bosses and their prey: How to identify and overcome abuse in the workplace.* New York, NY: Riverhead Books.

James, A. (2012). *Assholes: A theory.* New York, NY: Anchor Books.

Jenkins, M., Winefield, H., Zapf, D., & Sarris, A. (2011). Bullying allegations from the accused bully's perspective. *British Journal of Management,* 23 (4), 489-501. doi:10.1111/j/1467-8551.2011.00778.x

Kaplan, R. (1991). *Beyond ambition: How driven managers can lead better and live better.* San Francisco, CA: Jossey-Bass.

Leiter, M. P., & Maslach, C. (2005). *Banishing burnout.* San Francisco, CA: Jossey-Bass.

Levinson, H. (1978, May-June). The abrasive personality. *Harvard Business Review,* 86-94.

Ludeman, K., & Erlandson, E. (2006). *Alpha male syndrome.* Boston, MA: Harvard Business School Press.

Marais, S., & Herman, M. (1997). *Corporate hyenas at work!* Pretoria, SA: Kagiso.

Meadows, D. (1999). *Leverage points: Places to intervene in a system.* Hartland, VT: The Sustainability Institute.

Mezirow, J., & Associates. (2000). *Learning as transformation: Critical perspectives on a theory in progress.* San Francisco, CA: John Wiley & Sons.

Moustakas, C. (1994). *Phenomenological research methods.* Thousand Oaks, CA: Sage.

Murphy, A. (2004). *A grounded theory study of archetypal influences on workplace bullying: A long-term effect of early childhood abuse* (Doctoral dissertation). Retrieved from Proquest Dissertation and Theses database. (AAT 3174288)

Namie, G., & Namie, R. (2009). *The bully at work: What you can do to stop the hurt and reclaim your dignity on the job.* Naperville, IL: Sourcebooks.

Nielsen, M.F., & Einarsen, S.V. (2012). Outcomes of workplace bullying. A meta-analytic review. *Work and Stress*, 216(4), 309-332.

Nielsen, M.F., & Einarsen, S.V. (2018). What we know, what we do not know, and what we should and could have known about workplace bullying: An overview of the literature and agenda for future research. *Aggression and Violent Behavior*, 42, 71-83.

Oshry, B. (2007). *Seeing systems*. San Francisco, CA: Berrett-Koehler.

Pfeffer, J. (2018). *Dying for a paycheck*. New York, NY: Harper-Collins.

Rayner, C., Hoel, H., & Cooper, C. (2002). *Workplace bullying*. London, United Kingdom: Taylor & Francis.

Roscigno, V. J., Lopez, S. H., & Hodson, R. (2009). Supervisory bullying, status inequalities, and organizational context. *Social Forces*, 87(3), 1561-1589.

Ruderman, M., Hannum, K., Leslie, J., & Steed, J. (2003). Leadership skills and emotional intelligence. Retrieved from http://www.ccl.org/leadership/pdf/assessments/skills_intelligence.pdf

Senge, P. (1990). *The fifth discipline: The art and practice of the learning organization*. New York, NY: Doubleday/Currency,

Sperry, L. (2009). Mobbing and bullying: A consulting psychology perspective and overview. *Consulting Psychology Journal*, 61(3), 190-201.

Tucker, L.J. (2019) *A narrative inquiry with three formerly abrasive leaders: Stories of disruption, awakening, and equipping* (Doctoral dissertation). Retrieved from https://digitalcommons.acu.edu/etd/154

Workplace Bullying Institute. (2017). WBI US workplace bullying survey 2017. Retrieved from http://www.workplacebullying.org/wbiresearch/2017-wbi-national-survey/

Zimbardo, P. (2008). *The Lucifer effect: Understanding how good people turn evil*. New York, NY: Random House.

CHAPTER 7

THE IMPACT OF NEUROSCIENCE AND MINDFULNESS IN COACHING LEADERS IN VUCA CONTEXTS

Asma Batool
Fielding Graduate University

Abstract

To stimulate positive learning experiences for leaders, this chapter integrates the research in neuroscience and mindfulness and expands understanding for VUCA (Volatility, Uncertainty, Complexity and Ambiguity) challenges to be transformed to opportunities for cognitive peak performance. Coaching relationships characterized by curiosity, trust, and high level of acceptance make it easier for leaders to partner with the coach and enter the zone of discomfort to take advantage of the complexity and ambiguity, rather than struggle with it. A study of neural pathways illuminate the patterns of our perception as they were laid down neurologically in our formative years, and formed from earlier experiences. Mindfulness helps with improved attention to activate positive neural states for lasting changes to mental and emotional patterns of behavior. Coaches can support the client to nurture plastic mindset with mindful attention to reinterpret our reactions to change so that fresh perspectives emerge to lead more effectively in the VUCA world.

Keywords: Leadership development, VUCA, neuroscience, mindfulness, coaching, change, stress, cognition, amygdala, attention, memory, learning, growth mindset, paradoxical thinking.

Introduction

The term "change" has taken on a completely different meaning in today's world. It used to mean that we had encountered something new, something different in a relatively stable, complex but structured world. We could plan for change. This does not hold true anymore. Today, we live in an environment characterized by volatility, uncertainty, complexity and ambiguity (VUCA). The accelerated pace of change makes stability and planning obsolete. The once identifiable boundaries, which distinguished markets, industries and organizations, are now highly permeable. Magee describes VUCA as

"...a world order where the threats are both diffuse and uncertain, where conflict is inherent yet unpredictable, and where our capability to defend and promote our national interests may be restricted by materiel and personnel resource constraints. In short, an environment marked by volatility, uncertainty, complexity, and ambiguity (VUCA)" (1998, p. 1).

The magnitude of change presents unique challenges for leaders, as conventional leadership strategies and success frameworks do not account for the current realities. Given the dynamic environment, leaders require a quantum shift in their vision, approach, and strategy to effectively cope and lead in the current VUCA world.

Organizations need to review the role of leadership in today's rapidly changing and complex landscapes. "Many leaders are judging too soon and judging too simplistically. Others are deciding too late and paying a price for their slowness or lack of courage" (Johansen, 2012, pp. 1-2). Organizations now recognize that they must equip leaders with the right tools, strategies, and most importantly, identify and nurture the right behaviors to be effective in today's global workplace. To address the challenges and contribute to leadership objectives in the VUCA era, coaching has emerged as the most empowering approach to support leaders to lead in times of great change. The coaching orientation to leadership is to support the leader in creating new contexts where leaders can reframe perspectives, tap into their creative potential, and renew systems.

As Whitmore (2017) says, "Coaching is unlocking people's potential to maximize their own performance. It is helping them to learn rather than teaching them" (pp. 12-13). Coaching is the process of bringing out the best in an individual. It is about helping the client identify and nurture the learner within. It enables the clients to discover their own, unique path to success. Coaching addresses an important and growing need: expanding leader capabilities to work more effectively and cohesively in their environments in alignment with their sense of purpose. On one hand, coaching has witnessed rapid growth as a distinct field. On the other, it serves as a catalyst to leadership development activities.

Recent advances in neuroscience and mindfulness influence an evidence-based synergy to develop leadership competencies in a VUCA climate. Bossons, Riddell, and Sartain further elucidate, "An understanding of neuroscience might improve coaching in providing the rationale for ways in which behaviors can be changed for the better and by increasing our understanding of why some techniques work" (2015, p. 20). Neuroscience-based mindfulness or Neuro-mindfulness is a good fit with coaching as it maps human behavior in terms of activities of the brain and helps to focus attention in the direction of identified development. From the perspective of neuroplasticity, both the coach and the client can change the behavioral patterns to upgrade their capabilities and bring additional effectiveness to the coaching relationship. Mindfulness supports optimal functioning in the coaching relationship and influences coaching outcomes by "providing a foundation for healthy personality development and an intention to act authentically in the world" (Spence, 2019, p. 196). The study of neuroscience and mindfulness provides an understanding of those triggers that coaches can utilize to optimize brain performance. Embedding the linkages among the mind-body-brain interrelationships into the coaching domain, we can explore applications to create new options for effective VUCA leadership.

Exploring neuro-mindfulness to reframe effective leadership in VUCA context

How do we build a leadership mindset that enables leaders to dwell comfortably in uncertainty and to experiment with volatility? More importantly, how can coaches use findings from neuroscience and mindfulness to help leaders become positive change agents in a climate of constant change?

Neuroscience investigates the human brain to understand the biological mechanisms of brain-behavior interaction, as well as how the brain processes information. It is interesting to observe how the brain processes uncertainty in its environment. Our brain is hard-wired to survive and stay safe, which it does primarily by avoiding threats and seeking rewards. The motivation to avoid is stronger and far more important than the latter. As Breuning shares, "Our brain seeks rewards as enthusiastically as it avoids pain because rewards are necessary for survival. But in the state of nature, pain can kill you faster than missing out on rewards, so our brain prioritizes threat signals over reward signals" (2019, p. 20).

When the brain anticipates a novelty in the form of change, conflicts, or cognitive dissonance (inconsistent thoughts, beliefs, or attitudes), it fires a threat response. As a result of the perceived threat, the amygdala activates the stress response system. High levels of noradrenaline and dopamine are released which "impair the workings of the prefrontal cortex and simultaneously strengthen the amygdala functioning" (Arnsten, 2009, p. 4). The prefrontal cortex (PFC) responsible for higher-order cognitive processing regulating cognition and emotion is impaired, undermining cognitive performance. "The PFC is crucial in attention, working memory, and cognitive control processes, with damage to this region leading to impairments in planning, goal attainment, and problem-solving ability" (Hilt, Hanson,

& Pollack, 2011, p. 164). Since the amygdala is strongly activated during the process, it elicits a self-preserving impulse in the form of a fight-escape-avoidance-freezing response. While focused research (Duval, Javanbakht, & Liberzon, 2015; Stolier & Freeman, 2016) also points out the activation of certain regions in the insula that elicit similar responses, the amygdala is majorly considered to be the hub of avoidance and fear. Thus, the impairing of the PFC and strengthened activity of the amygdala induces primitive, survival instincts suppressing the higher-order, complex responses. The ability of the brain to deal with the complexity and turbulence in the VUCA world is hugely challenged and it throws us off balance.

One of the primary reasons why we struggle to adapt in VUCA is because for centuries we have survived and succeeded in a world which we considered predictable. Though influenced by complexity and gradual changes, we are used to a world that is largely organized around a stable context. This change—from something relatively stable to something fluid on the path of constant flux, which needs to be renewed over and over again—creates enormous amounts of stress for us. The impact of this change is that our brains can no longer seek patterns that they recognize, and predictability becomes a challenge. The absence of predictability is perceived by the brain as a threat from the environment. Thus, a vicious cycle is set into motion, in which the brain is dealing with an increasingly dynamic and ambiguous environment using only traditional, protective, survival-based safety mechanisms.

There exists a possibility of retraining the brain to emerge with positive learning experiences. Our brain's innate propensities can be influenced with conscious attention to create neuroplastic changes in the brain's structure. We now have compelling evidence of the brain's plasticity (Fuchs & Flügge, 2014; Zilles, 1992)—the brain's ability to undergo continuous structural and functional changes in response to internal and external stimuli from the environment. Of particular relevance to this discussion is self-directed neuroplasticity.

We can use our mind to change our brain and develop a mindset to deal with VUCA proactively and constructively. When the neural networks experience changes in behavior, there is a corresponding change in the neural architecture that produces the behavior (Byrge, Sporns, & Smith, 2014). With behavioral changes over sustained periods, the brain experiences continued activity across a distributed neural network. This results in new patterns of brain activation that cause lasting changes in the brain circuitry. Kleim and Jones (2008) state, "neural plasticity is the mechanism by which the brain encodes experience and learns new behaviors" (p. 225). This adaptive capacity of the brain can be used to create new pathways that lead to positive behavioral modifications over time.

Neuroscientific research continues to place mindfulness as the most proven way to rewire our brain architecture for lasting positive change. Boyatzis and Mckee (2005) define mindfulness as "the capacity to be fully aware of all that one experiences inside the self—body, mind, heart, spirit—and to pay full attention to what is happening around us" (p. 112). Mindfulness is the awareness of oneself in the experience of the moment. It is about bringing attention to the here and now "in a non-judgmental way" (Passmore & Marianetti, 2013, p. 132). By focusing our attention to a specific point of reference, we can "stimulate the firing in certain neuronal groups to establish new neural circuitry and reinforce the connections" along a specific, desired path (Widdett, 2014, p. 7). Mindfulness makes it possible for us to focus our attention to sculpt the brain in episodic as well as in permanent ways. Research has shown that mindfulness makes "measurable changes in brain regions associated with memory, sense of self, empathy, and stress" (McGreevy, 2011, para. 1). Mindfulness meditation enhances attention and activates neuroplasticity in a positive direction to strengthen wellbeing and quality of life. Most importantly, mindfulness taps into the benefits of neuroplasticity to inform and enhance awareness to focus and be present in the moment, a capacity so central to the exercise of dynamic leadership in the VUCA world.

The intersection of neuro-mindfulness and coaching in developing VUCA leadership

Does the research on neuro-mindfulness provide sufficient evidence for coaches to identify those mechanisms that facilitate learning and development in VUCA leaders?

Leveraging learning from a neuro-mindful perspective. Moving to a deeper context, let us take a look at learning how to learn— the neuro-mindful relationship between learning and development. Neuroanatomical research (Brem, Ran, & Pascual-leone, 2013; Engle, Tuholski, Laughlin, & Conway, 1999; Inda, Muravieva, & Alberini, 2011; Karpicke, 2016; Kyllonen & Stephens, 1990) prove that learning and memory are highly inter-related concepts, such that learning is the process of acquiring inputs and memory deals with the encoding, storage, and retrieval of these inputs. Memory gets encoded and stored in the central nervous system by changing the strength of synaptic connections between neurons. In other words, the strength of the previously existing connection is modified when memory is stored, retrieved, or encoded. We know that learning takes place when we pay attention, and attention forms new neural networks in the brain (Holland & Maddux, 2010; Posner & Rothbart, 2009; Posner, Sheese, Odludas, & Tang, 2006). When we pay attention, memories are formed, stored, and retrieved in a complex process that engages a set of overlapping regions in the brain. Research now shows (Hsu & Goh, 2016; Pessoa, 2018) that the brain involves different set of overlapping regions for cognitive reasoning and a separate set of brain regions are activated for social and emotional processing. Hence, discrete regions can be associated with discrete functions (Otero & Barker, 2014) that work together for cognitive functioning.

Fuster (2015) defines attention as the "the limitations of the nervous system to process an excessive amount of relevant or adaptive information at a given time" (p. 97). When we pay attention, the focus of our attention supports the brain in selecting information and internally representing the information for specific amount of time. This process

126

of selective attention focused on an internal representation is defined as working memory: the ability to hold and manipulate information for shorter intervals of time during cognitive functioning. Working memory can be viewed as "the subset of knowledge in long-term memory that is currently activated" (Cowan, 1995, p. 24). Multiple constraints placed on the operations of the working memory limits its capacity. Hence performance of the working memory may be reduced as a result of the numerous demands placed on a particular cognitive activity.

The temporal internal representations in the working memory are subject to spontaneous decay and possible interference (distraction), resulting in loss of information. However, the information can be retained for a further period of time with attentional mechanisms such as repetition, mental stimulation, constructing meaning by remembering and knowing (Tulving, 1985), or associating it with previously stored inputs (Brown & Craik, 2000). Motivation is an additional factor that intrinsically focuses attention on the acquired knowledge and enables retention (Pekrun, 1992; Seli, Wammes, Risko, & Smilek, 2016). The more the information is repeated or used, the more likely it is to be retained in long-term memory (Roediger & Karpicke, 2006). Memory gets consolidated and stabilized and is stored in a different part of the brain than the initial site of its encoding. Also, long-term memories experience structural modifications—changes in the structure of neurons that involve the growth of new processes and synapses. Thus, working memory is more of a base to hold information in short-term, and either gets lost, or with consolidation and retention is encoded into the long-term memory. The long-term memory is essentially a process by which gene expression, leading to protein synthesis, converts temporary traces into permanent memories (Bailey, Bartsch, & Kandel, 1996). Long-term memory is a permanent knowledge representation, which involves structural editing in neurons.

There is a lot of rigorous study on the interactive linkages between attention and working memory as these processes play a significant role in goal-driven processing. Working memory shows increased performance and cognitive abilities in areas associated with fluid intelligence (Engle, Tuholski, Laughlin, & Conway, 1999; Kyllonen & Christal, 1990), reasoning (Kyllonen & Christal, 1990), learning (Kyllonen & Stephens, 1990), verbal reading comprehension (Daneman & Carpenter, 1980), proactive control (Richmond, Redick, & Braver, 2015), and life event stress (Klein & Boals, 2001). Mental Time Travel (MTT), the capacity to mentally travel through past and possible experiences can be leveraged to optimize decision making and contribute to long-term goals (Boyer, 2008).

Mindfulness meditation has a significant co-relation to enhancements in cognitive performance and improving memory capacities. Mindfulness helps in focusing attention and to slow down the speedier response to external stimuli such that attention moves to the more subtle mind and body processes. Mindfulness helps us with a greater understanding of "tuning the autonomic nervous system" (Haule, 2011, p. 170) by "learning how to control and master the physiological processes that occur between the brain and the nervous system" (Rees, 2017, p. 197). Several studies have placed centrality on working memory, and working memory capacities and have shown improved processes in the brain's working memory system. In one study, participants were evaluated before and after a ten day mindfulness training and demonstrated significant improvements in working memory (Chambers, Chuen Yee Lo, & Allen, 2007). In another, a two week course in mindfulness meditation demonstrated reliable changes in GRE (Graduate Records Examination) reading comprehension and working memory capacity, while reducing mind wandering; thus, improving overall attentional focus for the participants (Mrazek, Franklin, Phillips, Baird, & Schooler (2013). "Working memory has been found to influence learning such that those with a greater working memory capacity learn more rapidly and are able to manipulate information, remember directions, and concentrate" (Entwistle & Shinaver, 2014, pp. 475-476).

Various studies have demonstrated that long term mindfulness practices can result in positive changes in brain and immune function (Davidson, Kabat-Zinn, Schumacher, Rosenkranz, Muller, Santorelli, Urbanowski, Harrington, Bonus, & Sheridian, 2003), attention regulation and increased self-awareness (Jha, Krompinger, & Baime, 2007), refined perceptiveness and affective processes (Nyklícek & Kuijpers, 2008), enhanced multitasking capabilities such as lower stress and better memory (Levy, Wobbrock, Kaszniak, & Ostergren, 2011), and improved emotion regulation (Nielsen & Kaszniak, 2006). Constant practice of mindfulness has shown to have long term impact in structural connectivity leading to neural plasticity.

Facilitating stress as an enhancing mechanism in learning interventions. A growing understanding in neuroscientific studies is the role of stress in improving cognitive performance. Stress is a form of neuroplastic adaptation in which our brain responds to stress in two ways: a "threat" mode or "challenge" mode. A stress situation is categorized as a "threat" when we understand that our brain and body do not have sufficient resources to cope with the environmental demands. We experience a heightened stress response system and high levels of noradrenaline and dopamine are released. The resulting impact is an overactive amygdala and underactive prefrontal cortex (Arnsten, 2009), and lower cardiovascular efficiency (Huang, Webb, Zourdos, & Acevedo, 2013) with decrease in cognitive ability (Arnsten, 2009). When we believe that our personal resources are sufficient to meet the stressful demands from the environment, we have a positive approach towards the stress, perceive the stress as a "challenge" and seek ways to effectively deal with and manage stress.

In the VUCA context, when leaders encounter stress in the form of unknown and ambiguous circumstances, they need to be equipped with resources that move them from operating in "threat" mode to functioning in "challenge" mode. Leaders are presented with uncertainty and failure a lot more often than predictability and success. Hence, they must challenge themselves by shifting their goals from the traditional objectives of striving for success to embracing failure and experimenting with uncertainty. Coaches must provide leaders with developmental resources that draw them out of their comfort zones and nudge them towards multi-frame thinking. Coaches must facilitate the understanding of threats as learning opportunities to develop the leaders' potential beyond their growth edges so that they consider VUCA as the playground to leverage their full potential and experiment with volatility.

In relation to stress, a subsequent understanding provided by neuroscience is that either too little or too much stress impairs the functioning of the prefrontal cortex. "The PFC is very sensitive to its neurochemical environment" (Brennan & Arnsten, 2008, p. 236). Catecholamines released in the PFC due to stress have an inverted U influence on the functioning of the PFC, whereby either too little or too much norepinephrine or dopamine impairs the cognitive abilities in the PFC. Since the PFC is essential for attention regulation, "optimal catecholamine actions in PFC are needed for focused, organized attention" (Brennan & Arnsten, 2008, p. 238).

The above neuroscientific base is also illustrated by the Yerkes-Dodson optimal arousal curve. The inverted U curve describes the relationship between stress-arousal (energy activation during stress) and performance. The curvilinear path demonstrates that performance improves as arousal increases until a point at which time it decreases. The mid-point of the curve is the peak at which performance is optimal or in flow, whereas too little or too much arousal degrades performance (Diamond, Campbell, Park, Halonen, & Zoladz, 2007).

It is crucial to understand what degree of challenge is effective to induce optimal performance rather than impede performance for leaders. Deci states, "this motivational mechanism (one's need to feel competent and self-determining) leads people to situations which provide challenges which make optimum use of their abilities" (1975, p. 57). Leaders should be provided the opportunities to engage in "challenge by choice." The element of choice works in multiple ways. It

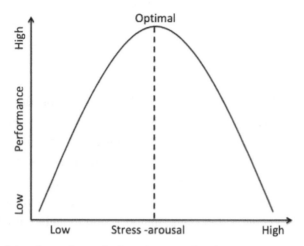

Figure 1: "The Relation of Strength of Stimulus to Rapidity of Habit-Formation" (Yerkes & Dodson, 1908). *Journal of Comparative Neurology.* Work in the public domain.

builds engagement towards the challenge, allowing leaders to perceive stress as an enhancer for growth. Leaders take accountability for their own growth and learning, and can easily be motivated to identify, utilize, and build more resources in the direction of their chosen development. Leaders find it much easier to move to the optimal point of performance, which results in impactful learning that is long term and sustainable. In a neuroscientific study, when participants were exposed to a laboratory social stressor designed to engender threat or challenge stress evaluations, "participants experienced boosts in cognitive flexibility and attentional bias towards happy faces only under challenge evaluations" (Crum, Akinola, Martin, and Fath, 2017, p. 391). Scientists also noted that while considering stress as a challenge rather than a threat may be beneficial, developing a stress-is-enhancing mindset "magnifies cognitive, emotional, and physiological attributes that may contribute to adaptive responses over the long-run" (Crum et. al., 2017, p. 390). As neuroscience provides evidence-based insights on brain-related processes that occur under all levels of stress, we must ensure that our coaching and development interventions are designed to enhance cognitive processes and result in optimal engagement of the leader's resources. Coaches can leverage optimal amounts of stress as vehicles for developing learning experiences for their clients. Having an accurate perception of a stressful reality helps the coach to leverage stressful environments as growth experiences for the leaders.

Neuro-mindful view on memory encoding, consolidation, and retrieval for leadership effectiveness. Neuroscientific research has led to a greater understanding on the significance of learning, attention, and memory as vital tools to generate awareness of information received from the external senses, and how the processes of learning and remembering further shape the experience of knowing, reflection, and action in context. Learning, memory, and thought are integral to the context of development.

The process of memory encoding, consolidation, and retrieval are not subjectively experienced but is more of an inference. However, a detailed understanding reduces the complexity of memory-related brain concepts to recognize positive and sustainable change triggers in leaders and their eco-systems.

Can coaches benefit from an understanding of memory-related insights and design interventions to help leaders improve their experiences with learning?

Human memory can store large amounts of information. Information is initially encoded as patterns of neural activity and is temporary and subject to change. How well we encode a memory is critical to how effectively we will be able to recall it at a future point. "Memory consolidation refers to the process by which a temporary, labile memory is transformed into a more stable, long-lasting form" (Squire, Genzel, Wixted, & Morris, 2015, para. 1). "New memories have to be stabilized or consolidated, if they have to persist" (LeDoux, 2007, p. 171). The process of memory consolidation strengthens the new memory traces, and there is ample evidence suggesting that "memory consolidation benefits essentially from a state of reduced sensory input, such as sleep and quiet wakefulness" (Abichou et al., 2019, para. 3). A research study with a student group proved that systems memory consolidation rapidly occurred with repeated rehearsal using words within one study session. Subsequent experiential demonstration provided evidence that sleep makes the consolidation stable and long lasting (Himmer, Schönauer, Heib, Schabus, & Gais, 2019).

Starting with encoding of information, the process is followed by short-term storage, consolidation and repeated reconsolidation from short-term memory to long-term memory, which results in successful long-term storage. "Consolidation is thought to occur in a structured way allowing for prompt and precise retrieval" (Brem, Ran, & Pascual-leone, 2013, p. 699). Retrieval is a collection of processes where memories are retrieved by cues, encounters with environmental or internal events, that have been previously associated with them. Some of these processes overlap with those used in encoding. Any retrieval event is also an encoding event and any encoding event involves some elements of retrieval. When an established memory is retrieved, it again becomes transiently labile. "Over time, it becomes resistant to disruption and this process that renders the memory stable is termed reconsolidation" (Inda, Muravieva and Alberini, 2011, p. 1635). Hence, new phase of consolidation can follow retrieval.

"New memories are formed on the background of a prior retrieved experience" (Sara, 2000, p. 73), as the new memory is dependent on the past memory to organize and provide meaning to it. Thus, new memory is an approximation of the original, past memory. Over time, the memories morph and we are unable to distinguish between the two. This process of cognitive reconstruction creates "coherent and integrated mental representations of complex concepts, the kind of deep learning necessary to solve new problems and draw new inferences" (Karpicke, 2016, para. 3).

A particular focus for coaches and development practitioners is to embed learnings for the long term. This requires us to encode learning such that leaders take time to process it. The lack of meaningful connection and processing time makes it difficult for the learner to retain information. Processing or connecting to the learning in their unique, meaningful ways is where learning happens. Memories are defined in terms of time. Likewise, stimulating learning that reflects on meaningful insights gained from experiences also takes time. Designing interventions for long-term impact enables leaders to consolidate memory, using sleep, quiet wake, and reflection on learning so that the desired learning sticks. Repeated reactivation increases the accessibility of information from the memory. Hence, learning that involves reinforcement of concept is important when designing a leadership intervention. The consistent reinforced practice results in learning that is a relatively permanent change in behavior. The reinforced learning forges a deeper and richer neural pathway, enhancing their cognitive processes. Learning is not just the process of grasping new behaviors. Repetitive exercise of the behaviors strengthens the memory traces in the new neural pathways until they transition and become more permanently embedded in the long-term memory, developing a new, embedded style of leadership for the leader.

Applications for neuro-mindful leadership development and coaching

Coaching is widely regarded as a means of augmenting leadership effectiveness. However, coaching has applications in many other leadership contexts. A more holistic focus for coaching is on innovative leadership and organizational transformation. Coaching can address multiple dimensions of the leadership experience to help leaders stay positive and engaged as learners—even in the midst of a VUCA context. Discussion of two such dimensions, growth mindset and paradoxical thinking, follows:

Growth Mindset. Leader's mindsets predict their performance in real-world settings. Mindsets are the inherent predispositions, taken-for-granted assumptions that shape our approach in which we view experience and take action in the world. As Dweck (2006) emphasizes, "the view you adopt for yourself profoundly affects the way you lead your life" (p. 6).

These mindsets influence in two ways:

(a) Fixed-mindset: a limited view, deficit-focused thinking which is blind to a broader perspective, works with routine, and change that is episodic and linear, or

(b) Growth-mindset: here, the basic orientation is towards an expanding mindset that embraces individualism, influences agility, and considers new possibilities. A growth mindset channels "the transformative power of effort—the power of effort to change your ability and to change you as a person" (Dweck, 2006, p. 42). This is an inquiring mind, which experiments with strategies and approaches, and believes that true potential can be discovered through repetitive and focused efforts. This results in examining habits of mind that are truly transformational. "The passion for stretching yourself and sticking to it, even (or especially) when it's not going well, is the hallmark of the growth mindset" (Dweck, 2006, p. 7).

To establish a growth mindset, coaches must work with the client to stimulate their heightened awareness of the assumptions underlying their actions and interactions. When their mental models become explicit, the clients can be placed at the center of their learning experiences. This orientation can produce a sharp difference in the way clients focus their efforts on specific developmental pathways where they experience profound change and work towards it. A coach-client relationship where the coach is a co-facilitator, and the client is both a co-facilitator and learner, enables self-directed comprehensive clarity for the client about their overall vision that fuels their personal and professional aspirations.

Research has shown that holding enhancing or debilitating mindsets produces corresponding changes in outcomes such as, "performance and productivity, health and well-being, and learning and growth" (Crum, Salovey, & Achor, 2013, p. 716). Mindsets at the level of core beliefs are dynamic and subject to change. Flexible mindsets can be

135

achieved by simply orienting people to different information (Blackwell, Trzesniewski, & Dweck, 2007). In a neuroscientific experiment where participants were shown a series of three three-minute videos on a "stress-is-enhancing" mindset, participants experienced "positive consequences relating to improved health and work performance" (Crum, Salovey, & Achor, 2013, p. 729). Building a growth mindset in elementary students using mindfulness practices demonstrated varied benefits, such as increases in self-efficacy, positive body image and confidence, and a resilient, capability-focused attitude (Kluk, 2017).

Langer, Djikic, Pirson, Mandenci, and Donohue (2010) experimented with an intervention to take advantage of the mindset that pilots have excellent vision. Participants were made to don the clothes of Air Force pilots and flew a flight simulator that was controlled by control participants. It was noted that the vision improved for the participants embodying the pilot mindset. When we read stories and engage closely with a character in the story, we pay close attention to the character's thoughts, feelings and experiences, which results in mindful attention. This changes our beliefs, our pre-defined assumptions that we hold on to, and opens our mind to varied possibilities. "Purposeful focusing on thoughts, feelings, sensations, and behavior in order to make meaning from those fragments of experience. The outcome of this reflection is to create new understanding which in turn may lead to: increasing choices, making changes, or reducing confusion" (Voller, 2010, p. 21).

Mindfulness deepens the attention for self-directed change and strengthens the mind's leadership to deal with external and internal challenges. A Scottish author, Caroline McHugh (2013), talks about True Mirrors—seamless mirrors that are placed at right angles to each other. She mentions,

> "The difference is when you look in a regular mirror you look for reassurance—that you're beautiful, or you're young, or you're tidy, or your bum doesn't look big in that. But when you look in a True Mirror you don't look at yourself, you look for

yourself. You look for revelation, not for reassurance. (2:36) Neuro-mindfulness is cultivating the penetrating awareness to "look for yourself" inside you, around you, and in the cosmos. Influencing a growth mindset in the coaching relationship helps both the coach and the client maintain the single-minded focus, yet seek multiplicity of perspectives to reach out to the next truth or the next experience."

Paradoxical thinking. Paradoxes are the competing forces that dissipate the leader's energies in two conflicting directions. The paradoxes could be in the form of competing values, conflicts, tensions, polarities, or opposing realities to name a few. A common understanding with paradoxes is that the conflicting forces demand a choice in one direction, resulting in either/or thinking. A better way of dealing with paradoxes is to move beyond the resistance to look at common synergies between the dualities and balancing the competing stimuli for complementary effectiveness in systems. Balancing extremities by holding interrelated and interdependent energies in dynamic equilibrium results in innovative possibilities and emergence of complex adaptive systems. The unique influence ushers "out of the box" thinking, helping the leaders become more innovative, flexible, and adaptive to the turbulent dynamics of the VUCA world.

Some paradoxes are cyclical in nature and result in iteration. For example, it takes too much time to resolve a problem, but by not resolving it, it stays forever. Another example is, to create something new, you must destroy the old. When the old is destroyed and new is created, the new is the old. Is not this what VUCA is all about?

When the cyclical, iterative paradoxes are not addressed, they become the wicked problems. Then situations are exacerbated and result in undesirable consequences. Grint (2008) illustrates the iterative, cyclical nature of wicked problems with this example:

"When global warming first emerged as a problem some of

the responses concentrated on solving the problem through science, manifest in the development of biofuels; but we now know that biofuels appear to denude the world of significant food resources so that what looked like a solution actually became another problem" (pp. 12-13).

A wicked problem morphs constantly and deals with the impossibility of finding an optimal solution. For example, poor countries are increasingly vulnerable to the impacts of climate change, particularly in reduced crop yields, lower nutritional levels, increased disease incidence, water scarcity, and coastal flooding. This alters the path of economic growth, worsens health, significantly increasing poverty, low levels of education, and lowering financial and socio-economic stability (OECD, 2010).

Paradox is a game-changer for organizations and leaders in the VUCA environment. When considered from a growth mindset, paradoxes stimulate a turn-around, a complete shift in thinking and developmental capacities, and provide untapped opportunities in systems around us. It is about taking a U-turn and getting behind the problem to understand its source. The best way to understand the growth edges for leaders is to look at the paradoxical conflicts inside them. In organizations, if you are looking at upping your game and creating new stories that have not been told before, look at the paradoxical elements that exist in the organizational eco-system.

Coaches need to fundamentally explore creating a shift in the leader's mindset to reframe boundaries and ensure the optimal performance of paradox in action. A fundamental strategy is to embrace both sides of the paradox and expand appreciation of the contradictory and conflicting demands. This calls for coaches to support leaders in moving from an either-or to a both-and mindset and create win-win strategies. With awareness of the paradoxical insights, coaches and trainers need to build capability in leaders to find actionable ground to accommodate opposing poles and ability to oscillate between the poles. We need to build interventions that promote synergistic thinking and facilitate reframing at a higher level of abstraction such that the system scans itself and learns how it learns.

How does neuro-mindfulness use paradoxical leadership and enable organizational leaders to view VUCA as an opportunity?

Neuroscience (Kruglanski, 1989; Epley & Gilovich, 2016) talks about motivated reasoning, a cognitive bias, in which our brain is prone to rationalization that conforms to our existing beliefs. This implicit emotional regulation is an attempt to shut down distress when faced with unpleasant realities. The motivation to avoid distress and approach biased, defensive reasoning results in positive reinforcement for the brain.

In a study conducted on 30 political activists during the U.S. Presidential election of 2004, when political participants were provided negative information about their chosen candidates, neuroimaging evidence captured activation in brain regions related to distress due to error detection. Subsequent evidence showed decrease in cognitive activity and increased emotional activity, resulting in emotionally biased conclusions. Participants provided contradictory statements and recruited false beliefs to exonerate their candidate of choice. This resulted in activation of reward circuits providing positive reinforcement for their biased reasoning (Westen, Blagov, Harenski, Kilts, and Hamann, 2006).

A second form of cognitive bias is cognitive tribalism. Our sense of self develops by knowing how we are distinct from others and where we fit in with others. The latter is a sense of belonging shaped by family beliefs, group expectations, and belonging/rebelling notions with a community. The group choices and levels of comfort/discomfort projects as personal choices and form the motivations for how we think, relate, decide, and perform. Cognitive tribalism is the need for fellowship with a group or community that we have either grown up with or strongly identify with—our political and cultural beliefs, value systems, hobbies, personal tastes, religion and spirituality, that manifests in our personality and mental outlook. These affiliations create the basis for our choice, judgment, and decision making when we are faced with the conundrum of polarized tensions. Interventions should be designed to challenge these affiliations to seek better approaches and newer directions in our line of sight. Learning interventions should be able to capture the reframing of boundaries and belief systems such that human cognition moves beyond the first-hand beliefs and learn to think and operate in multifaceted ways.

We frame our world so that it makes sense to us. Our human brains create filters that govern the way we want to see the world. Neuroimaging studies measure the data that emerges within the boundaries of these governing principles. The data that emerges is taken as certainty and new theories are built on top of this certainty. The filters that are used by our brain to perceive our assertions create a cognitive bias that supports us to access our version of the truth. This truth is further rationalized to build a "series of concatenated probabilities making it harder and harder to question the basic assumptions of the original truth" (Langer, 2013, p. 13). Mindfulness is the lens that enables us to pay attention to attention such that original truth and the associated filters can be seen as separate variables. When we separate the variables from the truth, can we hold steadfastly to our belief that our truth is original, or will the truth undergo a change?

Recommendations for future research

The field of coaching research has made good progress over the past two decades with the focus primarily on what happens in coaching and the facilitative/growth conditions that make coaching effective in certain contexts. We are now aware of a myriad of coaching behaviors that may influence coaching effectiveness—coach/client-behavior studies, coach-client relationship studies, coaching impact studies-organizational/individual (Passmore, & Fillery-Travis, 2011). While current research demonstrates the influence of coaching on learning and development, limited scientific evidence exists of the benefits of coaching (Jones, Woods, & Guillaume, 2016). We need to make coaching research more evidence based. "Neuroscience can shed light on the underlying mechanisms of coaching and provide important insights to facilitate development" (Boyatzis & Jack, 2018, p. 11). A neurological basis can provide deeper insights on those coaching variables that can produce positive outcomes. Further, both coaches and leaders would benefit from an understanding of those adaptive traits that are especially relevant for leadership in a complex, turbulent environment. It is important to draw on neuroscientific findings to identify the links among mindsets, behaviors, and skills best suited for adaptive performance in the VUCA world. Mindfulness is a potential resource that can help develop creative responses to the dynamic complexity. More research evidence is required to identify the mindfulness-related mechanisms in the brain that build lasting resources to promote physical and psychological well-being. Scientific findings from neuroscience and mindfulness can help us witness the potential of those brain capacities that flex and renew in order to be agile and adaptive in ambiguous times.

Conclusion

A coaching environment is an enabler of change. The coach helps the client identify their desired behavioral change and make it sustainable over time, thus facilitating the leader's capabilities to harness the opportunities inherent in the VUCA world. Neuroplasticity, our ability to alter neural structures and the physiology of our brain, allows us to adjust to and understand change, thus developing our capacity to hold ambiguity. Instead of reacting to neuro-conditioned reflexes, mindfulness can be leveraged to recognize the value of stillness and connection to experience a shift from living in the past to a center of gravity in the present moment. A mindset that embraces ambiguity and complexity can be nurtured with neuro-mindful attention that allows for deeper levels of concentration, cognitive flexibility, and emotional resilience to achieve sustainable change. When we see the mystery and messiness inherent in VUCA problems and our habitual orientation to these problems with neuro-mindful attention, we see them for what they really are. It allows clarity to emerge from the confusion painted by the mind's eye. Neuro-mindfulness facilitates an increasing openness to change. We refocus the lens of our habitual thinking "to create new neural connections and pathways, laying the groundwork for new habits that lead to changes in behavior" (Anderson, 2013, para. 7). A neuroscientific perspective supports us to embrace mindful attention for lasting, positive transformation in the VUCA world.

About the Author

Asma Batool's career has been defined by her relentless search and zeal for personal and professional transformations. For more than nineteen years, Asma has been helping leaders define and reach their goals. She is a leadership coach and L&D educator specializing in vertical leadership development, developing emotional and authentic leadership, and supporting executives in transition and change. She also enjoys conducting research on whole-person transformational development of individuals, teams, and organizations. Asma has coached leaders in the IT, healthcare, retail, ecommerce and banking industries as well as nonprofits and academia. She was awarded the World's Best Top 100 Global Coaching Leaders by CHRO Asia and World Coaching Congress in 2017. She has a Master's degree in Organizational Development and Leadership from Fielding Graduate University, USA and Bachelors in Computer Science. She is an accredited, certified coach with the International Coaching Federation. She is passionate about helping individuals use themselves as instruments of change, and excited about possibilities for collaboration.

References

Abichou, K., La Corte, V., Hubert, N., Orriols, E., Gaston-Bellegarde, A., Nicolas, S., & Piolino, P. (2019). Young and older adults benefit from sleep, but not from active wakefulness for memory consolidation of what-where-when naturalistic events. *Frontiers in Aging Neuroscience*, 11, 58.

Anderson, J. B. (2013). Mindfulness and the Process of Change. *Coaching World.* Issue 7.

Arnsten, A. (2009). Stress signaling pathways that impair prefrontal cortex structure and function. *Nature Reviews Neuroscience*, 10(6), 410–422.

Bailey, C. H., Bartsch, D., and Kandel, E. R. (1996). Toward a molecular definition of long-term memory storage. *Proceedings of the National Academy of Sciences of the United States of America*, 93(24), 13445-13452.

Blackwell, L. S., Trzesniewski, K. H., & Dweck, C. S. (2007). Implicit theories of intelligence predict achievement across an adolescent transition: A longitudinal study and an intervention. *Child Development*, 78, 246 –263.

Bossons, P., Riddell, P., and Sartain, D. (2015). *The Neuroscience of Leadership Coaching*. London: Bloomsbury Press.

Boyatzis, R. E., & McKee, A. (2005). *Resonant Leadership: Renewing yourself and connecting with others through mindfulness, hope, and compassion*. Boston: Harvard Business School Press.

Boyatzis, R. E., & Jack, A. I. (2018). The neuroscience of coaching. *Consulting Psychology Journal: Practice and Research*, 70(1), 11–27. https://doi.org/10.1037/cpb0000095

Boyer, P. (2008). Evolutionary economics of mental time travel? *Trends in Cognitive Sciences*,12, 219–224.

Brem, A. K., Ran, K., & Pascual-leone, A. (2013). Brain Stimulation: Learning and memory. In Aminoff, M. J., Boller, F., & Swaab, D. F. (Eds.). *Handbook of Clinical Neurology*. (pp. 693-737). Amsterdam: Elsevier.

Brennan, A. R., & Arnsten, A. (2008). Neuronal mechanisms underlying attention deficit hyperactivity disorder: The influence of arousal on prefrontal cortical function. *Annals of the New York Academy of Sciences*, 1129(1), 236-245.

Breuning, L. G. (2019). *Tame your anxiety: rewiring your brain for happiness*. Lanham, MD: Rowman & Littlefield.

Brown, S. C., & Craik, F. I. M. (2000). Encoding and retrieval of information. In Tulving, E., & Craik, F. I. M. (Eds.). *The Oxford handbook of memory*. (pp. 93-107). New York: Oxford University Press.

Byrge, L., Sporns, O., & Smith, L. B. (2014). Developmental process emerges from Extended brain-body-behavior networks. *Trends in cognitive sciences*, 18(8), 395–403. doi:10.1016/j.tics.2014.04.010.

Chambers, R., Chuen Lee Yo, B., & Allen, N. B. (2008). The impact of intensive mindfulness training on attentional control, cognitive style, and affect.

Cognitive Therapy and Research Volume, 32(3), 303-322.

Cowan, N. (1995). *Attention and memory: An integrated framework.* New York: Oxford University Press.

Crum, A. J., Akinola, M., Martin, A., & Fath, S. (2017). The role of stress mindset in shaping cognitive, emotional, and physiological responses to challenging and threatening stress. *Anxiety, Stress, & Coping,* 30(4), 379-395, doi: 10.1080/10615806.2016.1275585.

Crum, A. J., Salovey, P., & Achor, S. (2013). Rethinking stress: The role of mindsets in determining the stress response. *Journal of Personality and Social Psychology,* 104(4), 716–733. doi:10.1037/a0031201

Daneman, M., & Carpenter, P. A. (1980). Individual differences in working memory and reading. *Journal of Verbal Learning and Verbal Behavior,* 19, 450–466.

Davidson, R. J., Kabat-Zinn, J., Schumacher, J., Rosenkranz, M., Muller, D., Santorelli, S. F., Sheridian, J. F., Urbanowski, F., Harrington, A., & Bonus, K. (2003). Alterations in brain and immune function produced by mindfulness meditation. *Psychosomatic Medicine,* 65, 564–570.

Deci, E. L. (1975). *Intrinsic motivation.* New York: Plenum Press.

Diamond, M. D., Campbell, A. M., Park, C. R., Halonen, J., and Zoladz, P. R. (2007). The Temporal Dynamics Model of Emotional Memory Processing: A Synthesis on the Neurobiological Basis of Stress-Induced Amnesia, Flashbulb and Traumatic Memories, and the Yerkes-Dodson Law. *Neural Plasticity,* 60803.

Duval, E. R., Javanbakht, A., & Liberzon, I. (2015). Neural circuits in anxiety and stress disorders: a focused review. *Therapeutics and Clinical Risk Management,* 11, 115-126.

Dweck, C. S. (2006). *Mindset: The new psychology of success.* New York: Random House.

Engle, R. W., Tuholski, S. W., Laughlin, J. E., & Conway, A. R. A. (1999). Working memory, short-term memory and general fluid intelligence: A latent-variable approach. *Journal of Experimental Psychology: General,* 128, 309–331.

Entwistle, P. C., & Shinaver, C. (2014). Working Memory Training and Cogmed. In Goldstein, S., & Naglieri, J. A. (Eds.). *Handbook of Executive Functioning.* (pp. 495-508). New York: Springer.

Epley, N., & Gilovich, T. (2016). The Mechanics of Motivated Reasoning. *Journal of Economic Perspectives,* 30(3), 133-140.

Fuchs, E., & Flügge, G. (2014). Adult neuroplasticity: more than 40 years of research. *Neural plasticity,* 541870. doi:10.1155/2014/541870

Fuster, J. M. (2015). *The Prefrontal Cortex* (5th ed.). New York, NY: Academic Press.

Grint, K. (2010). Wicked Problems and Clumsy Solutions: The Role of Leadership. In: Brookes, S., & Grint, K. (eds.). *The New Public Leadership Challenge.* (pp. 169-186). London: Palgrave Macmillan.

Haule, J. R. (2011). *Jung in the 21st century: Evolution and Archetype.* Sussex: Routledge.

Hilt, L. M., Hanson, J. L., and Pollak, S. D. (2011). Emotion Dysregulation. In Brown, B. B., and Prinstein, M. J. (Eds.). *Encyclopedia of Adolescence.* (pp. 160-169). London: Elsevier.

Himmer, L., Schönauer, M., Heib, D. P. J., Schabus, M., & Gais, S. (2019). Rehearsal initiates systems memory consolidation, sleep makes it last. *Science Advances.*

Holland, P. C., & Maddux, J. M. (2010). Brain systems of attention in associative learning. In Mitchell, C. J., & Le Pelley, M. E. (Eds.). *Attention and Associative Learning. From Brain to Behaviour.* (pp. 305-350). New York: Oxford University Press.

Hsu, C. W., & Goh, J. O. S. (2016). Distinct and Overlapping Brain Areas Engaged during Value-Based, Mathematical, and Emotional Decision Processing. *Frontiers in Human Neuroscience,* 10. doi: 10.3389/fnhum.2016.00275

Huang, C. J., Webb, H. E., Zourdos, M. C., and Acevedo, E. O. (2013). Cardiovascular reactivity, stress, and physical activity. *Frontiers in Physiology*, 4, 314.

Inda, M. C., Muravieva, E. V., & Alberini, C. M. (2011). Memory retrieval and the passage of time: from reconsolidation and strengthening to extinction. *The Journal of Neuroscience,* 31(5), 1635–1643.

Jha, A. P., Krompinger, J., & Baime, M. J. (2007). Mindfulness meditation modifies subsystems of attention. *Cognitive Affective Behavioral Neuroscience,* 7(2), 109–119.

Johansen, R. (2012). *Leaders make the future: Ten new leadership skills for an uncertain world.* San Francisco: Berrett-Koehler Publishers.

Jones, R. J., Woods, S. A., & Guillaume, Y. R. F. (2016). The effectiveness of workplace coaching: A meta-analysis of learning and performance outcomes from coaching. *Journal of Occupational and Organizational Psychology,* 89(2), 249–277. https://doi.org/10.1111/joop.12119

Karpicke, J. D. (2016). A powerful way to improve learning and memory. APA *Psychological Science Agenda.* Retrieved from: https://www.apa.org/science/about/psa/2016/06/learning-memory

Kleim, J. A., & Jones, T. A. (2008). Principles of experience-dependent neural plasticity: Implications for rehabilitation after brain damage. *Journal of Speech Hearing and Language Research,* 51, 225-239.

Klein, K., & Boals, A. (2001). The relationship of life event stress and working memory capacity. *Applied Cognitive Psychology,* 15, 565–579.

Kluk, A. R. (2017). Fostering a Growth Mindset: Elementary Teacher Experiences Using Mindfulness Practices.

Kruglanski, A. W. (1989). The Psychology of Being "Right": The Problem of Accuracy in Social Perception and Cognition. *Psychological Bulletin,* 106(3), 395–409.

Kyllonen, P. C., & Christal, R. E. (1990). Reasoning ability is (little more than) working- memory capacity? *Intelligence,* 14, 389–433.

Kyllonen, P. C., & Stephens, D. L. (1990). Cognitive abilities as determinants of success in acquiring logic skill. *Learning and Individual Differences,* 2, 129–160.

Langer, E. J., Djikic, M., Pirson, M., Mandenci, A., & Donohue, R. (2010). Believing is Seeing: Using Mindlessness (Mindfully) to Improve Visual Acuity. *Psychological Science,* 21(5), 661-666.

Langer, E. J. (2013). Mindfulness Forward and Back. In. Le, A., Ngnoumen, C. T., & Langer, E. J. (Eds.). *The Wiley Blackwell Handbook of Mindfulness.* (pp. 7-20). Chichester: Wiley-Blackwell.

LeDoux, J. E. (2007). Consolidation: Challenging the traditional view. In Roediger III, H. L., Dudai, Y., & Fitzpatrick, S. M. (Eds.). *Science of Memory: Concepts.* (pp. 171-176). New York: Oxford University Press.

Levy, D.M., Wobbrock, J.O., Kaszniak, A.W. and Ostergren, M. (2011) Initial results from a study of the effects of meditation on multitasking performance. *Extended Abstracts of CHI 2011:* ACM Press, 2011-2016.

Magee, R. R., & Army War College (U.S.). (1998). *Strategic leadership primer.* Carlisle Barracks, PA: Dept. of Command, Leadership, and Management, United States Army War College.

McGreevy, S. (2011). Eight weeks to a better brain. *The Harvard Gazette.* Retrieved from: https://news.harvard.edu/gazette/story/2011/01/eight-weeks-to-a-better-brain/.

McHugh, C. [Tedx]. (2013, Feb 15). The art of being yourself. [Video File].

Mrazek, M. D., Franklin, M. S., Phillips, D. T., Baird, B., & Schooler, J. W. (2013). Mindfulness Training Improves Working Memory Capacity and GRE Performance While Reducing Mind Wandering. *Psychological Science,* 24 (5), 776-781.

Nielsen, L. and Kaszniak, A.W. (2006) Awareness of subtle emotional feelings: A comparison of long-term meditators and non-meditators. *Emotion,* 6 (3), 392-405.

Nyklícek, I., & Kuijpers, K. F. (2008). Effects of mindfulness-based stress reduction intervention on psychological well-being and quality of life: Is increased mindfulness indeed the mechanism? *Annals of Behavioral Medicine,* 35(3), 331–340.

OECD. (2010). Climate Change: Helping Poor Countries to Adapt. In *Development Co-operation Report* 2010, 65-74. Paris: OECD Publishing. doi: https://doi.org/10.1787/dcr-2010-8-en.

Otero, T. M., & Barker, L. A. (2014). The Frontal Lobes and Executive Functioning. In Goldstein, S., & Naglieri, J. A. (Eds.). *Handbook of Executive Functioning.* (pp. 29-44). New York: Springer.

Passmore, J. & Fillery-Travis, A. (2011). A critical review of executive coaching research: A decade of progress and what's to come. *Coaching: An International Journal of Theory, Practice & Research.* 4(2), 70-88.

Passmore, J., & Marianetti, O. (2013). The role of mindfulness in coaching. *The Coaching Psychologist,* 3(3), 131-138.

Pekrun, R. (1992). The impact of emotions on learning and achievement: towards a theory of cognitive/motivational mediators. *Applied Psychology,* 41, 359–376. doi: 10.1111/j.1464-0597.1992.tb00712.x

Pessoa, L. (2018). Understanding emotion with brain networks. *Current opinion in behavioral sciences,* 19, 19–25. doi:10.1016/j.cobeha.2017.09.005.

Phelps, E. A. (2007). Learning: Challenges in the merging of levels. In Roediger III, H. L., Dudai, Y., & Fitzpatrick, S. M. (Eds.). *Science of Memory: Concepts.* (pp. 45-48). New York: Oxford University Press.

Posner, M. I., & Rothbart, M. K. (2009). Toward a physical basis of attention and self regulation. *Physics of life reviews,* 6(2), 103–120. doi:10.1016/j.plrev.2009.02.001.

Posner, M. I., Sheese, B. E., Odludas, Y., & Tang, Y. (2006). Analyzing and shaping neural networks of attention. *Neural Networks,* 19, 1422–1429.

Rees, B. (2017). The use of Mindfulness in a Traumatic VUCA World. In Nandram, S. S., & Bindlish, P. K. (Eds.). *Managing VUCA Through Integrative Self-Management: How to Cope with Volatility, Uncertainty, Complexity and Ambiguity in Organizational Behavior.* (pp. 193-206). Cham: Springer International Publishing.

Richmond, L., Redick, T. S., & Braver, T. S. (2015). Remembering to repare: The benefits (and costs) of high working memory capacity. *Journal of Experimental Psychology: Learning, Memory, and Cognition,* 41(6), 1764-1777.

Roediger, H. L., & Karpicke, J. D. (2006). The power of testing memory: Basic research and implications for educational practice. *Perspectives on Psychological Science,* 1(3), 181-210. doi:10.1111/j.1745-6916.2006.00012.x.

Sara, S. J. (2000). Retrieval and reconsolidation: toward a neurobiology of remembering. *Learning Memory,* 7(2), 73–84.

Seli, P., Wammes, J. D., Risko, E. F., & Smilek, D. (2016). On the relation between motivation and retention in educational contexts: the role of intentional and unintentional mind wandering. *Psychonomic Bulletin & Review,* 23, 1280–1287. doi:10.3758/s13423-015-0979-0.

Spence, G. B. (2019). Mindfulness in Coaching: a self-determination theory perspective. In Palmer, S., & Whybrow, A. (Eds.). *Handbook of coaching psychology: A guide for practitioners.* (pp. 195-205). Oxon: Routledge.

Squire, L. R., Genzel, L., Wixted, J. T., & Morris, R. G. (2015). Memory consolidation. *Cold Spring Harbor perspectives in biology,* 7(8), a021766.

Stolier, R. M., & Freeman, J. (2016). The Neuroscience of Social Vision. In Absher, J. R., and Cloutier, J. (Eds.). *Neuroimaging Personality, Social Cognition, and Character,* (pp. 139-157). San Diego: Elsevier.

Tulving, E. (1985). Memory and consciousness. *Canadian Psychology/Psychologie canadienne,* 26(1), 1-12. doi: 10.1037/h0080017.

Voller, H. (2010). *Developing the understanding of reflective practice in counselling and psychotheraphy.* [Unpublished dissertation]. University of Middlesex.

Westen, D., Blagov, P. S., Harenski, K., Kilts, C., & Hamann, S. (2006). Neural bases of motivated reasoning: an FMRI study of emotional constraints on partisan political judgment in the 2004 U.S. Presidential election. *Journal of Cognitive Neuroscience,* 18(11), 1947-58.

Whitmore, J. (2017). *Coaching for performance: The principles and practice of coaching and leadership* (5th ed.). London: Nicholas Brealey.

Widdett, R. (2014). Neuroplasticity and Mindfulness Meditation. *Honors Theses.* Paper 2469.

Zilles, K. (1992). Neuronal plasticity as an adaptive property of the central nervous system. *Annals of Anatomy,* 174(5), 383–391.

CHAPTER 8

SEARCHING FOR SOUL AND FINDING SELF

Ann L. Clancy, PhD and Jacqueline Binkert, PhD

Abstract

The Appreciative Coaching® approach rests on a key premise: begin where the client is. However, practitioners can only begin where the client is by also discovering where they begin with their own thoughts, beliefs, and experience. Knowing the practitioners' role to be instruments of change, our search to reveal and understand our own foundational theories and existential beliefs became essential. In this search, we explored multiple approaches, reflected on our own lived experiences and personal evolutions, and conducted evidence-based coaching research about what enables deep human change. We looked at how theory influences who coaches are, thereby influencing how they coach. Many coaches we worked with were unaware of the findings from the phenomenological, generative, and quantum sciences. In this search for the "soul" of coaching, we sought to build a conceptual bridge to new scientific assumptions about self that matched the real-time experience of clients as dynamic, energy-based beings in continual process.

> "We shall not cease from exploration
> And the end of all our exploring
> Will be to arrive where we started
> And know the place for the first time."
> — T. S. Eliot, *Four Quartets*

Introduction

Early in our careers as coaches and organization development (OD) consultants, we found a disconnect between what we were experiencing and some of the traditional theories and approaches to change; especially those focused on the problem-solving model and Newtonian mechanistic assumptions about human capacity. Questioning these assumptions was part of an overall movement in the 1980s and 90s to challenge the status quo of the Newtonian perspective with quantum science findings. Educated in OD at Fielding, it was impressed upon us how we are the instrument for change. This resonated strongly with us, leading to a years-long exploration of alternative existential beliefs, life experiences, and evidence-based research, beginning with our dissertations on exploring a phenomenological holistic concept of time (Clancy, 1996) and the impact of existential beliefs on group performance (Binkert, 1995).

We were drawn toward process, generative, and energy-based foundations to understanding human change. This led to creating a generative coaching model, Appreciative Coaching (Orem, Binkert & Clancy, 2007), based on the philosophy, principles and stages of appreciative inquiry (as well as positive organizational scholarship, positive psychology, and solution-focused brief therapy). Practicing and training with this model of coaching requires an awareness of one's worldview, an essential component of human nature that represents one's beliefs and assumptions about reality, human nature, and the meaning and nature of life itself (Koltko-Rivera, 2004). Worldview not only shapes who we are, but also determines that our behavior is consistent with our worldview.

We realized that one's "stance" towards human change (whether practitioner or client) consists of unconscious existential beliefs. We began to explore the ways these viewpoints about change could be linked together to yield greater understanding. How could we build a conceptual bridge from the unconscious Newtonian assumptions based on determinism, linearity, objectivity and reductivity to the newly emerging existential beliefs arising from the phenomenological, generative and quantum sciences? We identified three main areas where beliefs about change differ dramatically: how one defines "self," how one defines "life in motion," and how one understands the "movement of meaning-making." This chapter explores the different dimensions of self-underlying approaches to change and weaves together new perspectives of change as process; that is, life and meaning-making as motion. This suggests a significantly different stance for practitioners, moving from the perspective of "use of self" to "self as instrument."

Defining dimensions of "self"

One of the foundations of Appreciative Coaching® is to begin where the client is. Given that all humans have unconscious existential beliefs, this premise also implies that practitioners can only begin where they are; hence, "self as instrument" encompasses not only the parts of ourselves we know about but also the shadows we glimpse and the areas we are blind to or unaware of. Research of how practitioners "use" themselves in the helping professions is primarily based on how one defines "self." The literature review below is representative of different perspectives on how to define "self" as an instrument of change in the areas of OD, psychology and coaching.

OD/Psychology practitioner research

Organization development literature has focused on "use of self" to describe the role of change agent as one who intentionally seeks to understand her intentions, needs, styles, patterns, habits, skills, shadows and defenses to increase self-efficacy, functionality and embodied presence (Jamieson, Auron, & Shechtman, 2010; Jamieson & Davidson, 2019; Seashore, et al., 2004).

Kennedy (2012) comprehensively reviewed the psychological "use of self" literature, mentioning its historical roots in Sigmund Freud's diagnostic work, Carl Rogers' humanistic support, and Virginia Satir's study of a person's inner landscape. According to Kennedy, key tenets found in "use of self" have been self-awareness, self-knowledge, self-differentiation, agency, self-efficacy and presence. She highlights three models that combine most of these elements: the Seashore, Shawver, Thompson and Mattare (2004) model that self is an ongoing construction built from a continuous learning loop; the Jamieson, Auron, and Shechtman (2010) model that self is seen from the perspective of core competencies; and the Davidson (2006) model that self is comprised of intrapersonal and interpersonal intelligences.

Gestalt psychotherapy provides a different theory of self as being relational and emergent within a given field or situation (Chidiac & Denham-Vaughan 2009). The self is recognized as "the system of contact at any moment" (Perls, Hefferline & Goodman, 1951/1994, p.11). Chidiac and Denham-Vaughn describe self as process (not substance) that is embedded in the situation or in the given context in which it is in contact. It is at one with its relationships and environment. They note how new discoveries in physics support self as process rather than substance and that this concept is at the core of the Gestalt training programs, providing a unique perspective of self-as-instrument.

Organization development practitioner Cheung-Judge (2012) refers to "self as instrument" as being a cornerstone for the future of OD. She supports the Gestalt perspective that "the purpose of the self is to organize the emerging and changing experiences to make it meaningful" (p. 42). Thus, the self is capable of changing and adjusting according to the situation in which it finds itself and is at the heart of practitioner uniqueness and effectiveness. Organization development consulting requires a high degree of self-knowledge and personal development throughout one's professional life; it is the practitioner's "prime asset in achieving the helping relationship" (p. 44). She offers four categories for practitioners to consider in their own self-work: developing life-long learning habits, working through issues of power, building emotional and intuitive self-awareness, and committing to self-care.

Cheung-Judge also identified three groups that practitioners seem to fall into based on her over ten years of supervising and mentoring OD consultants:

1. Consultants whose effectiveness is inconsistent because they rely more on a highly professional image and technical expertise rather than attending to human processes such as trust, dependency and ethics.

2. Effective consultants who experience burn out because their high performance is costly and unsustainable. Such consultants do not put equal time and energy on knowing themselves better and creating a robust self-care package to minimize the personal cost of their high performance.

3. Effective consultants who are in optimal condition most of the time because they engage in self-work activities.

Coaching practitioner research

Some research perspectives on "use of self" from the coaching field forego a definition of "self" in favor of theoretical influences that can impact on how a coach may shape his or her approach. Barner and Higgins (2007) focus on four implicit theories to guide the coaching process and, depending on which one is adopted, to likely shape a practitioner's coaching practice: the clinical model, the behavioral model, the systems model, and the social constructionist model. Their premise is that while coaches can be eclectic in their methods, they tend to center their expertise in one of the four models which then informs and shapes their assessments and interventions. Instead, coaches should look carefully at these theory models so they can bring to light their own implicit expectations of how the change process works. Marshak (2012) proposes generative conversations as a method for coaches to help clients address their limiting assumptions. His premise is that people experience the world through nonconscious cognitive structures that "organize" both what is experienced and any resulting comments, behaviors, and actions. His focus is on the client and does not address in this article the nonconscious cognitive structures that coaches also bring to their work.

Hunt (2009) proposes an integral coaching approach based on helping clients both transcend and include their current way of being into a new way of being based on a developmental model drawn from the works of Ken Wilbur (1980) and Robert Kegan (1982). She points at how significant it is for coaching schools to be based on specific underlying belief structures regarding change. Hunt uses a four-quadrant mapping of common belief structures for change on a subjective-objective and individual-group matrix drawn from Wilbur's integral model. While each quadrant has merit, it is also partial in its understanding. For embodied change to occur, coaches need to focus on all four perspectives in an interconnected fashion. She draws on the subject-object theory of both Wilbur's and Kegan's work: how the subject at one level becomes the object of the subject at the next level, bringing an individual to greater levels of development and evolution. She implies that coaches need to have the training and experience to negotiate among these different belief structures to lead clients to greater depths of change.

Reflecting on self dimensions

One of the most foundational unconscious existential beliefs is how one defines "self": as object? as process? For years, it has been the norm for many in the field of psychology to accept the nature of human beings as mechanistic, fixed and deficit based. Humans were seen as objects that could be predetermined, measured and controlled externally. The view of self as object is also embedded in those theories of development which present the self as an independent unit within a social context. This self consists of body, mind and spirit shaped by the environment and "contained" as a defined, open system. Self as object still underlies some of the OD/Psychology "use of self" research.

In contrast, recent neuroscience tells us we have a self-transforming brain/mind that is awakening and which remains open to change throughout our lifespan (Hanson & Mendius, 2009). The self keeps changing, arising, and adapting depending on its relationships and situations and actually has no independent existence (Hanson & Mendius, 2009). In this chapter, we make the distinction between "use of self" as described in much of the OD and psychology literature and "self as instrument," our preference for connoting self as a process, a catalyst, a creator. See Table 1 for a comparison between the Newtonian-based coaching concept of "self" and the quantum-based coaching concept of self.

TABLE 1: Newtonian-based vs. Quantum-based Coaching Concept of Self

Newtonian-based Coaching Concept of Self	Quantum-based Coaching Concept of Self
• Self as discrete entity or object to be viewed objectively	• Self as process indistinguishable from its relationships and environment
• Self as neutral onlooker	• Self as participating observer
• Self as having content and issues (problem story) which constitutes a Newtonian "mass" (weight); moving the mass is seen as logical and mechanical, but more focus spent on moving the "mass" in a determined direction creates more resistance	• Self as process which can be re-oriented by shifting client focus to a new story or solution, spending little time on client problem story and thereby reducing resistance
• Self as coaching neutrally around the content of others	• Self as coaching within the context and process of others
• Self as coaching through observing and witnessing but not influencing or sharing responsibility for results	• Self as coaching through co-creation, both individuals as participating observers of reality and co-sharing responsibility

Table 1: Newtonian-based Versus Quantum-based Coaching Concept of Self
(Adapted from Cardon 2017a, 2017b, 2017c)

Affirmation of life as motion

For us, "self as instrument" incorporates the "soul" of coaching by drawing on these foundations: movement as quantum, self-organizing, and evolutionary; phenomenology of lived experience; and levels of hermeneutic understanding—all of which support new existential beliefs of self as process in movement. The researchers, theorists, and fields of study indicated below (Table 2) provide more expansive explanations of human capacity that move beyond the limitation of Newtonian-based psychological principles. These theorists share an underlying perspective of life as generative, self-organizing process in evolutionary movement:

TABLE 2: Theorists supporting non-Newtonian principles of human change

William James (1890/1950): Focus on inner process and subjectivity that combines philosophy and psychology to understand human change as pragmatic and functional, purposive and selective.

Hans-Georg Gadamer (1960/1997): Theory of interpretation and understanding of the unconscious process of human change in which experience itself is a process that cannot be explained by the natural sciences model of seeking similarities, regularities and conformities.

Alfred Whitehead (1929): Assertion "that the actual world is a process" (p.22) and that life itself is motion. An entity is a process and is not describable in terms of the morphology of a "stuff" (p.41).

Martin Heidegger (1962): Hermeneutic circle of understanding, a process to discover meanings not immediately apparent or which need interpretation due to unique life experiences.

Kenneth Gergen (1978, 1994): A generative theory of human capacity to adapt in which he criticizes traditional embedded scientific biases (i.e., the mechanistic approach that humans are machine-like, limited, head-oriented).

David Bohm (1980): Post-Newtonian quantum paradigm that the ultimate nature of reality is an undivided whole in perpetual flux, made of parts that merge and unite in a constant flow and change called holomovement.

Robert Kegan (1982): Constructive-developmental approach in which evolutionary motion of change is the way humans make meaning for greater coherence.

Spencer McWilliams (2016): Pragmatist stance that theories are changeable and that human activity can be seen in terms of its usefulness and continual evolution. Perspective of reality as an ever-changing interactive process in which humans develop knowledge, interpret experience and are impacted by their historical contexts (constructivism). Knowledge is therefore temporal, practical, and revisable, making human lives more meaningful.

Transformative phenomenology (Rehorick & Bentz, 2008): Description of direct experience as a source of knowledge, leading to a deepening of embodied awareness that is itself a process of transformation as well as a way of knowing.

Developmental and evolutionary change theorists (LaLoux, 2014; Beck & Cowan, 2006; Wilbur, 2000; Wade, 1996; Graves, 1981): Perspective of historically emerging stages of human consciousness leading to ever greater levels of human complexity, summarized by LaLoux as Impulsive-Red consciousness (tribal); Conformist-Amber consciousness (traditional, agrarian); Achievement-Orange consciousness (scientific, technical, multi-national), Pluralistic-Green consciousness (empowerment, culture-driven, diversity, inclusion); and Evolutionary-Teal consciousness (self-organizing, adaptive, wholeness, purpose).

Evolutionary movement: first tier to second tier stages of consciousness

Humanity is currently experiencing and witnessing a powerful evolutionary movement and paradigm shift from a Newtonian mechanistic view of life as organized, predictable and knowable to that of a quantum, constructivist perspective of life that is expansive, generative and self-organizing. Graves (1974) challenged the Newtonian perspective with his description of human nature as an open, constantly evolving system that moves from one steady state to the next through quantum leaps. According to Wilbur (2000), these evolutionary movements or stages are not rigid levels, but flowing waves which overlap and interweave in a dynamic spiral of consciousness unfolding into higher order systems.

These transformations in consciousness occur in humanity as a whole and each stage or wave has a different set of values, needs, motivations, morals, worldviews, ego structures, social types, and cultural networks (Wilbur in LaLoux, 2014). Developmentalists explain that later stages are not better than earlier ones, but rather they are more complex ways of dealing with the world; each new stage transcends and includes the previous ones in their nested ordering. Thus, the complexity of human evolution cannot be reduced to a single stage and the many dimensions of human development such as cognitive, moral, psychological, social and spiritual, do not necessarily grow at the same pace. We operate out of more than one type of paradigm at any given time. We see a significance for practitioners, given their role as instruments for change, to be aware of this particular movement in consciousness, as all developmentalists seem to agree that the current paradigm shift represents a different type of consciousness from all the previous stages. The earlier stages or waves have been described as "subsistence levels" with "first-tier thinking" (Wilbur, 2000, p. 8). Based on Maslow's hierarchy of needs, these previous stages of human consciousness have been focused on meeting humanity's more basic needs.

LaLoux (2014), an evolutionist who focuses on organizational contexts, summarizes the emergence of the worldview described as Evolutionary-Teal as a second tier stage of consciousness that acts out of a sense of radical abundance and trust rather than fear. Developmentalists agree this is a monumental leap in meaning for human evolution. All previous first tier stages are described as operating out of a sense of lacking, scarcity, and deficiency and see their specific worldview as the only valid one. The shift toward second tier thinking moves out of this rigidity to a new focus on human "being" and welcomes the interplay of spirituality and science, shows respect for the holistic wisdom of living systems, prefers integrative and open systems, and accepts the inevitable flow of nature (Beck and Cowan, 2006).

The Evolutionary-Teal worldview is compelling for the field of coaching. It describes life as a journey of unfolding, which incorporates a shift from external to internal yardsticks and from a deficit to a strength-based paradigm. For deeper level coaching, it offers a foundation for helping clients better access their inner wisdom and strive for wholeness with life and nature. Coaches bring greater relevance when they are aware of the evolution of multiple worldviews in a nested hierarchy, co-existing, with each successive stage not "better" but rather a broader and more complex way of dealing with life.

Reflecting on life as motion

Newtonian influence in coaching approaches is based on some of the following existential beliefs: linear time, incremental change, client and coaching engagement as objects for study, quantitative evaluation, singular causality, goal orientation, and time and space separation. Because existential beliefs are concerned with the nature of reality, personal beliefs and values follow from our existential beliefs, and our behavior is directly influenced by our values (Narasimhan et al., 2010). Thus, how we coach is founded on our existential beliefs, and these foundational beliefs evolve as new worldviews emerge. Below is a summary highlighting some of the distinctions of coaching based on Newtonian existential beliefs and quantum existential beliefs (Cardon 2017a, 2017b, 2017c).

Meaning-making as movement

The perspectives above describe human change as process and as evolutionary motion. We believe there are three foundations in understanding the soul of coaching that support meaning-making as movement: Kegan's spiral model of constructive-development, the embodied awareness of transformative phenomenology, and the power of embracing deeper hermeneutic levels of understanding. These all support practitioners opening to new existential beliefs about the holistic nature of human change and about their role in helping clients find greater coherence through the felt experience of the motion of change, e.g., Kegan's emergence from embeddedness.

TABLE 3: Newtonian-based Coaching vs. Quantum-based Coaching

Newtonian-based Coaching (Red-Amber-Orange-Green: First Tier)	Quantum-based Coaching (Teal: Second Tier)
• Machine nature of universe	• Holographic nature of universe
• Space and time separated	• Space and time collapse into one continuous dimension
• Single causal explanations	• System orientation, multi-causal
• Incremental change, client postponement strategies slow change	• Power of disruption and interruption to break client fractal patterns to move them forward
• Linear Absolute Time (past has more weight than present and future)	• Expanded time in which the "now" simultaneously incorporates past, present and future, and synchronicity is entwined with environment
• Mirroring as a mentalist approach to mimic gestures and facial expressions to create a therapeutic connection with client	• Mirroring as the subconscious intimate synchronization and shared presence that happens at the physical, emotional and mental levels between coach and client
• Predominantly reliant upon cognitive or mental mode of knowing	• Embracing multiple modes of knowing: intuition, somatic knowing, instinct, social and creative intuition, direct knowing, enactive knowing, tacit knowing

Table 3: Newtonian-based Versus Quantum-based Coaching
(Adapted from Cardon 2017a, 2017b, 2017c)

Kegan's meaning-making spiral of movement

Kegan sees "human being as an activity" based on two major premises: constructivism, in which humans and systems construct their reality; and developmentalism, in which organic systems evolve through stages based on consistent principles of stability and change (1982, p. 8). He explains that both these notions require us to recognize that behind the form "there exists a process which creates it, or which leads to its coming into being" (p. 8-9). According to Kegan, it's not so much that we make meaning as that the activity of being a human is actually "the meaning-making context" (p. 11). Kegan defines meaning as a physical activity (grasping, seeing), a social activity (requiring another), and a survival activity (by doing it, we live). It is, therefore, "the primary human motion, irreducible" which cannot be separated from the body, the social experience, or the actual survival of the organism (p. 19). Kegan's constructive-developmental framework is what he uses to study the "evolution of meaning" which he proposes is "the fundamental motion in personality" (p. 15). This motion is based on the process of differentiation and adaptation, of emergence from embeddedness, of creating an object out of what was a subject and is observable.

For Kegan, meaning also depends on relationship (on someone who recognizes you). He is awed by how touched he is in the presence of a person engaged in this "astonishingly intimate activity—the activity of making sense" (p. 16). Two tenets of Kegan's approach offer coaching practitioners new or highlighted existential beliefs about human change. First, Kegan stresses how his fundamental orientation toward the person he is working with stems from his convictions about the activity or process he shares with the client in that very moment— not a process unknown to him or something he once experienced. He emphasizes that in that moment: "we are bound by a single fate, and we do not share it so much as it shares us" (p. 265). Second, he stresses how limited our interventions can be as practitioners if they are addressed "to a stage rather than a person, an address to made meanings rather than meaning-making" (p. 277). To Kegan, clients are not their stages or their stories, but "they are the creators, the meaning-makers, not the made-meaning" (p. 277). Kegan's constructivist approach focuses on the actual moment and process of meaning-making which differs significantly from the Newtonian reality of being objective, static and linear.

Embodied Awareness of Transformative Phenomenology

In phenomenology (the study of lived experience), the past takes on unexpected, diverse and abundant new meanings because time and history are seen as fluid, creative and indeterminate, unable to be predicted with certainty (Rehorick & Bentz, 2017). Newtonian change is inextricably linked with linear absolute time in which the past is considered predictive (Clancy, 1996). This linear view cannot explain how humans experience multiple perspectives of time, such as synchronicity, intuition, sudden leaps of insight or discontinuous change. According to Rehorick and Bentz, life is reinterpretable and its emotional, physical, and geographical dimensions are interwoven with our thinking and feeling in the present moment. We physically and energetically live only in the present, visiting the past from the present and anticipating the future from the present. Transformative phenomenology is about the lived experience of humans whose lives are embodied in energy and movement and in which the present and future are equal influencers of change. It's not possible to be prescriptive about change from this perspective. It is instead a way of knowing in which self cannot be extracted from what it studies. We find this reinforces the importance of "self as instrument" as we understand the poignancy of revealing deeply held existential beliefs that influence us, whether we are conscious of them or not.

Hermeneutic/Interpretive Levels of Understanding

Hermeneutics is the study of interpreting and understanding something that "appears" in personal experience. The origin of the word hermeneutics is from the Greek "to interpret" and originally referred to the study and interpretation of the written word, as in biblical texts. But philosophers such as Martin Heidegger and Hans-George Gadamer evolved its meaning into "the theory and practice of interpretation and understanding (Verstehen) in different kinds of human contexts" (Odman, 1988, p. 63). Heidegger (1962) viewed existence as being-in-the-world in which many of the elements that shape us are hidden, and require interpretation for our lives to be understood. His concern was to uncover these hidden phenomena of human lives and their meanings in order to reveal what is not immediately apparent. For Gadamer (1960/1997), hermeneutics was a way of being in the world and a willingness to undergo a process so that "what is" may emerge and show itself. Underlying hermeneutics is the premise that every individual's experience is unique and influenced by one's preconceptions.

Hermeneutics offers a process that deepens understanding of how clients become open to the "revealing" of their own inner process and offers practitioners new existential beliefs about how humans evolve and make meaning. Gadamer points out how our use of language is primarily unconscious and that one of the tasks of hermeneutics is to question things in order to detect and make conscious their actual meaning.

For Gadamer, the movement of understanding is constantly from the whole, to the part, and back to the whole—like a single word belonging in the complete context of a sentence. He saw hermeneutics as a unified process of three elements—understanding, interpretation and application—which then yields "sharing in a common meaning" (p. 303). For practitioners, the element of understanding can be seen as analogous to watching a wild horse from a distance and describing its context and characteristics. The element of interpretation is akin to approaching the wild horse, observing how it interacts with other horses and its environment. The element of application is equivalent to getting on and riding the wild horse, taking the risk to end up in a place the practitioner did not expect, letting the horse become the guide. (Horse analogy courtesy of phenomenologists Rehorick & Benz, 2008.)

Reflecting on meaning-making as movement

From a quantum perspective, coaching is the mutual intent to move clients to a more expanded and generative view of their situation from whatever stage of consciousness they occupy. This perspective recognizes both coach and client as energy-based beings in continual process and relationship. For Kegan, human life is an evolution of meaning, a continual process of emergence from embeddedness that practitioners support by paying attention to the meaning being transformed in the moment, not by a focus on past meaning.

Transformative phenomenology shows practitioners how clients are embodied in energy and movement, influenced as much by the present and future as by the past. Hermeneutic levels of understanding show practitioners how they can join clients in a shared space and time of mutual influence, which can lead to solutions or reframing that could not have been anticipated individually. The third level of hermeneutic understanding (riding the horse) is similar to Kegan's focus on meaning-making in the moment. Other generative tools that help support meaning-making include directing attention, using appreciative and positive inquiry, and applying priming strategies to trigger new connections in unconscious associative memory networks.

Implications for practitioners

The coaches' existential beliefs about life lead to the values they hold, which in turn influence their behavior (Narasimhan et al., 2010). The implications for coaching are profound in that, from a quantum perspective, "self as instrument" is holographic. Holographic coaches are participating observers that have influence and are influenced in a shared, intimate embodied presence with their clients. The entire relationship and experience is one of ever-changing process in which related patterns are fractals, repeating across time and space. From this worldview, coaches are not neutral and objective. A useful metaphor in quantum science to capture this holographic model of transformational change is the Möbius loop, demonstrating that what is inner is also outer.

Expanding on self as instrument

Hovell (January, 2019), drawing on the work of Cheung-Judge (2012), offers nine clusters that define in greater detail how different areas of use of self can help practitioners focus on a deeper inner work stance. The nine clusters below have been organized into the three main areas presented in this chapter as new existential beliefs about human change:

PHOTO 1: Möbius Loop

Definition of self as process

• Values cluster: appreciation of diversity, commitment to equality and inclusion, commitment to democratic processes, maintaining a learning and development stance, holding justice and fairness, commitment to scientific inquiry in balance with a with client-centric focus

• Affiliative/emotional cluster: awareness and ability to express own emotions, especially in relation to others' emotions; showing a depth and range of empathy and grace for others and their situations; holding positive regard, showing compassion, being willing to extend oneself in service of others

• Character cluster: mental and moral qualities distinctive to the individual, trustworthiness, ability to show humility, respectful to others, grounded level of confidence, desire to serve others

Affirmation of life as motion

• Cognitive cluster: ability to see and think through situations, perceive and express strategic insights, see from a systems perspective, and tolerate ambiguity

• Skills cluster: depth and range of listening skills, ability to leverage similarities and differences across people; ability to conduct experiments on the go, using inquiry to build relationships

• Courage cluster: daring to take evocative and provocative stances when necessary, daring to differentiate and hold own opinion, having courage to put "self" on the line

Meaning-making as movement

• Self-work cluster: ability to work on self by increasing sense of awareness of self and others, maintaining sense of groundedness, authenticity by being real and transparent, continually expanding range of mindfulness and awareness by working on unresolved issues of one's own life; willing to invest in doing own inner work to stay choiceful and intentional with oneself (one helps/heals/cures oneself first in order to serve others)

• Discipline (self-management) cluster: emphasis on focus, seeking feedback and learning opportunities, undertaking supervision and cultivating habits that increase one's ability for generative thoughts and emotional renewal, learning when to share; practicing one's ability to stay non-reactive to challenging situations and people, separating own needs from those of others

• Continuous self-work and growth cluster: continual practice and growth of one's self-work; staying curious about one's evolving self, noticing one's own behavior/thought patterns; intentionally and choicefully growing one's range in skills and self-management, being a reflective practitioner who notices one's own thoughts, words and actions, especially managing boundaries

Kegan talks about the "life-long theme of finding and losing," the process of differentiation that creates the possibility of integration (p. 81). He describes this as evolutionary activity that is a felt experience of a motion—the fundamental motion of human personality. Such new existential beliefs about human change merit focus and discussion

(Clancy & Binkert, 2017). Consider the expanded concept of self as process, life as evolutionary movement into a second tier of consciousness based on trust and abundance, and the transformative ways open to practitioners in the actual moments of meaning-making with their clients.

The human evolutionary spiral is aimed at ever greater coherence for the human species, which is also a desirable aim for practitioners. The ability to coach from a particular worldview depends on one's own evolutionary development. According to Beck and Cowan (2006), much of the world's population still lives in the first tier (or mechanistic) perspective. The coaching field engages with organizations that are still primarily Achievement-Orange or Pluralistic-Green in the first tier perspective. A number of coaching approaches also occur at these levels. In this chapter, we hope to share with our colleagues the opportunity to broaden perspectives and be open to exploring second tier (quantum) coaching. Understanding that each of the worldviews has intrinsic value on its own, practitioners can seek to expand their own coaching relevance and depth by opening themselves to the capacity to deal with a new tier of consciousness that embraces more complex ways of relating to life. Then practitioners have greater fluidity in beginning with where their clients are.

About the Authors

Ann L. Clancy (HOD '96) specializes in executive coaching, strategic planning, and leadership and team development. Ann has over thirty years of experience in working with organizations, teams and individuals to create positive change. She is researcher and co-author of Appreciative Coaching: A Positive Process for Change (2007) and Pivoting: A Coach's Guide to Igniting Substantial Change (2017), both of which present a researched, evidence-based approach to coaching. She coaches from an appreciative philosophy based on the assumption that inquiry into and dialogue about strengths, successes, hopes and dreams is itself a transformational process. Her clients come from a broad range of industries including: banking, education, economic development, energy, engineering, financial services, government, healthcare, natural resources (mining, refining) non-profit agencies, professional organizations, publishing, technology, and transportation. She is an international speaker and trainer in Appreciative Coaching® and Igniting Substantial Change working in countries such as Thailand, Japan, Nepal, Brazil, Chile, Switzerland, Turkey, the Netherlands, Norway, and South Africa. She offers online classes on Igniting Substantial Change and has offered online courses for Appreciative Coaching through the Fielding Graduate University. She is an international faculty adviser for doctoral students in management and organization development at Assumption University, Bangkok, Thailand.

Jacqueline Binkert (HOD '95) is an Executive Coach specializing in helping leaders realize the potential of their teams and organizations by leading from their best selves. For over thirty years, she has worked with a diverse range of clients: non-profit organizations, international corporations, educational institutions, health care organizations, utilities, and manufacturing, including the executive development center of a Fortune 50 company. Clients benefit from her in-depth knowledge of psychology, leadership effectiveness, organizational behavior and change, and team dynamics. She co-authored the books Appreciative Coaching: A Positive Process for Change (2007) and Pivoting: A Coach's Guide to Igniting Substantial Change (2017), both of which present a researched, evidence-based approach to coaching founded on advanced theories of human development and consciousness. She is a scholar practitioner who has led workshops and on Appreciative Coaching® internationally and nationally to coaches, consultants, HR practitioners, executives, and managers interested in transforming their own leadership and the cultures of their organizations. She has offered online courses for appreciative coaching through the Fielding Graduate University and has been an international faculty adviser for doctoral students in Management and Organization Development at Assumption University, Bangkok, Thailand.

References

Barner, R., & Higgins, J. (2007). Understanding implicit models that guide the coaching process. *Journal of Management Development*, 26(2), 148-158.

Beck, D. E., & Cowan, C. C. (2006). *Spiral Dynamics: Mastering values, leadership, and change*. Oxford, UK: Blackwell Publishing.

Binkert, J. (1995). *Group-level existential beliefs: Mustang case study* (Doctoral dissertation). Fielding Graduate University, Santa Barbara, CA.

Bohm, D. (1980). *Wholeness and the implicate order*. London: Routledge & Kegan Paul.

Cardon, A. (2017a). Quantum Coaching I: Space-time warps. Paris: Metasysteme S.A.S. Retrieved from https://www.metasysteme-coaching.eu/english/quantum-coaching-i-space-time-warps/

Cardon, A. (2017b). Quantum Coaching II: Speed is of the essence. Paris: Metasysteme S.A.S. Retrieved from https://www.metasysteme-coaching.eu/english/quantum-coaching-ii-speed-is-of-the-essence/

Cardon, A. (2017b). Quantum Coaching III: Synchronicity, fractals and systemic coaching. Paris: Metasysteme S.A.S. Retrieved from https://www.metasysteme-coaching.eu/english/quantum-coaching-iii-synchronicity-fractals-and-systemic-coaching/

Cheung-Judge, M-Y. (2012). The self as an instrument: A cornerstone for the future of OD. *OD Practitioner*, 44(2), 42-47.

Chidiac, M-A, & Denham-Vaughan, S. (2009). An organizational self: Applying the concept of self to groups and organizations. *British Gestalt Journal*, 18(1), 42-29.

Clancy, A.L. & Binkert, J. (2017). *Pivoting: A coach's guide to igniting substantial change*. New York: Palgrave Macmillan.

Clancy, A. L. (1996). *Toward a holistic concept of time: Exploring the link between internal and external temporal experiences* (Doctoral dissertation). Fielding Graduate University, Santa Barbara, CA.

Davidson, D. A. (2006). *Teaching therapeutic use of self to future occupational therapists: A survey of current educational practices*. Available from ProQuest Dissertations and Theses. (UMI No. 3237402)

Gadamer, H. (1960/1997). *Truth and method* (2nd Rev. ed., J. Weinsheimer & D. G. Marshall, Trans. Rev.). New York: Continuum.

Gergen, K. J. (1978*). Toward generative theory*. Journal of Personality and Social Psychology, 36(11), 1344-1360. doi: 10.1037/0022-3514-36.11.1344.

Gergen, K. J. (1994). *Toward transformation in social knowledge* (2nd ed.). Thousand

Oaks: CA: Sage.

Graves, C. W. (1974). Human nature prepares for a momentous leap. *The Futurist*, 8(2), 72-87.

Graves, C. W. (1981). *Summary statement: The emergent, cyclical, double-helix model of the adult human biopsychosocial systems.* Handout for presentation to World Future Society, Boston, MA. (Compiled for Dr. Graves by Chris Cowan).

Hanson, R., & Mendius, R. (2009). *Buddha's brain: The practical neuroscience of happiness, love & wisdom.* Oakland, CA: New Harbinger Publications, Inc.

Heidegger, M. (1962). *Being and time* (J. Macquarrie & E. Robinson, Trans.). San Francisco: Harper & Row.

Hovell, J. (2019, January 3). Advancing your OD practice, Part 3: Self as instrument for OD. [Web log post]. Retrieved from http://spaceforlearning.com/advancing-your-od-practice-part-3/

Hunt, J. (2009). Transcending and including our current way of being: An introduction to Integral Coaching. *Journal of Integral Theory and Practice*, 4(1), 1-20.

James, W. (1890/1950). *The principles of psychology* (Vol. 1). New York: Dover Publications.

Jamieson, D. W., Auron, M., & Shechtman, D. (2010). Managing use of self for masterful professional practice. *OD Practitioner*, 42(3), 4-11.

Jamieson, D. W., & Davidson, J. E. (2019). Advancing thinking and practice on use of self. *Organization Development Journal*, 37(1), 39-53.

Kegan, R. (1982). *The evolving self: Problem and process in human development.* Cambridge, MA: Harvard University Press.

Kennedy D. L. (2012). *The impact of development on coaches' use of self as instrument* (Doctoral dissertation). Fielding Graduate University, Santa Barbara, CA.

Koltko-Rivera, M. E. (2004). The psychology of worldviews. *Review of General Psychology*, 8(1), 3-58.

LaLoux, F. (2014). *Reinventing organizations: A guide to creating organizations inspired by the next stage of human consciousness.* Brussels, Belgium: Nelson Parker.

Marshak, R. J. (2012). Generative conversations: How to use deep listening and transforming talk in coaching and consulting. In J. Vogelsang (Ed.), *Handbook for strategic HR: Best practices in Organization Development from the OD Network* (pp. 206-214). New York: AMACOM.

McWilliams, S. (2016). Cultivating constructivism: Inspiring intuition & promoting process & pragmatism. *Journal of Constructivist Psychology,* 29(1), 1-29.

Narasimhan, N., Bhaskar, K., & Prakhya, S. (2010). Existential beliefs and values. *Journal of Business Ethics,* 96, 369-382. doi: 10.1007/s10551-010-0472-7

Odman, P. J. (1988). Hermeneutics. In J. P. Keeves (Ed.), *Educational research methodology and measurement: An international handbook* (pp. 63-70). New York: Pergamon Press.

Orem, S.L., Binkert, J. & Clancy, A.L. (2007). *Appreciative Coaching: A positive process for change.* San Francisco: Jossey-Bass.

Perls, F. S., Hefferline, R. F., and Goodman, P. (1951/1994). *Gestalt Therapy: Excitement and growth in the human personality.* New York: Gestalt Journal Press, Inc.

Rehorick, D., & Bentz, V. M. (2017). *Expressions of phenomenological research: Consciousness and lifeworld studies.* Santa Barbara, CA: Fielding University Press.

Rehorick, D., & Bentz, V. M. (Eds.) (2008). *Transformative phenomenology.* New York, NY: Lexington Books, Rowman & Littlefield Publishers, Inc.

Seashore, C. N., Shawver, M. N., Thompson, & Mattare, M. (2004). Doing good by knowing who you are: The Instrumental Self as an agent of change. *OD Practitioner,* 36(3), 42-46.

Wade, J. (1996). *Changes of mind: A holonomic theory of the evolution of consciousness.* New York: State University of New York Press.

Whitehead, A. N. (1929). *Process and reality: An essay in cosmology.* New York: The Free Press.

Wilbur, K. (2000). *Theory of everything: An integral vision for business, politics, science and spirituality.* Boston: Shambhala.

Wilbur, K. (1980). *The atman project: A transpersonal view of human development.* Wheaton, IL: Quest Books.

CHAPTER 9

TRANSFORMATIONAL COACHING: THE USE OF METAPHORS, ARCHETYPES, AND LIFE STORY IN EMBODIED KNOWING

Annabelle Nelson, PhD, Fielding Graduate University; João Noronha, M.A., M.A., Consultancy and Coaching for Change at INSEAD; Lee Palmer, PhD, Palmer Leadership; Kristen Truman-Allen, PhD, PULP Leadership Coaching

Abstract

Transformational coaching taps clients' creative force to solve current dilemmas and tensions in work and personal life. Drawing on both Mezirow's transformative learning and Torrance's creativity research, transformational coaching uses human's symbolic faculty and kinesthetic knowing to catalyze client's insight. This chapter presents four transformational coaching techniques. Firstly, Metaphor and Somatic Resonance coaching invites clients to self-generate a metaphor symbolized in the body. With a life of its own, the metaphor shifts and resolves tensions between disparate metaphors for an enhanced perspective. Second, metaphor and movement coaching takes an active role using questions to prompt an artistic and verbal response to a word. This is then deepened through experiential learning. Third, life narrative coaching taps clients' imaginations to help them create a coherent structure in their life and a clearer view of their identity to resolve problems. Fourth, archetypal imagery coaching leads clients to find an archetype in imagery exercises, and then to use this archetype in the visualization of a recent difficult event to shift perspectives. All of these coaching techniques use human symbolic faculties to prompt creative insight for transformation.

Introduction: A Deeper Dive for Coaching

Transformational coaching takes the coaching process to a deeper level in using methods to tap a client's creativity and intuition sometimes even outside of conscious awareness to accelerate and sustained change. This is the unique contribution of transformational coaching, acceleration, and sustainability of change through embodied knowing.

Coaching is a conversation and partnership that is intended to co-create a new reality (Barner & Higgins, 2005). Whether a situation, a dilemma or a new achievement goal, the coach and the client contract to work together for positive change (Whitworth, Kimsey-House & Sandahl, 1998). The coach is the expert in the process, and clients are the experts of their own life. Together they evoke possibilities to discover and maximize the client's expertise to foster transformation. The following quote captures the coach's job:

> "... create a safe environment; acceptance; presence; no-judgment; asking thought provoking questions/deep inquiry for critical reflection; challenge false beliefs and assumptions; accountability; active listening; modeling behavior" (Sammut, 2014, p. 48).

Transformational coaching adds creativity to this basic coaching paradigm. Torrance defines creativity as novelty (1962). Through transformational coaching clients gain insight to see something in a new way. Rogers (1961) describes the process of healing and positive growth as a result of tapping a person's creative force, the source of inner wisdom. There are several conceptual frames that explain the process that can catalyze such creative transformation.

First is Mezirow's theory (2003) of transformative learning, detailing how cognitive schemas shift to become more inclusive, allowing multiple perspectives or the novelty of new ideas. Torrance (1962), a foundational researcher in creativity, established that divergent thinking facilitates creativity, while on the other hand convergent thinking is counterproductive to creativity. Divergent thinking allows a person to come up with new ideas, similar to Mezirow's more flexible schemas, ideas that the mind has been closed to before.

Psychologists give the techniques to accomplish this. Symbolic thinking which is found in imagery, metaphors, and story give what Jung and others (Jung, von Franz, Henderson, Jacobi & Jaffe, 1964) say is a way of expressing what humans don't understand. Certainly, before there is creative transformation there is something that is not immediately understood. Therefore, the symbolizing faculty can help reveal what needs to be understood. If symbolic knowing is combined with kinesthetic or embodied knowing (Houston, 2000), then there is even more power for the coach to facilitate clients to find novel insights to everyday or intractable dilemmas.

Nelson's wise mind-body model (Nelson, 2014) demonstrates that coaching techniques using symbols and body awareness tap an inner creative force for transformation.

In Nelson's Wise Mind-Body model, there are four bodies: spiritual, physical, emotional, and mental. The physical body and the emotional body are both connected to intuition and when sensed, can give unexpected insights. These insights give new perspectives, either through something like Mezirow's dilemmas, as a surprising perspective that doesn't fit previous understanding; or as a divergent idea, tapping creativity for health and growth. In other words, body awareness and emotions are important messengers to prompt transformation. Evidence-based coaching techniques of metaphors (Cox, 2018 & Truman, 2013), life story (Barner, 2018), and archetypal imagery (Nelson, 2007) are tools to use both symbols and embodied knowing for insight and transformation.

Certainly, when dealing with the emotions of embodied knowing techniques, coaches must navigate the boundary between coaching and therapy, and applying these evidence-based coaching techniques can give structure for sessions to create emotional safe environments.

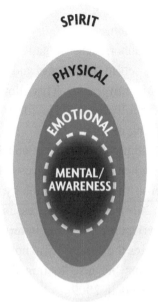

The Wise Mind-Body

Figure 1: The Wise Mind-Body

Specifics of four coaching techniques are defined in the following sections: metaphors and somatic resonance, metaphor and movement, life story, and archetypal imagery. The common elements that make these transformational are as follows: (1) the use of symbol as in metaphors created by the client or suggested by the coach; and (2) imagery in a life story or the visualization of an archetype created by the client. All include an emotional and body sense. Further these techniques allow a transformation shift in awareness by the client for accelerated and lasing change.

Metaphors and Somatic Resonance
João Noronha

Metaphors and somatic resonance employ the symbols of client generated metaphors and checks in with the client for an emotional or body sense to them. During the coaching process, often metaphors emerge that represent a tension or conflict; these can merge to create a new one resolving this tension.

Coaching with metaphors and somatic resonance invites the client to bring the whole self to the process and to experience internal metaphorical and somatic movements. This allows the best version of the client to emerge, to be fully lived and to liberate hidden capabilities, facilitated by this coaching method.

Metaphorical and somatic resonance coaching is a rich and effective process to use when the client aspires to have significant shift in worldviews, the sense of self, epistemology, ontology, behavior, or capacity (Hoggan, 2016). Because the essence of a metaphor is understanding and experiencing one thing in terms of another (Lakoff & Johnson, 2003), it creates the possibility to not only transfer meaning between different domains but also to transform meaning through novel re-combinations (Modell, 2009).

As metaphors also exist apart from language in gestures, visual images, feelings, and bodily sensations (Modell, 2009), coaching allows for the shift in cognitive, emotional, and embodied dimensions. Because of that, it facilitates clients' transformations with greater impact when compared to pure language coaching methods. In contrast, this method uses engaging embodied knowledge (Claxton, 2015; Cox, 2018), imagery work (Berry, 2000; Jung, 1997; Nelson, 2011, 2014) and emotional exploration.

Primary metaphors (Lakoff & Johnson, 2008) are created by direct physical sensations, since they have physical correlates of emotion, for example warmth and joy. Inviting the client to move from the metaphor into the somatic and emotional space, the coach allows the for possibility to stay with the direct apprehended experience in the body. This can lead to a deep emotional shift that, when processed, will lead to a cognitive reappraisal.

Metaphors can bridge the conscious and the unconscious mind (Lakoff & Johnson, 2008) and the sensory and language systems (Modell, 2009; Lakoff & Johnson, 2008). Metaphors are also the bridge between the individual and the collective spaces, the self and the others, the different representations of the self, the self and life, the body and the mind, as well as other combinations (Modell, 2009). For example, a client may identify that anxiety is like a black hole in the chest, and at the same time the client visualizes a pump with the energy needed to overcome the anxiety. In this case, the two metaphors together create the possibility for a somatic resolution of an important tension that was possibly held for several years. When the black hole metaphor was transformed by the pump, the client reported changed imagery of an immense landscape with mountains and rivers. This change created an emotional release (release of anxiety) and a somatic shift (a significant shift in the temperature of the body and the release of the tension in the chest).

Transformation is the possibility to discriminate differences and integrate them. This explains how metaphors can be a wonderful tool to do that. As Modell (2009) argued, they have the intrinsic capacity to find similarities in apparent different dimensions that can only be connected through the use of a metaphor. In the above-mentioned case, the perceived difference between anxiety and the need to move a project forward were depicted differently (black hole and pump), and integrated when the two metaphors merged into a third (landscape). The most common process to work with metaphors and somatic resonance follows a natural sequence of stages: (1) entry points; (2) deepening the experience; (3) core metaphorical shift; (4) integration.

The client's transformation starts with offering different entry points (dilemmas, stories, life transitions, core themes, sensorial experiences or emotions) from which it is possible to start the process and prepare the conditions for the next phase, deepening the experience. There are also instances in which the client brings the self into the metaphor, saying for example, "I am all over the place," "I am scattered," or "This has been a big burden." In this case the metaphor is already part of the natural discourse of the client (and related imaginal representation of the situation he or she is living). As the metaphor emerges naturally even before the coaching conversation, it is important in the coaching session to create the space for the client to imagine interacting with the metaphor.

There are instances in which the entry point is the felt-sense, a term coined by Gendlin (2007, p. 37), that describes a bodily (somatic) feeling that is the source and the result of awareness of a situation, a person, an event, or any combination of the three. Felt-sense is an important concept because, "[a]n internal aura that encompasses everything you feel and know about a given subject at a given time, not a mental experience but rather a physical one" (Gendlin, 2007, p. 37).

If more than one metaphor is part of the client's imaginal landscape, it is also possible to invite the metaphors to interact and, by letting them move or create connections, create the conditions for a metaphorical shift. For example, one client held a tension between two possible decisions, one represented by a tightness in the throat visualized as a worm, and another visualized as a metal plate representing a constriction in the chest. The coach invited the client to stay with the two images, and the plate converted into a small net that wrapped around the worm and, suddenly the client started to cough. After a few seconds neither the tightness in the throat nor constriction in the chest were still felt. Although visibly relieved, the client felt a bit disoriented and wanted to progress the conversation about what to do regarding his decision. The coach suggested rest after the somatic and metaphorical exploration. During that evening, the client dreamt about a third and new solution for the problem he was facing.

There is also a possibility that the metaphor is not "prepared" to do its work, which normally means there is some unconscious resistance to let the transformation occur. In those cases, it is important to respect that "will," and it is possible to come back to the felt-sense and stay in the sensorial space to continue the exploration to see if something emerges from there. An interesting case happened with a client that had a goal and, when the coach asked how the goal could be represented, he came with the image of a small sphere. When the coach asked where that sphere was the client said that he felt the sphere in his belly. When the client was invited to imagine approaching the sphere, the sphere moved to a different place. This happened three times, after which the coach suggested to pause. A few sessions later, a different sphere (larger and with a different color) appeared during the session, and the client was able to come closer, to touch, and even move inside the sphere. In that moment, an important somatic and emotional shift happened, and the coaching "issue" was dissolved.

Once the metaphorical process finishes (marked by the integration or dissolution of the metaphor) the client experiences a somatic or emotional shift that could lead to a shift in identity, expressed by any of its dimensions (worldview, Self, epistemology, ontology, behavior or capacity) or any combination of them. Transformative learning markers are sufficient to understand the depth and stability of the client's transformation, that together represent a shift in the client's identity. This will allow the client to relate to the original story, dilemma, or theme in a different way and to have a different resonance (emotional, imaginal and somatic through the felt-sense). The process culminates in the integration of the new identity into the daily life of the client, bringing a revised version of the story to mind, the resolution of the theme or dilemma and a new competency to live similar situations with a new response and a new emotional and somatic resonance.

Metaphors and Movement
Kristen Truman-Allen

In metaphors and movement coaching, the symbol is a metaphors suggested by the coach after beginning dialogue often with just one word. The emotional and physical response includes art and physical experiences in nature. A shift in awareness happens as the client transforms with renewed energy to accomplish a goal.

Truman's (2013) "cycle of self-generated change" prompts a coach to help a client choose a metaphor which creates an emotional and physical shift and becomes a symbolic reminder for transformation.

The metaphor can symbolize the goal of the coaching exercise and be used for engagement in a physical experience. During the coaching dialogue, the client draws an illustration of the metaphor and notes words that come to mind, followed by a physical experience with the metaphor. Physical experiences vary in time from walking, hiking, snowshoeing, paddle boarding or strength training, to name a few. During the physical experience, the coach asks the clients to notice, to be present and to consider the situation that they are working on in their coaching and be open to new information in their environment.

Coaching is a partnership for transforming reality, thinking, doing, and new ways of being. The coaching process is perpetuated by use of tools to maximize critical reflection to alter the way individuals perceive things and to create new learning. Metaphor is a tool that coaches can use to generate new perspectives (Schon, 1979; Seto & Geither, 2018). Coaches explore metaphor by listening to language, and through the imagery and symbols gather a shared understanding and clarity of what a client is experiencing (Lawley & Tomkins, 2000). This evokes clients' intuitive knowing into their awareness. It creates a consciousness, a mental shift, and a transformation. It is a symbolic way of remembering and recreating insight that can then consciously apply to tasks and actions as well as a way to describe a shift in their bodies (Grisoni & Page, 2010). Metaphor brings information from unconscious knowing to conscious awareness as a way to embody and stimulate meaning and action.

Truman (2013) found that when metaphor is used in coaching conversations, clients experience a process in which metaphor creates a new awareness, shifts their perspective, informs, and often transforms clients' way of being. This creates both an emotional and physical shift. The metaphor becomes a symbolic reminder for ongoing transformation.

In this experience-based coaching methodology, metaphor is consciously used to walk clients through the cycle of accelerated change. Metaphors are elicited from symbolic representation of their

180

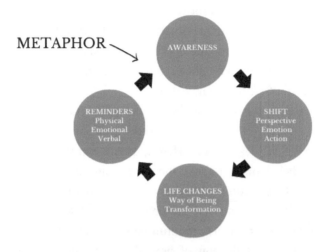

Figure 2. Cycle of self-generated change (Truman, 2013)

experience as well as elicited through physical movement to help clients get to transformation, embody their experience, and ultimately keep them moving toward ongoing transformation.

Clients (individual or in groups), begin by determining a metaphor based on the goal of the coaching session, followed by engagement in a physical experience. To access a metaphor, the coach asks for one directly by asking something like, "What is the metaphor for your experience?" The coach may instead choose a word that represents the goal of the coaching situation and ask, "What comes to mind when I say _____". For example, when working with a group of physicians with the goal of maximizing resilience, the following question could be used: "What image comes to mind when I say 'adaptation'?" Clients could then be asked to draw their image and use words to describe it. This is a type of symbolic modeling intended to identify the client's unique metaphoric landscape (Lawley & Tompkins, 2000). In this example, the metaphors will all be unique, and usually range from things like cellular activity, trees shaped by the wind, or evolution for example. The clients could then share the image that comes to mind when a word is reflected to them based on their stated goals, desires or situation. The metaphor is a tool which allows clients a detached, objective way of looking at their situation, a safe way to express themselves, and a great way for the coach to understand their initial perspective and shape their own understanding (Grisoni & Page, 2010; Lynch & Fisher-Ari, 2017; Sammut, 2014).

Introducing the metaphor early in the coaching process allows clients to quickly access their situation or their goal objectively, with clarity and with visual description (Heron, 1992). Exploring a new metaphor brings their situation above the surface and identifies their situation in ways they hadn't previously considered or articulated (Grisoni & Page, 2010). Creativity is tapped for novel solutions and more open schemas. After clients are intuitively clear about their own imagery and their own definition of how they conceptualize their situation symbolically (in this example, "adaptation"), the coach asks them to identify how their image represents their leadership style or personal strengths. The coaching open-ended question looks like: "How does your description of 'adaptation' apply to your way of being?" By using what the client knows about their conceptual and imagistic representation and applying it to their situation, the metaphor is then a tool to generate transparency and clarity (Schon, 1979, Sammut, 2014).

With their current metaphor and situation in mind, the coach then incorporates the client's metaphor into a physical experience. As noted above, physical experiences vary in time from walking, hiking, snowshoeing, to paddle boarding or strength training, for example. Introducing an experience with the identified metaphor and evoking new metaphors shifts the client's awareness and their perspective and actively disrupts the current way of thinking (Bacon, 1983; Lynch & Fisher-Ari, 2017).

The goal in this experiential coaching model is to consciously use the metaphors to attribute learning from the experience to new learning in a client centered goal. This approach is in line with Kolb's (1984) experiential learning model, in which the client engages in an activity or experience followed by a reflection to explore the effect of the experience and perpetuate the learning. During the experience there is plenty of space, and sometimes silence, to simply be present and play without thinking or discussing goal related topics. The coach listens and observes for a notable or emotional moment where the client has critical decision making, or hesitation, similar to what Mezirow & Associates (2000) referred to as a disorienting event or what Haan et al. (2010) recognized as a critical moment. Notable moments might include falling off of a paddleboard, summiting a mountain, losing your way on a trail, or having difficulty moving through the deep snow in snowshoes.

At the conclusion of the experience, or when there are notable moments that elicit emotion, the coach engages in reflective dialogue to help clients interpret meaning in their experience and discover how the interpretation or effects of their physical experience applies to their current coaching situation. By taking what is known now about themselves in the experience and applying it to their coaching goals, a new metaphor is generated (Schon, 1979). Antle, Corness, & Droumeva (2009) refer to these new sensory-motor metaphors as embodied metaphors, and suggest that this interaction improves learning. The transformation of one or more preliminary metaphors to a new one depicts new awareness from embodied knowing, as in Noronha's Metaphors and Somatic Resonance. In addition, the unique experience that these clients have is very personal and the metaphors they create gives them an opportunity to express their changed perspectives in meaningful ways (Lynch & Fisher-Ari, 2017).

The memory of the experience is embodied and becomes a physical and emotional symbolic reminder to keep the changes alive and may even foster transformation faster (Florin, 2015). Acceleration and sustainability are hallmarks of transformational coaching. The whole-body experience contains embedded feelings and beliefs which represents the client's whole being (Grisoni & Page, 2010). Clients attribute aspects of the emotional experience to their situation, which generates metaphor (Schon, 1979) as a point of reflection to their current situation to increase their self-knowledge and shift their perspective (Fullagar & O'Brien, 2012).

The initial metaphor, the subsequent experience, and the critical reflection with coaching discourse, bring underlying meaning above the surface to transform the elements of the experience to something useful and applicable to their current situation (Grisoni & Page 2010). In this movement-based metaphoric coaching approach, which follows the cycle of self-generated change, new metaphors, symbols, and imagistic representations create a new awareness and shift perspective. Using the metaphor as a point of reflection stimulates a new way of thinking and challenges perspectives. The metaphors create a catalyst or some discomfort or disorientation to generate critical reflection to facilitate transformational learning. The metaphor is transformational in that it generates emotion that continues to be an embodied emotional and physical reminder of their goals and inspired action.

Life Story Coaching
Lee Palmer

In the life story coaching method, symbols are endemic to story as characters and scenes represent greater meaning than factual information. Stories are from the heart of a client to the heart of the coach and are rife with emotional content. Moving into the mythic realm of story, clients tap into collective embodied knowing to gain perspective and clarity of live events. Transformation happens as clients move their lives into story and gain a cohesive view of life patterns to see meaning and solve problems.

Human beings are storytellers by nature (Bruner, 1986). It is common for people to make sense of their lives and the lives of others through story. According to Lakoff and Johnson (1980), the life-is-a-story metaphor is deeply rooted in culture and society. The psychological and spiritual assumption that lives are structured like stories can facilitate a level of coherence and perspective. Damasio (1999) wrote: "Consciousness begins when brains acquire the simple power of telling a story" (p. 10). A person's dynamic life story is an essential component to his or her individuality, which is situated among particular family, friends, and acquaintances (Thorne, 2000), and living in a society at a particular historical moment (Gregg, 1991).

One powerful way for transformation to occur in coaching is through the skillful utilization of life story and life narratives, positioned as a gateway to navigate certain experiences and construct them into meaningful patterns. Life story is described as an economic summary of life's experiences (Anderson & Conway, 1993; Bluck & Habermas, 2000). As Barner (2018) says, "when it comes to constructing our narratives, each of us carries around an active editor in our head" (p.14). Conceptually, related life events consist of a combination of cognition and emotion that can be used to understand and make sense of events that have occurred in people's lives (Pillemer, 2001). This narrative summarization, with a "distinct, temporal causation" (Sarbin, 1986), is used as a structure that allows leaders to maintain a sense of personal identity (McAdams, 2001; Neimeyer & Metzler, 1994). The narrative coaching approach assumes that a person feels, thinks, and acts from a "meaning system" that enables him or her to analyze and interpret reality in a way that gives it a personal meaning (Kegan & Lahey, 2009). Narratives are not records of historical facts, but they represent a meaning-making system that makes sense out of the chaotic mass of perceptions and experiences of a life (Josselson & Lieblich, 1993). Simply stated, a personal narrative is the manifestation and expression of the events as perceived and interpreted by the individual that experienced them (Widdershoven, 1993). Narrative psychology advocates for life stories as an important component of personal identity, used as a means of explaining how an individual's identity has either changed or remained consistent through time (Kober & Habermas, 2017; McAdams, 2001; Polkinghorne, 1991).

Life narratives also serve two other key functions (Bluck, 2003) which are directly related to coaching as a process and a profession. First, meaningful events used to construct life narratives serve directive functions, providing life lessons which define goals, causes, actions, and context (Baumeister & Newman, 1994; Pillemer, 2003). Research suggests that when people are exposed to crises (particularly complex, challenging events) they are likely to apply life narratives as a mechanism for understanding and responding to new events (Bluck & Staudinger, 2001; Pillemer, 1998; Reiser, Black, & Abelson, 1985). Second, life narratives provide a way for leaders to communicate personal understanding of their lives in relation to the current situation (Alea & Bluck, 2003; Fitzgerald, 1996). This communication allows the clients who are leaders to test and refine their understanding of a situation in terms of its implications for themselves and others, based on feedback and consequential behavior (Barclay, 1995).

Storytelling is the vehicle by which coaching dialogue emerges. Clients narrate personal or workplace experiences in the form of a story, and coaches listen and respond to the story told to them. Only in recent years has narrative coaching (Mattingly, 1998; Anderson, 2004; Baldwin, 2005; Drake, 2007, 2016) made a substantial contribution to reframing our understanding of how telling stories can address the challenges and complex issues of everyday life. This stems from the research of scholars such as Abma (1999), Mattingly (1991), Mishler (1992), Pals (2006) and Rappaport (1993), who laid down a strong foundation of narrative analysis in related disciplines from which coaching could benefit. There is a body of research (Vogel, 2012; Drake, 2016; Drake and Lanahan, 2007; Polkinghorne, 1991) maintaining that stories help coaches and their leader clients think narratively. The narrative imagination captures the interplay between language and discourse and helps us to order our thoughts in a clearer, more coherent structure. Drake's (2007, 2016) research, in particular, makes a powerful case for storytelling as a means of conceptualizing our position in the workplace and of resolving professional problems. His theory is that stories make visible an individual's identity and that they are valuable for what that person includes and excludes. As individuals construct themselves in the coaching process, they aim to create an orderly and meaningful narrative.

Coaching conversations are social interactions that hold space for ongoing dialogue where clients reflect, interpret, and reinterpret their situations. These interactions use language to influence the construction of the client's reality (Barner & Higgins, 2005). This theory suggests that reality is what drives actions and that conversations can be used as interventions to construct, deconstruct, and reconstruct reality to achieve different results. This is meaningful for purposes of coaching delivery, as coaches need strategies to navigate the complex issues that their clients encounter. The 21st century organizational leaders are experiencing an upheaval and high degree of uncertainty because of forces involving global competition, rapid evolution of technology, increased need for competent human capital, government's regulatory business policies, and the shifting nature of the economy (Park and Kim, 2015). Using narrative strategies, coaches can help the client work through these various leadership challenges.

Barner (2018) states that every leader "is walking around with an interconnected series of significant life stories in his or her head, and these stories help shape their effectiveness as leaders" (p.14). In coaching engagements, there is always an initial phase of client assessment and data gathering. This intake process can commence in several different ways; however, it is typical that the coach asks targeted questions on subjects such as where the client fits into the organizational structure, the leader's span of control, or key performance accountabilities. While this information is important, it doesn't necessarily provide the coach with a coherent picture of the coaching client. This is where life story becomes valuable. Barner and Ideus (2017) suggest that a better approach is to make use of broad questions that encourage the client to tell his or her story in any way that works for him or her. Certain questions can be used to deconstruct the clients' past, present, and future stories, such as: "Could you tell me how you came into your organization, and where you think that journey has taken you so far? What else do I need to know about your story that might help us in this coaching relationship? What has been omitted from what I've heard?" The client's responses to these questions, including tone, opinions, language, and level of openness, can provide valuable information to the coach (Barner, 2018). In this way, life stories or narratives reveal much about the client's self-image, leadership tendencies, and the general perspective of the world in which they live.

A life story coaching example could be when a client expresses frustration and disappointment over a particular setback or rejection. The coach prompts the client to recall other instances in their past which involved similar circumstances or feelings of defeat. This creates an opportunity for the client to access the feelings, thoughts, and actions which reside in their own story. Looking back on past disappointment or rejection can help to put those feelings into context and eventually move forward in a productive way. The coach guides the client through a thorough reflective thought process (comparing the current situation with past situations) to identify either useful or detrimental narratives, which can then be retained or discarded by the client. The coach asks questions such as, "Did that (past) perspective serve you in that circumstance of rejection? Knowing now how that past event transpired, what wisdom did you gain? What implicit narrative would have served you better? How can that be applied to this current situation?" This form of taking action can mitigate disappointment and helps the client channel the associated feelings into motivation for positive change.

In addition to the time of client intake, the use of life story can also occur at other points along the arc of the coaching engagement, as needed. At any time in the coaching conversation, for the various reasons mentioned above, coaches can support leaders through a guided process of life story reflection. Ultimately, it is up to the individual coaching practitioner to make an informed decision about when and how to effectively utilize life story in the coaching experience.

Archetypal Imagery
Annabelle Nelson

An archetype is an energy pattern in the collective unconscious that connotes a given characteristic; as such, archetype is a symbol and conveys multiple meanings depending on people's perception. In archetypal imagery, embodied know is used by prompting clients to visualize a recent uncomfortable situation and find the evoked emotion in their body. Imagery exercises prompt the visualization of an archetype, and the introduction of such an archetype into the visualization of a recent situation gives the client a new perspective. The archetype can symbolize characteristics such as confidence for example, which can transform emotions. As with other transformational coaching techniques, symbols, and in this case the visualization of the archetype and the emotion in the body, accelerates transformation; cognitive understanding and incorporation comes after the shift.

Storytelling moves the client to the liminal realm (Campbell, 2008) where the client is automatically identifying with an archetype as they are telling their story, since archetypes are the main characters in stories. Archetypes symbolize a given characteristic that a client can embody by using imagery (Achterberg, 1985; Nelson, 1993). Imagery speaks to the limbic system (Pribram, 1981), which expands the field of perception in consciousness, thereby calming the client. Through the relaxation prompted by imagery, a person can embody the characteristic of an archetype and reflect on action to solve a current issue. Imagery can then be extended to include a current work or interpersonal scene where the archetype offers awareness for transformation to shift patterns and prompt insight into solutions.

Carl Jung (Edinger, 1992; Woodman & Dickson, 1996) said that all people live in front of an archetype. As children develop, they seek an energy pattern to organize their personalities. This happens outside of conscious awareness. Rediscovering the archetype in front of which one lives opens a channel to embodied knowing. It is like opening up a window to hidden potential. In day-to-day life, coaching clients only perceive a small portion of reality. However, coaches can help clients contact their deep wisdom so they can see a dilemma clearly; archetypal imagery can do this.

Figure 3: The Greek goddess Gaia

As noted, an archetype is an energy pattern that conveys a given characteristic. Usually one recognizes an archetype right away; the characteristic pops comes to mind immediately. For example, the Greek goddess Gaia conveys protection (Olson, 1994). In Gaia's story, she protects life even when her mate, Ouranos, tells her to kill their deformed child (the one-eyed cyclops). She does so again when her son, Cronos, wants her to kill his son, Zeus, because of the prophecy that Zeus will take over Cronos' throne. Gaia protects life even though pressured by her husband and son.

In its quest for stability, the ego keeps consciousness tied up with a busy mind. But the ego likes archetypes, since they are part of a natural psychodynamic for organizing personality. Visualizing an archetype

190

quiets the ego to open the mind to deep wisdom. Thomas Aquinas, a 13th century theologian (Hartelius, Caplan & Rardin, 2007), said that wisdom could be defined as "lifeability," or making one's life work. Coaches can help their clients gain this lifeability to solve problems. Often, this means figuring out how to map out and face life's adversity. Unfortunately, difficulties happen frequently. Archetypes give hope. Even though negativity happens in life, one can foster the wisdom to roll with the punches and come out adept at making life work. Visualizing archetypes is a tool to develop such wisdom since archetypes embody characteristics that can help solve current issues. Stories show tried and true patterns of lifeability.

It is not complicated to help coaching clients find an archetype, since it can happen in a playful and intuitive way using imagery. Imagery is a magical way to relax the mind (Achterberg, 1985; Nelson, 1993, 2014; Armstrong, 2015). Coaches can lead the client on a guided imagery exercise. Effective imagery techniques include using relaxing music, leading a client to relax the body, using all senses (sight, sound, touch, movement and smell) to evoke a vivid beginning scene, and giving the client time to let the imagery move. Coaches can visualize as they lead the process in order to ensure an ideal pace. At the end of imagery, it is good to "close it" by thinking of a quiet scene and visualize a comforting image, such as being in a comfortable chair and covering up with a throw. To use imagery to help a client find an archetype, after relaxation, the client can be led to visualize an outdoor scene, somewhere the client has been before. The client is led to find a relaxing place in nature and visualize that an entity is coming. The entity means the client no harm and can be an animal, a deity, a friend, or someone who has passed. The coach gives time for the imagery to play out, and to resolve the scene. For example, the entity may have something to say or a gift or conveys a feeling. The entity is the client's archetype.

A client's archetype can be engendered spontaneously from an imagery exercise like the one above or, alternatively, the coach can

Figure 4: The archetype of the world

suggest an archetype to the client. For example, the archetype of "the world" could be used. Its main characteristic is fulfillment. Once the archetype is identified, the coach can lead clients to use its characteristic to transform an emotional pattern in a recent uncomfortable situation. Humanistic and Jungian psychologists (Nelson, 2014) note that a recent emotional event is tied to emotional patterns or stories stored in the unconscious that are limiting (such as, "I'll never be loved" or "I'm not as smart as these people I work with"). Clients can be led to visualize a recent situation that was difficult and find the emotion evoked in their body. The coach can vivify visualizing the emotion in the body with prompts. For example, "Where is it? How big is it? Is it inside the body? Is it smooth? What color is it?" Once that is done, the coach can ask the client to return to the visualization of the difficult situation, but this time to bring in the archetype into the imagery. Prompts can lead the client to transform the image, using the archetype's characteristic. "What would happen if you had the archetype's characteristic or had the archetype's point of view?" There is often a shift in the emotion in the body, and the coach can take the client back to the visualization, asking, "What does it look like now?" Clients realize that they did their best or that the next time the situation occurs they would do something differently. It is a possible that a fundamental shift and an opening in the self for greater inner resources emerges with this shift of awareness.

An example is a veteran who was working in a support group for vets at a university. His difficult emotional situation was doing counseling with another vet and feeling incapable of helping. He saw a knotted fist in his stomach. During the initial imagery session, the entity or archetype that came to him was a golden warrior-monk. When he brought the golden warrior-monk into the difficult emotional situation imagery, he realized he had empathy and more importantly had great compassion to help other vets. The fist in his stomach released its grip and disappeared. He gained confidence in his work.

Usually the mind is full of worries or other sensations, but visualizing an archetype quiets the mind and helps a person embody a specific characteristic. This is important since the archetypes in stories hold characteristics of human wisdom built over centuries to create lifeability. The archetypes prompt clients to be reflective and bring their characteristics to bear on life's ups and downs.

Conclusion

The four coaching techniques in this chapter may seem disparate, but there is an underlying core of using natural human cognitive capabilities to open new vistas generated by clients themselves. Rather than using logical problem solving or conscious goal setting, the four coaching techniques approach the whole person, from Nelson's (2014) wise mind-body model. Both the physical and the emotional bodies are activated to prompt an individual's creative force to generate insight that can be transformational. The "aha" comes from not logical reasoning, but from a felt sense in the body that includes emotional markers. Metaphor and somatic resonance prompt a coach to create an environment free of the coach's preconceived notions of what might be best for the client, and allows a client to engender visualizations of feelings in the body. Of particular note to this technique is the opportunity for the tension of competing choices to be represented, and in the client's own time, allow these to shift for transformation. With metaphors and movement, a coach may take a more direct approach in proposing a specific word that prompts an individual to create a metaphor. The unique process here is to use art and physical activities to embody the metaphor that accelerates its incorporation to a shift in perspective propelling action. Life narratives may seem out of flow with these others, but stories come from the heart of the storytelling, engendering an emotional component to see one's life as a cohesive whole that makes sense and can lead to clarity and create new perceptions for solving dilemmas. Finally, archetypes are essentially metaphoric symbols that have an emotional component, allowing individuals to embody characteristics that they didn't see in themselves before for strength and clarity.

Creativity is the thread that weaves these coaching techniques into an effective coaching tool kit that will not only solve problems but change the client from the inside out. These can lead a client to see coherence in life, gain new perspectives, build strength, and find purpose to transform their personal and work lives.

About the Authors

Annabelle Nelson, PhD is a psychology professor, author, researcher and dynamic speaker. Nelson is now a professor at Fielding Graduate University. She has presented at many international and U.S. conferences, completed a Fulbright in India, and published five books and many journal articles. This experience gives Nelson the expertise to create transformational learning in teaching and coaching to tap deep wisdom. Her innovative and effective imagery technique is documented in *Archetypal imagery and the spirit self: techniques for coaches and therapists*, 2014, published by Jessica Kingsley Publishers.

Social service has been integral to Nelson' career. Her commitment to child advocacy has led her to create a nonprofit, the WHEEL Council (Wholistic, Health, Education and Empowerment for Life, www. wheelocoucil.org) which creates storytelling curriculum to empower youth with their unique wisdom.

João Noronha, M.A., M.A. has a mission to help individuals, groups and organizations to tap into their source of energy, insight and creativity and, from there, libertate their full potential. Individuals and organizations worldwide are benefiting from his first experience as consultant in strategy, organizational development, knowledge management, and transformation and his fifteen years' experience in leadership development, individual, and team coaching. João holds a Master's in Consultancy and Coaching for Change (INSEAD) and he is currently a PhD student in Human Development (with a coaching concentration) at Fielding Graduate University. João uses metaphorical coaching and non-intrusive questioning as a tool for his clients to tap into their conscious and unconscious wisdom through their metaphorical landscape and embodied knowledge and, from there, to liberate, nurture and develop the best version of themselves. His passions include poetry, chess, swimming and Tai Chi.

Lee Palmer, PhD is a leadership coach, facilitator, and researcher who thrives on helping others to optimize themselves personally and professionally. She believes the human connection is the key component to success and happiness in the workplace. She has over fourteen years of experience in psychology-based instruction of leadership training, team training, emotional intelligence (EQ), and relationship/life skills. Lee's experience as a certified teacher and coach in the US, Europe, and Australia has proven successful in guiding students and clients to significant personal and professional gains. She is committed to helping individuals and organizations achieve their goals through their personal, interpersonal, and group competencies. Her B.A. in

Psychology, M.A. in Leadership & Organizational Development, and doctoral work in Human Development & Leadership Psychology has been the key to success in her field of work. She is currently completing her PhD dissertation and her areas of focus include personal mastery, high performance teaming, leadership psychology, evidence-based coaching, and self-actualization.

Kristen Truman-Allen, PhD is on a mission to ensure that every leader and the people they serve live a fully engaged and integrated whole life. Kristen brings her experiences as health care administrator, emergency nurse, outward bound expeditionary learning instructor and organization development professional into her coaching for executives and formal leaders in organizations. With a PhD in Human Development and a Master's in Human and Organization Systems, Kristen uses metaphor and intuition in her coaching of organizations and individual leaders to help them have the energy to integrate what's most important to them. Kristen balances her family of 6, travel, adventure, business and play and is passionate about evoking inspiration and impact in our world.

References

Abma, T. A. (1999). Powerful stories: The role of stories in sustaining and transforming professional practice within a mental hospital. In Josselson, R. & Lieblich, A. (eds.) *Making meaning of narratives.* Thousand Oaks, CA: Sage.

Achterberg, J. (1985). *Shamanism and modern medicine.* Boston and London: Shambhala.

Alea, N., & Bluck, S. (2013). When does meaning making predict subjective well-being? Examining young and older adults in two cultures. *Memory,* 21(1), 44-63. doi:10.1080/09658211.2012.704927

Anderson, S. J., & Conway, M. A. (1993). Investigating the structure of autobiographical memories. *Journal of Experimental Psychology: Learning, Memory, and Cognition,* 19(5), 1178.

Anderson, T. (2004). "To tell my story: configuring interpersonal relations within narrative process", in Angus, L.E. and McLeod, J. (Eds), *Handbook of* narrative and psychotherapy: Practice, theory and research. Sage, Thousand Oaks, CA, pp. 315-329.

Antel, A., Corness, G, & Droumeva, M. (2009). What the body knows: Exploring the benefits of embodied metaphors in hybrid physical digital environments. *Interacting with Computers,* 21, 66-75.

Armstrong, C. (2015). *The therapeutic "aha": 10 strategies to get your clients untuck.* N.Y. ,N.Y.: W.W. North & Co.

Bacon, S. (1983). *The conscious use of metaphor in Outward Bound.* Denver, CO: Type Smith.

Baldwin, C. (2005). *Storycatcher: Making Sense of our Lives through the Power and Practice of Story,* Novata, CA: New World Library.

Barner, R. (2018). Creating stories that work. *Training,* 55(1), 14-15. Retrieved from https://fgul.idm.oclc.org/docview/2009453720?accountid=10868

Barner, R., & Higgins, J. (2005). A social constructionist approach to leadership coaching. *OD Practitioner,* 37(4), 4-9.

Barner, R. & Higgins, J. (2007). Understanding the implicit models that guide the coaching process. *Journal of Management Development,* 26, 148–158.

Barner, R., & Ideus, K. (2017). *Working deeply: Transforming lives through transformational coaching.* Emerald Publishing Limited.

Baumeister, R. F., & Wilson, B. (1996). Life stories and the four needs for meaning. *Psychological Inquiry,* 7(4), 322-327.

Berry, P. (2000). An approach to the dream. In B. Sells (Ed.), *Working with images: The theoretical base of archetypal psychology* (pp. 91–111). Woodstock, Connecticut: Spring Publications.

Bluck, S. (2003). Autobiographical memory: Exploring its functions in everyday life. *Memory,* 11(2), 113-123.

Bluck, S. & Habermas, T. (2000). Getting a life: The emergence of the life story in adolescence. *Psychological Bulletin,* 126(5), 748-769. doi:10.1037/0033-2909.126.5.748

Bruner J. (1986). *Actual Minds, Possible Worlds.* Harvard University Press: Cambridge, MA.

Campbell, J. (2008). *The collected works of Joseph Campbell.* New World Library.

Claxton, G. (2015). *Intelligence in the flesh: Why your mind needs your body much more than it thinks.* Yale University Press. conversation. Fielding Graduate University, ProQuest Dissertations Publishing, 2013.

Cox, A. M. (2018). Embodied knowledge and sensory information: Theoretical roots and inspirations. *Library Trends,* 66(3), 223-238. doi:10.1353/

lib.2018.0001

Damasio, A. R. (1999). *The feeling of what happens: Body and emotion in the making of consciousness.* Houghton Mifflin Harcourt.

Drake, D. & Lanahan, B. (2007). The story-driven organization. *Global Business and Organizational Excellence,* May/June, 36-46.

Drake, D. B. (2007). An integrated approach to coaching: The emerging story in a large professional services firm. *International Journal of Coaching in Organizations,* 5(3), 22–35.

Drake, D. B. (2015). *Narrative coaching: Bringing our new stories to life.* Petaluma, CA: CNC Press.

Edinger, E. (1992). *Ego and archetype.* Boston: Shambhala.

Florin, W. (2015). Creating change faster: Convergence and transformation acceleration. *Journal of practical consulting.* 5(2), 29-37.

Ford, J. D. (1999). Organizational change and shifting conversations. *Journal of Organizational Change Management,* 12, 480-500.

Fullagar, S. & O'Brien. (2012). Immobility, battles, and the journey of feeling alive: Women's metaphors of self-transformation through depression and recovery. *Qualitative Health Research,* 22(8), 1063-1072.

Gendlin, E. T. (2007). *Focusing.* New York: Bantam Books.

Gregg, G. (1991). Themes of authority in life-histories of young Moroccans. In S. Miller & R. Bourgia (Eds.), *Representations of power in Morocco.* Cambridge, MA: Harvard University Press.

Grisoni, L. & Page, M. (2010). Two to the power of three: An exploration of metaphor for sense making in (women's) collaborative inquiry. *Organization Management Journal,* 7, 13-25.

Haan, E. et al (2010). Client's critical moments of coaching: Toward a "client model" of executive coaching. *Academy of Management Learning & Education* 9(4), 607-621.

Hartelius, G., Caplan, M., & Rardin, M. A. (2007). Transpersonal psychology: Defining the past, *The Humanistic Psychologist,* 35 (20), 135-160

Hoggan, C. (2016). Transformative learning as a metatheory: Definition, criteria, and typology. *Adult Education Quarterly,* 66(1), 57–75.

Heron, J. (1992). *Feeling and personhood: Psychology in another key.* London: Sage publications.

Houston, J. (2000). Myths of the future. *The Humanistic Psychologist.* 28 (1-3), 43-58. http://dx.doi.org/10.1080/08873260701274017

Josselson, R., & Lieblich, A. (Eds.) (1993). *The narrative study of lives.* Thousand Oaks, CA: SAGE Publications.

Jung, C. G., von Franz, M-L, Henderson, J.L., Jacobi, J. & Jaffe, A. (1964). *Man and his symbols.* Random House.

Jung, C.G. (1970). *Analytical psychology: its theory and practice.* New York: Vintage.

Kegan, R., & Lahey, L. L. (2009). *Immunity to change: how to overcome it and unlock potential in yourself and your organization.* Boston: Harvard Business School Publishing Corporation.

Köber, C., & Habermas, T. (2017). How stable is the personal past? Stability of most important autobiographical memories and life narratives across eight years in a life span sample. *Journal of personality and social psychology,* 113(4), 608.

Kolb, D. A (1984). *Experiential learning: Experience as a source of learning and development.* Englewood Cliffs, NJ: Prentice Hall.

Lakoff, G. & Johnson, M. (1980). *Metaphors we live by.* Chicago, IL: Chicago University Press.

Lawley, J., & Tompkins, P. (2000). *Metaphors in mind: Transformation through symbolic modeling.* Highgate, London, UK: Developing Company Press.

Lynch, H, & Fisher-Ari, T. (2017). Metaphor as pedagogy in teacher education. *Teaching and Teacher Education.* 66, 195-203.

Maslow, A. (1970). *Motivation and personality.* New York, NY: Harper and Row.

Mattingly, C. (1998). *Healing Dramas and Clinical Plots: The Narrative Structure of Experience.* Cambridge University Press, New York, NY.

Mattingly, C. (1991). Narrative reflections on practical actions: Two learning experiments in reflective story-telling. In: Schön, D. A. (ed.) *The reflective turn: Case studies in and on educational practice.* New York, NY: Teachers College Press.

McAdams, D.P. (2001). The psychology of life stories, *Review of General Psychology,* 5,100-123.

Mezirow, J. (2003). Transformative learning as discourse. *Journal of Transformative Education,* 1(1), 58-63.

Mezirow J. D., and Associates. (2000). *Learning as transformation: Critical perspectives on a theory in progress.* San Francisco, CA: Jossey-Bass.

Mishler, E. G. (1992). Work, identity, and narrative: An artist-craftsman's story. In: Rosenwald, G. C. & Ochberg, R. L. (eds.) *Storied lives: The cultural politics of self-understanding.* New Haven, CT: Yale University Press.

Modell, A. H., M.D. (2009). Metaphor-the bridge between feelings and knowledge.

Psychoanalytic Inquiry, 29(1), 6-11. doi:http://dx.doi.org.fgul.idm.oclc.org/10.1080/07351690802246890

Neimeyer, G. J., & Metzler, R. E. (1994). Personal identity and autobiographical memory. In V. Neisser & R. Fivush (Eds.), *The remembered self: Accuracy in the self-narrative* (pp. 105–135). New York, NY: Cambridge University Press.

Nelson, A (1993). *Living the wheel: working with emotions, terror and bliss with imagery.* York Beach, Maine: Samuel Weiser.

Nelson, A. (2007). The spacious mind: using archetypes for transformation towards wisdom. *The Humanistic Psychologist.* 35, 235-246.

Nelson, A. (2014). *Archetypal imagery and the spiritual self: techniques for coaches and therapists.* London and Philadelphia: Singing Dragon.

Olson, C. (1994). *The book of the goddess: Past and present, an introduction to her religion.* New York: Crossroad.

Pals, J. L. (2006). Narrative identity processing of difficult life experiences: Pathways of personality development and positive self-transformation in adulthood. *Journal of Personality,* 74, 1079–1109.

Park, S. & Kim, E. (2015). Revisiting knowledge sharing from the organizational change perspective. *European Journal of Training and Development,* 39(9), 769-797.

Perls, F. S. (1992). *Gestalt therapy verbatim.* Gouldsboro ME: Gestalt Journal Press.

Pillemer, D.B. (1998). *Momentous events, vivid memories,* Cambridge, MA: Harvard University Press.

Pillemer, D.B. (2001). Momentous events and the life story. *Review of General Psychology,* 5(2), 123-134.

Pillemer, D. B. (2003). Directive functions of autobiographical memory: The guiding power of the specific episode. *Memory,* 11(2), 193-202.

Polkinghorne, D. (1988). *Narrative knowing and the human sciences.* Albany, NY: State University of New York Press.

Polkinghorne, D. (1991). Narrative and self-concept. *Journal of Narrative and Life History,* 1(2-3), 135-153.

Pribram, K. H. (1981). *Languages of the brain: experimental paradoxes and principles in neuropsychology.* New York, NY: Brandon House.

Rappaport, J. (1993). Narrative studies, personal stories, and identity transformation in the mutual help context. *Journal of Applied Behavioral Science,* 29, 239–256.

Reiser, B. J., Black, J. B., & Abelson, R. P. (1985). Knowledge structures in the organization and retrieval of autobiographical memories. *Cognitive Psychology,* 17, 89–137.

Restak R. (2010). *Think smart: a neuroscientist's prescription for improving your brain's performance.* New York, NY: Riverhead Trade.

Rogers, C. (1961). *On becoming a person: a therapist's view of psychotherapy.* New York, NY: Merrill.

Sammut, K. (2014). Transformative learning theory and coaching: Application in practice. *International Journal of Evidence Based Coaching and Mentoring,* 8, 30-54.

Sarbin, T. (1986). *Narrative psychology: The storied nature of human conduct.* New York, NY: Pager.

Schon, D . (1979). Generative Metaphor: A perspective on problem-setting in social policy. In Ortney, A. (Ed.), *Metaphor and Thought.* New York, NY: Cambridge University Press.

Seto, L. & Geithner, T. (2018). Metaphor magic in coaching and coaching supervision. *International Journal of Evidence Based Coaching and Mentoring,* 16(2), 99-111.

Thorne, A. (2000). Personal memory telling and personality development. *Personality and Social Psychology Review,* 4, 45–56.

Torrance, P. (1962). *Guiding creative talent.* Englewood Cliffs: N.J.: Prentice-Hill, Inc.

Truman, Kristen Marie (2013). *Evocative imagery: the experience of metaphor in the coaching conversation.* Fielding Graduate University, ProQuest Dissertations Publishing, 2013. 3604637.

Vogel, M. (2012). Story matters: an inquiry into the role of narrative in coaching. *International Journal of Evidence Based Coaching and Mentoring,* Vol. 10 No. 1, pp. 1-12.

Von Franz, M.-L. (1996). *The interpretation of fairy tales.* Boston: Shambhala.

Whitworth, L., Kimsey-House., & Sandahl. (1998). *Co-active coaching: New skills for coaching people toward success in work and life.* Palo Alto, CA: Davies-Black.

Widdershoven, G. A. (1993). The story of life: Hermeneutic perspectives on the relationship between narrative and life history. *The narrative study of lives,* 1, 1-20.

Woodman, M. & Dickson, E. (1996). *Dancing in the flames: The dark goddess in the transformation of consciousness.* Boston: Shambhala.

CHAPTER 10

CO-CREATING A NEW SHARED REALITY: EXPLORING INTERSUBJECTIVITY IN EXECUTIVE COACHING RELATIONSHIPS

Alex Eunkyeong Yu, PhD, PCC
ITIM International, Korea

Abstract

Bringing attention to the intersection of two subjectivities, the inquiry of intersubjectivity explores how two individuals with their differences can cocreate a new meaningful, shared reality in moments of interaction. This study inquired of six seasoned executive coaches how they experience and create intersubjectivity with their coachees. Phenomenology and neuroscience were integrated as conceptual foundations, and a multifaceted research design was adopted. Findings revealed that when the coach and the coachee were connected, their feelings and thoughts were in concert with each other and with the topic of the conversation. The sense of alignment brought in reframing moments which expanded their shared reality. Intersubjectivity is a choice of how much and on what our attention is going to be assigned, and how to make meaning out of the experience. Its major underpinnings include deep interest and care for the other, embracing uncertainty, and trust in self, other, and process.

Keywords: Intersubjectivity; executive coaching relationship; establishing trust and intimacy with client; coaching presence; coaching as improvisation.

Introduction

What is in the space between the coach and the coachee that enables dialogues leading to insight and transformation? When walking out of sessions in which the coachees created expanded possibilities from the impossibilities of moments ago and found a better version of themselves, what triggers this positive shift?

Given the inherent complexity of the individual human mind, the possibility of what may happen in the space where two or more individuals with their own subjective minds meet is nearly infinite. Intersubjectivity attends to the intersection of two subjective minds, "the experience of joining two subjective inner worlds with each other" (Siegel, 2012b, p. 23-1), and as a competence it is "one's ability to interact with others in a reciprocal and meaningful fashion" (Grinnell, 1983, p. 185). Tankink and Vysma (2006) defined intersubjectivity as "the symbolic space that is created when two subjectivities meet and a shared reality comes into being" (p. 2). Intersubjectivity, in this study, referred to how two individuals with their unique differences cocreated a new meaningful, shared reality in the moments of interaction.

The possibility of intersubjectivity in coaching space was brought to my attention as a by-product of other research focused on intercultural competence. Searching for interactional competences in intercultural situations to complement the popular dimensionalized model approach, and looking into the phenomenological concept of intersubjectivity, I realized that my best possible experience of intersubjectivity was usually in coaching space.

The dyad interaction in coaching is a unique human relationship. Executive coaches intend to bring in unconditional positive regard for the client's development (Rogers, 1967/2004), and create a safe space for the client to discuss his or her vulnerabilities. When coaches create unique bonding with respect and trust, the dialogue goes deep with focus and presence. In such a deep connection of intersubjective space, mutual learning and transformation happen.

This study focused on how other coaches, with their different life

203

experiences, cocreated a new meaningful, shared reality with their coachees in the moments of coaching interaction. The question central to the study was, "What is the experience and impact of intersubjectivity in the executive coaching space, if any?"

Intersubjectivity in Phenomenology

Intersubjectivity has been a main theme in phenomenology. Husserl was the first philosopher to employ the term and established the subject as a foundational concept for phenomenology (Tankink & Vysma, 2006; Thompson, 2005). Phenomenology contemplates how self relates with other and consciously experiences getting connected with the other. Genuine intersubjectivity is conditional upon the sense of mutuality and simultaneity of experiences. Schutz (1970) presented a genuine experience of intersubjectivity through his concept of "we-relationship." When two individuals share spatial and temporal immediacy and when all individuals involved intend to grasp the existence of the other in the mode of original self, it leads to the experience that the individuals "sympathetically participate in each other's lives for however short a time" (Schutz, 1970, p. 186). Merleau-Ponty (1945/2012) presented how two subjectivities can coexist as "collaborators in perfect reciprocity" (p. 370) and encouraged exploration of the dynamic of mutually exclusive, yet equally compelling, differences through synergetic dialogue. Phenomenology maps the way to enter the lived essence of intersubjectivity. Van Manen (1990) postulated that action will flow from phenomenological thoughtfulness, and in turn, that attitude creates a presence that will make a difference to interaction, as in the coaching space.

Research Design and Data Interpretation

Phenomenology is a system of interpretation (Wagner, 1983), and extracts the essence of experience asking for meanings and significance of certain phenomena (van Manen, 1990). Using a phenomenological interview allows deep exploration of how the participants of the research experience and make meaning out of establishing deep connection with others.

Six executive coaches were recruited for the study and formed into three dyads. The research consisted of two rounds of individual phenomenological interviews, one at the beginning and at the end, with two reflections in the middle, that included a peer coaching dyad exercise with joint reflection afterwards. Each participant took turns as both coach and coachee as they conducted a 30-minute coaching session, followed by joint critical reflection on what had been made between them while we listened to the recorded session, if necessary. I observed the sessions and facilitated the refection afterwards. The peer coaching exercise introduced the dyad's interpretation of the dyad experience, with an added third-person perspective through my observation. It checked the possibility of dangerous learning, which can be induced from the limitation of incorporating only first-person subjective interpretation on a second-person dyadic practice (Arieli, Friedman & Agbaria, 2009; Torbert, 2000). In addition, joint critical reflection provided feedback on the participant's relational competence; therefore, could be an incentive to participate in the research.

Table 1
Research Flow

Research Design		
Variable	Coach	Coach
Step 1	Interview on their experience of intersubjectivity in the coaching space	Interview on their experience of intersubjectivity in the coaching space
Step 2	Peer coaching dyad exercise with joint reflection afterwards. I observe this dyad interaction and facilitate joint critical reflection.	
Step 3	Reflection journal: upon transcripts and their experience so far	Reflection journal: upon transcripts and their experience so far
Step 4	Follow-up interview	Follow-up interview

Research data were analyzed following the steps from interpretative phenomenological analysis (Smith, Flowers, & Larkin, 2009). Validity of the research was focused on participant validation for phenomenological data (Moustakas, 1994), and eliminating the validity threats of researcher's bias and reactivity, along with transparently illustrating the research process and my own commitment and ethics as a researcher.

Six Coaches and Three Faces of Intersubjectivity

Introducing the Coaches

Following Moustakas' (1994) essential criteria for selecting phenomenological research partners, I needed participants who were proficient at creating intersubjectivity in coaching space. I searched for executive coaches with credentials from an established coaching organization, such as the PCC level of International Coach Federation, or with five years or more working experience as an executive coach. I chose five years based on my experience of accumulating hours for the PCC. Periods were negotiable, and I relied mostly on my observation and reference from others for this. I was fortunate to work with six highly seasoned executive coaches who value the relational aspects of coaching. Three coaches had more than ten years of coaching experience, and the rest had four to seven years of experience. Hashida, who had the least years of coaching experience, was an executive working as an internal coach, and the other five were professional executive coaches. All of them are dedicated to their personal and professional growth and were willing to be coresearchers.

They are presented in chronological order of the interviews and dyad exercises. Participants chose their own pseudonyms, which were either related with their own coaching presence or their nicknames in the hosting countries.

Three Faces of Intersubjectivity

Participants brought real coaching topics to the dyad exercises that revealed their vulnerabilities and complexities. Prominent themes of how they cocreated a shared reality are included.

Bob Weaver and Hashida: Expanding each other's bubble. When I asked Bob Weaver and Hashida to each recall an experience of executive coaching with unique bonding and deep connection, they both talked about their working experience with each other. Weaver coached Hashida four years ago, which became the most memorable coaching experience for both of them. Hashida wanted an environment of freedom to expand his bubble, and Weaver created the space for him to be in control and just kept "pushing and prodding at him [Hashida] to expand his own bubble." They built deep trust towards each other and also about themselves during this time.

Allowing not knowing: Embracing uncertainty. Their previous coaching engagement was unlike how most coaching projects unfolded, at least in Bob Weaver's experience. Starting from the contract, Hashida did not want to include "specific and measurable objectives." He wanted to see how it evolved and even "banned the word, process" during the session. Considering that even more structured coaching conversations have lots of uncertainties in terms of how the conversation would evolve, this is like jumping into a vast sea of uncertainty. Initially, Bob Weaver heard the background noise coming from anxious feelings. "I have no idea what's happening. I'm lost . . . am I helping, am I adding value here to this person?"

The "aha!" moment came "in the confusion of it, on the anxiety of the stomach, hmm, what am I doing here?" It took courage to embrace uncertainties, and Bob Weaver checked in with Hashida when it became too much. With Hashida's confirmation of the value of the conversation, he learned to trust himself to "include [himself] and his thinking in the conversation," to "trust Hashida and his own judgment of it being helpful," and "not to worry about what was happening." This trust of coach, coachee, and process made possible the "cocreation of

Hashida being able to just launch himself through the questions that I would ask him."

Hashida appreciated their "unique way of interacting which was based on trust and freedom." He trusted that Bob Weaver put him into that state of mind that "has nothing to fear and that there are only opportunities." Bob Weaver created a space for Hashida to venture into the uncertainties of new territory, pushing his limits and growing his boundary—expanding his bubble. They cocreated an environment of uncertainty and thrived there, expanding each other's bubbles, and both stated trust as the factor that made it possible.

Language game: Creating a shared reality around metaphor. Observing their interactions was like watching a game in which two players enjoy each other and push each other's limits, because they know this will build their muscles. Hashida encouraged Bob Weaver to delve into his issue with persistent visualizing and repeating the focused question, "what else?" Bob Weaver pushed Hashida with penetrating and provocative questions until he reached a different perspective toward his issue.

Metaphors were central elements in both rounds, creating the turning points for the topic. Once they created a shared language, they built new reality by playing around the metaphor and reframed the issue from different perspectives. For example, when Hashida identified Bob Weaver's issue as beginning, Bob Weaver brought in the experience of running, and then Hashida's questions were built around reviving the experience of running around the topic. "So how can you put your (running) shoes on?" "Can you describe to me the feeling of putting your shoes on for this project?" Bob Weaver emphasized that "if you can share a metaphor you can also share the same feeling . . . that resonates with the other person." It is also a part of the process to create a shared understanding of what is happening around them. The use of metaphors throughout their interaction created unique bonding between them and facilitated cocreation of a new reality based on resonant feeling and their own unique shared understanding.

With their embracing uncertainty and playing around with metaphor, their interaction looked close to improvisation. Hashida and Bob Weaver both were well-versed in coaching grammars and tools. Their previous working experience provided ample cues (e.g., facial expressions, body gestures, and language) to each other about how to respond to those cues. With well-established trust and history, their interactions were well-coordinated with each other. They cocreated the new narratives through metaphors which stimulated each other's development. Their interaction was close to Merleau-Ponty's intersubjectivity, based on a balanced bilateral interaction. Two selves here were "collaborators in perfect reciprocity" (Merleau-Ponty, 1945/2012, p. 370) and cocreated a dialectic single fabric in dialogue.

Morning Sun and Gold Digger: See and being seen. Morning Sun and Gold Digger were casual acquaintances without working experience together. Morning Sun, as coachee in the first round of peer coaching, described Gold Digger's intervention as the "riverbank" that provided protection for her to flow safely and she felt "permission to be herself" which was a strong form of recognition.

The second round started with high energy for both of them. They greeted each other with laughter and their voices were on a high note. However, within less than ten minutes, I noticed Morning Sun became smaller physically and her voice became quieter. As their dialogue continued, Gold Digger became smaller with his voice lower as well. At the end of the dialogue, they were sitting nearly head to head, whispering to each other. I could almost see the circle that encompassed two of them inside and was reluctant to call an end to the coaching dialogue.

Limbic resonance: Let me experience you. "The front of your body is actually clay and let your client make an impression on you" (Gold Digger, Interview 2). That was what Morning Sun demonstrated. Gold Digger wanted the conversation to flow rather than drive to a solution, and "with that, he had [her] total focus, and [her] senses were fully open to his words, his body language, as well as his emotions"

(Morning Sun, Reflection). She experienced and reflected the complex layers of Gold Digger's current status of being within the short coaching dialogue.

> By focusing on what you were saying, actually, I'm not thinking about much of anything. And I was sensing where you were at. I have this sense of wanting to be your own person and also have this sense of uncertainty. . . Also sense of responsibility. And that is a lot to take on. And there's a little bit of weariness, even in the exploration. And my heart just went out to you and I can feel it, and I thought there is, along the way, you had forgotten a part of where all the efforts and all the qualities and all of the gifts that you came here with. (Joint Reflection 2)

Morning Sun acknowledged Gold Digger's courage "in spite of weariness" when she wrapped up the coaching conversation. Gold Digger confirmed that when she used the word weariness, he "really felt seen by [her] . . . and that [she] was picking up on something that was underlying the whole thing." Gold Digger recounted the experience as he:

> . . . became very calm physically. Your quietness really got over me. And that also allowed me to rest in my subject. I did not be too wowed by it, I just kind of could rest in that subject. So that's physical, very somatic . . . I am also kind of more compassionate with myself. . . . So what was half an hour ago, a sort of head scratcher, is now a cool thing to deal with. (Joint Reflection 2)

It was a "seeing of human-to-human . . . [with] a degree of safety and intimacy" (Gold Digger). Morning Sun was not lost in her empathetic resonance with Gold Digger. While she kept in touch with him, "[she] was touching with the topic and [she] was not losing touch with reality," which provided a platform for Gold Digger to look at his topic with a fuller heart. She also brought his courage and talent out so he could take off with more confidence. It is one thing that the coachee took courage to show and acknowledge his vulnerability, and another thing that the coach did it in a respectful and honoring way that could leave the other on a high note.

What made their resonance strong was they experienced what they valued most from the interaction. That created strong chemistry and amplified their resonance. Morning Sun shared during her first interview that the real potential of coaching is to experience having "someone to believe in us." Gold Digger asserted that "with my personality type, something really important is the aspect that we all want to be seen . . . every individual wants to be recognized as a wholesome, beautiful being." They saw and felt seen by each other with mutual honoring, which created strong resonance coming from their hearts.

I had never observed such a strong resonance between two individuals which permeated the atmosphere. Another thing that stood out from their interaction, especially from the meaning-making of joint reflection after the dyad exercise, was both recognition and acknowledgement of each other's being and help. Their appreciation to each other expanded their attention (Fredrickson & Branigan, 2005), and they even acknowledged my presence as an observer. Resonance between Morning Sun and Gold Digger was very palpable, even from my observer's stance; it reminded me of Schutz's (1970) we-relationship, that the individuals "sympathetically participate in each other's lives" (p. 186). There was the "spatial and temporal immediacy" (Schutz, 1967, p. 163) on the foundation of reciprocal "thou-orientation" (Schutz, 1970, p. 185) and "mutual tuning-in" (Schutz, 1964, p. 161).

Tai Chi Teacher and Jerry: It takes more than two to tango. Tai Chi Teacher and Jerry were strangers before the dyad exercise. They met an hour before the dyad exercise to get acquainted, and then spent the whole afternoon together.

211

While I left the first and second dyads with the feelings of fun and warmth respectively, my feeling at the end of the third dyad exercise was confusion. The first round of coaching dialogue and joint reflection was smooth. Jerry felt "listened to and supported with undivided attention" and the coach's practical questions urged her to tap into her resources. Both agreed that they made "connection." I also felt that they were adding blocks to build trust.

The second coaching dialogue was as good as the first round to my observation. Jerry was good at paraphrasing and tagging along with the coachee's thoughts with her own questions. Tai Chi Teacher was developing and refining ideas at the speed of a bullet train as coachee.

The locus of intersubjectivity. I thought I saw intersubjectivity from their coaching dialogue through a well-synchronized brainstorming. However, in joint reflection, Tai Chi Teacher and Jerry did not voice the sense of cocreation much. Tai Chi Teacher admitted the value of their coaching conversation, and he stated that he intentionally "kept her at arm's length" (Interview 2) because what was coming out was of value to him. If coaching is all about providing value to the coachee, as Tai Chi Teacher affirmed many times, it was a successful coaching dialogue.

If beauty is in the eye of the beholder, it must be the participants who have the last say about what happened in their intersection. Tai Chi Teacher put it as "a kind of one and a half as opposed to one plus one equals three." Jerry "felt the same." She "was not in flow with Tai Chi Teacher," nor he with her. "We enjoyed laughing together and the challenge of the new exercise . . . [but] did not reach that level of empathy." Powerful as it is, intersubjectivity may just be one way to cultivate coaching results.

This also made me aware of my criterion to either find intersubjectivity or not from a one-time interaction. I am looking into the intersection of two complex individuals in a complex context. Intersubjectivity is not just a tango between two participants. Given the role of coach and coachee, and within an evolving contextual setting, the range of possible outcomes is like turning a kaleidoscope. Sometimes one may see a pattern emerging, and at other times, may see just fuzzy dots and colors which are on the way to form something.

In sync or out of sync: How it affects. Conditions that made them feel less connected were blocked physical alignment, focus on cerebral activity, and the context of meeting for the first time for a one-time coaching within a short time frame. As in the example of Tai Chi Teacher's heavy note taking, not being in physical alignment, and blocked space created by the fact that Tai Chi Teacher was left-handed, created a "choppier" flow. When the interaction is more cerebral, "more of a process of head," the experience is summarized as "self-brainstorming with support" (Joint Reflection 2). Similarly, Hashida shared that focusing on problem solving prevented him from being in flow, and Morning Sun also commented her narrowing-in happens less when the coaching agenda is technically oriented, process oriented, or requires cerebral thinking. There is more chance for the participants to create the experience of intersubjectivity if there is emotional or limbic connection. This concurs with Boyatzis' and Jack's (2018) observation that analytical thinking mostly engages a task-positive network while turning off the brain regions essential for empathy.

More importantly, there was no mutual tuning in (Schutz, 1964), and public testing during the joint reflection was swaying between being honest and being polite. Jerry shared that she felt "slightly hurtful" from Tai Chi Teacher's "quite blunt and frank" feedback. When she revealed her feelings during the follow-up interview, I wondered how it would be different if she tested publicly her feelings toward Tai Chi Teacher's feedback. Tai Chi Teacher was a bit apologetic during the joint critical reflection; however, his choice as a coachee was to keep the coach at arm's length. It was a successful coaching conversation, and not with the strong evidence of intersubjectivity as that was the participants' choice based on the context of the interaction.

Lived Experience and Creation of Intersubjectivity

Establishing meaningful interaction with the client is the foundation of coaching dialogue, with its dedication to the client's development and intensity of focus. Out of the participants' experiences, as well as my observation and interpretation of them, several themes emerged in relation to the research question. Table 2 is a summary of these themes, and the following section describes each theme. Focusing on the lived experience of intersubjectivity, I identified three themes: sense of connection, sense of congruence, and sense of expansion. Creation of trinity space was the subsequent impact. This phenomenology of intersubjectivity is explained from the perspective of recent developments in neuroscience.

The original research (Yu, 2013) included the additional question of the executive coach's capacity for intersubjectivity, which is captured briefly in Table 2. Coaches did foundational work on themselves in order to create meaningful interaction, which included embracing uncertainty, courage, and putting trust on self, other, and process. The other bridging capacities which facilitated deep engagement were from the coaches' total investment of intentional attention on the interaction in the moment. Coaches intended to meet their coachees in their original selves, believing in their best selves with full empowerment. Full attention started from emptying out other details of life that might distract them during the coaching dialogue. This undivided attention was embodied as listening, and cocreated reframing moments through mirroring back unnoticed parts of reality.

Sense of Connection

Themes to describe deep connection were derived from the somatic markers participants used to report their experience. Frequently named physical sensations were warm, light, floating, comfortable, open, no constraint, no fear, effortless, and freedom. Of these, the most notable one was sense of warmth. This comes from a sense of connection, and the metaphors of onsen (Japanese hot spring) and sunshine were used

214

Table 2
Summary of Themes

Questions	Themes		
The lived experience and impact of intersubjectivity	Sense of connection Sense of congruence Sense of expansion Creation of trinity space		
Creating intersubjectivity	Foundation	Embracing uncertainty Courage Trust in self, other, and process	
	Bridging	Intention	Thou-orientation Lifting up Cocreation
		Attention	Emptying out Marrowing in Listening Mirroring with microscope
	Intersubjectivity as a choice		

(Hashida). It is a feeling that comes from "being totally with others" (Hashida), "gripped by each other" (Jerry), and when there is "intense intimacy" (Gold Digger) between the two. The feeling is about seeing and being seen as a "wholesome, beautiful human being" (Gold Digger) in which a coach serves others and the coachee is allowed the safety to be vulnerable, with the coach's undivided attention. Both are grateful for the space and the connection.

Sense of Congruence

The moment of connection brings out a sense of congruence. "When there is a deep connection, something intuitive that you are really aligned with the coachee, you seem to really know or feel as if with your imagination, your intuition, you can understand what they are telling you" (Jerry). It is "on the same wavelength with the client" (Tai Chi Teacher), like the moment when we find the right frequency for a radio station using a manual dial. Your body, thoughts, and feelings are aligned and in concert, not just with the others but also with the topic of conversation. The moment of connection prompts a sense of congruence, which offers new perspective on the topic and creates an opportunity. When the client feels the alignment, has that "aha!" moment, it brings a reframing of the topic or the situation.

It is a moment in which a new, shared reality emerges. In Morning Sun's and Gold Digger's coaching dialogue, they cocreated the space of "exploratory walk" triggered by the experience of being seen by the coach, and the coachee reframed "a head scratcher" thirty minutes ago to "a cool thing to explore." Hashida and Bob Weaver's language game based on metaphors facilitated cocreation of a new reality based on resonant feeling and their own unique shared understanding.

Sense of Expansion

The sense of connection develops more energy to tackle a challenging situation, expanding possibilities. Hashida recounted how he received good energy from what he was doing with Bob Weaver, like sunshine on plants, and continued "this discovery experience." Tai Chi Teacher described how the sense of connection made him motivated to bring out more service orientation towards the client, wanting to be "as helpful as possible." When the coach maintained the balance of power holding the coachee accountable, the exploration became cocreation and generated a more powerful sense of expansion.

> It's a sense of feeling really good and warm and a sense that there is really nothing to fear and that there are only opportunities. . . And he [Bob Weaver] made sure he also took some autonomy on continuing some effort we are doing together. So he gave me the direction, the momentum, trust to be with myself and find my own solution. And when you are in those conditions, it's like being in paradise in a sense. It's like wow. I was going to say sky has limit, but I think there is no limit in that state of mind. So everything is possible. And it's just so amazing, so great. You feel it. (Hashida)

This sense of expansion combined with a sense of potency creates another space in the coaching container. Morning Sun expressed it as "almost like trinity. You have the coach and the coachee. And this space. It is not just the coach and the coachee. You expand that universe."

Creation of Trinity Space and the Use of Self

I noticed from Hashida's interview that he used three phrases almost synonymously: "being with self," "being with the other," and "being in the moment." All three worked together to expand his universe. Morning Sun and Gold Digger also mentioned tripartite constitution in the coaching space, how coach and coachee work together to create something bigger than their sum. When two subjectivities connect, it is like self, other, and universe coexist in the moment of connection, congruence, and expansion. The experience of intersubjectivity affects all three dimensions, and transformation happens for all three tripartite parts. To facilitate this transformation, coaches would attend to all three voices in order to cocreate a powerful new reality. What made Morning Sun and Gold Digger's coaching dialogue powerful was the fact that Morning Sun resonated with the coachee's state of being, she listened to how the resonation affected her, and she also did not lose touch with reality.

Self plays a crucial role in the formation of the trinity space. To create a sense of connection and expansion, coaches need to understand and be deeply in touch with self, as it provides the foundation from which to build connection with the other. Hashida confirmed that "if the coach is not deeply connected with himself or herself, it will probably reduce the outcome of the coaching relationship." Gold Digger asserted that while he needs his self for resonance and rapport, he also needs to be ready to let go especially of his smaller self, because as the coach drops his (small) self, he expands both his and his coachee's universe. The paradox here is that you have to find self in order to lose it, and

217

when you lose some part of self, your self becomes bigger. This is the moment when "me" becomes "we."

Neuroscience of Intersubjectivity

Recent developments in neuroscience support the phenomenological experience and impact of intersubjectivity in coaching space. Dweck (2006/2016) posited that our brain is able to reorganize itself throughout life, and what drives this neuroplasticity are our emotions, behaviors, and experiences. Our brain, connected with body, is an emotional and social sense organ (Blake, 2018). Our social experiences shape our neural architecture, and the neural integration directs our self-regulation and the flow of consciousness (Siegel, 2012a).

What is possible inside one human brain can influence another brain though transfer of energy and information. Two differentiated individuals become linked as part of a resonating whole when mirror neurons fire, and interpersonal integration happens. As mirror neurons are a part of our mammalian limbic brain, thus it is called limbic resonance. Blake (2018) described limbic resonance as "the unconscious syncing up of brainwaves and bodily rhythms that underlie the felt sense of attunement" (p. 174). When there is a sense of connection, emotions and limbic states can leap between minds and allow reception of the contents of other's minds (Lewis, Amini, & Lannon, 2005). It works as "the door to communal connection" (Lewis et al., 2005, p. 64), and this silent reverberation is contagious and draws us into almost immediate emotional congruence.

The function of limbic resonance can also shed a light on how the sense of connection extends to the sense of congruence and expansion. Located centrally in the brain is the limbic system (Siegel, 2012a) and it can work like a bridge to affect other areas of the brain, both reptilian and homo sapiens brain structures. Limbic resonance can quell the amygdala of the reptilian brain through trust, empathy, and feelings of support induced from the sense of connection (Glaser, 2014). Glaser (2014) also noticed that mirror neurons, located right below the prefrontal cortex, form a bridge of empathy and insight with another being. When noise from the brain's fear state is calmed, and when there is limbic connection, it opens access to the prefrontal cortex, the homo sapiens brain, which can create reframing by endowing different meaning-making to the issue.

When connected, we participate in the other's reality. When there was the sense of being heard and understood, as in the coaching between Morning Sun and Gold Digger, it created the sense of intersubjectivity and also functioned as the highest acknowledgment of another's being. The felt sense of respect of one's own being makes the coachee more motivated to change (Boyatzis & Jack, 2018).

Blake (2018) suggested safety, connection, and respect as the three essential nutrients for our brain, which corresponds to the needs of the triune brain. When intersubjectivity fires mirror neurons in the limbic system, it provides all the nutrients for our brains to work at their best, thus supporting and maximizing the client's personal and professional potentials. Siegel (2012a) also confirmed that "when interpersonal communication is fully engaged—when the joining of minds is in full force—there is an overwhelming sense of immediacy, clarity, and authenticity" (p. 377). In sum, the experience of intersubjectivity can result in more facing of challenges than avoiding, better decision-making, wider vision, foresight, and so forth, which all result in a better coaching outcome.

Concluding Thoughts—Intersubjectivity as a Choice

One of the most powerful moments during the study was observing Morning Sun and Gold Digger's coaching session. Two persons who started coaching conversation with high energy became smaller and quieter and influenced the whole atmosphere. What generated limbic resonance in Morning Sun's coaching was her utmost intentional attention set on the coachee's development. It is this attending with undivided attention and without the coach's personal agenda that creates the powerful impact of intersubjectivity in coaching space.

The concept of flow explains that their experience of intersubjectivity is an outcome of total investment of attention in the moments of coaching interaction. Nakamura and Csikszentmihalyi (2002) pointed out that our subjective experience is shaped by our attentional process, and "what to pay attention to, how intensely and for how long, are choices that will determine the content of consciousness" (p. 92). Two choice points divided the coaches' final remarks on their experience of intersubjectivity. First was the coach's decision regarding how much attention, how deeply, and on what she was going to commit to the experience in the moment. Second was how to make meaning out of the experience after the interaction. Context affecting the choices included factors of purpose, timeframe, and level of intimacy.

In sum, intersubjectivity is an evolving concept with ongoing processes of selective attention and meaning making through the interaction. As seen from the third dyad, intersubjectivity may not be requisite to create successful coaching dialogue. However, when two people cocreate a new shared context and meaning, it activates more parts of the brain and leads to reframing moments which cast different and wider perspectives on the topic. Having intersubjectivity alive in the coaching space opens up more possibilities of positive transformation for the coachee.

This study looked closely at how dealing with uncertainty, metaphors, limbic resonance, and positive psychology both affect and create intersubjectivity in the moments of coaching interaction. Results of my study may benefit executive coaches by supporting them in bringing the strengths of their presence into the session and utilizing their interactional competencies. Additional studies in how intersubjectivity plays out and affects virtual coaching may be of use. Equally interesting would be to investigate how team and group coaching, with more participants involved in interactions, could leverage the lived experience of intersubjectivity.

About the Author

Alex Eunkyeong Yu is an executive coach and organizational development consultant with primary areas of focus on global leadership, executive team development, culture change and transition, and other subjects related with organizational effectiveness. Her main focus in coaching is to enable leaders to function at their highest potential while also being mindful of systemic concerns. As a trained thinking partner, she works with leaders to find the real levers behind phenomena, and then supports them to transfer their best competencies into different cultural contexts, including national and organizational cultures.

Consulting, coaching, and facilitating since 2004, she has worked with C-suite/senior level executives across a wide range of sectors including consumer products, luxury, hospitality, financial services, pharmaceuticals, and IT. Most recently, she has been representing a Finnish consulting firm in Korea. Prior, she was a Senior Consultant at a Shanghai-based consulting firm. As a Certified Coaching Supervisor, she serves as faculty for a coaching education program at another Shanghai-based coaching firm.

Alex holds both PhD and MA in Human and Organizational Systems from Fielding Graduate University. She also holds an MBA in International Management from Thunderbird School of Global Management with the honors of Beta Gamma Sigma and Phi Sigma Iota.

References

Arieli, D., Friedman, V. J., & Agbaria, K. (2009). The paradox of participation in action research. *Action Research, 7*(3), 263-290.

Blake, A. (2018). *Your body is your brain: Leverage your somatic intelligence to find purpose, build resilience, deepen relationships and lead more powerfully.* USA: Trokay Press, imprint of Embright, LLC.

Boyatzis, T. E., & Jack, E. (2018). The neuroscience of coaching. *Consulting Psychology Journal: Practice and Research, 70*(1), 11-27.

Dweck, C. S. (2016). *Mindset: The new psychology of success.* New York, NY: Ballantine Books. (Original work published 2006.)

Glaser, J. E. (2014). *Conversational intelligence: How great leaders build trust and get extraordinary results.* New York, NY: Routledge.

Grinnell, F. (1983). The problem of intersubjectivity: A comparison of Martin Buber and Alfred Schutz. *Human Studies*, 6, 185-195.

Fredrickson, B. L., & Branigan, C. (2005). Positive emotions broaden the scope of attention and thought-action repertoire. *Cognition and Emotion*, 19(3), 313-332.

Lewis, T. L., Amini, F., & Lannon, R. (2005). *General theory of love*. New York, NY: Vintage Books.

Merleau-Ponty, M. (2012). *Phenomenology of perception* (D. A. Landes, Trans.). New York, NY: Routledge. (Original work published 1945.)

Merleau-Ponty, M. (1968). *The visible and the invisible* (A. Lingis, Trans.). Evanston, IL: Northwestern University Press. (Original work published 1964.)

Moustakas, C. (1994). *Phenomenological research methods*. Thousand Oaks, CA: Sage.

Nakamura, J., & Csikszentmihalyi, M. (2002). The concept of flow. In C. D. Snyder & S. J. Lopez (Eds.), *Handbook of positive psychology* (pp. 89-105). New York, NY: Oxford University Press.

Rogers, C. (2004). *On becoming a person: A therapist's view of psychotherapy*. London, England: Constable & Robinson. (Original work published 1967.)

Schutz, A. (1964). Making music together: A study in social relationship. In A. Schutz, *Collected papers, Vol. 2: Studies in social theory* (pp. 159-178). The Hague, Netherlands: Martinus Nijhoff.

Schutz, A. (1970). *On phenomenology and social relations*. Chicago, IL: University of Chicago Press.

Siegel, D. J. (2012a). *The developing mind*. New York, NY: Guilford Press.

Siegel, D. J. (2012b). *Pocket guide to interpersonal neurobiology*. New York, NY: Norton.

Smith, J. A., Flowers, P., & Larkin, M. (2009). *Interpretative phenomenological analysis: Theory, method and research*. Thousand Oaks, CA: Sage.

Tankink, M., & Vysma, M. (2006). The intersubjective as analytic tool in medical anthropology. *Medische Antropologie*, 18(1), 249-265.

Thompson, M. G. (2005). Phenomenology of intersubjectivity: A historical overview of the concept and its clinical implications. In J. Mills (Ed.), *Intersubjectivity and relational theory in psychoanalysis*. Hillsdale, NJ: Jason Aronson. Retrieved from http://www.michaelguythompson.com/Library/Downloads/2005_PhenomenologyIntersubjectivity.pdf

Torbert, B. (2000). The challenge of creating a community of inquiry among scholar-consultants critiquing one another's theories-in-practice. In F. Sherman & W.

Torbert (Eds.), *Transforming social inquiry, transforming social action* (pp. 161-188). Boston, MA: Kluwer Academic.

van Manen, M. (1990). *Researching lived experience: Human science for an action sensitive pedagogy* (2nd ed.). London, Ontario, Canada: Althouse Press.

Wagner, H. (1983). *Phenomenology of consciousness and sociology of the life-world: An introductory study.* Edmonton, Alberta, Canada: University of Alberta Press.

Yu, A. E. (2013). *Cocreating a shared reality: Exploring intersubjectivity in intercultural interaction through executive coaching relationship* (Unpublished doctoral dissertation). Fielding Graduate University, Santa Barbara, CA.

CHAPTER 11

EMBODIED AWARENESS: TRANSFORMATIVE COACHING THROUGH SOMATICS AND PHENOMENOLOGY

James Marlatt, MBA, PhD, CEC, Marlatt Coaching & Consulting;
Valerie Malhotra Bentz, MSSW, PhD, School of Leadership Studies,
Fielding Graduate University.

Abstract

Transformative coaching focuses on the co-creation of reflective spaces for consciousness raising for personal, professional, organizational and social transformations. Coaching from a somatic and phenomenological foundation acknowledges "being" as the primary instrument of change through communicative embodied awareness. Somatics promotes whole-bodied communication, and phenomenology—the study of consciousness—increases self-awareness through reflective understanding of the "lifeworld" for both coach and coachee. Transformative Phenomenology—a somatic-hermeneutic-phenomenology put into action in the "lifeworld"—is offered as a foundation for transformative coaching practice. Our work expands the definition of evidence-based coaching to include somatic-phenomenological "essence-based" coaching as a process of facilitating transformation. Phenomenological coaching strategies including bracketing, imaginative variation, and horizontalization, among others, that are used to unveil themes that can be used as information to understand lived experience and promote transformation through dialogue.

Keywords: Coaching, somatics, phenomenology, consciousness, transformation, surrender-and-catch.

Introduction

Embodied awareness is the capacity for knowing from within. The "being" of both the coach and coachee becomes the primary instrument of change. Several scholarly traditions inform the practice of transformative coaching from an embodied perspective. Somatics is a powerful approach with a long scholarly tradition that promotes whole-bodied communication. Phenomenology also has long scholarly roots and is the study of consciousness. Phenomenologically informed conversations increase the coachee's self-awareness and enhances their understanding of the "lifeworld" in which they live and work. The capacity for guiding the communicative construction of meaning creates a sense of collaborative action for change. Put together, communicative-embodied-awareness processes offer coaches and coachees new tools for improving the well-being and effectiveness of participants in change efforts.

Somatic phenomenological coaching is offered as an approach to support consciousness-raising for personal, professional, organizational, and social transformations. The transformative potential of this type of coaching is founded in somatics and phenomenology. Historically, the social sciences followed the path of the physical sciences taking an objectivist view, governed by positivist assumptions (Bentz & Shapiro, 1998). Phenomenology, the study of consciousness, sought to fill this gap by paying careful attention to how we know everything from within our senses, brains, and bodies in connection with other beings. Somatic psychology brought on practical techniques of knowing from within (Hanna, 1988). Schütz' lifeworld phenomenology (Wagner, 1970) also provides a framework for looking at social life from within. Recent discoveries from neuroscience (Damasio, 1999) and ancient insights from yoga and Vedanta (Shankaracharya, 1946) affirm and intensify somatic phenomenology. Over two decades of experience of Fielding Graduate University scholar-practitioners who have engaged with transformative phenomenology demonstrates how a somatic-phenomenological orientation can lead to transformations (Bentz,

Rehorick, Marlatt, Nishi, & Estrada, 2018; Rehorick & Bentz, 2017a; Rehorick & Bentz, 2008). Studies over the past decades also reveal the power of somatic phenomenology as contemplative inquiry and practice for change (Bentz & Giorgino, 2016). The adoption of a phenomenological attitude in the lifeworld can support transformative that can be facilitated, in part, through the emergence of personal openness arising from the practice of transformative phenomenology. Rehorick and Bentz (2012) refer to this openness as "inner spaciousness" which they relate to Husserl's transcendental ego (pure consciousness; self before perception and thought), and with reference to its inventor, Mary Beth Haines (1999), refer to it as "a sense of openness in the inner mind and heart."

Significant ineffable elements rooted in a natural connection between the coach and coachee that are based in trust and authenticity, and that are rooted in somatic and phenomenological practice, can play a critical role in the process of transformation that is supported through the coaching relationship. Our work expands the definition of evidence-based coaching to include somatic-phenomenological "essence-based" coaching, seeking the "whatness" of experience beyond the taken-for-granted in the world of everyday life—the lifeworld.

We divide our chapter into three parts. In part one, we describe the foundation for somatic phenomenological coaching through the practice of professional coaching and the adoption of a humanistic stance for coaching. A description of transformative phenomenology follows, to define the origins of somatic phenomenological coaching. Some of the qualities of coaches who practice coaching from a somatic phenomenology foundation are illustrated. We end part one with a description of the phenomenologically oriented process of surrender-and-catch as a mode of somatic phenomenology coaching that has emphasis on creating openings for the emergence of coachee insights and transformative "ah-ha" moments. In part two, we introduce a process model for somatic-phenomenological coaching through the lens of surrender-and-catch. Finally, in part three we describe some methods of somatic phenomenological coaching in practice. We close with a commentary on how somatic phenomenological coaching relates to evidenced-based coaching practice.

Part 1: Somatic and Phenomenological Coaching Foundations

From empirical evidence (discrete and measurable outcomes) to the inclusion of essence-based evidence (somatic-phenomenological insights)

In this section we describe somatic and phenomenological foundations for coaching within the context of the professional coaching that is focused on developing a humanistic coaching relationship. Evidence-based coaching (Stober & Grant, 2006) is offered as a mantle to somatic phenomenological essence-based coaching (Figure 1). Coaches practicing from somatic and phenomenological foundations rely on communicative embodied awareness to bring their whole self to the coaching engagement. The coach seeks to reveal personal, cultural, and historically sculpted prejudgments and prejudices, making them visible and explicit within the coaching process. They seek to discover the essence or the "whatness" of the lived experience of the coachee's phenomenon of interest that is situated in the world of everyday life. Through the phenomenological and somatic methods of bracketing (holding theory, practice, and prejudices in abeyance), mindfulness (through deep listening and awareness of felt bodily sensations), and approaching the conversation with openness and wonderment, attention is devoted to recognizing the emergence of dialogic openings (Marlatt, 2012). These openings offer the potential for consciousness raising and personal transformation through insights emerging from open-ended questioning and somatic interaction. In some instances, the coachee obtains revelatory insight beyond the everyday taken-for-granted. With this catalyzing awakening, theory and practice can be deployed to assist and promote learning and transformation.

227

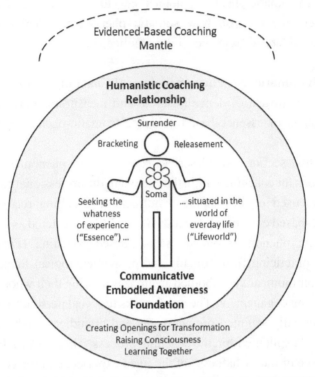

Figure 1: Communicative Embodied Awareness Foundation for Coaching, © 2020 James Marlatt, Used with Permission, Original Artwork.

What is Professional Coaching Practice?

Coaching practice can be described as a professional and confidential relationship between a coach and a coachee with the goal of identifying challenges and turning them into opportunities for personal and professional growth. From a humanistic perspective the process is appreciative, nondirective, and is driven by the client's desires and goals. The coach facilitates confidential conversations by asking open-ended questions and providing feedback and insights in a trusting and unbiased fashion. A coach facilitates coachee learning based on the coach's life and professional experience, specialized training in a coaching process, and through an understanding of human behaviour in social and organizational settings. Opportunities for learning are

228

founded on the development of a trusting, compassionate, and caring relationship, focused listening, questioning, curiosity, affirmation, challenges, and a call-to-action. The focus of coaching is on self-directed learning in the specific context of the learner's situation (Knowles, Holton III, & Swanson, 2005; Merriam, Caffarella, & Baumgartner, 2007; Rogers, 1995). The coaching system encompasses the coach-as-thinking-partner, coachee, and their collective response to external environmental stimulus, as shared and understood through a confidential, and trusting, relationship. Research into coaching encompasses humanistic, behavioural, and cognitive perspectives. It can also embrace constructive developmental, psychoanalytical, and adult learning theories (Stober, 2006).

What is the Humanistic Coaching Relationship?

A coach may be faced with many choices about how to engage a coachee in practice. These may be influenced by training, work and life experience, and motivations. These choices often revolve around shifting roles involving the acts of listening, telling, and guiding. Professional coaches develop personalized coaching models that are rooted in the personal experience of the coach and the coachee, as well as in theory. Humanistic coaches can utilize positive psychology, and are taught to set aside their value systems and ego-driven opinions in support of instilling greater self-awareness and transformation in the coachee. Coaches move the coachee from a position of stasis towards a position of conscious choice. "Humanistic interventions share the view that in order to understand another, practitioners must attempt to understand the phenomenological experience of the other (Stober, 2006, p. 26)." Coaching from a humanistic perspective is focused on facilitating positive change and moving forward in life or work on small or grand scales, in contrast to the remedial focus of the therapeutic medical counseling models. The coach maintains a selfless focus on the needs, wants, goals, and vision of the coachee. Coaches become process experts, instead of content experts (Stober,

2006). A coach needs to understand the state-of-affairs of the coachee from these perspectives. "The faith in the client's potential results in the humanistic coach's disinclination to be directive, but rather to act in ways that free clients to find their own directions, solve their own problems, and evolve in ways that are congruent to them" (Stober, 2006, p. 20).

What is Transformative Phenomenology: Communicative Embodied Awareness

Transformative phenomenology (Marlatt, Rehorick, & Bentz, 2020) is a somatic-hermeneutic-phenomenology that is put into action in the lifeworld that promotes embodied awareness. It is an application of phenomenology—the study of consciousness and phenomena—that can lead to personal, professional, organizational, and social transformations. It is also a form of applied socio-cultural research and practice that supports positive change. Transformative phenomenology emerged from extensive applied phenomenological doctoral research supervised by David Rehorick and Valerie Malhotra Bentz from 1996-2016 during the "Silver Age" of phenomenology at Fielding Graduate University. It is founded on the essence-based phenomenology of Edmund Husserl, the social phenomenology of Alfred Schütz, the embodied phenomenology of Maurice Merleau-Ponty, the ontologic-existential phenomenology of Martin Heidegger, and the reflective interpretative hermeneutic methods of Hans-Georg Gadamer. Transformative phenomenologists seek transformations in the world of everyday life and exhibit qualities, including the adoption of phenomenology, as a way of being and embracing embodied consciousness, wonderment, and authenticity (Bentz et al., 2019; Husserl, 1931; Rehorick & Bentz, 2017; Rehorick & Bentz, 2008; Schutz, 1970).

Transformative phenomenology is a way of knowing that includes enriched and embodied awareness. A person's view of the world of everyday life, understandings, and situations with others can be clouded by preconceptions, scientific and popular constructs, and media images and distortions. Over time, these may blind us to what is apparent to the unclouded phenomenological eye. Phenomenology directs us to the fullness of experience rather than a remote or pro forma accumulation of information and facts. The creative capacity is enhanced by the opening of vision resulting from immersion in the subject matter, rather than limiting the researcher to the traditional mode of observation or data gathering at a discrete distance.

The aim of the study of phenomena (objects of consciousness) is to bring about awareness and understanding of direct experience. Unlike traditional methods of inquiry, phenomenology involves an enriched awareness of our own consciousness. It challenges one to let phenomena reveal themselves, rather than predetermining what phenomena are. Phenomenology seeks to portray the essential, or necessary structures of phenomena, and to uncover the meaning of lived experience within the world of everyday life.

Somatics is an approach, with a long scholarly tradition, that promotes whole-bodied awareness and communication where the capacity for knowing from within becomes the primary instrument of change. Hermeneutics involves the reflective search for meaning through the interpretation of texts and life that include conversations, relationships, and social interaction. The interpreter seeks to reveal personal, cultural, and historically sculpted prejudgments and prejudices, making them visible and explicit within the research process.

Phenomenological inquiry is a way of being as well as a way of knowing. It involves a practice of "bracketing," through which prior judgments and categorizations are suspended so that one's vision opens to what is occurring. Another phenomenological strategy is to change one or more elements of the phenomenon using imagination, so that one may see how things may be different, thus freeing the mind's grip on perceptions and feelings. Transformative phenomenology is what Swami Vivekananda called Jnana Yoga, or the yoga of knowledge, by

231

discriminating what one's essence is from the superficial aspects of lived experience.

According to Alfred Schütz, social phenomenology is a way of looking beyond the taken-for-granted in the world of everyday life—the lifeworld (Wagner, 1983). Social phenomenology offers approaches to connect with social and cultural worlds from the perspectives of an individuals' motivation, sense of topical relevance, the typification of others, relationships, and other vantages. Schütz's social phenomenology springs from the interpretive sociological tradition created by Max Weber, who differentiated between the sciences of explanation and of understanding.

What are the Qualities of Somatic Phenomenological Coaches?

Rehorick and Bentz (2017) identified qualities of transformative phenomenologists based on their analysis of applied phenomenological research. Coaches who practice from somatic phenomenological foundations also embrace many of these qualities (Figure 2). Qualities of transformative phenomenologists include adopting phenomenology as a way of being and embracing embodied consciousness, wonderment, and authenticity. Phenomenological scholar-practitioners focus on looking beyond the taken-for-granted, with awareness that lifeworlds are constructed through patterns of communication. Transformative phenomenologists seek to transcend the reality of everyday lived experience in service of generating common understanding among others. They focus on the creation of transformative spaces through a practice that offers ways of raising consciousness and healing, and creating change in persons, organizations, and society. Transformative phenomenologists address practical concerns in the lifeworld from the diverse vantage of the coach, human development professional, leadership specialist, company executive, directors of medical organizations, professional musician, community social innovators, and more.

Figure 2: Qualities of Coaches Working from Somatic Phenomenological Foundations, © 2020 James Marlatt, Used with Permission, Original Artwork.

Surrender-and-catch: Creating space for coaching transformations

The phenomenological philosopher Martin Heidegger describes Gelassenheit ("releasement" or "letting-be") as the essence of what it means to be human. It is a state that "precedes and exceeds" the commanding human will-to-power that is the will-to-master and the will-to-being-superior-to-others—to preserve and enhance power and increase territory in the technological world that orders things as objects of standing reserve for more and more power. Gelassenheit releases one from this state of willingness toward a state of non-willingness. This is a state of "staying within being," "attentive waiting that surmises," "thoughtful remembrance," "attentively releasing someone into their own," and requiring a "thoughtful participation" with others. The careful non-willing "interpersonal attunement" and openness of Gelassenheit releases and lets others be who they are. This is a radically different state than that created by willing "passive neglect" or "expectation" or "aggressive interrogation" or "active leaping in." Through releasement or letting-be we can stay open to the mystery of being and its withdrawal into concealment, and support the processes of un-concealment as we participate in generating "clearings of truth"— and within the context of coaching, create spaces for transformation through embodied awareness (Davis, 2014; Heidegger, 2010).

Kurt Wolff's concept of surrender-and-catch offers an avenue to understand the nature of creating "space" or "clearings" for transformation through the coaching relationship (Wolff, 1976). Wolff's concept helps to inform what humanistic coaching is, and what transformative learning can be, and how they might be realized in relationship. Surrender-and-catch might be a philosophy available to some, a pre-phenomenological research methodology of a kind, and perhaps a research method of engagement of the "other" that is deeply humanistic. So how are humanistic coaching, surrender-and-catch, and transformation conceptually and practically intertwined?

Wolff depicted surrender-and-catch as encompassing the ephemeral and existential experience that rises out of cognitive love. The experience of surrender can be understood as transformation, grace (Stehr, 2007), flow (Csikszentmihalyi, 1991), peak experience (Maslow, 1999), being in the "coaching zone," the coachee's "ah-ah" revelation, or any number of other descriptions. An intense existential experience might be categorized as a case of surrender. The recognition and exploration of existential surrender in the form of a cognitive catch is an act of meaning making. When linked to theory it can become an act of knowledge creation (Backhaus, 2003).

Wolff (1976, pp. 22-24) posits that several things stem from the concept of surrender as cognitive love. These include total involvement, suspension of received notions, the pertinence of everything, identification, and the risk of being hurt. With total involvement, "as in love, differentiation between subject, act, and object disappears." Through bracketing we suspend our received notions. With pertinence of everything we encounter "the infinity of experience" at surrender.

234

Through identification we understand the "aim of the surrender, not the aim of the catch," and "the love of the catch." The risk of being hurt can arise from surrender itself, or through the risk of false surrender. This risk can be surrender aborted where the received notion takes too much of a hold and can't be suspended. Or, surrender betrayed where the surrenderer loses him- or herself in "the faith in the possibility of surrender" itself, making surrender itself impossible. These are challenging existential concepts that point to why a consensus about the nature of surrender-and-catch has not yet been reached (Nasu, 2007). Nasu also suggests that surrender might be a limit concept and unreachable in practice, although he goes on to emphasize that it is worthwhile to try to achieve it.

In the act of surrender-to, we experience another person, or thing, in her, his, or its essence, without preconceptions. This is done through an attitude of extreme bracketing that takes us out of our common everyday taken-for-granted way of understanding things around us (Backhaus & Psathas, 2007). As we surrender-to we bracket with great intention and intensity, but within the context of a critical stance, as we understand our deep concern for the state of the world and others in the world. We can surrender-to something in response to an egregious act, from which our humanity and curiosity emerges. From this stance we can recognize the vulnerability of another person. From the act of surrender-to rises the potential for the ephemeral, affective, and existential experience of surrender.

In the state of surrender the dichotomy of subject and object dissolves into a unity, and the potential of the catch appears. This is an unpredictable, transformative change or outcome of surrender that can emerge from the "radical commitment" to another. It marks a break with the past (Godway, 2007) that can lead "to personal changes of increased 'openness, tolerance, and compassion' and their political relevance" (Ludes, 2007, p. 171).

The catch emanating from surrender might be recognized through reflection. "Through words, the abyss from the meaning-less" (of

235

surrender) "to meaning-ful" (of the catch) "is 'jumped'" (Backhaus, 2003, p. 316). This involves transcending the boundary from the subjective and existential realm of surrender, where the everyday world is bracketed, to the everyday world where the catch is more fully recognized (Backhaus, 2003, p. 312).

Some of the elements of Kurt Wolff's concept of surrender-and-catch can be related to the fields of humanistic coaching, transformative learning, human development, and transformative phenomenology (Table 1). The humanistic coaching process and surrender-to are sympathetic in describing why surrender can happen. Theories of transformative learning generally depict how transformative learning happens. Human developmental theories generally depict what happens.

Humanistic coaching is aligned with the radical commitment of surrender in the critical response to a condition of the lifeworld. For example, the humanistic coach understands that an existential lens trumps epistemic lens in the search for understanding born out of a crisis or disorientation. In the search for understanding, the humanistic coach focuses on positive psychology, unconditional positive regard, is non-directive, sets aside ego driven and value based opinions in favor of deep listening, has a phenomenological focus, and has a selfless focus on the needs, wants, goals, and vision of the coachee. In alignment, Hisashi Nasu (2007) posits that surrender is also born out of crisis, or an extreme situation, and requires that conceived notions are suspended. To surrender is "to study, as intimately as possible, a given human being ... as the unique things they are" ... "to be totally involved, identified or identical with what is happening" (Nasu, 2007, p. 139).

Surrender-to can bring a coach's existential moment into juxtaposition with the coachee's existential moment. Coaching can catalyze the coachee's transformative catch. The break with the past as experienced through surrender has some of the hallmarks of constructive human development through transformative learning

(Kegan, 1983; Mezirow, 2000). It is a process by which we transform our taken-for-granted frames of reference (meaning perspectives, habits of mind, mind-sets) to make them more inclusive, discriminating, open, emotionally capable of change, and reflective so that they may generate beliefs and opinions that will prove more true or justified to guide action (Mezirow, 2000, p.7). The catch is indicative of an individual's evolution towards a different way of being. There are many synergies evident between surrender-and-catch, humanistic coaching, and theories of learning and human development that warrant further investigation.

Domain	Mapping Transformation	Outcome of Transformation	Some Influential Scholars
Humanistic Coaching Practice & Surrender & Catch	The humanistic coaching process can depict why transformation happens (surrender-to)	Shift in way of doing, seeing or being	Carl Rogers, Kurt Wolff, Donald Polkinghorne, Aristotle
Transformative Learning Theory	Learning theory generally depicts how transformation happens	Shift in our Habits-of-Mind	Jack Mezirow, Robert Boyd, John Dirkx, Patricia Cranton, Jürgen Habermas
Human Development Theory	Developmental theory generally depicts what happens in development (change)	Shift in our Logics-of-Action (Individuation; Self-Actualization)	Jean Piaget, Robert Kegan, William Torbert, Susanne Cook-Greuter
Transformative Phenomenology Foundation to Coaching	Phenomenology can illuminate elements of transformation for exploration through the theories of development & learning, & coaching practice (the essence of lived experience before theory and practice).	Consciousness Raising Looking Beyond the Taken-for-Granted in the World of Everyday Life	Edmund Husserl, Alfred Schütz, Hans-Jorg Gadamer, Max van Manen, David Rehorick, Valerie Bentz

Table 1: A framework for relating Transformative Phenomenology to other domains. After (Marlatt, 2011). Some references for influential scholars: (Boyd & Myers, 1988; Brown, 2009; Cook-Greuter, 1999; Cranton, 2006; Dirkx, 2000; Eriksen, 2003; Kegan, 1983; Mezirow, 2009; Natanson, 1973; Palmer, 1969; Polkinghorne, 2004; Rehorick & Bentz, 2008; C. R. Rogers, 1995; Torbert, 2004; van Manen, 1997).

Part 2: A Phenomenological Coaching Model

A humanistic coaching methodology based on Kurt Wolff's pre-phenomenological concept of "surrender-and-catch" and founded on the qualities stemming from engagement with transformative phenomenology is illustrated in Figure 3 (Marlatt, 2012, 2017). The methodology offers an ontological foundation from which to understand and follow a phenomenological approach to coaching that embraces a free-flowing critical dialogue in support of transformation, as opposed to a more directive and goal-focused agenda.

Surrender can be an unexpected, intense, existential experience leading to a revelatory, recognizable, transforming, cognitive catch. In the act of surrender-to we experience another person, or thing, in its essence, without preconceptions, through an attitude of extreme bracketing that takes us out of our common taken-for-granted way of understanding things around us (Backhaus & Psathas, 2007). As we surrender-to we bracket with great intention and intensity but within the context of a critical stance, as we understand our deep concern for the state of others in the lifeworld. From this stance we can recognize the vulnerability of another person. From the act of surrender-to rises the potential for the ephemeral, affective, and existential experience of surrender-and-catch can emerge.

A model for surrender-and-catch in the coaching relationship is introduced in Figure 3 (Marlatt, 2012, 2017). Marlatt utilizes this model in his coaching practice.

A phenomenological description of the coaching model follows, with reference to Figure 3.

I surrender-to my coachee as a humanistic coach fully focused on serving my coachee. As I surrender-to my coachee, I create a coaching environment that might be conducive to surrender. I understand the nature of surrender as a methodology that is also aligned and synonymous with my humanistic coaching method—surrender in anticipation of an existential awakening in response to some-thing. I

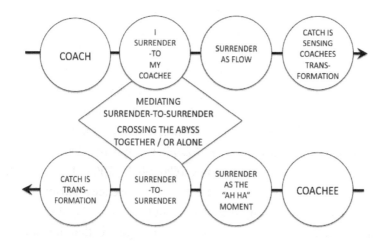

Figure 3. A model of surrender-and-catch in the coaching relationship. Reprinted with prem-ission from Marlatt, J. (2012). When executive coaching connects: A phenomenological study of relationship and transformative learning. (PhD Dissertation), Fielding Graduate University, Santa Barbara, CA., 2012, © James Marlatt, 2012.

enter the coaching conversation with intuitive vacillations in and out of different coaching modalities—mentor, consultant, and humanistic coach. In surrendering-to my coachee I adopt an open and wondrous attitude toward their interests and dilemmas (phenomenological epoché). My attitude is content with looking behind the taken for granted, sometimes from an agenda-less perspective. I hold in abeyance my preconceptions and biases and knowledge of theory and practice (phenomenological bracketing, explication, reduction). As we interact, my coachee and I may encounter "flow" which is a hallmark of being in sync; where time stands still—I surrender-to "flow." We may reach a mutual understanding, initially with or without words, a felt experience, and move toward recognizing the potential of an existential experience—the recognition of the coachee's "ah-ha" moment. My cognitive catch, as a coach, is in sensing the potential germination of the coachee's transformative potential through their "ah-ha". Through the sometimes ineffable nature of the coaching conversation my coachee recognizes an existential and ephemeral "ah-ha" moment that can range from momentous to trivial. For the coachee, the cognitive, affective, and somatic process of meaning making through their catch requires a surrender-to-their-surrender-experience (Wolff, 1976, pp. 168-169), in this instance an existential awakening through their "ah-ha." For some, crossing the abyss to their transformational catch stemming from their "ah-ha" can be deeply personal, hidden, cathartic, life altering, lengthy and transformational. It can be akin to traversing the road of trials illuminated in Joseph Campbell's description of mankind's mythopoetic life journey (Campbell, 2008; Lash, 2002). The coach can play a role in mediating the coachee's surrender-to-surrender and in supporting the coachee in traversing the abyss, once the "ah-ha" moment is reached, although it is arguable that the journey should, or must, be a solitary journey of transformation and learning. (James Marlatt, personal account)

Part 3: Somatic Phenomenological Coaching in Practice

Transformative phenomenology is both a methodology and method for phenomenological and hermeneutic research into the social and human sciences. What fundamentally differentiates this form of phenomenological inquiry is its relationship to transformation. The coach who works in this form of inquiry values the process of Husserlian essential phenomenology and Schützian social phenomenology. Communicative embodied awareness processes focus on exploring the inner world of the coachee to understand the essential nature of the coachee's lived experience associated with the coaching topic. The exploration of the social, relational, world of the coachee from a view-from-within seeks to understand and acknowledge the habits-of-mind and blind spots that can block transformation.

An illustration of the process of coaching from a somatic and phenomenological foundation is presented in Figure 4. Here we contrast conversation in general, with coaching from a somatic and phenomenological foundation. The phenomenological qualities inherent in the being of the coach are involved in catalyzing the emergence of a safe and trusted coaching space. The coach relies on a variety of phenomenological techniques to help the coachee to build awareness of the essential elements associated with phenomenon of interest in the coaching encounter. For the coach, this involves the temporary bracketing of preconceptions, prejudices, and theory. By this we mean that our thoughts and evidence-based theories relevant to coaching are held in abeyance, in favor of free-flowing open-ended conversations and embodied awareness of the coach and coachee in the coaching encounter. The emergence and recognition of dialogic openings (the "ah-ha") lead to additional conversations that attempt to identify insights into the essence of the coachee's dilemma. Then the coach can consider the value of starting to un-bracket and bringing the evidence-base into the conversation to assist in consolidating learning, change, and transformation.

Somatic phenomenological coaching techniques that stem from transformative phenomenology and that are relevant to coaching involve communicative embodied awareness and the phenomenological techniques of bracketing, imaginative variation, horizontalization, typifications, and relevances, among others. With bracketing we set aside preconceptions and biases with the goal of looking beyond taken-for-granted assumptions to understand the lived experience. Horizontalization helps to gain clarity by making the elements in a situation of equal value and thinking about them from a distance without bias or assumptions. With imaginative variation, components of the experience are varied to understand what is essential for the situation to exist. Lived experience can be understood from embodied perspectives building awareness of habituated ways of thinking and acting through consideration of experience through the lenses of lived space, lived body, lived time, and lived human relationship. Recognizing how we habitually label or typify ourselves, others, and groups in general is another avenue for exploration; identifying the different ways that we understand the relevance of things we pay attention is yet another. Things become relevant when we freely turn our attention to them, or when something is imposed on us, or when can no longer take things for granted. Asking coaching questions from these perspectives can help coachees to understand habits of mind and identify blind spots, leading to consciousness raising. See Table 2 with reference to (Rehorick & Bentz, 2008; van Manen, 1997; Wagner, 1983).

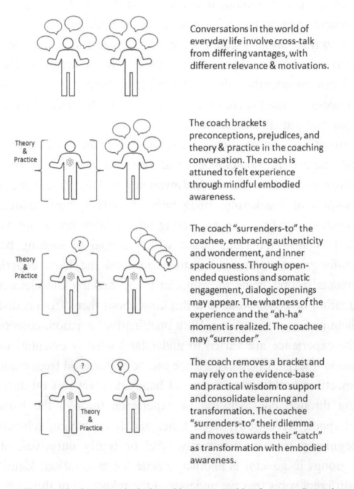

Figure 4. The somatic phenomenological coaching process with reference to Surrender-and-Catch, © 2020 James Marlatt, Used with Permission, Original Artwork.

Coaching Objective	Some Coaching Techniques & Coaching Questions
Exploring the Inner World (Essential Phenomenology & Embodied Awareness)	**Bracketing:** Setting aside preconceptions and biases with the goal of looking beyond taken-for-granted assumptions to understand the lived experience. Bracketing theory and practice to stay away from habitual thinking and access the pre-reflective world to get to the meaning of things. Question: What biases do you bring to the table when you consider you experience? How do things appear when you set the assumptions aside?
Discover the essential elements of the coachee's lived experience (understand what must be present for the experience to exist)	**Horizontalization:** Gaining clarity by making the elements in a situation of equal value and thinking about them from a distance without bias or assumptions. Question: What if you placed equal weight on each side of the "equation"? What happens if you stand back and look at things from the other point of view? **Imaginative Variation:** Imaginatively vary components of the experience to understand what is essential for the situation to exist. Use imagination to shift away from the factual nature of the situation to get to the essence of the situation. Question: What would things look like if you reversed roles? You are the president, and the president is now walking in your shoes?
Exploring the Social World from Within (Social Phenomenology & Embodied Awareness)	**Lifeworld Essentials:** Understanding the experience from embodied perspectives can build awareness of habituated ways of thinking and acting (lived space, lived body, lived time, lived human relationship) Question: How would you describe your sense of space in your encounter? How would you describe your physical or bodily presence? Where do you feel it in your body? Describe your felt sense of time; did it speed up, slow down, stand still? What was your felt impression of the other person? **Typification:** People tend to typify or label themselves, others, and groups in general. Typification is an important feature of thinking and communicating in everyday life. Understanding typifications can build awareness of habituated patterns of thinking and communicating. Question: How would you name the other people that you are in conflict in a word or two? How does that label serve you?
Understand the lived experience of the coachee as experienced in the taken-for-granted world of everyday life (the lifeworld). Connecting with social and cultural worlds.	**Relevances:** Things become relevant when we freely turn our attention to them, or when something is imposed on us, or when can no longer take things for granted. It is only in retrospect that we can reflect on our motivation for engaging in a relevant activity. Understanding motivation can lead to a break-away from habituated ways of thinking and acting. Questions: Why is this significant to you? What factors led to your focus of attention? What is motivating you to explore this? Would others around you see this as a relevant issue?

Table 2: A Selection of Somatic Phenomenological Coaching Techniques to build awareness of habits and taken-for granted assumptions in the world of everyday life. With contributions from Joao Noronha (personal communication).

Returning to the Evidence-Base

The humanistic coaching stance relies on practical wisdom and an iterative process of asking questions in a spontaneous and unscripted manner that recognizes the contextual, specific, and phenomenological nature of the conversation. It is a judgment-based practice. Alternatively, the evidence-based coach engages the client from a more theoretical and presumptive perspective with a more defined pattern of goal attainment.

Judgment is necessary given the uniqueness of value-focused human beings in action. Human beings are open to multiple futures stemming from complex value sets. They are focused on specialized over-generalizable life trajectories that stem from unique emotional and imaginative life contexts. Human beings also often rely on unique affective modes as catalysts for action. A judgment-based practice attends to the uniqueness of individuals seeking change. (See: Marlatt, 2012.)

Donald Polkinghorne (2004) suggests that the focus on instrumental rationality and the drive to achieve outcomes through efficient and effective processes has led to the adoption of efficiency and effectiveness as values in their own right. These values have been transferred into societal practice. Efficiency is about controlling human action, and unique human values do not form part of this value proposition in a meaningful way. Instrumental rationality is aligned with positivist approaches to developing theory and technologies in the arena of the natural science. Max Weber argued that the values and action that involve ethical and spiritual judgments are subordinated, as is:

...[the] desire to live a meaningful life...within a rationalized society...Practices involving human-to-human interaction cannot be readily reduced to technical-rational approaches. Because of the unique, emerged characteristics of human beings, successful practice with them requires improvisation and ongoing adjustments informed by situated practitioner judgment...Practitioners of care are social actors who have been reared in a culture that values technical solutions. (Polkinghorne, 2004, p.36 & p.94)

Returning to the role of the evidence-base in coaching, we ask the question: Where does the best generalizable knowledge come from? Numerous epistemic coaching lenses are related to the fields of psychology, adult learning, adult development, social views of adult development, intelligence, culture and gender, communication, human systems, therapy, neuroscience, leadership, and organizational systems. There is a wide range of theoretical orientations that the evidenced-based coach can draw on in practice. The coaching focus can be directed towards helping the client to self-actualize, grow through reflection, develop learning plans, understand possibility, be authentic, change behavior, and understand human systems, among other possibilities. The coaches challenge is to know when and how to deploy theoretical knowledge (Marlatt, 2012).

In closing, we refer to Dianne Stober (2006), who may be correct in suggesting that evidence-based coaching methods can be more effectively deployed as a manifold over the core humanistic coaching foundation, when the requisite relational coaching conditions are in place (See Figure 1). We see our work as an expansion of the definition of evidence-based coaching to include somatic-phenomenological "essence-based" coaching—with a focus on seeking the "whatness" of experience beyond the taken-for-granted in the world of everyday life, in support of personal and professional transformations.

About the Authors

James Marlatt, MBA, PhD, P.Eng., Certified Executive Coach is an Institute for Social Innovation Fellow at Fielding Graduate University. Jim is an executive coach and leadership development consultant with coaching credentials from Royal Roads University and the Fielding Graduate University evidence-based coaching program. He is a graduate of Fielding Graduate University, holding a PhD in Human and Organizational Systems with a dissertation related to coaching: *When coaching connects: A phenological study of transformative learning and relationship.* Jim's publications include a chapter about coaching: "The transformative potential of conversations with strangers" in the Fielding monograph *Expressions of phenomenological research* edited by David Rehorick and Valerie Malhotra Bentz, and a co-authored chapter: "The silver age of phenomenology at Fielding" in *The Fielding Scholar Practitioner: Voices from 45 years of Fielding Graduate University.* He is active in the Fielding Somatics, Phenomenology and Communicative Leadership community-of-practice and is the Research Coordinator for the 2019 Fielding international and multi-institutional "From Strangers to Collaborators" participatory action research project led by Professor Valerie Bentz. Contact: jmarlatt@email.fielding.edu.

Valerie Malhotra Bentz, MSSW, PhD is Professor of Human and Organization Development, Fielding Graduate University, where she served as Associate Dean for Research. Her current interests include somatics, phenomenology, social theory, consciousness development, and Vedantic theories of knowledge. Her books include: *Contemplative social research: Caring for self, being, and lifeworld,* with Vincenzo M. B. Giogino; *Transformative phenomenology: Changing ourselves, lifeworlds and professional practice,* with David Rehorick; *Expressions of phenomenological research,* with David Rehorick; *Mindful inquiry in social research,* with Jeremy Shapiro, and *Becoming mature: Childhood ghosts and spirits in adult life.* She also authored a philosophical novel, *Flesh and mind: The time travels of Dr. Victoria Von Dietz.* She is a Fellow in Contemplative Practice of the American Association of Learned Societies. Valerie was editor of Phenomenology and the Human Sciences (1994–98). She has served as president and board member of the Clinical Sociology Association, the Sociological Practice Association, and the Society for Phenomenology and the Human Sciences. She founded and co-directed an action research team and center in Mizoram, India. Valerie was co-founder of the Creative

Longevity and Wisdom program at Fielding. She is the Director of the Doctoral Concentration in Somatics, Phenomenology, and Communicative Leadership (SPCL). She has twenty years experience as a psychotherapist and is a certified yoga teacher and certified massage therapist.

References

Backhaus, G. (2003). Vindication of the human and social science of Kurt H. Wolff. *Human Studies, 28,* 309-335.

Backhaus, G., & Psathas, G. (2007). *The sociology of radical commitment: Kurt H. Wolff's existential turn.* Lanham, MD: Lexington Books.

Backhaus, G., & Psathas, G. (Eds.). (2007). *The sociology of radical commitment: Kurt H. Wolff's existential turn.* Lanham: Lexington Books.

Bentz, V., Rehorick, D., Marlatt, J., Nishi, A., & Estrada, C. (2018). Transformative Phenomenology as an Antidote to Technological Deathworlds. *Schutzian Research*(10), 189-220.

Bentz, V., Rehorick, D., Marlatt, J., Nishii, A., Estrada, C., & Buechner, B. (2019). The Silver Age of Phenomenology at Fielding Graduate University. In K. S. Rogers & M. L. Snowden (Eds.), *The Fielding Scholar Practitioner: Voices from 45 years of Fielding Graduate University* (pp. 179-204). Santa Barbara, CA: Fielding Press.

Bentz, V., & Shapiro, J. (1998). *Mindful inquiry in social research.* Thousand Oaks, CA: Sage Publications.

Bentz, V. M., & Giorgino, V. M. B. (Eds.). (2016). *Contemplative social research: Caring for self, being, and lifeworld.* Santa Barbara,CA: Fielding University Press.

Boyd, R. D., & Myers, J. G. (1988). Transformative Education. *International Journal of Lifelong Education, 7*(4), 261-284.

Brown, L. (Ed.) (2009). *The Nicomachean ethics / Aristotle (L. Browne Trans.).* New York, NY: Oxford University Press, Inc.

Campbell, J. (2008). *The hero with a thousand faces* (3rd ed.). Novato: New World Library.

Cook-Greuter, S. (1999). *Postautonomous ego development: A study of its nature and measurement.* (Ed.D), Harvard University.

Cranton, P. (2006). *Understanding and promoting transformative learning: A guide for educators of adults.* San Franscisco, CA: Jossey-Bass.

Csikszentmihalyi, M. (1991). *Flow: The psychology of optimal experience.* New

York, NY: Harper Perennial.

Davis, B. W. (2014). Will and Gelassenheit. In B. W. Davis (Ed.), *Martin Heidegger: Key concepts* (pp. 168-182). New York: Routledge.

Dirkx, J. M. (2000). Transformative Learning and the Journey of Individuation. ERIC Digest No. 223

Eriksen, E. O. (2003). *Understanding Habermas: Communicating action and deliberative democracy.* New York, NY: Continuum.

Godway, E. (2007). Surrender and catch and the question of reason: Kurt Wolff and John Macmurray. In G. Backhaus & G. Psathas (Eds.), *The sociology of radical commitment: Kurt H. Wolff's existential turn* (pp. 80-91). Lanham: Lexington Books.

Haines, M. B. (1999). *Interior spaciousness: The hidden openess of some who walk a mystical path with practical feet.* (PhD), The Fielding Institute, Santa Barbara, CA.

Hanna, T. (1988). *Somatics: Reawakening the mind's control of movement, flexibility, and health.* Cambridge, MA: Da Capo Press.

Heidegger, M. (2010). *Country path conversations* (B. W. Davis, Trans.): Indiana Unuversity Press.

Husserl, E. (1931). *Ideas: General introduction to pure phenomenology* (W. R. B. Gibson, Trans.). Woking, Great Britain: George Allen and Unwin Ltd.

Kegan, R. (1983). *The evolving self: Problem and process in human development.* Cambridge, MA: Harvard University Press/Triliteral.

Knowles, M. S., Holton III, E. F., & Swanson, R. A. (2005). *The adult learner: The definitive classic in adult education and human resource development* (6th ed.). Burlington, MA: Elsevier.

Lash, R. (2002). Top leadership taking the inner journey. *Ivey Business Journal, 66*(5), 44.

Ludes, P. (2007). Individual transcendence, media transformations, and collective experiences: An introduction to my 1984 interview with Kurt H. Wolff. In G. Backhaus & G. Psathas (Eds.), *The sociology of radical commitment: Kurt H. Wolff's existential turn.* Lanham: Lexington Books.

Marlatt, J. (2011). *When executive coaching connects: A phenomenological study of relationship and transformative learning.* Paper presented at the 2011 Annual Meetings of the Society for Phenomenology and the Human Sciences, Philadelphia, PA.

Marlatt, J. (2012). *When executive coaching connects: A phenomenological study of relationship and transformative learning.* (PhD Dissertation), Fielding Graduate University, Santa Barbara, CA.

Marlatt, J. (2017). The transformative potential of conversations with strangers. In D. Rehorick & V. Bentz (Eds.), *Expressions of phenomenological research: Consciousness and lifeworld studies* (Vol. 10, pp. 313). Santa Barbara, CA: Fielding University Press.

Marlatt, J., Rehorick, D., & Bentz, V. (2020). Transformative Phenomenology. In A. Possamai & A. J. Blasi (Eds.), *SAGE Encyclopedia of Sociology of Religion.* Thousand Oaks, CA: SAGE.

Maslow, A. (1999). *Towards a psychology of being.* New York, NY: John Wiley & Sons.

Merriam, S. B., Caffarella, R. S., & Baumgartner, L. M. (2007). *Learning in adulthood: A comprehensive guide* (3rd ed.). San Francisco, CA: Jossey-Bass.

Mezirow, J. (2000). Learning to think like an adult: Core concepts of transformative theory. In J. Mezirow & Associates (Eds.), *Learning as transformation: Critical perspectives on a theory in progress.* San Francisco: Jossey-Bass.

Mezirow, J. (2009). Transformative Learning Theory. In J. Mezirow, E. W. Taylor, & Associates (Eds.), *Transformative learning in practice: Insights from community, workplace, and higher education.* San Francisco, CA: Jossey-Bass.

Nasu, H. (2007). Scope and limits of Wolff's world of "Surrender". In G. Backhaus & G. Psathas (Eds.), *The sociology of radical commitment: Kurt H. Wolff's existential turn* (pp. 137-151). Lanham, MD: Lexington Books.

Natanson, M. (1973). *Edmund Husserl: Philosopher of infinite tasks.* Evanston, IL: Northwestern University Press.

Palmer, R. E. (1969). *Hermeneutics: Interpretation theory in Schleiermacher, Dilthey, Heidegger and Gadamer.* Evanston, IL: Northwestern University Press.

Polkinghorne, D. (2004). *Practice and human sciences: The case for a judgement-based practice of care.* New York, NY: State University of New York Press.

Rehorick, D., & Bentz, V. (Eds.). (2017). *Expressions of phenomenological research: Consciousness and lifeworld studies* (Vol. 10). Santa Barbara, CA: Fielding University Press.

Rehorick, D. A., & Bentz, V. (Eds.). (2008). *Transformative phenomenology: Changing ourselves, lifeworlds, and professional practice.* Lanham, MD: Lexington Books.

Rehorick, D. A., & Malhotra Bentz, V. (2012). Re-envising Schutz: Retrospective reflections & prospective hopes. *Annual Meetings of the Society for*

Phenomenology and the Human Sciences (SPHS).

Rogers, C. (1995). *On becoming a person: A therapist's view of psychotherapy*. New York: Houghton Mifflin Company.

Schutz, A. (1970). Phenomenological baseline. In H. Wagner (Ed.), *Alfred Schutz on phenomenology and social relations* (pp. 53-71). Chicago: University of Chicago Press.

Stehr, N. (2007). How I came to sociology and who I am: A conversation with Kurt H. Wolff. In G. Backhaus & G. Psathas (Eds.), *The sociology of radical committment: Kurt H. Wolff's existential turn* (pp. 37-61). Lanham, MD: Lexington Books.

Stober, D. (2006). Coaching from the humanistic perspective. In D. R. Stober & A. M. Grant (Eds.), *Evidence based coaching handbook: Putting best practices to work for your clients*. Hoboken, NJ: John Wiley & Sons, Inc.

Stober, D., & Grant, A. (2006). *Evidence based coaching handbook: Putting best practices to work for your clients*. Hoboken: John Wiley & Sons.

Torbert, W. R. (2004). *Action inquiry: The secret of timely and transforming leadership*. San Francisco, CA: Berrett-Koehler Publishers, Inc.

van Manen, M. (1997). *Researching lived experience: Human science for an action sensitive pedagogy*. London, Ontario: Althouse Press.

Wagner, H. R. (1983). *Phenomenology of consciousness and sociology of the life-world: An introductory study*. Edmonton, Canada: The University of Alberta Press.

Wagner, H. R. (Ed.) (1970). *Alfred Schutz: On phenomenology and social relations*. Chicago, IL: The University of Chicago Press.

Wolff, K. (1976). *Surrender and catch: Experience and inquiry today*. Boston, MA: D. Reidel Publishing.

CHAPTER 12

SETTING THE STAGE FOR LEARNING AND CHANGE THROUGH GROUP COACHING

Erek J. Ostrowski, PhD, PCC
Fielding Graduate University

Abstract

Coaching in an "unaffiliated" group setting, where members do not belong to the same work team and share no affiliation outside the coaching group, requires an understanding of the complex social processes that shape learning and change in groups. What makes group coaching effective? How does coaching in this type of group environment differ from one-on-one coaching? What do coaches need to know in order to work with this kind of group?

Ostrowski's (2018) dissertation study explored group coaching as a setting for learning and change in entrepreneurs. It revealed five background conditions or group characteristics that when present set the stage for meaningful learning and change. This chapter outlines these findings, explores their connections to related theory and research on group psychotherapy, and discusses implications for coaches who wish to work with groups.

Keywords: Coaching, Group Coaching, Entrepreneurship, Entrepreneurial Learning, Group Learning, Group Psychotherapy.

Introduction

Despite a recent increase in research on dyadic (one-on-one) coaching, knowledge of group coaching lags far behind (O'Connor & Cavanagh, 2017). Group coaching includes the coaching of intact work teams in organizations (team coaching), as well as coaching that involves other types of groups that may or may not have an organizational focus (Brown & Grant, 2010; Thornton, 2010). To date, researchers have given more attention to the study of organizational team coaching than to other types of coaching groups. However, in its latter form group coaching is becoming increasingly popular among practitioners and consumers (Britton, 2013).

Coaching in "unaffiliated" groups, where members do not belong to the same work team and share no affiliation outside the coaching group, requires an understanding of the complex social processes that shape learning and change in groups (Kets de Vries, 2014; Thornton, 2010). What makes group coaching effective? How does coaching in this type of group environment differ from one-on-one coaching? What do coaches need to know in order to work with groups?

Thornton (2010), Kets de Vries (2011, 2014), and others have begun to answer these questions by tracing group coaching's connections to knowledge from related fields such as group psychotherapy (Yalom & Leszcz, 2005) and group analytic theory (Foulkes, 1948, 1986). Ostrowski's (2018) dissertation study on group coaching as a setting for entrepreneurial learning (EL) builds on this work by making these connections more explicit. Using narrative methods of inquiry and analysis, the study explored the experiences of eight entrepreneur participants in four different coaching groups. The study uncovered five background conditions that helped set the stage for group members' meaningful learning and change: *cohesiveness, commonality, social support, exchange, and accountability.* This chapter describes the study's findings, explores their connections to related theory and research, and offers recommendations for further research and practice in the group domain.

Conceptual Framework

The study intersects the literatures on entrepreneurial learning and group coaching. At the individual level of analysis, past research on entrepreneurship has focused primarily on the psychology (personality traits and characteristics) of individuals (Watson, 2009). However, the study of entrepreneurial personalities has been criticized for failing to acknowledge an entrepreneur's ability to learn and change over time and through experience (Rae, 2000; Watson, 2009). In the wake of this critique, researchers have turned to the learning and developmental processes of entrepreneurship (Deakins & Freel, 1998, 2012; Wang & Chugh, 2014).

Entrepreneurial Learning (EL)

Entrepreneurs engage with a different set of challenges than the organizationally employed—one that requires different avenues for learning and problem solving (Brett, Mullally, O'Gorman, & Fuller-Love, 2012). First, entrepreneurship is fundamentally dynamic and non-linear (Cope, 2003; Deakins & Freel, 1998). The turbulence and uncertainty that entrepreneurs face influence the development of their learning practices (Higgins & Aspinall, 2011). EL is less likely to occur in a planned or programmatic way, and more likely to occur as a result of knowledge accumulated over time and through reactions to specific situations or experiences (Deakins & Freel, 1998).

Second, while owning a business can be significantly rewarding, the rewards often come at a high cost. Entrepreneurs describe stress, responsibility, and long hours as potential down sides of entrepreneurship (Alstete, 2008), along with loneliness and isolation, immersion in business, and people problems (Boyd & Gumpert, 1983). Although entrepreneurs are often surrounded by others (employees, vendors, customers, competitors, etc.), their isolation and loneliness stem from not having anyone with whom to discuss business problems or share their deep concerns (Gumpert & Boyd, 1984; Zhang & Hamilton, 2009).

Finally, many entrepreneurs feel the need to project an image of strength, health, and reliability to suppliers and customers (Zhang & Hamilton, 2009), to hide weakness from competitors, and to convey confidence to employees (Gumpert & Boyd, 1984). As a result, they often lack colleagues or peers with whom they feel comfortable sharing ideas, processing experiences, or even simply commiserating. Since learning in small firms is dependent on social interaction (Higgins & Aspinall, 2011), these pressures create a need for entrepreneurs to search for and find social contexts that can foster their learning and development.

Learning from experience. Learning from experience is understood to be a key ability in entrepreneurship (Deakins & Freel, 1998). Entrepreneurial knowledge is most often gained through action taken in response to lived experiences and real-world situations, rather than through formal instruction (Higgins & Aspinall, 2011; Zhang & Hamilton, 2009). These *critical learning events* provide a catalyst for learning specific entrepreneurial competencies, as well as for learning that leads to new awareness or new perspectives (Deakins & Freel, 1998). Learning occurs when reactions to critical events require the entrepreneur to process information in new ways, to adapt strategy, and to make important decisions.

Learning with and from other entrepreneurs. Although research suggests that entrepreneurs often feel isolated and alone, social processes play a key role in EL (Cope, 2005; Higgins & Aspinall, 2011). Personal (peer) networks are one important social learning domain for entrepreneurs (Brett et al., 2012; Zhang & Hamilton, 2009). The term "peer learning" encompasses many types of organized peer interaction in which individual (versus collective) EL is the focus. Entrepreneurial peer groups can provide a fertile context for learning by removing barriers or constraints on EL (Brett et al., 2012). For example, peer networks can help ease isolation and loneliness, spread useful knowledge and ideas, and foster critical reflection and vicarious learning (Florén, 2003; Gumpert & Boyd, 1984; Zhang & Hamilton, 2009). The role of peers is not necessarily to solve an individual's problems, but to help them clarify their thinking, consider alternative points of view, and resolve complex decisions.

Constructing and negotiating entrepreneurial identity. Through the lens of identity, EL is about the construction and maintenance of an entrepreneurial sense of self (Higgins & Aspinall, 2011; Rae, 2000). Entrepreneurs create and negotiate their identities socially, pulling from various cultural and discursive resources to position themselves in relation to others and to achieve desired ends (Down & Warren, 2008; Watson, 2009). From a sociocultural perspective, this requires them to learn and engage in the language, behavior, and other practices of their entrepreneurial communities; in other words, to learn the language of entrepreneurship (Higgins & Aspinall, 2011; Watson, 2009).

Group Coaching

For the purposes of this study, group coaching is defined as the application of coaching principles to a small group, across multiple sessions, facilitated by a skilled professional, and in service of individual, collective, personal, and/or organizational learning and goals. Despite recent advances in coaching research, knowledge of the subdiscipline of group coaching is still in its infancy (O'Connor & Cavanagh, 2017; Stelter, Nielsen, & Wikman, 2011; Van Dyke, 2012). As a result, the literature base is limited, and conceptions of group coaching differ according to a variety of theoretical perspectives.

This study explored the experiences of independent entrepreneurs (not affiliated with the same organization) who come together as a group and engage a professional coach for the purpose of advancing their individual capability as business owners. O'Connor and Cavanagh (2017) noted the potential benefits such groups can hold for their members. For example, a coach can help individuals in the group draw from the challenges, learning, and experience of other group members. New relationships and understandings can emerge out of group interaction, linking individuals across their different situations and contexts. These relational learning and change processes do not exist in dyadic coaching, which makes groups of this nature a new and different practice environment for many coaches (Britton, 2013; Kets de Vries, 2014).

A search of the coaching literature revealed four examples of studies focused on unaffiliated group coaching (UGC). Van Dyke (2012) explored the experiences of executives who participated virtual group coaching programs. She found that participants used their coaching groups as structures of accountability, as sounding boards for the discussion of business challenges, and as opportunities to gain perspective and learn from others. Stelter et al. (2011) studied group coaching for young people who participate in elite sports. They found that group coaching facilitated social support measured in terms of social recovery, which resulted in the formation of durable social networks and the cultivation of social capital among group members.

Whitley (2013) showed that group coaching can be designed to facilitate needed lifestyle changes in people with long-term health conditions. Participants in her study reported that their groups helped them practice the skills needed to achieve their health goals, thereby supporting them to make changes in their lives, and to cope with and manage their health conditions. Finally, Scamardo and Harnden (2007) implemented group coaching for managers as part of an employee assistance program (EAP) at the University of Texas at Austin. Participants reported that their groups helped them achieve their individual goals for management skills development, while also providing some of the psychotherapeutic benefits of group work discussed by Yalom and Leszcz (2005), including universality, altruism, and the installation of hope.

Mechanisms of group learning and change. Although there is no single, unifying theoretical perspective on group coaching, authors such as Thornton (2010) and Kets de Vries (2011, 2014) have highlighted the usefulness of applying psychoanalytic theory as a lens for understanding the mechanisms of learning and change at work in UGC. These include holding and exchange, connectedness and belonging, mutual identification, and vicarious learning.

Holding and exchange. Thornton (2010) stated "All coaching is founded in a developmental relationship blending enough safety in the relationship to enable an encounter with new information" (p. 28). The potential for deep learning and change though group coaching is fundamentally connected to the coach's ability to create a safe, trusting, and intimate group environment (Kets de Vries, 2011; Thornton, 2010). Such an environment allows for meaningful dialogue, and fosters interdependence among group members (Cockerham, 2011).

Thornton (2010) explained this principle using two terms from psychoanalytic and group analytic theory—*holding* and *exchange*. The term "holding" was coined by Winnicott (1971) and represents the nurturing relationship that forms between mother and infant. A holding environment is the space of trust and safety that arises out of this nurturing relationship. When an environment of sufficient safety is created in a coaching relationship, it allows for an encounter with something new. This type of encounter is called *exchange*—a term borrowed from group analytic theory (Foulkes, 1948, 1986). There can be no change and development without an encounter with difference, or something that is new or unknown. At the same time, individuals must be able to stand on safe ground when they are challenged (Thornton, 2010).

Connectedness and belonging. Thornton (2010) explained that connectedness and belonging are closely linked with the concept of holding. Groups that are "well-held" enable members to feel connected to one another and exude a sense of forward progress. Members of a cohesive group convey mutual acceptance and support, and are likely to form meaningful relationships with one another, as well as positive regard for the group and its work (Thornton, 2010). This state of connectedness and the accompanying feeling of belonging act as a major catalyst for change (Kets de Vries, 2014).

Mutual identification. Kets de Vries (2014) explained that while listening to the stories of others, participants "may come to realize that they are not alone... and that others... struggle with similar problems" (p. 89). In group psychotherapy, this phenomenon is called "universality" (Yalom & Leszcz, 2005), and is defined as the realization that one is not alone in her/his struggles, and that others experience similar challenges (Holmes & Kivlighan, 2000). This realization in itself can be a huge relief, but it can also open up new opportunities to explore a situation from different perspectives (Kets de Vries, 2011).

Vicarious learning. Group members learn through observing and reflecting on others' experiences (Kets de Vries, 2014; Thornton, 2010). In a comparative study of the therapeutic factors of group and individual psychotherapy, Holmes and Kivlighan (2000) found that individuals experienced the therapy of other group members—both through observation and through direct participation. More recently, Kivlighan (2011) found that individuals experience greater session depth when other group members engage in vicarious learning.

In summary, this study was framed conceptually by an understanding of the experiential and social processes that influence entrepreneurial learning, as well as by an understanding of the psychoanalytic and psychotherapeutic mechanisms of learning and change that characterize unaffiliated coaching groups. The study explored the experience of group coaching as a setting for entrepreneurial learning and change. The research question was "given the impact of social processes on learning and identity, what does it mean to entrepreneurs to navigate their learning-related challenges in the context of a coaching group?" An exploration of the study's methods and findings follows.

Methods

This qualitative study used narrative methods of inquiry and analysis. Narrative research explores the stories or storied descriptions of events that take place in the lives of individuals (Pinnegar & Daynes, 2007). Narrative researchers seek to gather rich, storied descriptions of lived experience. They place attention on the sequence and consequences of human activity, and on the context(s) surrounding the production of storied data (Riessman, 2008). Narrative studies can lead to general knowledge about a phenomenon or to knowledge of the uniqueness of specific situations. Where research on entrepreneurship is concerned, recent works have established the validity and appropriateness of a narrative approach for developing new insights into the nature of entrepreneurship and the lived experiences of entrepreneurs (Rae, 2000; Watson, 2009).

Selection of Participants

Recruitment for the study involved finding and contacting coaches who provide group coaching for entrepreneurs, ensuring their coaching programs and program participants met the criteria for inclusion, and then inviting individual group members to participate in the study. Nine participants met the criteria for inclusion and chose to participate in the study. Two participated in a pilot study and seven in the main study. Data from one of the pilot interviews were later added to the main study, bringing the total number of participants in the main study to eight (five female and three male). Six participants in the main study were referrals from two different groups led by the same coach. The other two were each referred by different coaches and participated in separate group coaching programs.

Data Collection

Data collection took place via one-on-one, semi-structured narrative interviews with each participant. Six interviews were conducted face-to-face, and three (including two pilot interviews) were conducted via Zoom web conference (audio only). The interviews ranged from 60-90 minutes in length. The interview protocol for this study was designed according to Kvale's (2007) recommendations for conducting semi-structured life-world interviews, and Chase's (2003) advice on interview questions in narrative research.

Analysis

The data were interpreted using separate and sequential narrative/ performative and thematic analytical methods (Braun & Clarke,

2006; Polkinghorne, 1995; Riessman, 2008) to produce an in-depth, multi-dimensional understanding of the data. The goal of a narrative/ performative analysis is to configure the data elements into an over-arching and emergent higher-order plot or explanatory story of each interview. This involved reviewing the interview transcripts noting speech elements and their use, "scenes" portraying unfolding action and its results, and relevant contextual information. The emergent plot of each interview is then mapped, developing rich explanatory stories supported by quotes and specific examples from the data. Such an analysis brings to the surface "truths unique in their particularity" and grounded in human experience (Josselson & Lieblich, 2003).

In contrast, the product of thematic analysis is a set of common elements of categories that stretch across multiple stories, participants, and events (Riessman, 2003, 2008). Braun and Clarke's (2006) method involved coding the transcript data and searching for themes; then reviewing, defining, and naming the themes and weaving them together to create an overall story of the analysis.

Findings

The study revealed three types of phenomena that participants either directly associated with their group coaching experiences or that they illustrated through their stored accounts. The first includes the background conditions or characteristics that participants associated with their coaching groups and what happens in them. The second includes a range of "process moves" reflected in participants' stories of their personally meaningful or defining moments in group coaching. The third is comprised of the discursive moves or actions performed within the relational context of the interview itself that contributed to participants' meaning-making processes. This chapter focuses exclusively on the background conditions. A separate publication, Ostrowski (2019), focuses exclusively on the process moves.

Five common conditions or characteristics of the coaching group and its activities formed a backdrop for group members' memorable experiences, setting the stage for meaningful learning and change (see figure 1). These background conditions fell broadly into two categories: characteristics of the social environment of the group and characteristics of the social processes at work in the group.

Figure 1.
Five Characteristics of Effective Coaching Groups

© 2020 Erek Ostrowski, Used with Permission, Original Artwork.

Social Environment

Meaningful experiences in group coaching rest importantly on the other people in the room. The stories that participants told bring to light two interrelated aspects of the group social environment: cohesiveness and commonality. Group cohesiveness, as defined by Yalom and Leszcz (2005), refers to the "groupness" or "attractiveness of a group for its members" (pp. 54-55). I use the term here to represent the spirit of belonging and togetherness that participants described through their stories about their coaching groups. I use the term "commonality" here to refer to the sense that one's experience is shared and/or deeply understood by others; in other words, the sense that one is not alone in her/his experience.

Cohesiveness. Entrepreneurs form close relationships with their peers in the group. Where cohesiveness is concerned, most participants described their groups in terms of the warm and caring relationships they developed with other group members, their fondness for the group itself, and their sense of belonging. Several participants described their peers in the group as friends or close friends despite never having met before joining their groups.

One participant indicated that her coaching group had become an enduring resource for friendship and caring relationships in her life, both business and personal in nature:

> P1: I didn't know the other members of the group at first. But, um, no, now... we're like a really close-knit group... I mean, it's a group of people that I think you develop relationships with that are looking out for you personally and for your business.

Another participant was surprised to find himself valuing a feeling of belonging more than the structure of accountability he had initially sought through group coaching:

> P2: The longer I would go and we would have interaction, it became comfortable. And when I became comfortable then, yeah... this is our group, you know? I belong, we belong, you know, all that.

Commonality. Meaningful bonds between group members emerge through shared experience. Several participants made reference to feeling as though others in the group understood and could relate to their entrepreneurial experiences. In particular, they noted feeling that their peers share similar goals and challenges, feeling a "common bond" with their peers in the group, and feeling as though they are not alone. One participant talked about her struggles with other business-related group situations and how she found her coaching group to be a very different type of experience:

> P3: Networking, that's very difficult for me... but the group coaching, because we were in similar situations and had likeminded goals and objectives... and we're experiencing the same kinds of challenges... that didn't feel like it was a networking group. It didn't feel like I was out there selling myself. It felt like I was there to support someone who was going through something difficult and giving the expertise that I had... and I was getting that in return.

Several participants shared an initial skepticism or resistance to their groups that they eventually overcame. One admitted that his reluctance stemmed from his concern that being in a group meant less time devoted to his own challenges, and hence less value overall. Here he explains his shifting view:

> P5: Basically you're... involving yourself in a partnership, and... there's a sense of community when you start sharing your... story with other people, and I was super surprised at all the common themes. I really shifted gears... not coming from the perspective so much of, "What am I going to get out of this? How much can I get out in the shortest amount of time?" ...but embracing the fact that... you're in an environment where the whole point is to share your vulnerabilities.

He went on to explain that by being honest about his shortcomings and listening to others admit their own, he ultimately felt less alone and less embarrasses about the challenges he was experiencing.

Social Processes

Meaningful experiences in group coaching arise out of specific types of social interaction between group members. Throughout the interviews, participants frequently described or made reference to three types of social processes at work in their coaching groups: *social support, exchange,* and *accountability.* In the context of their stories, social support refers to acts of personal and/or emotional support and encouragement. Some participants talked about receiving this type of support, while others talked about providing it. The term *exchange* is used here to describe an interchange of ideas, information, and feedback between group members. *Accountability* refers to a process whereby group members hold one another to their word for the actions and/or goals to which they commit.

Social support. Entrepreneurs benefit greatly from receiving emotional support and encouragement from their peers. Overwhelmingly, participants described their coaching groups not only as a source of business knowledge and expertise, but also as a source of personal and/or emotional support and encouragement. They spoke of this type of support as a meaningful and potent aspect of their group experiences—whether they were giving or receiving it, and regardless of whether the focus of the support was business-related or personal in nature. This aspect of the groups prompted some comparisons to therapy:

> P4: Personal stuff comes into it too. Like... one of the other people in our group... his spouse, you know, has a lot of issues with his entrepreneurial side... it's more than just your business, it's like, "Business is affecting my family, my spouse. You know, how am I gonna deal with this?" And so sometimes it turns into more like therapy in a way.

> P1: The group has been very supportive and—and it's just nice to have that outlet... it gives you a place to unload some of your baggage but also... to reload some support and, you know, know that there are people out there that care.

Another participant remarked that he liked the fact that his group prioritized its members' most pressing needs above any planned agenda. He described a session in which his group bypassed their planned agenda in order to support a group member who was going through a difficult time.

For participants in this study, social support also encompasses encouraging and validating group members' ideas and choices. One participant described how her group encouraged and supported her when she decided to start her tech business:

P6: So I took it to my group and I said, "I think I'm gonna try this. I don't know how, I don't—I can't develop software, I need resources, I've never done this before. This is completely out of my element. I know how to market it, but I don't really know the foundations of building it. And I've got the go-ahead at home." They were like, "That is awesome. Totally think you should do that. That would be great." So supportive.

Exchange. A vibrant interchange of ideas, information, and feedback functions as an engine of learning and change for group members. Several participants described or told stories about meaningful interactions of this nature. These encounters were seen as a central component of the groups' regular and ongoing activities. Participants noted the reciprocal nature of exchange in their groups (receiving and giving), and the fact that it can occur either during or outside of group coaching sessions.

In one such example, a participant talked about getting an idea to create a guidebook on employee turnover to help clients of her HR consultancy cope with their staffing challenges. The idea came from another group member who had created a guidebook for parents of troubled children who were clients of her therapy practice. In addition to exchanging concrete ideas for generating business and managing relationships with customers and staff, several participants described exchanging information and advice with other group members. For example, a participant spoke about learning from other group members how to use social media to market her business after her recent move to a new state.

Some of the participants specifically emphasized the reciprocal nature of exchange in their groups. They indicated that they value the opportunity to provide input into other people's challenges:

> P6: I also loved giving input. Who doesn't like to give their opinion? I love to give my opinion! [laughs] Just give me an invitation! So... we'd sit around the table and they'd be like, "Oh, I'm really struggling, I'm trying to do this," —it's an opportunity to motivate people, it's an opportunity to have input into a different area of life that maybe you've never dabbled in before.

Finally, the processes involved in exchange include giving and receiving feedback to and from other group members. This feedback can be either affirming or challenging in nature. Feedback can function as a sounding board for group members' ideas and/or as a mirror for their behaviors and choices. In addition, group feedback sometimes functions as an interruption or a challenge to modes of thinking and/or action that group members consider to be unproductive or ineffective. For example, a group member recalled an incident that pushed her to challenge a group member's relationship with a business partner:

> P4: One woman just joined our group and she has a... business partner. And they're already having issues, like, three months into their partnership. And, you know, it's the kind of place where you can say, "This is alarming. Like, this might be an indicator that you need to cut ties with this woman and do this." And I expect the same from them. And you need that. I mean, sometimes you just need somebody to call you out.

Accountability. Entrepreneurs crave accountability and find this through group coaching. Accountability refers to a process whereby group members hold one another to their word for the actions and/or goals they commit to. Participants repeatedly mentioned accountability as an important function of their groups and a useful source of motivation. In the excerpt below, a participant talked about the structures his group uses to set and manage group members' goals and commitments:

> P7: Every time we meet... there are forms we get that challenge us to reflect on things or to do homework for the next time... you know... definite steps. Quarterly we look at where are..., what have we accomplished, are we taking steps to truly... grow... and the group holds you accountable to that.

Interestingly, the social expectation of accountability was held collectively by all group members, not by the coach alone. This carried implications not only for action, but also for identity negotiation. Some participants described their concerns about how they would be perceived by their peers if they failed to take the actions they had promised. Thus, they found themselves motivated to take actions they wouldn't otherwise take in order to maintain their social standing in the group:

> P1: I feel like it helps, having these other people that are watching me and paying attention to whether or not I'm reaching my goals... How does that make me look if I'm not reaching them? How... [are my peers] going to talk about me if I'm not getting somewhere towards my goals? You know... if they keep seeing me being lazy or failing or whatever the case may be, how is that fair?

No Guarantees

Even when the background conditions are present, group members do not always learn or change in ways they find meaningful. Participants' stories suggest a twofold relationship between the presence of the background conditions and the experience of meaningful learning and change. First, individual member perceptions of background conditions appear to influence whether they experience opportunities for learning and change. Group members who do not experience these conditions (even if others in the group do) are unlikely to experience meaningful learning or change as a result of their participation. Such was the case for one participant who described her coaching group as lacking the common bond of friendship and the relevant information that had made another group she belonged to a more meaningful source of learning and change.

Second, the presence of the background conditions doesn't guarantee results. Even for a group member who experiences these conditions, learning and change may not take place. Despite the meaningful sense of belonging that P2 experienced with his group, he struggled to recall any specific experiences which resulted in learning or change. These counter narratives suggest that additional factors (e.g., the group member's level of self-awareness, the degree of relevance of peers' experiences and feedback, etc.) may influence whether an individual learns from her or his experiences in group coaching. The conditions appear to set the stage, but do not automatically precipitate learning and change.

Discussion

The study contributes to an understanding of where or under what conditions EL unfolds in a group coaching context. It revealed that certain characteristics of the social environment of the group and the social processes at work in the group create an environment that supports learning and change. These background conditions are consistent with theory shown in the group psychotherapy literature

(Foulkes, 1948, 1986; Yalom & Leszcz, 2005) and adapted by group coaching scholars (Kets de Vries, 2011, 2014; Thornton, 2010). This study helps fortify these important connections by explicitly linking group coaching experience with relevant theory and research from group psychotherapy.

Cohesiveness and Commonality

Participants highlighted the roles of *cohesiveness* and *commonality* in shaping their meaningful experiences that led to learning. For members of a cohesive group, the group itself offers a source of warmth, comfort, and belonging which are fundamentally important to personal growth (Yalom & Leszcz, 2005). Fusco, O'Riordan, and Palmer (2015), who studied group coaching for senior organizational leaders, referred to group cohesion as "the bedrock upon which all further individual and group work was to take place" (p. 137). The current study suggests that group cohesiveness can be a catalyst for EL also.

Past EL research has shown that social bonding and friendship play a key role in supporting social learning among students of entrepreneurship (Preedy & Jones, 2017); and that long-term, stable peer groups help members overcome their competitive mentalities and form strong relationships that foster information sharing (Zhang & Hamilton, 2009). The close relationships that form through group work promote group social processes that may serve as a foundation for individual learning (Preedy & Jones, 2017). This study confirms these findings and suggests that such relationships bridge the divide between business and personal support. The study also shows that these caring relationships can develop and support learning despite group members' initial reluctance or skepticism about joining a peer group.

Commonality, meanwhile, closely resembles the group psycho-therapeutic factor of universality (Yalom & Leszcz, 2005). Past research has shown that peer learning groups can help entrepreneurs overcome barriers to learning by reducing their isolation. This happens precisely because entrepreneurs share the same types of challenges and can relate to one another's experiences (Kuhn, Galloway, & Collins-Williams, 2016; Zhang & Hamilton, 2009). Likewise, participants in group therapy often benefit from meeting people with similar problems, comparing their difficulties with others, and realizing that their own cases are not as extreme as they had imagined (Danino & Shechtman, 2012). Scamardo and Harnden (2007) found that the experience of universality helped resolve group members' isolation in a managerial context and temper their unrealistic self-expectations. The present study supports these findings and suggests that the rich personal connections group members form with one another over time contribute to a sense of commonality or a common bond.

Social Support and Exchange

The conditions of social support and exchange closely resemble the psychotherapeutic mechanisms of holding (Winnicott, 1971) and exchange (Foulkes, 1948, 1986). Thornton (2010) argued that these two principles constitute the basis for effective learning in both dyadic and group coaching. Sufficient levels of safety and trust (holding) allow group members to engage openly with difference and the unknown (exchange). In groups however, holding and exchange become even more complex. An effective group coach must create a holding environment large enough for multiple people, must be able to process difficult feelings that arise for group members, and must create sufficient safety for group members to engage in the risks associated with learning. At a group level, exchange is characterized by a multiplicity of perspectives and assumptions, requiring a "continuous iterative process" (p. 40) of absorbing new information and its implications.

Participants in this study explained that the emotional support and encouragement they received from their groups allowed them to view group coaching as a resource for support and helpful information, rather than as an evaluative, critical, or competitive environment. This safe and encouraging atmosphere led to a reciprocal interchange of ideas, information, and feedback (exchange) between group members.

Accountability

The study showed that accountability in group coaching is held collectively by group members and may hold implications for identity management. Identity work, according to Sveningsson and Alvesson (2003), involves "forming, repairing, maintaining, strengthening or revising the constructions" that result in a coherent and distinctive sense of self (p. 1165). For some study participants, taking action or making progress was a way of maintaining their personal standing in the group and managing their self-presentation among group members. When individuals in a group vicariously observe another group member behaving inconsistently (not doing what they said they would, etc.), the resulting conflict can be a source of dissonance within the group (Norton, Monin, Cooper, & Hogg, 2003). Cognitive dissonance, resulting from a mismatch between speech and action, can be a powerful motivator for change in individuals (Festinger, 1957).

Further Research

Coaching researchers have only recently begun to explore the possibilities of group coaching, so the opportunities for future research in this area are vast. More research is needed, for example, in order to find out (a) how coaches are already using work with groups to enhance their practices, (b) how members of these groups experience their participation and its impact, and (c) what mechanisms of learning and change (including and/or beyond those explored in this study) help shape group members' experiences.

In particular, future research should aim to cultivate a more complete understanding of coaching in unaffiliated group settings, given the potential of this modality for fostering learning and change. For example, what populations, situations, or specific problem constellations stand to benefit most from this type of intervention? In what ways do they benefit (or not)? Also, what approaches, techniques, and/or theoretical perspectives are most relevant and important to practice in this setting? How, if at all, do these differ from coaching in organizations, work teams, or dyadic settings?

Implications for Practice

A psychological perspective was highly useful for interpreting and understanding participants' group coaching experiences. This suggests that coaches who wish to practice in the group domain would do well to familiarize themselves with the literatures on group counseling and group psychotherapy. Group counseling also deals with the group as a context for learning and problem-solving. Unlike most group psychotherapy, counseling groups tend to focus on conscious problems and short-term issues rather than severe psychological problems (Corey, Corey, & Corey, 2010). However, as discussed above, the group psychotherapy knowledge base also includes a rich and illuminating array of resources for learning to work in unaffiliated group settings. These include Yalom and Leszcz' (2005) ideas on group psychotherapeutic factors, and Winnicott's (1971) notion of the holding environment. Coaching educators and others involved in coach training and education should also consider incorporating these resources into their curriculum designs where group coaching is concerned.

About the Author

Erek J. Ostrowski, PhD, PCC is a leadership and business coach, coach educator, and the founder of Verve Coaching. He is recognized for his innovative work advancing group coaching knowledge and practice in entrepreneurship and management education. His study interests include entrepreneurial learning, identity development, group coaching, and narrative theory. In his professional practice, he partners with entrepreneurs and executives to help them become skillful, impactful leaders in the organizations and communities they serve. He is also an adjunct instructor at the University of Pennsylvania and at the Grenon School of Business at Assumption College. Erek received his PhD in Organizational Development and Change from Fielding Graduate University. He also holds a Graduate Certificate in Evidence-Based Coaching and a Master of the Arts in Human and Organizational Systems from Fielding. He is a credentialed coach with the International Coach Federation (ICF) and the Center for Credentialing and Education (CCE). He is a member of the Institute of Coaching (IOC) at Harvard/McLean Hospital and a board member of the Graduate School Alliance for Education in Coaching. In 2017, he was awarded a Harnisch Fellowship from the Institute of Coaching for his original research on navigating entrepreneurial challenges through group coaching.

References

Alstete, J. W. (2008). Aspects of entrepreneurial success. *Journal of Small Business and Enterprise Development,* 15(3), 584-594. doi:10.1108/14626000810892364

Boyd, D. P., & Gumpert, D. E. (1983). Coping with entrepreneurial stress. *Harvard Business Review,* 61(2), 44-64.

Braun, V., & Clarke, V. (2006). Using thematic analysis in psychology. *Qualitative Research in Psychology,* 3(2), 77-101.

Brett, V., Mullally, M., O'Gorman, B., & Fuller-Love, N. (2012). The role of action research in the development of learning networks for entrepreneurs. *Action Learning: Research and Practice,* 9(2), 125-143. doi:10.1080/14767333.2012 .685699

Britton, J. J. (2013). *From one to many: Best practices for team and group coaching.* Somerset, NJ: John Wiley & Sons.

Brown, S. W., & Grant, A. M. (2010). From GROW to GROUP: Theoretical issues and a practical model for group coaching in organisations. *Coaching: An International Journal of Theory, Research and Practice,* 3(1), 30-45.

Chase, S. E. (2003). Learning to listen: Narrative principles in a qualitative research methods course. In R. Josselson, A. Lieblich, & D. P. McAdams (Eds.), *Up close and personal: The teaching and learning of narrative research* (pp. 79-99). Washington, DC: American Psychological Association.

Cockerham, G. (2011). *Group coaching: A comprehensive blueprint.* Bloomington, IN: iUniverse.

Cope, J. (2003). Entrepreneurial learning and critical reflection: Discontinuous events as triggers for 'higher-level' learning. *Management Learning,* 34(4), 429-449.

Cope, J. (2005). Toward a dynamic learning perspective of entrepreneurship. *Entrepreneurship: Theory & Practice,* 29(4), 373-397.

Corey, M. S., Corey, G., & Corey, C. (2010). *Groups: Process and practice* (8th ed.). Belmont, CA: Brooks/Cole.

Danino, M., & Shechtman, Z. (2012). Superiority of group counseling to individual coaching for parents of children with learning disabilities. *Psychotherapy Research,* 22(5), 592-603. Retrieved from http://www.ncbi.nlm.nih.gov/pubmed/22694319

Deakins, D., & Freel, M. (1998). Entrepreneurial learning and the growth process in SMEs. *The Learning Organization,* 5(3), 144-155. doi:10.1108/09696479810223428

Deakins, D., & Freel, M. (2012). *Entrepreneurship and small firms* (6th ed.). Maidenhead, UK: McGraw-Hill.

Down, S., & Warren, L. (2008). Constructing narratives of enterprise: Clichés and entrepreneurial self-identity. *International Journal of Entrepreneurial Behavior & Research,* 14(1), 4-23. doi:10.1108/13552550810852802

Festinger, L. (1957). *A theory of cognitive dissonance.* Evanston, Ill.: Row.

Florén, H. (2003). Collaborative approaches to management learning in small firms. *Journal of Workplace Learning,* 15(5), 203-216.

Foulkes, S. H. (1948). Introduction to group analytic psychotherapy. In S. L. Garfield & A. E. Bergin (Eds.), *Handbook of psychotherapy and behaviour change* (3rd ed.). New York, NY: Wiley.

Foulkes, S. H. (1986). *Group analytic psychotherapy: Method and principles.* London, UK: Karnac Books.

Fusco, T., O'Riordan, S., & Palmer, S. (2015). Authentic leaders are... conscious, competent, confident, and congruent: A grounded theory of group coaching authentic leadership development. *International Coaching Psychology Review,* 10(2), 131-148.

Gumpert, D. E., & Boyd, D. P. (1984). The loneliness of the small-business owner. *Harvard Business Review,* 62(6), 18-24.

Hamilton, E. (2014). Entrepreneurial narrative identity and gender: A double epistemological shift. *Journal of Small Business Management,* 52(4), 703-712. doi:10.1111/jsbm.12127

Higgins, D., & Aspinall, C. (2011). Learning to learn: A case for developing small firm owner/managers. *Journal of Small Business and Enterprise Development,* 18(1), 43-57. doi:10.1108/14626001111106424

Holmes, S. E., & Kivlighan, D. M. (2000). Comparison of therapeutic factors in group and individual treatment processes. *Journal of Counseling Psychology,* 47(4), 478-484. doi:10.1037/W022-OI67.47.4.478

Josselson, R., & Lieblich, A. (2003). A framework for narrative research proposals in psychology. In R. Josselson, A. Lieblich, & D. P. McAdams (Eds.), *Up close and personal: The teaching and learning of narrative research* (pp. 259-274). Washington, DC: American Psychological Association.

Kets de Vries, M. F. R. (2011). *The hedgehog effect: The secrets of building high performance teams.* San Francisco, CA: Jossey-Bass.

Kets de Vries, M. F. R. (2014). The group coaching conundrum. *International Journal of Evidence Based Coaching and Mentoring,* 12(1), 79-91.

Kivlighan, D. M. (2011). Individual and group perceptions of therapeutic factors and session evaluation: An actor–partner interdependence analysis. *Group Dynamics: Theory, Research, and Practice,* 15(2), 147-160.

Kuhn, K. M., Galloway, T. L., & Collins-Williams, M. (2016). Near, far, and online: Small business owners' advice-seeking from peers. *Journal of Small Business and Enterprise Development,* 23(1), 189-206. doi:10.1108/jsbed-03-2015-0037

Kvale, S. (2007). *Doing interviews.* Los Angeles, CA: Sage.

Norton, M. I., Monin, B., Cooper, J., & Hogg, M. A. (2003). Vicarious dissonance: Attitude change from the inconsistency of others. *Journal of Personality and Social Psychology,* 85(1), 47-62. doi:10.1037/0022-3514.85.1.47

O'Connor, S., & Cavanagh, M. (2017). Group and team coaching. In T. Bachkirova, G. Spence, & D. Drake (Eds.), *The Sage handbook of coaching.* Thousand Oaks, CA: SAGE Publications.

Ostrowski, E. J. (2018). *Coming in from the cold: The experience of group coaching as a setting for entrepreneurial learning and change.* (Doctoral dissertation). Retrieved from ProQuest Dissertations and Theses database. (UMI No. 10746488)

Ostrowski, E. J. (2019). Using group coaching to foster reflection and learning in an MBA classroom. *Philosophy of Coaching: An International Journal,* 4(2), 53-74.

Pinnegar, S., & Daynes, J. G. (2007). Locating narrative inquiry historically. In D. J. Clandinin (Ed.), *Handbook of narrative inquiry: Mapping a methodology.* Thousand Oaks, CA: Sage Publications.

Polkinghorne, D. E. (1995). Narrative configuration in qualitative analysis. *International Journal of Qualitative Studies in Education*, 8(1), 5-23. Retrieved from http://dx.doi.org/10.1080/0951839950080103

Preedy, S., & Jones, P. (2017). Student-led enterprise groups and entrepreneurial learning. *Industry and Higher Education*, 31(2), 101-112. doi:10.1177/0950422216689349

Rae, D. (2000). Understanding entrepreneurial learning: A question of how? *International Journal of Entrepreneurial Behavior & Research*, 6(3), 145-159. doi:10.1108/13552550010346497

Riessman, C. K. (2003). Narrative analysis. In M. S. Lewis-Beck, A. Bryman, & T. Futing Liao (Eds.), *The Sage encyclopedia of social science research methods* (Vol. 1-3). Thousand Oaks, CA: Sage Publications.

Riessman, C. K. (2008). *Narrative methods for the human sciences*. Los Angeles, CA: Sage Publications.

Scamardo, M., & Harnden, S. C. (2007). A manager coaching group model. *Journal of Workplace Behavioral Health*, 22(2-3), 127-143.

Stelter, R., Nielsen, G., & Wikman, J. M. (2011). Narrative-collaborative group coaching develops social capital – a randomised control trial and further implications of the social impact of the intervention. *Coaching: An International Journal of Theory, Research and Practice*, 4(2), 123-137.

Sveningsson, S., & Alvesson, M. (2003). Managing managerial identities: Organizational fragmentation, discourse and identity struggle. *Human Relations*, 56(10), 1163-1193.

Thornton, C. (2010). *Group and team coaching: The essential guide*. New York, NY: Routledge.

Van Dyke, P. (2012). *Virtual group coaching: The experience of business professionals in the process*. (Doctoral dissertation). Retrieved from ProQuest Dissertations and Theses database. (UMI No. 3546895)

Wang, C. L., & Chugh, H. (2014). Entrepreneurial learning: Past research and future challenges. *International Journal of Management Reviews*, 16(1), 24-61. doi:10.1111/ijmr.12007

Watson, T. J. (2009). Entrepreneurial action, identity work and the use of multiple discursive resources: The case of a rapidly changing family business. *International Small Business Journal*, 27(3), 251-274.

Whitley, S. (2013). Group coaching as support for changing lifestyle for those diagnosed with a long-term condition. *International Journal of Evidence Based Coaching and Mentoring* (Special Issue 7), 82-89.

Winnicott, D. W. (1971). Playing and reality. London, UK: Penguin.

Yalom, I. D., & Leszcz, M. (2005). *The theory and practice of group psychotherapy* (5th ed.). New York, NY: Basic Books.

Zhang, J., & Hamilton, E. (2009). A process model of small business owner-managers' learning in peer networks. *Education + Training*, 51(8/9), 607-623.

CHAPTER 13

THE LEADERSHIP COACH AS CATALYST OF CULTURAL TRANSFORMATION

Kristin E. Robertson, M.A., M.M., PCC
CEO, Brio Leadership

Abstract

Leaders are the primary shapers of culture, either to the positive or the negative (Sathe & Davidson, 2000; Bolman & Deal, 2003; Martin, 2007; Schein, 2010; Schroeder, 2010). Because leadership coaches work directly with executives and managers to improve their performance, leadership coaches can view themselves as catalysts for transforming organizational culture. It is important for coaches to understand that culture represents the values, underlying beliefs and behavioral norms of the organization (Cooke & Szumal, 1993), or the "the way we do things around here" (Deal & Kennedy, 2000, p. 4). Knowing that, coaches should explore culture-specific items with their clients, including personal and organizational values, behavioral norms of the organization and how to model new, more positive behaviors that can shape the culture or sub-culture.

Keywords: Company culture, organizational culture, leadership development, leadership coaching, executive coaching, company culture transformation, organizational culture transformation, company culture shaping, organizational culture shaping, organizational culture catalyst, company culture catalyst

Statement of Problem

The importance of leadership coaching is supported in the

literature, that confirms the concept that leaders are integral to shaping the organization's culture. One of the most powerful ways to transform an organization's culture is to change the way leaders lead, ensuring they demonstrate behaviors consistent with the values and purpose of the organization (Schein, 2010). The leader's culture-shaping tools include what they pay attention to, what they reward and punish, how they set the standards of conduct with their own actions, how they allocate resources, how they react in times of crisis, and hiring and firing employees according to their ability to uphold the cultural norms (Trice and Beyer, 1993; Schein, 2010). In designing culture transformation initiatives, organizational development experts would be wise to include leadership training and coaching programs with the goal of enacting behavioral change in the executive suite. The coaching component can be done with a combination of team coaching (especially for the C-Suite), group and individual coaching, all of which can be a primary intervention in cultural transformation initiatives. Coaches themselves must be aware of their role in cultural change and of the transformation tools available to their clients. Coaches can pay attention to broadening the capacities of their clients to enact cultural transformation by supporting them in increasing self-awareness, active listening capabilities and leadership savvy.

Argumentation of the Findings
What is culture?

Culture is a popular term in current management literature. Culture can be defined as the underlying values and deeply seated beliefs of an organization, and the behavioral norms members must adopt to fit in (Cooke & Rousseau, 1988). Schein (2010, p. 18) offers a lengthier definition of culture: "a pattern of shared basic assumptions shared by a group as it solved its problems of external adaptation and internal integration, which has worked well enough to be considered valid and, therefore, to be taught to new members as the way to perceive, think and feel in relation to those problems". More simply, organizational

279

culture can be referred to as "the way we do things around here" (Deal &Kennedy, 2000, p. 175).

With the popularization of culture, a problem has emerged in that "everything has become culture" (Kuppler & Cooke, 2016). Culture must be differentiated from and not confused with organizational climate, which is the "shared perceptions and attitudes of the members of the organization" (Kuppler & Cooke, 2016) and "how people feel about working at the company" (Golman, Boyatzis and McKee, 2002). Some instruments on the market today that claim to be culture indicators are climate indicators; indeed, every engagement or employee satisfaction survey is a measure of climate, not culture (Cooke & Szumal, 1993; Denison, 1996). Climate is vitally important in identifying corrective actions that may eventually result in culture transformation. However, culture (underlying assumptions, beliefs, values and behavioral norms) is enduring, hard to change and difficult to measure whereas climate (employee perceptions, emotions and attitudes) is transitory, easily changed and measurable.

Does culture make a difference?

One reason that culture has become a popular subject is that several longitudinal studies show that positive, performance-enhancing cultures contribute to financial success (Sisodia, Sheet & Wolfe., 2014; J. Collins, 2001; Kotter & Heskett, 1992; Mackey & Sisodia, 2014; Rhoades, Covey, & Shepherdson, 2011). In for-profit business, profitability and shareholder value are the ultimate goals of a company and must be the expected results of initiatives that executives will fund. Sisodia et al (2014) report that the public companies on their firms of endearment list returned "1,026 percent for investors over the 10 years ending June 30, 2006, compared to 122 percent for the S&P500; that's more than a 8-to-1 ratio!" (p. 16). Firms of endearment are companies who actively align all stakeholders' interests and consider corporate culture their most important asset (pp.8-11). Kotter & Heskett (1992) conducted an 11-year study and found that high-performance companies with cultures that focus on all key constituencies (customers, stockholders and employees) outperformed their competition by large margins (p. 11).

The case for leadership coaching as a cultural catalyst

Researchers have identified actions that can shape organizational culture. Here are six commonly agreed-upon ways to transform a culture (Trice and Beyer, 1993; Schein, 2010):

1. What leaders pay attention to and control
2. Role modeling & teaching positive behavioral norms
3. Exemplifying emotional maturity and teamwork in a crisis situation
4. Hiring and firing, both of which signal the kind of values and behaviors that are tolerated by the organization
5. Allocating resources such as money, headcount and tools
6. Creating reward and punishment systems, including the compensation structure

Cooke (as cited in Jones et al, 2011, p. 126) summarizes and condenses Schein's change modalities into two: change the way the leaders lead and change the compensation & rewards programs. Deal and Kennedy (2000, p. 175), in recommending how to change culture, includes the exhortations to managers to "make transition rituals" and "provide transition training in new and behavior patterns."

Leadership coaches can change culture, one conversation at a time, by helping leaders redefine their values and modify their behaviors, knowing that they set the example for their team members. Coaching can provide a sounding board for leaders to think through their culture-shaping actions according to Schein's (2010) six ways to transform culture (see above). For example, the leadership coach can inquire into what clients pays attention to, how they react in times of crisis, what criteria they use to hire and fire and how they reward and punish employees.

Building a Coaching Culture

The International Coach Federation, in partnership with Human Capital Institute, (2018) found that if a company can say yes to five of the following six factors, it is sixty-one percent more likely to have improved talent outcomes (like engagement surveys and internal promotions) AND improved business outcomes (like shareholder value, profitability and customer satisfaction):

1. Employees value coaching
2. Senior executives value coaching
3. Leaders and internal coaches receive accredited coach-specific training.
4. The organization includes internal coaches, external coaches and managers/leaders using coaching skills
5. Coaching is a line item in the budget
6. All employees have equal access to coaching, either internal or external

Coaching is a Culture-Shaping Intervention

As coaches, we know intuitively that cultures are shaped by the work we do with leaders. Fortunately, the literature supports our gut instincts. For example, Kolodziejczak (2015, p. 329) found that the "use of coaching in organizational management can gradually model or change the organizational culture." This is because coaching changes behaviors, increases creativity and help leaders make plans and take action (Kolodziejczak, 2015). Cultural change is enacted over time rather than with a revolutionary or rapid transformation. Rock and Donde state that coaching can shift the culture "by transforming the quality of every conversation," "by improving retention and engagement" and by enabling "personal and organizational performance change" (2008, p. 2). Rock and Donde identify the purpose of coaching as improving performance, and their research shows that improving a leader's performance creates positive change that ripples through the organization.

Research has shown that it is not sufficient to have only a charismatic and highly effective leader at the top to build a positive and performance-enhancing culture; rather successful organizations are "the product of distributive, collective and complementary leadership" (Kets de Vries, 2007, p. 5). This supports the ICF/HCI findings, mentioned above (2018), that creating a coaching culture in which all team members have access to coaching is key to cultural transformation and business success. Kets de Vries (2007, p. 5) continues: "Leadership coaching can be a catalyst for the creation of a new cultural environment."

In a professional service firm, Bianco-Mathis and Schurgin (2014) found that coaching improved "engagement, career development, interpersonal interactions, performance, people decisions, and client service." While some of these results are climate measures, they nonetheless contribute to long term culture transformation and behavioral change.

How coaches help clients navigate and shape the organizational culture

The essence of coaching is in asking questions, rather than advising or telling. ICF cites "powerful questions" as one of eleven core competencies for credentialed coaches (International Coach Federation, 2019), demonstrating the importance of asking questions to inspire independent thinking on the part of clients. Asking questions has been proven to be more effective in behavioral change than giving advice (Rock, 2006).

Leaders need help in both navigating the prevailing culture to advance agendas that aid the organization (DeLuca, 2002, p. 49) and to shape the culture, or at least the sub-culture of that leader's team. Coaches need to keep in mind these needs of their clients.

Following are some questions coaches might use to examine and shape the culture their clients are operating in:

1. What values do you wish to hold dear in your work and private life?

As a coach, I provide clients with a values identification

exercise to complete before our first meeting. A copy of this exercise is included in Appendix A. It is important that clients identify their personal or true self values as opposed to the values that they must adopt to conform to the organization's norms. This helps the client accurately assess their fit with the organization's culture. In addition, research has shown that employee's understanding of their own value system produces higher levels of engagement than clarity of the organization's values (Kouzes & Posner, 2017). Therefore, it is incumbent on the leadership coach to clarify personal values with their clients and help them find alignment (or not) with the operational values of the company.

2. In examining the values of your company, how closely do you see leaders around you align with them?

There is a difference between espoused values and operational values, the values that are put into action. Even Enron, the failed energy company, had espoused values that an employee could be proud of. Those values were communication, respect, integrity and excellence (Lencioni, 2002). Yet, this company declared bankruptcy after a massive account fraud scheme was revealed (Enron Fast Facts, 2019) – a breach of integrity to be sure. How comfortable is your client with the integrity of their colleagues' actions?

3. What actions can you start, stop or continue to align your behaviors with your values?

It's great to identify your values, and it's even better to spend time examining how to align your actions with values. "Credibility is the foundation of leadership," as Kouzes and Posner (2017) state. In other words, walk your talk and align actions with your values. This alignment makes your client a believable leader.

4. When you first came to the company, what unwritten rules about acceptable behavior did you observe? What actions or words could draw negative attention to yourself?

Explain that cultures are learned by imitating the behavior of those you work with, and that a leader's behavior and mood have an outsized influence on the group (Goleman, Boyatzis, & McKee, 2013). In one company, an unwritten rule is that no one can leave for the day until the boss does. In another company, a rule is that it is not OK for women executives to cry. These are the unwritten rules that you violate at your peril. How aware are your clients of these behavioral norms and expectations? How can they adapt their behavior to them?

5. During your tenure at this organization, describe a time that you were deeply excited, passionate or proud of what you were doing? How can you describe the essence of that experience?

The flavor of this question is taken from Appreciative Inquiry (Cooperrider & Whitney, 1999), the school of thought that posits that change comes about easiest and best through building on strengths. Asking the client to remember a time when they felt deeply engaged and positive about their work is affirming both to the client and the organizational culture. Several follow-on lines of inquiry are possible, such as asking: 1) How often have you achieved that state recently; 2) What actions can you take to achieve that state more frequently; 3) How can you create the right environment so your team members can feel excited, passionate or proud?

6. If you had a magic wand and could change something about your organization's culture overnight, what would that be?

Again, this is a question inspired by Appreciative Inquiry (Cooperrider & Whitney, 1999), which helps the coach and client identify what aspects of the culture are most worrisome.

To dig deeper, the coach might ask 1) What would it take in real life to make that change; 2) What resources do you have at the ready to enable that change; and 3) What one step can you take to start the change, if only in your team?

7. How can you use political savvy to navigate the unwritten norms in your organization?

Political savvy is best described as an ethical, active player who "puts the organization first, believes in and cares about the issue at hand, sees a career as an outcome rather than a goal, plays above board and legitimizes the task: avoids the political blind spot." (DeLuca, 2002, p. 49) Some techniques that help increase a client's savvy is to understand the priorities of those you wish to influence, creating a supportive coalition, and linking agendas (DeLuca, 2002). How can you, as a coach, help clients navigate their culture using some of these tools?

8. What behaviors of yours might your team members emulate? How positive are those behaviors?

This is a "look in the mirror" question that helps clients with self-awareness. Encourage them to self-observe for signs of actions that might send a mixed message or be in violation of their values. One helpful practice is to suggest an end-of-day or nightly review of the day in which the client remembers, in reverse order, their activities each hour. In thinking through their day, they might ask questions like, Did I show up as my best self? Did I act in accordance with my values? What characteristics did I exemplify and were those the best for the situation? What did I especially enjoy, or when did I get the most satisfaction during my day?

9. How much are active listening skills taught and practiced in your organization? How skilled are you at actively listening?

Because it is counter to today's pervasive distraction-obsessed business culture (emails, texts, social media, etc.), listening is both an under-employed skill in today's workplace and a powerful leadership tool (Asree, Zain & Razalli, 2010) that can shape culture. Active listening could be the keystone to better leadership effectiveness for a client. According to Fernández-Aráoz, (2015), "Great leaders are great listeners, who make their employees feel valued, see the bigger picture and feel a part of something important." A coach might headline that they are changing roles to that of a teacher and introduce a client to the steps of active listening, such as the LAFF method of listen, ask questions, focus on the issues, and find a first step (McNaughton & Vostal, 2010).

10. What goals might we set to help you achieve alignment with your values and your actions?

Rock and Donde assert that "Coaching is the art of improving performance" (2008, p. 3). By helping clients set goals, coaches can hold their clients accountable and improve their performance.

11. When I see or hear you acting in a way that supports the values you hold dear, how would you like me to congratulate you? How can I best support you in this endeavor?

Even for the crustiest of executives, we know from neuroscience that encouragement or appreciation strengthens learning in the brain (Hamid, Pettibone, Mabrouk, Hetrick, Schmidt, Vander Weele, ... & Berke, 2016) and provides a surge of dopamine, the reward neurotransmitter, in the recipient. Dopamine, which is activated by either giving or receiving appreciation, increases arousal, movement, mood and executing abilities (Miller, 2019). Therefore, the coach can use appreciation and encouragement to enhance learning and executing abilities in their client, and in the doing, increase their own reward system. This is a reason that coaches love their work – when coaches express appreciation and encouragement to their clients, a surge of dopamine makes them feel good.

The coaching process

What follows is a common and well-researched process (Kets de Vries, 2008; O'Neill, 2011) in conducting an effective coaching program that will enhance the organizational culture, one conversation at a time (Rock and Donde, 2008).

1. Contracting

Per International Coach Federation core competencies (The Gold Standard in Coaching, n.d.), establishing the coaching agreement is the important first step. In this phase, the coach, client and organization (if applicable) will clarify expectations for coaching, the confidentiality agreement, fees, duration and structure of the coaching process (Thach, 2002).

2. Assessment Phase

Thach calls this the "data collection' period (Thach, 2002, p. 206), that includes both 360 and personality assessments. Smerek, Luce, Kluczynski, & Denison observed that 360 assessments without coaching fail in achieving their intended outcome (2009, p. 5), whereas 360 assessments followed by coaching is highly effective in producing leadership behavioral change. Many leaders today lack self-awareness (Wigglesworth, personal communication, August 7, 2019), which hinders their ability to lead effectively and produce results. Hildebrand (2019) recommends using personality assessments in various ways. He identifies two areas of essential tools for leadership coaching:

a. Personality assessments: Birkman Signature Suite, Hogan 360, Enneagram (from various providers), WorkPlace Big Five, Myers-Briggs Type Indicator, DiSC

b. Leadership 360 instruments: personal interviews of 360 raters, Leadership Circle Profile, Korn Ferry 360, Social Emotion Intelligence Profile, Benchmarks 360 (Center for Creative Leadership), DiSC 363 (Wiley).

The case for the effectiveness of 360 assessment has been well researched (Jones, Dunphy, Fishman, Larne & Canter, 2011; Kets de Vries, 2005). Thach (2002, p. 206) contends that "the use of 360 feedback is one of the best methods to promote increased self-awareness of skills strengths and deficiencies in managers." Wasylyshyn observes that the use of 360 feedback allows coaches to "pull the behavior change levers quickly" (2003, p. 100) when working with executives. The delivery of 360 results can be an eye-opening experience that can elicit defensive reactions (Jones, Dunphy, Fishman, Larne & Canter, 2011) but ultimately paves the way for true behavioral change. Kym (2014) found that a combination of 360 feedback and coaching can enhance the effectiveness of coaching. Luthans and Peterson (2003) contend that the use of 360 feedback by itself produces mixed results while adding coaching focused on self-awareness and managerial effectiveness resulted in improvements in employee satisfaction, retention and commitment and, indirectly, profitability. The 360 is typically used as a basis for creating a development plan for each leader. Coaches as enablers of culture transformation need to include 360 instruments in their program (Kets de Vries, 2005).

3. Development plan

Using the knowledge gained in the assessment phase, the client creates an individual development plan to guide and measure the rest of the coaching. My research shows that development plans typically include the following elements and are depicted in a matrix structure like this:

Goal:	What will success look like?	Action items to achieve goal:	Measure ments of success:
#1.		1	1
		2	2
		3	3
		etc.	etc.
#2.		1	1
		2	2
		3	3
		etc.	etc.
#3.		1	1
		2	2
		3	3
		etc.	etc.

4. Coaching

This is the phase that is longest in duration, spanning 4-10 or more months depending on the contractual agreement. This is the time for the coach to go deep with their clients, addressing the clients' day-to-day situations in context of their development plan. I request that my clients come to the coaching call with a situation in mind to work on. It is the coach's job to hold the client's agenda but not the content of the conversation (Kimsey-House, Kimsey-House, Sandahl, Whitworth, 2011), which points to the need for the client to arrive at the meeting with an agenda in mind.

5. Engagement Completion: Measuring improvement

In this phase, the coach re-surveys the 360 participants to measure changes in the client's behavior. One way to do this is to list behavioral issues identified in the Assessment phase and ask participants to rate the client's actions from 12 months ago. Then, re-state the behavioral issues in the present tense and ask participants to rate the client's behavior in the past 2 months. The delta in the ratings can be produced to measure improvement in the client's behaviors. This can be done easily using commercially available survey programs that you

290

customize to the client.

Some coaches re-conduct the original 360 assessment to measure improvements. In my experience, this is an effective method to conclude the coaching engagement for highly analytical or skeptical clients.

Team Coaching in Cultural Transformation

According to ICF and HCI research (2018, p. 14), team and group coaching are the least accepted coaching modalities in the companies studied. Deaton and Williams (2014, p. 147) acknowledge that "group and team coaching is less familiar" than individual coaching. However, approximately 40% of the companies that ICF/HCI studied plan to incorporate team and group coaching in the future (2018, p. 14). Team and group coaching are growing trends in these organizations.

Team coaching is a type of group coaching that is directed to an intact team in an organization, such as the CEO and direct reports (C-Suite) or a manager and the team. When seen through a cultural lens, a benefit of team coaching is the alignment achieved throughout the leadership team (Anderson, Anderson & Mayo, 2008). This is an effective way to ensure that leaders are focusing on advancing the overall organization's goals in cooperation with each other, and that they are leading from similar levels of self-awareness and leadership effectiveness.

Group coaching is a coaching engagement in which a group of leaders, usually at similar levels in the organization, are coached together. In both instances, the group is coached as an entity in conversation with all members present. There is a distinction between group facilitation, which is process-oriented, and group coaching, which is goal-focused (Brown & Grant, 2009). Brown & Grant also found that group or team coaching has the potential to create "goal-focused change in organizational contexts" (p. 37). In other words, group or team coaching can influence culture change. Individual coaching could be used as an adjunct modality during either group or team coaching, as well as peer coaching, (Deaton & Williams, 2014). Peer coaching among the team provides a safe space for participants to practice their own coaching skills (ICF, 2018).

Several case studies in the literature provide fascinating support for the effectiveness of team coaching. The first is Kets de Vries' exposition on group coaching (2008) in which he details the process he uses in coaching an executive team, including personality audits, 360 feedback, and conducting a multi-day, in-person debriefing with the team. He asserts that group/team coaching has the highest payoff in terms of "high-performance organizations; results-oriented and accountable people; boundaryless organizations; and true knowledge management" (p. 75).

The second case study explores the cultural change at Caterpillar's North American Commercial Division (NACD) (Anderson, Anderson & Mayo, 2008). The newly appointed vice president and head of the division set out to change the culture: first by employing an executive coach for himself, and then by expanding the coaching for his direct reports, and team coaching for the executive suite. The leader wanted to make the leadership team more effective by developing a "leadership expectations guide" (p. 41) and defined the cultural/behavioral tone he wanted his team to set. Results of the team coaching were higher performance, more collaboration, self-awareness of leader's style and effectiveness, higher level of coaching skills, and achievement of the cultural journey.

Conclusion

The leader as primary culture shaper is the most common model throughout the literature (Bolman & Deal, 2003; Sathe & Davidson, 2000; Schroeder, 2010). This supports the need for coaching to enable leaders to make cultural change. Research shows that the three modalities of coaching (using internal coaches, external coaches and managers using coaching skills) in a comprehensive coaching program is beneficial for the culture and the bottom line (ICF, 2019). The leadership coach can use powerful questions to help their clients both navigate and shape the culture to the better.

Recommendations for Further Research

More research is needed to establish best practices for how coaching affects organizational culture. It would be interesting to use a highly researched and validated culture assessment, such as the Organizational Culture Indicator from Human Synergistics (Cooke & Szumal, 1993), to measure the before and after states of a wide-spread coaching initiative. In addition, it would be fascinating to study the efficacy of coaching, either group or individual, through a Diversity and Inclusion lens. Women and minorities often fail to achieve promotions and leave organizations sooner and more often than do white males (McKinsey, 2013). How might coaching in the early stages of their careers help these populations understand the cultures of their organizations, especially the unwritten rules around deportment, assertion and competition?

Appendices

Appendix A: Identifying your Core Values and Mapping them to your Company's Values

The following are steps to take to identify and define your company's core values. This exercise is to identify YOUR top five values, not those of the organization.

Research shows that awareness of one's own personal values and how they correlate to company values is a positive indicator of employee engagement. For this reason, you might consider offering this exercise to each of your team members and ask them to identify their core values.

1. Using the following list of suggested values, circle the top ten values that you wish to honor in your life.

Possible Values (or create your own):

Accountability	Efficiency	Humility	Power
Achievement	Environmental	Humor/fun	Respect
Balance	responsibility	Independence	Responsibility
(home/work)	Ethics	Integrity	Risk-taking
Commitment	Excellence	Initiative	Self-discipline
Compassion	Fairness	Innovation	Self-esteem
Competence	Family	Intuition	Serving others
Continuous learning	Financial gain	Learning	Social justice
Cooperation	Forgiveness	Love	Success
Courage	Friendships	Making a difference	Survival
Conflict resolution	Fun	Mentoring others	Teamwork
Cooperation	Future generations	Open communication	Trust
Courtesy	Generosity	Openness	Vision
Creativity	Harmony	Personal fulfillment	Wealth/profit
Customer service	Health	Personal/profess-ional	Winning
Enthusiasm	Honesty	growth	Wisdom

2. Place a ☐ next to each value that is somewhat important to you.

3. Place a – next to each value that is not so important to you.

4. Select your top five values, prioritize and define each one.

5. Note your five top values and their definitions in this matrix:

My Five Core Values:

Value:	What this means to me/Definition:
1.	
2.	
3.	
4.	
5.	

Next, map your personal core values to those of your organization. If your organization doesn't have explicit core values, list 4 or 5 that you see exemplified in the behaviors of the leaders and colleagues. Considering the definition of your values and the definitions of your company's core values, map any correlation from one to the other. Here is an example:

294

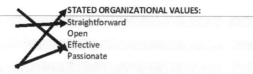

MY PERSONAL VALUES:	STATED ORGANIZATIONAL VALUES:
EXCELLENCE	Straightforward
COMPASSION	Open
WORK/LIFE BALANCE	Effective
INTEGRITY	Passionate
MAKING A DIFFERENCE	

In this example, the organizational values are Straightforward, Open, Effective and Passionate. Four out of five of this person's personal values can be mapped, or is similar, to the four core values of the company. Even though Work/life balance is not a shared value, this person found enough of a match between personal values and company values to work well.

You can fill in the matrix with your own values, your company's values and draw arrows to show similarities.

MY PERSONAL VALUES:	STATED ORGANIZATIONAL VALUES:

About the Author

Kristin Robertson, CEO of Brio Leadership and graduate of Fielding Graduate University with an MA in Organizational Design and Leadership, is the Happy Mondays Coach. Ms. Robertson is the 2020 President of the International Coaching Federation – North Texas chapter, where she has served for three years as the Programs Chair and President-Elect. She is the founder and president of the Dallas Company Culture Consortium, a professional organization dedicated to providing education, best practices and community-building to local culture shapers. Before founding her own companies, Kristin held numerous executive positions at Advent Software, where she built the client service culture that enabled an Initial Public Offering, and Fidelity Investments, where she won the President's Award for her transformational work. She is credentialed as a Professional Certified Coach and a mentor coach by the International Coaching Federation, is certified to conduct the Organizational Culture and Effectiveness Indicators from Human Synergetics and is a trained spiritual director. Her calling is to change the world by helping leaders create positive, productive and performance-enhancing businesses. Her latest book, called *Your Company Culture Ecosystem*, guides leaders in growing vibrant organizational cultures. Kristin can be reached at kristin@BrioLeadership.com.

References

Anderson, M. C., Anderson, D. L., & Mayo, W. D. (2008). Team coaching helps a leadership team drive cultural change at Caterpillar. *Global Business and Organizational Excellence*, 27(4), 40–50. doi: 10.1002/joe.20212

Asree, S., Zain, M. and Rizal Razalli, M. (2010), "Influence of leadership competency and organizational culture on responsiveness and performance of firms", *International Journal of Contemporary Hospitality Management*, Vol. 22 No. 4, pp. 500-516. https://doi-org.fgul.idm.oclc.org/10.1108/09596111011042712

Bianco-Mathis, V. & Schurgin, W. (2014) Transform organizational culture through coaching. *Talent Development*, 68(8), 26-29.

Bolman, L. G., & Deal, T. E. (2008). *Reframing organizations: Artistry, choice, and leadership.* San Francisco, CA: Jossey-Bass.

Brown, S. W., & Grant, A. M. (2010). From GROW to GROUP: Theoretical issues and a practical model for group coaching in organisations. *Coaching: An International Journal of Theory, Research and Practice*, 3(1), 30-45.

Collins, J. (2001). *Good to great: Why some companies make the leap...and others don't* (1st ed.). New York, NY: HarperBusiness.

Cooke, R. A., & Szumal, J. L. (1993). Measuring normative beliefs and shared behavioral expectations in organizations: The reliability and validity of the Organizational Culture Inventory. *Psychological Reports*, 72(3_suppl), 1299-1330.

Cooke, R. A., & Rousseau, D. M. (1988). Behavioral norms and expectations: A quantitative approach to the assessment of organizational culture. *Group & Organization Studies*, 13(3), 245-273.

Cooperrider, D. L., & Whitney, D. (1999). *Appreciative inquiry.* San Francisco, CA: Berrett-Koehler.

Deal, T., Kennedy, A., (2000). *Corporate cultures: The rites and rituals of corporate life* (1ˢᵗ ed.). Cambridge, Mass: Basic Books.

Deaton, A. V., & Williams, H. (2014). *Being coached: Group and team coaching from the inside.* Broad Run, VA: MAGUS Group LLC.

DeLuca, J. R. (2002). *Political Savvy: Systematic approaches to leadership behind the scenes.* Berwyn, PA: EBG Publications.

Denison, D. R. (1996). What is the difference between organizational culture and organizational climate? A native's point of view on a decade of paradigm wars. *The Academy of Management Review*, 21(3), 619–654. http://doi.org/10.2307/258997

Enron Fast Facts. (2019). Retrieved from https://www.cnn.com/2013/07/02/us/enron-fast-facts/index.html

Fernández-Aráoz, C. (2015). Creating a Culture of Unconditional Love. Retrieved from https://hbr.org/2014/01/creating-a-culture-of-unconditional-love

Gender diversity in top management: Moving corporate culture, moving boundaries. (2013). Retrieved from https://www.mckinsey.com/featured-insights/gender-equality/women-matter-2013.

Gold Standard in Coaching, The: ICF - Core Competencies. (n.d.). Retrieved from https://coachfederation.org/core-competencies

Gold Standard in Coaching, The: ICF - Building a Coaching Culture. (2018). Retrieved from https://coachfederation.org/research/building-a-coaching-culture

Goleman, D., Boyatzis, R. E., & McKee, A. (2002). *The new leaders: Transforming the art of leadership into the science of results.* London: Little, Brown.

Goleman, D., Boyatzis, R. E., & McKee, A. (2013). *Primal leadership: Learning to lead with emotional intelligence.* Boston, MA: Harvard Business School Press.

Hamid, A. A., Pettibone, J. R., Mabrouk, O. S., Hetrick, V. L., Schmidt, R., Vander Weele, C. M., ... & Berke, J. D. (2016). Mesolimbic dopamine signals the value of work. *Nature Neuroscience*, 19(1), 117.

Hildebrand, T. (2019, May) How to Effectively Use and Choose Assessments. Poster presented at Coaching Conference and Alumni Reunion. Fielding Graduate University, Santa Barbara, CA

Kets De Vries, M. F. (2005). Leadership group coaching in action: The zen of creating high performance teams. *Academy of Management Perspectives,* 19(1), 61–76.

Kets De Vries, M. F. (2007). Decoding the team conundrum: The eight roles executives play. *Organizational Dynamics,* 36(1), 28-44.

Kets De Vries, M. F. (2008). *Leadership coaching and organizational transformation: Effectiveness in a world of paradoxes.* Retrieved from https://flora.insead. edu/fichiersti_wp/inseadwp2008/2008-71.pdf

Kets De Vries, M. F. (2015) Leadership coaching for organizational transformation. *Reflections on Groups and Organizations,* 197–223. doi: 10.1002/9781119206484.ch9

Kym, S. (2014). Assessing the influence of managerial coaching on employee outcomes. *Human Resource Development Quarterly,* 25(1), 59–85. doi: 10.1002/hrdq.21175

Kotter, J.P., Heskett, J. L. (1992). *Corporate culture and performance.* New York: Free Press.

Mackey, J., Sisodia, R., & George, B. (2014). *Conscious capitalism: Liberating the heroic spirit of business* (2nd ed.). Boston, Massachusetts: Harvard Business Review Press.

Miller, K. (2019). 14 Health Benefits of Practicing Gratitude According to Science. Retrieved from https://positivepsychology.com/benefits-of-gratitude/

Jones, Q., Dunphy, D., Fishman, R., Larne, M., & Canter, C. (2011). *In great company: Unlocking the secrets of cultural transformation.* Sydney, NSW: Human Synergistics International.

Kołodziejczak, M. (2015). Coaching across organizational culture. *Procedia Economics and Finance,* 23, 329-334.

Kimsey-House, H., Kimsey-House, K., Sandahl, P., Whitworth, L. (2011). *Co-active coaching: Changing business, transforming lives* (3rd ed.). Boston: Nicholas Brealey Pub.

Kouzes, J. M., & Posner, B. Z. (2017). *The leadership challenge* (6th ed.). San Francisco, CA: Jossey-Bass.

Kuppler, T., & Cooke, R. (2016). Clarifying the elusive concepts of culture and climate. Retrieved from https://www.humansynergistics.com/blog/constructive-culture-blog/details/constructive-culture/2016/12/20/clarifying-the-elusive-concepts-of-culture-and-climate

Lencioni, P. M. (2002). Make your values mean something. *Harvard Business Review,* 80(7), 113-117.

Luthans, F., & Peterson, S. J. (2003). 360-degree feedback with systematic coaching:

Empirical analysis suggests a winning combination. *Human Resource Management: Published in Cooperation with the School of Business Administration, The University of Michigan and in alliance with the Society of Human Resources Management*, 42(3), 243-256.

Martin, J. (2007). *Organizational culture: Mapping the terrain.* Thousand Oaks: Sage Publ.

McNaughton, D., & Vostal, B. R. (2010). Using active listening to improve collaboration with parents: The LAFF don't CRY strategy. *Intervention in School and Clinic,* 45(4), 251-256. doi:http://dx.doi.org.fgul.idm.oclc.org/10.1177/10534512093534

O'Neill, M. B. (2007). *Executive coaching with backbone and heart: A systems approach to engaging leaders with their challenges.* San Francisco, CA: Jossey-Bass.

Rhoades, A., Covey, S. R., & Shepherdson, N. (2011). *Built on values: Creating an enviable culture that outperforms the competition* (1st ed,). San Francisco: Jossey-Bass.

Rock, D., & Donde, R. (2008). Driving organizational change with internal coaching programs: part one. *Industrial and Commercial Training,* 40(1), 10-18.

Rock, D. (2006). *Quiet leadership: Six steps to transforming performance at work; Help people think better – Don't tell them what to do!* New York: Harper.

Sathe, V., & Davidson, E. J. (2000). Toward a new conceptualization of culture change. *Handbook of organizational culture and climate,* 117129.

Schein, E. H. (2010). *Organizational culture and leadership* (4th ed.). San Francisco, Calif: Jossey-Bass.

Schroeder, P. J. (2010). Changing team culture: The perspectives of ten successful head coaches. *Journal of Sport Behavior,* 33(1), 63-88.

Sisodia, R. S., Sheth, J. N., & Wolfe, D. B. (2014). *Firms of endearment: How world-class companies profit from passion and purpose* (2nd ed.). Upper Saddle River, New Jersey: Pearson FT Press.

Smerek, R. E., Luce, K., Kluczynski, P., & Denison, D. R. (2009) Executive Coaching: Does leader behavior change with feedback and coaching? *Linkage Leader,* 1-7.

Sun, S. (2008). Organizational culture and its themes. *International Journal of Business and Management,* 3(12), 137-141.

Thach, E. C. (2002). The impact of executive coaching and 360 feedback on leadership effectiveness. *Leadership & Organization Development Journal,* 23(4), 205-214.

Trice, H. M., & Beyer, J. M. (1993). *The cultures of work organizations.* Englewood

Cliffs, NJ: Prentice Hall.

Wasylyshyn, K. M. (2003). Executive coaching: An outcome study. *The Wisdom of Coaching: Essential Papers in Consulting Psychology for a World of Change,* 79–89. doi: 10.1037/11570-008

CHAPTER 14

COACHING AS AN INTERVENTION TO SUPPORT CONSTRUCTION

ON ITS JOURNEY TO BECOME AN INDUSTRY WHERE EVERYONE CAN THRIVE

Kate McAlpine, PhD

Abstract

Women and minorities who work in construction do not always thrive. This paper describes how coaching has been used as a research tool to understand people's lived experience of working in construction, and how it may be used as a tool to build inclusive organizational cultures. Research was conducted with a construction company who want to "build a workforce that is the best." Data was collected in conversation: coaching conversations with women, narrative interviews with people working on building sites, and group facilitation of the Immunity to Change process.

The company values individual agency. The emphasis on personal drive as a route to success comes at a cost, particularly for women. Participants are motivated to be part of the company. But they self-censor, assuming they need to silence themselves in order to get ahead. This dissonance could be confronted and resolved in coaching conversations that nurture the organization on its inclusion journey.

Keywords: Construction, Coaching, Women in construction, Inclusion, Equality, Diversity, Integral Theory, Narrative Research, Grounded Theory

Introduction: Not everyone thrives in construction.

Construction in the United Kingdom has changed rapidly within the last ten years, and the industry increasingly recognizes that success is all about people. However, construction continues to be a tough industry with an image problem, where claimed values of inclusion are not consistently practiced. "Middle aged white men" (according to one interviewee) continue to hold the power and women and minorities struggle to thrive. The challenge lies in building organizational practices that enable everyone to feel included. Those grappling with this challenge typically do so through the lens of equality, diversity and inclusion (EDI).

What is EDI?

A review of the literature on equality, diversity and inclusion in engineering, major projects, and construction (Accuracy Market Research, n.d.; BBC, n.d.; CIPD, 2018; Eagly & Chin, 2010; Fanshawe, 2013; Vivienne Hunt, 2015; Peters, n.d.; Quinn, 2018; Royal Academy of Engineering, 2015.), defines the terms as follows:

Equality is access to opportunity, so that structural and practical disadvantages are removed. It is a legal requirement, that in the United Kingdom takes the form of the UK Equalities Act, the Sex Discrimination Act, and the Equal Pay Act ('What equality law means for you as an employer: pay and benefits | Equality and Human Rights Commission', 2019).

Diversity demands a recognition and an appreciation of individual differences and worldviews. This has four dimensions;

1. Perspective taking: how individual traits, intelligences, developmental stages, and belief systems inform people's mindsets (Beck & Cowan, 2005; Gardner, 1983; Wilber, 2011).

2. Toolbox: how individuals' neuro-processing, skills, knowledge, and behaviors inform what they do and how they do it.

3. Networks: how group representation, relationships, social ties and bonds, and inter and intra group politics inform people's relationships

302

with others.

4. The Firm: how the commercial, technical, and procedural functioning of the organization and/or sector informs the individual in the context of the institution.

Inclusion is a relational experience, whereby individuals feel included. It demands an organizational culture that is characterized by trust, openness, representation, and an equal distribution and flow of resources, including information.

This paper explores what needs to happen for more people to feel included in the construction industry, and does so via two lenses. One is from the perspective of the individual, exploring the experience of women and men who work in the industry and their assumptions about how change may happen in construction. The other is an organizational development perspective that theorizes what needs to change at an organizational level for women and minorities to thrive. Throughout, I endeavor to show the power of conversations to explore these questions. I conclude by proposing how coaching could be used as an intervention to shift the industry so that everyone can be their best.

Not everyone thrives in the world of work because the status quo serves those with power. The literature on EDI reveals that not everyone thrives in construction because of intersecting structural and behavioral barriers (Accuracy Market Research, n.d.; Amaratunga, Shanmugam, Haigh, & Baldry, 2008; Jamieson, 2018). These result in a lived experience where people are silenced. They experience a myriad of discriminatory practices, that are legitimized and perpetuated by a social environment that continues to value the *White Western Male* and a world of work that values visibility over results. Given that race, gender, and organizational life are social constructs, and that people are typically blind to their beliefs and bias, the scene is set for resistance to change both inside and outside the organization (DiAngelo, 2019; Eddo-lorge, 2018). In construction, these dynamics manifest in an industry that has a negative public image, a leaky recruitment and retention pipeline, and a worrying skill shortage.

The case for greater inclusion is pressing. But it is the legal and business case that is being made and not the social or moral case. The case for investing in equality, diversity, and inclusion currently takes two forms. The one focusses on compliance with workplaces' legal responsibility to ensure equal access to opportunity. The other adopts a business case that assumes that there is a correlation between EDI and organizational flourishing. The literature evidences this assumption by demonstrating that team functioning and productivity improves once diversity and inclusion is taken seriously. People demonstrate improved commitment, problem solving, creativity, thinking, and decision making, when the organization is more diverse (Vivian Hunt, Prince, Dixon-Fyle, & Yee, 2018). In turn, innovation and differentiation improve, driving a competitive advantage that results in profitability, growth, and a better bottom line (ACAS, n.d.; Thomas, 2004).

What the literature does not do, is make a moral case for investment in EDI. The literature describes the problems faced in getting traction for inclusion across the construction industry, but it does not explain the drivers behind resistance. Nor does the literature articulate a clear EDI vision or theorize directions of travel that would generate solutions to the inclusion challenge in the industry. The literature does not identify agents or processes for change, thinking instead in terms of tactics that businesses can adopt rather than ways to upend the unfair system.

This paper describes research that was conducted in the UK with a family-owned, 150-year-old construction company. The company has expressed a commitment to "build a workforce that is the best" and its leadership believes that investing in EDI aligns with their company values. They recognize that there is no inevitability towards greater inclusion and that the mission needs to be actively fostered. This research was co-created with the company to explore people's lived experience of work and to theorize what would need to shift so that all its staff could flourish.

Research design

The research sought to understand why some people do not thrive in construction. The underlying epistemology is called "Integral Activist Research" (IAR) (McAlpine, 2014).

This framework:

• Adopts an Integral lens (Wilber, 1996) that argues that it is impossible to fully understand the experience of being human without exploring the domains of the individual's subjective and objective experience and the group's inter-subjective and inter-objective worlds. These four domains are the fundamental dimensions of all phenomenon.

• Supports researchers who also identify as activists, to ground themselves as both scholars and change agents, and to conduct studies that have personal integrity, that generate meaningful social change, and that are practical and credible.

• Uses a Classic Grounded Theory research method. Grounded theory is a process that generates ideas that are grounded in data about participants' problems. The intention is to build abstract theoretical understanding of latent patterns of behavior. It is essentially a codified method for generating theory that consists of systematic, yet flexible guidelines for collecting, analyzing and constructing theories (Glaser, 1967). Data is collected, coded, and analyzed in an iterative process. As the researcher codes, categories and their properties begin to emerge, and the researcher begins to generate hypotheses about the relations among the categories and the key variable starts to become clear. Grounded theory allows the researcher to go beyond verifying facts and describing experience to generating an explanation of them and theorizing how change may occur.

Data Collection

Data was collected in conversation. The fundamental human need is to be truly heard. Conversation, underpinned by unconditional positive regard, was at the heart of all the data collection approaches. Unconditional positive regard refers to accepting and supporting another exactly as they are, without evaluating or judging them. At the heart of the concept is the belief that every person has the personal resources within to help themselves, if they are offered the environment of acceptance to foster their own recognition of this idea (Rogers, 1980).

Coaching conversations were held with six women in construction over a period of nine months. Coaching is a helping conversation where each partner holds equal power. The relationship is underpinned by an assumption that the client has the self-efficacy to solve their own challenges. The coach is a thought-partner who listens deeply. In doing so, the coach creates a safe space and holds up a mirror up to the client. This helps them to reflect deeply, find their voice, surface their assumptions, think through how to behave in different scenarios, and practice new behaviors.

Narrative interviews (Chase, 2005; Clandinin & Connelly, 2000; Josselson & Lieblich, 2014) were conducted with twenty staff members based in construction sites in London and Newcastle. They included women, men, people with disabilities, and minority ethnic groups. I interviewed project managers, package engineers, design managers, planners, community managers, supply chain representative and a works supervisor. In an hour-long open-ended interview, I asked them to explore their motivation and journey into construction, which is the subjective emotional domain of Wilber's integral framework. I asked them to share the actions they take to navigate the workplace, which is the observable behaviors in Wilber's schema. I asked them to speak about the company's claimed values on equality, diversity, and inclusion, and to assess the company's actual practice, which is the institutional functioning as Wilber would put it. Finally, I asked them to consider how cultural change could happen at the company, which is Wilber's domain of collective relationships.

The narrative interviews were neither coaching nor therapeutic conversations. But this approach does assist interviewees to create a coherent narrative, and that can be liberating. By putting our story into words so that we can convey it to another, people integrate past experiences into a cohesive sense of how the world works and who one is (Siegel, 2012).

I facilitated Kegan and Lahey's (2009) Immunity to Change process with twenty staff, working in two groups of ten. This is not what Kegan and Lahey recommend, but I did this deliberately to urge participants to move beyond describing their experience of construction and to start to explain the reasons for their lived experience. Having already used the narrative interviews with individuals to build a sense of safety, I felt that the group setting was supportive and symbolic of my desire for participants to build a shared sense of meaning and to generate some solidarity. Kegan and Lahey argue that the ability to change is elusive because desire and motivation are insufficient to change habitual behavior, and because behavior change is blocked by our own beliefs; many of which are unconscious. Their process supports a systematic conversation whereby participants

• Identify their self-improvement goals.

• Describe what they are doing or not doing to achieve those goals.

• Deepen their appreciation that what they are not doing reveals other goals to which they are committed.

• Surface fears that they may have about the consequences of actively pursuing their self-improvement goals.

• Name the underlying, big assumptions that they hold about themselves, their organization and the consequences of behaving differently.

Next steps are co-created with the research participants and company leadership.

The final step in the research involves sharing the research findings with the participants and with the company's leadership. In doing so, the findings are validated, and space is created to have a generative conversation about their implications for the company's practice. These meetings have yet to be held, but possible outcomes include:

• A decision to commission new research on additional construction sites, and so to saturate the data and deepen the analysis, with a focus

on sites that are resistant to the EDI agenda;
• A decision to proceed with the coaching and the narrative interviews with potential leaders on sites where EDI is being resisted, with a view to these individuals acting as change agents;
• A recognition that advancing inclusion in construction is a cultural change intervention that should bear fruit over the long-term and not a quick fix that can be handled tactically.

Findings: Participants' main concern is to build a culture where everyone can be their best.

Participants envision a construction industry where people are defined by their potential, and where individuals can progress to the very top, irrespective of their identity or background. They envisage a fair company culture, *"a place for everyone"* where profit-making is never at the expense of its people.

However, the research reveals that there is a fundamental tension between the inclusive vision and the value placed on individual agency in the company.

Individual agency is valued, but it comes at a personal cost. The research revealed that construction attracts people who are driven by an intrinsic motivation to be part of something bigger than themselves, as reflected in participants' comments such as, "it is a 'privilege to build a legacy,' but I also want to 'get my hands dirty' and 'make my family proud'." Work plays a vital role in how these individuals self-identify. They are tough on themselves and have high expectations of others, as in, "I am my own worst critic," and, "Underestimate me at your peril."

There is a clear alignment between these participants and the company's values. Personal agency, drive, talent, and craft are expected to be demonstrated if someone is to get ahead. In the company, career pathways are opaque, and progression is up to the individual.

Do not rock the boat. Despite a claimed commitment to inclusion, participants are committed to not rocking the boat. The Immunity to Change process revealed that the espoused value, revealed in the group's improvement goal, is to build an organizational culture where everyone feels welcomed, accepted, listened to, and guided, and where they have a work-life balance. However, the values in action (Argyris, 1993) include failing to prioritize time to talk to people; not using the personal development plan process to consider purpose, motivation, or longer-term career objectives; avoiding conversations about appropriate recognition; not looking after themselves and switching off; and not finding time for their own development.

What is not being done reveals a fear of failure, of others' judgement, of having to move out of the comfort zone. These fears indicate that participants are also committed to a belief that collective success requires them to put their heads down and avoid confrontation. They are strongly committed to others' approval. This is the competing commitment that paralyses and undermines efforts to achieve the participants' espoused improvement goals.

This fear reveals a heretofore unconscious assumption; namely that success for the business requires people at the frontline to compromise their wellbeing in service of the interests of those who pay the company. There is also an assumption that they are not valued and will be judged negatively for putting down limits; that it is impossible to advance in one's career if "I tell people things they don't want to hear."

The personal cost for women is being under-appreciated by men who think that women thrive. Men think that women thrive in the company, but in reality, the latter carry a hidden burden as they navigate the workplace. This is partly a matter of numbers, whereby they are in a minority, but learn to ignore that fact over time, as in: "I don't notice I'm the only female," or "I'm quite comfortable with men."

Men often advocate for women in construction. A number actively sponsor women's career progression and will positively change their behavior when around women, as some women observed: "I've found men with daughters are particularly nurturing," and, "Stand near something heavy and look like you needed it moving."

But, at the same time young women quickly learn that progression requires them to deflect micro-aggressions and to be 100% on top of their brief. Confidence grows with experience and skills, but women only thrive in the company if they are committed to working harder to get their own self-respect and that of men. Toxic masculinity occurs from time to time, and men will often critique young women. Typically, women ignore the behavior, rationalizing that it not worthwhile to make a scene and to cause someone to lose their job. It doesn't feel right to "tell tales." Women describe how they indulge men's egos in meetings, framing questions as, "I may be wrong, but what about...?"

Women do not consider a successful career as necessarily involving a race to the top. In contrast to many men who will clamor for the project manager role, success is more nuanced. It is about projecting confidence, gaining experience, feeling that you are on top of the brief and fulfilling personal motivation.

Do the right thing vs. do things right. A commitment to inclusion demands that the company does the right thing, rather than just doing things right; and this poses dilemmas. The challenge emerges at the intersection between organizational values that recognize and reward individuals based on their personal drive and agency, and a claimed desire to be inclusive of everyone. Inclusion is experienced in relationship, and it demands an organizational culture that is collegiate, fair, and transparent.

The research revealed that whilst participants are intrinsically motivated and enthused to be part of the company, they also self-censor because they are making an unconscious assumption that they need to silence themselves in order to get ahead. This poses organizational questions that need to be confronted and resolved.
• At the level of leadership, how open is the leadership to the implications of inconvenient diversity and to designing out homophily from decision-making? Homophily is the tendency for people to have

ties with and therefore to prefer people who are similar to themselves (Friedman & Lauriston, 2019).

• At the level of relationships, how can the company help its people to see the world through others' eyes?

• At the level of resources, what is the company's stance when regressive client demands risk the company's commitment to its people?

Diversity means accommodating difference that may be unwelcome, and that will certainly challenge the status quo. The company's leadership team and Board will be required to work on themselves and to grapple with the unintended consequences of diversity. This may include considering changes to the organizational structure in ways that support a flatter and more networked organizational form. Leaders will have to practice what they preach, and this requires that they reflect on and question their own privilege and habitual behaviors. Given the company's commitment to be "identity blind", creating affinity groups based on identity as a lever for conversations about diversity may not be the most generative approach. The key is to get people talking across identity groups and this requires an emphasis on commonality, rather than on difference.

Conclusion: Coaching could be used strategically to support the construction industry in its inclusion journey.

Coaching potentially has two roles to play in construction's inclusion journey. The first is at an individual level where it can provide a safe space for people who are grappling with what it takes for them to thrive in the business. This is typically how coaching has been deployed by companies. The second, is as intervention that supports organizational cultural change. This proposition has been informed by this research into people's experience of working on construction, but there is no reason why it could not equally benefit other industries embarking on a journey towards greater inclusion. The final section of this paper theorizes how coaching could be used as a resource for building inclusive organizational cultures.

Coaching helps women in construction address the leadership challenge of Doing the Right Thing, and not just doing things right. The women who participated in the coaching conversations referenced here contend that in order to consistently do the right thing, and to do so authentically, women in construction need to proactively take control of their destiny. This requires them to create conditions that enable them to be their best.

Rather than waiting for employers or the system to create conditions where they can thrive, participants believe that women in construction need to draw on their own agency to create change. To do so demands that they invest in their own development—and this is where coaching has a role to play.

Coaching conversations become the safe space for women in construction to:

• Pause from their habitual busyness; to move away from a state of reactivity and to reflect on themselves and their situation.

• Consider whether there is alignment between their personal and organizational goals; and where there is not, to set a course for change.

• Think and prepare for presentations, strategic change, and role transitions; so that they can work intentionally and perform at their peak.

• Work with their shadows and the unintended consequences of their strengths.

In industries where people are constantly on the go, where they are trained and rewarded for fixing problems quickly and efficiently, they have little time and few incentives to slow down, take a deep breath and reflect. Coaching is the pause button. And it is in the pause that we re-discover ourselves and generate the energy for self-development.

Proposal: use coaching as a resource for building inclusive organizational cultures.

Every organization is a system, the elements of which can be mapped on a matrix that supports practitioners to identify the key question in a given domain, and to consider interventions that may assist in resolving that question. The higher the level in the matrix the less tangible the domain, but the more powerful the intervention in shifting the system.

Table 1 draws on the EDI literature review and the dilemmas that were articulated by research participants to map out the form that an inclusion journey could take and the potential role of coaching in that journey.

Tables 1 and 2. EDI good practice & opportunities for coaching to support the inclusion journey

EDI GOOD PRACTICE REQUIRES	COACHING IS A SPACE FOR GENERATIVE CONVERSATIONS	RESULTING IN
AN ENVIRONMENT WHERE DISCRIMINATORY NORMS ARE CHALLENGED	WITH thinkers, leaders & advocates TO EXPLORE the systemic nature of resistance to change & how to disrupt that.	Solidarity and a collective voice for change.
	....	
IDENTITY THAT HOLDS EDI AS BEING INTEGRAL	WITH management & team leads TO EXPLORE how to position new initiatives so that they are received by people as making life simpler & thus adding value.	A reduction in change cynicism that enhances the chances of initiatives having a positive impact.
	....	
LEADERSHIP DRIVING THE AGENDA & MODELLING DESIRED BEHAVIORS	WITH the leadership team & Board TO EXPLORE how to accommodate unwelcome difference, and what needs to shift in their worldview and behavior.	Leaders authentically practice what they preach.
	....	
RELATIONSHIPS THAT BUILD CONNECTIONS ACROSS NETWORKS	WITH *the Western White Male* TO EXPLORE the experience of living as other.	Empathy imbues the organization.
	....	

EDI GOOD PRACTICE REQUIRES	COACHING IS A SPACE FOR GENERATIVE CONVERSATIONS	RESULTING IN
STRATEGY BASED ON EVIDENCE	WITH Leadership & Management TO EXPLORE the coherence, relevance & effectiveness of strategies.	Assumptions and strategies are systematically tested and validated.
PROCEDURES THAT DESIGN OUT BIAS	WITH construction sites, HR +/or EDI unit. TO EXPLORE what works and under what conditions before roll-out, and how to create, celebrate and share good practice between sites.	New initiatives "land" and achieve proof of concept before being rolled out.
ACTIVITIES THAT PUT ORGANIZATIONAL VALUES INTO ACTION	WITH individuals & teams across the business. TO EXPLORE how to shift from busyness to intentional action.	Individuals deploy their Engineering mindset to solve problems more effectively.
RESOURCING OF AN ORGANIZATIONAL UNIT TO DRIVE THE EDI AGENDA	WITH Human Resource +/or EDI unit. TO EXPLORE how systems do not work for everyone, & the implications of this for practical action.	Unconscious bias is recognized & owned.

Companies' inclusion journeys need to be resourced with an organizational unit that drives the EDI agenda. Once in place, coaching can be of service in helping the staff in that unit to deeply reflect on the systemic nature of discrimination and the implications for this in terms of practical actions that they will take. Creating consciousness about their individual privilege will enable these practitioners to recognize and own their unconscious bias and will support intentional action.

People in construction like to solve problems and take action. They are habitually busy. Coaching is a useful space for all individuals and teams to pause; and to intentionally draw on their Engineering mindset which enthuses them with a desire to solve problems. It is important to do so, however, in a measured way and in service for putting the organization's values into action.

The default position of construction companies when faced with the EDI agenda is to roll out new procedures (ACAS, n.d.). There is a role for procedures that design out bias, but Human Resources and/ or EDI units need to be wary about initiative overload. The coaching conversation can be a useful space where these staff explore what works and under what conditions, before rolling-out initiatives. Construction is an industry where project sites have large degrees of autonomy from the center. At the discretion of the project manager good practices are often demonstrated. Coaching is also an opportunity for the centralized HR and EDI units to learn from sites about what is working and why, and to co-create plans for celebrating and sharing good practice across the business.

EDI strategies need to be based on evidence and not purely on aspiration. Coaching can be useful to help leadership and management explore the coherence, relevance, and effectiveness of strategies, and, in doing so, to systematically test the assumptions that are being made. Similarly, coaching can be used as a conduit to explore how to position new initiatives so that they are received by people as making life simpler, as being more than a gimmick, and as adding value to them personally and to the company. Thinking through the mechanics of rolling out change initiatives is critical if change cynicism is to be avoided, and new initiatives are to land in a way that has a positive impact.

An effective inclusion journey requires that leaders drive the agenda and model desired behaviors. Whilst EDI sounds like an appealing, modern proposition, it has consequences with which many more conservative leaders may be uncomfortable. For example, more women on the team shifts the dynamics and expectations about what is acceptable behavior. People on the team who are neuro-atypical do not necessarily manifest emotional intelligence in the way that is routinely valued by leaders. Coaching can be an opportunity to work with leaders to explore their own biases in a safe space where they can reveal and resolve their own discomfort at the novelty they are experiencing as the workplace becomes more diverse. The aim is that leaders become able to authentically practice what they are preaching with regards to inclusion.

Similarly, relationships throughout the company need to be nurtured and connections built across networks so that people move out of their silos and generate collective action for cultural change. This does require the archetypical *Western White Male* to explore the experience of living as other; and in turn to become more empathetic to the women and minorities. The foundational premise of coaching is unconditional positive regard for the client, and it in this judgement-free conversation that individuals may feel the safety to have their own assumptions about others constructively challenged.

Finally, there is a role for coaching thinkers, leaders and advocates in the wider industry who are challenging discriminatory norms. There is a small UK based community of practice working in major projects who are concerned to advance the EDI agenda. Coaching would be an affirming space in which they can explore the systemic nature of resistance to change and how to disrupt that; and in doing so build greater solidarity and a collective voice for change.

Recommendations for future research

Not everyone thrives in construction because the status quo serves middle-aged white men who hold power in the industry. Experts across project delivery make the case that mega-projects have the potential to better enable conditions of equality and inclusivity in society (Carter, H; Miles, E et al; 2019). But this will require cultural change within individual organizations and across the broader construction industry. Coaching could be used strategically to support the construction industry in its inclusion journey, but there is also a need for broader research and understanding.

Future lines of inquiry that I am pursuing include investigating how to challenge monocultures. This includes using the coaching conversation as an opportunity to understand the types of leadership style and behaviors that drive culture change.

Engineers are drawn to measurement and at the event on Equality participants sought answers to their question "how do you measure inclusive cultures?" Is it even possible to measure an ethos? What are the key social impacts valued by members of the workforce and the communities that are affected by large infrastructural projects? Measurement drives change and if we want to build an industry where people flourish, we need to be careful about measuring the wrong things and creating unintended negative consequences. The success criteria in construction is often framed in the narrow terms of delivery on time and on budget. But if mega-projects can be a force for social good, we need to better understand the dimensions of human flourishing and to integrate those into the success criteria for projects.

The coaching conversation can be a non-judgmental, generative space to have the types of conversation that support individuals to articulate their values; to connect their work in construction with a larger social purpose; and to take ownership of their own unconscious bias, interactions and leadership style, so that they contribute to an organizational culture where everyone can thrive.

About the Author

Dr Kate McAlpine applies her training in Evidence Based Coaching and Human and Organizational Development and 20+ years in the development sector in East Africa to the child protection, governance, civil society and construction sectors. Highly experienced at group facilitation and designing strategy, she is driven by a desire to help organizations and individuals thrive, enabling people to do the right thing in their community or workplace. She is also a social entrepreneur, working via Citizens4Change (www. citizens4change.net) and ConnectGo (www.connectgo.co.uk) to demonstrate that there is a groundswell of East Africans who are taking action to improve the lives of children. Kate's research practice seeks out citizens' voices, explores their realities, and uses civic tech to demonstrate their social impact. Her website is kate@katemcalpine.org.

References

ACAS. (n.d.). *Equality and diversity in the workplace, Toolkit.*

Accuracy Market Research. (n.d.). *Women in the construction industry.*

Amaratunga, D., Shanmugam, M., Haigh, R., & Baldry, D. (2008). Construction and Women. In H. Smyth & S. Pryke (Eds.), *Collaborative Relationships in Construction* (pp. 224–244). https://doi.org/10.1002/9781444301069. ch10

Argyris, C. (1993). *Knowledge for Action, A Guide to Overcoming Barriers to Organizational Change.* Jossey-Bass Publishers.

BBC. (n.d.). *Diversity and Inclusion Strategy* 2016-20.

Beck, D. E., & Cowan, C. C. (2005). *Spiral Dynamics: Mastering Values, Leadership, and Change* (Kindle edition). Wiley-Blackwell.

Carter, H; Miles, E (2019) *Building Equality: Are mega-projects creating a better world?* Conference at the Bartlet, UCL. London, UK.

Chase, S. E. (2005). Narrative inquiry: Multiple Lenses, Approaches, Voices. In N. K. Denzin (Ed.), *The SAGE handbook of qualitative research.*

CIPD. (2018). *Neurodiversity at Work.*

Clandinin, J., & Connelly, M. (2000). *Narrative Inquiry: Experience and Story in Qualitative Research.* San Francisco: Jossey-Bass.

DiAngelo, R. (2019). *White Fragility: Why It's So Hard for White People to Talk About Racism.* Penguin.

Eagly, A., H., & Chin, J. L. (2010). Diversity and leadership in a changing world. *America Psychologist,* 65(3), 216–224.

Eddo-lorge, R. (2018). Why I am no longer talking to white people about race. Bloomsbury Publishing PLC.

Fanshawe, S. (2013, October 17). Why waste time whistling from the scaffolding when you could be more diverse and win contracts. Retrieved 4 March 2019, from Diversity by Design website: https://diversitybydesign.co.uk/why-waste-time-whistling/

Friedman, S., & Lauriston, D. (2019). *The Class Ceiling: Why it Pays to be Privileged.* Retrieved from https://books.google.co.tz/books/about/The_Class_Ceiling. html?id=hURvDwAAQBAJ&printsec=frontcover&source=kp_read_button&redir_esc=y#v=onepage&q&f=false

Gardner, H. (1983). *Frames of mind: Theory of multiple intelligences.* New York:

Basic Books.

Glaser, B. (1967). *Discovery of grounded theory: Strategies for qualitative research.*

Hunt, Vivian, Prince, S., Dixon-Fyle, S., & Yee, L. (2018). *Delivering through Diversity* (p. 42). McKinsey & Company.

Hunt, Vivienne. (2015). Why Diversity matters. *McKinseys & Company.* Retrieved from https://www.mckinsey.com/business-functions/organization/our-insights/why-diversity-matters

Jamieson, J. (2018). Our kids will look back and ask: Why did diversity take so long? *Construction News.* Retrieved from https://www.constructionnews.co.uk/analysis/expert-opinion/our-kids-will-look-back-and-ask-why-did-diversity-take-so-long/10037671.article?search=https%3a%2f%2fwww.constructionnews.

Josselson, R., & Lieblich, A. (2014). *Interviewing for narrative research.* Presented at the Narrative Matters, Universite Paris Diderot.

Kegan, R., & Lahey, L. (2009). *Immunity to change: How to overcome it and unlock the potential in yourself and your organization.* Harvard Business Review Press.

McAlpine, K. (2014). Integral Activist Epistemology: A Model for Researchers to Act on Personal Values. *Journal of Integral Theory and Practice*, Fall 2014.

Peters, J. (n.d.). *Equality and diversity: good practice for the construction sector A report commissioned by the Equality and Human Rights Commission.* Equality and Human Rights Commission.

Quinn, L. (2018). How to break the deadlock on diversity. *Construction News.* Retrieved from https://www.constructionnews.co.uk/analysis/expert-opinion/how-to-break-the-deadlock-on-diversity/10033477.article?sm=10033477

Rogers, C. R. (1980). *A way of being.* Boston & New York: Houghton Mifflin Company.

Royal Academy of Engineering. (2015.). *Diversity and inclusion in engineering survey report 2015 including trends, similarities and differences with the highways and transportation sector.*

Siegel, D. J. (2012). *Pocket Guide to Interpersonal Neurobiology: An Integrative Handbook of the Mind (Pocket Guides).* W. W. Norton & Co.

Thomas, D. A. (2004). Diversity as a Strategy. *Harvard Business Review.*

What equality law means for you as an employer: pay and benefits | Equality and Human Rights Commission. (2019, February 14). Retrieved 14 February 2019, from https://equalityhumanrights.com/en/publication-download/what-equality-law-means-you-employer-pay-and-benefits

Wilber, K. (1996). *A brief history of everything*. Dublin: Gill & Macmillan.

Wilber, K. (2011). *Integral Psychology: Consciousness, Spirit, Psychology, Therapy*. Shambhala Publications; 1st paperback. ed edition.

Appendix: Interview Guide

NB: These questions are prompts for a dialogue and should not be slavishly followed in sequence.

Please tell me about yourself

What is your current role?

Tell me about your journey?

What are the strengths + capacities that you bring to your role and to the wider industry?

What role does work play in fulfilling your wider desires for life?

Navigating construction

How have you navigated your career?

What helped to build your confidence?

How did you make yourself visible?

How does it feel to be in a minority / majority?

What biases does this reflect about minorities in construction?

What is valued in the industry if you are to get ahead?

Do you think EDI is a priority? If so, whose priority is it? And why is it a priority?

Who is effective at communicating the business case for inclusion? And why are they effective?

Within the industry what criteria is used to identify people with potential?

How is the minority pipeline being developed?

What actions are taken to attract, retain and promote minority groups?

How do people access professional development opportunities?

Who mentors whom? To what effect

What sort of conversations happen with line managers?

What [if any] is the challenge you personally face that prevents you flourishing in construction?

What adversities have you overcome? What helped you?

Have you experienced unfairness? How was it addressed?

If or when power is mis-used, what is the employers' theoretical duty of care and what actually happens?

Envisaging change

What is the change you want to see in construction?

How does change happen in the industry?

Who has power to effect change? What is their interest + influence in this agenda?

Currently, who is championing this agenda? How? Any men?

How change ready do you think the industry is? Why?

What everyday steps for change are being taken?

How would one resolve a possible tension between hierarchical bureaucracy and increased diversity of thinking?

What needs to happen to shift mindsets and move beyond lip service?

Personally, how do you influence?

What everyday steps for change are you taking?

Any more questions? Anything to ask me?

Thank you!

CHAPTER 15

CHASING THE SHADOW: COACHING FOR EQUITY IN EDUCATION

Mary Ann Burke, PhD, EdD, MFT
Coaches Evolve, LLC

Abstract

How can transformational coaching be a powerful tool to help educators increase their ability to discern, disrupt, and remedy inequities in Pre-K-12 school culture and practices? This chapter presents key findings from Burke's research (Norwood & Burke, 2013) into this question. Burke used critical inquiry to investigate possible hegemonic and non-hegemonic barriers to the potential of transformational coaching to bring about radical and sustainable change of current inequitable educational practices. She found that two aspects of school culture have the greatest impact on the viability of educational coaching: 1. administrators' ability and willingness to understand, support, and facilitate coaches' work, and, 2. educators' widely divergent levels of awareness of, and openness to, equitable practice. Each area is fertile ground for well-trained coaches.

Burke's research was part of a collaborative dissertation co-authored by Burke and Norwood (see Norwood's companion chapter that follows this one). Norwood interviewed world thought leaders of five unique visionary approaches to coaching: Julio Olalla (Ontological Coaching), Sara Orem (Appreciative Coaching), Robert Hargrove (Masterful Coaching and Triple-Loop Learning), Four Arrows (Indigenous Approaches to Deep Learning), and Art Costa, Robert Garmston, and Jane Ellison (Cognitive CoachingSM). Of these five, only Cognitive CoachingSM has been used in schools. Through these interviews, Norwood tapped into a visionary collective wisdom that uncovered new dimensions and possibilities for educational coaching that constitute a true paradigm shift in how coaching is applied in the schools.

Through Burke and Norwood's cooperative argumentation, a third body of knowledge emerged. They concluded that cross-fertilization of research, theory, knowledge, and practice from fields other than education hold possibilities to enrich and broaden coaching potential in education. As coaches cultivate mastery in an eclectic range of coaching theories and practice and learn to detect and mitigate hegemonic and non-hegemonic barriers to coaching in their schools, they will be better equipped to help educators move through their fears and doubts toward a transformed level of praxis.

Keywords: Educational Coaching, Transformational Coaching, Hegemony, Institutional Scripts, Shadow, Transformation, Equity, Refugees, Principals, Teachers

Introduction

"Reforming the social structures which perpetuate poverty and the exclusion of the poor first requires a conversion of mind and heart." Pope Francis (2015)

Through both educational research literature as well as their own experiences, educators have long been aware of the importance of closing the racial skill and achievement gap between so-called minority and Caucasian students. Fryer (2010) argued that "closing the racial [skill] achievement gap is the most important civil rights battle of the twenty-first century" (p. 31): "Eliminating the racial skill gap will likely have an important impact on income inequality, unemployment, incarceration, health, and other important social and economic indices. The problem, to date, is that we do not know how to close the achievement gap" (p. 30). After decades of initiatives to close achievement gaps, which are often correlated with gaps in the rates of disciplinary actions for minority students versus their white counterparts (Pearman, Curran, Fisher, & Gardella, 2019), the differences persist.

Achievement testing data is but one measure of the consequences of inequitable educational practices. Perhaps an even more important measure than testing data is the comparative dropout rates of minority students versus Whites: "In 2017, the American Indian/Alaska Native (10.05 percent), Hispanic (8.2 percent), and Black (6.5 percent) status dropout rates remained higher than the White (4.3 percent) status dropout rate" (The National Center for Educational Statistics Report, 2019). While students give many reasons why they drop out, it seems likely that an important factor is that they simply do not see the value in going to school. On the contrary, students who consistently perform poorly in school may feel shamed and devalued by a system that somehow cannot supply what they need to succeed. For these students, school might well look like a poor investment of time and effort.

Students are not alone in feeling discouraged. Educators also experience the weight of inequitable practices and often, as Kegan and Lahey have voiced, feel in over their heads (1994) when it comes to knowing what to do about it. Institutional racism—embedded in discriminatory practices, entrenched belief systems, policies, and current power structures—often seems insurmountable. Research literature shows that equity issues have a strong impact on leaders and teachers. Principal leadership has momentous implications for students' experiences and teacher retention. Principal turnover results in higher teacher turnover, lower student achievement, and negatively impacts school culture. The data on principal and teacher turnover are grim. The average national tenure of a principal in a single school is 4 years, with 35 % leaving within two years and 18% leaving after only one year; low income schools fare even worse where 21% move on after only one year (Levin, & Bradley, 2017, p. 146). The lack of stable leadership has a strong effect on teachers' willingness to remain in their jobs. Teachers leaving the profession entirely are the cause for

90 % of the annual demand for new teachers. A staggering two-thirds of those teachers leave the profession for reasons other than retirement. The turn-over rate of all teachers in Title I schools ranks 50% higher than the national average, and is 70% higher for math and science teachers, and 80% higher for teachers who received their certification through alternative teacher training programs (Carver-Thomas & Darling-Hammond, 2017).

How, then, can the nation's schools—especially Title I schools—keep their students motivated and engaged in their education if the principals and teachers themselves are struggling to maintain their own morale? How can schools retain educators who are experienced, well-trained, and enthusiastic about educating the students entrusted to them? The whole system cries out for deep-seated, radical transformation, a systemic "conversion of mind and heart" (Pope Francis, 2015). This chapter, in combination with Norwood's companion chapter in the next section, considers the question of whether transformational educational coaching could help initiate this conversion, and if so, then how it might look in actual practice.

Discussions of what practitioners of transformational learning do are rare. As DeSapio (2017) rightly observed,

> Nearly all of the literature that was surveyed lacked any thorough discussion of how practitioners might promote or implement transformational learning. It seems that much of the discussion is related to what transformational learning is, or what it is that catalyzes transformation from within a person, but not what can be done to make transformational learning happen in the workplace or various other institutions of society. (p. 60)

Perhaps what makes the *how* of transformational learning so elusive is that it involves "these intangible qualities [that] move beyond traditional understandings" (p. 61). The current chapter explores how those qualities resist description and transformation because they are rooted in hegemony, what people "don't know that they don't know" (Norwood and Burke, 2013, p. 205).

In the pages that follow, Burke will explore findings from her research on some of the substantive hegemonic barriers to coaching for equity in educational practices. In the following chapter, Norwood will discuss her own research on coaching theories that go well beyond the standard instructional coaching approaches that are commonly applied in educational settings. She will consider how these theories suggest possibilities for moving beyond talk into action. The authors encourage the reader to read these chapters together, as transformation requires a twofold approach. First, Burke considers how to unearth the source of inequity, the invisible deeply buried roots of people's inequitable beliefs and practices. This is the Shadow, the conglomerate of suppressed fears, shame, and anger that compel otherwise well-meaning people to make hurtful and hateful choices. This is what must be transformed. The second part is Norwood's discussion of what to do with the onslaught of information and emotions that surely follow the first encounter with one's shadow. This is *how* transformational coaching begins.

Burke's Research

As the first collaborative dissertation in the history of Fielding Graduate University, Norwood and Burke's dissertation (2013) was the product of years of ongoing dialogue between the two of them concerning the importance and feasibility of transformational coaching in education. Norwood has long asserted that ongoing transformational coaching is imperative for producing sustainable change in schools. Burke, on the other hand, has argued that such coaching, however worthwhile it could be, might not be supported within the organizational dynamics of a typical school community. In their dissertation they tested their ideas through scholarly research and then continued that conversation based on their findings. They aimed to integrate practice and research by deeply grounding coaching theory and training as a living theory-in-practice. While this dissertation uncovered multiple avenues for further exploration, this chapter, as well as the one that follows, focuses on aspects of the findings that hold possibilities for addressing inequitable practices in Education.

Burke's research consisted of in-depth interviews with administrators, coaches, and teachers in a single school district that had had an active coaching program for 6 years. This district was selected primarily because of its ongoing experience with and commitment to their educational coaching program. All schools had some degree of involvement in the coaching program. Coaching was a component of this district's self-proclaimed academic focus on training staff to work collaboratively in their PLCs to improve the academic success of all students.

The district also presented an intriguing set of cultural, socio-economic, and demographic features that offered an opportunity to examine how coaches perceived their work in extremely challenging circumstances. Situated in a suburban community near a major U.S. city, the district has historically enjoyed strong community support, and many of the teaching staff grew up in the community and were themselves students in the schools. Over the course of only a few years, the community had experienced a pronounced demographic shift away from White middle-class families to economically challenged non-English-speaking refugees from other countries, many from Nepal and Burma. At the time of the interviews, there were 37 different languages represented in the schools. English Language Learners (EL students) made up 20% of the district and at the elementary level they comprised an average of 30-40% of the student population.

Although the minority student population had grown exponentially, the composition of the teaching staff remained exclusively White and middle class. Their sense of rootedness in the community went deeper than for teachers in many other districts, mostly because the history of the district was also their own personal history. As one participant observed,

There are so many staff members who went to school here themselves or they've married people who were here and they live in the district, and so there is really that strong sense of [school district name] pride, and the teachers and that group of teachers and individuals have definitely been part of the middle class group that lived in the district, which is not the primary group that lives here anymore. And so culturally the [district name] area is having a shift without shifting, and everything is changing around and within us, so bringing that dialogue [about inequity] to light is very personal for a lot of people. (Norwood & Burke, 2013, p. 111)

Analysis of the interview data revealed one fundamental barrier to the coaching program, School and District Culture. Two core sub-areas emerged as contributors to cultural barriers, Administrator Role and Accountability, and Equity, as the following breakdown illustrates. Listed under Administrator Role and Accountability are those barriers that referred to areas of school life that fell within the bailiwick of administrators, whether in each school or across the district.

Findings	
Administrator Role & Accountability	**Equity**
Priorities/Expectations/Goals/Focus	Fewer professional development opportunities for EL teachers
Understanding Coach Role	Poor principal supervision and support for EL staff
Support for Coaches	Predominantly White staff
Time/Money	"Our kids" (White) vs. "Their kids" (non-White)
PLC Coaching Format	
Lack of Training	
Fear	
Teachers' Union	
Autonomy	

While equity is the focus of the present chapter, it is important to keep in mind the role of Administrators in establishing the cultural tone, setting the priorities, and allocating the program funding for their schools. Principals have an important role in deciding what initiatives are worthy of their resources. Programs that they deem more important receive more of their support in the form of money and endorsement. Some of the principals interviewed in Burke's research stated that they personally had a difficult time maintaining focus on every school goal. They elected to emphasize those goals that seemed most critical to them. If principals do not care or know as much about certain programs as opposed to others, they are more likely to neglect them, leaving the teachers in those areas to fend for themselves. Some respondents to Burke's (Norwood & Burke, 2013) interview questions addressed this issue, noting principals' influence on programs targeting English Language Learners (EL):

"[EL] It's the step-child in the district. It's not a priority." (p. 204)
"The EL teachers have often been left out of the loop when it comes to coaching and professional development." (p. 204)
"The importance of that additional support for ELs is not there. So, I don't think principals walk through EL teacher classrooms. They do literacy walkthroughs and don't see the relevancy or the importance in walking through EL teachers' classes" (p. 204).

The lack of support for programs designed to meet the needs of English Language Learners seems odd, given the crisis caused by the burgeoning number of these very students in the district. Why wouldn't administrators recognize the importance of supporting EL teachers in any way they could, including offering coaching to them? One coach voiced an opinion on this incongruity: "I think if principals knew more about ELD [English Language Development] I think they would be

329

more willing to discuss coaching with them [ELD staff] because they would know of some of the support that they might need" (p. 205).

Assigning coaches to EL teachers would not be enough, however. One coach noted, ""The largest barrier I've had really has been administration, it's always the boss" (Norwood & Burke, 2013, p. 225). This statement referred to this coach's experience that administrators often assign coaches to teachers and then fail to follow-through to verify that coachees are meeting with their coaches and are making progress on their goals. Many coaches asserted in their interviews that principals' ability to remain consistent in what they expect of their coaches and coachees was a major factor in creating an effective coaching culture in their schools. Failure to do so, on the other hand, became an important barrier to coaches' ability to do their job.

The year prior to Burke's interviews, the former superintendent of this district initiated a survey to assess instructional priorities and goals that included staff as well as members of the community. Staff accounted for at least 80% of the respondents. This survey was prompted at least in part by an earlier state-generated report that suggested that there were inequities in the district regarding the frequency and severity of disciplining African American students versus White students. Burke was given access to the data, and was intrigued by responses to the question on the survey about instructional equity: "How important is it for schools to have the same high expectations for ALL students, regardless of ethnicity, economic circumstances or special needs?"

Respondents' answers revealed that for at least one-fourth of them this goal was less vital than other priorities, and for some it even seemed objectionable: 73% rated this goal as *very important*; 18% rated it as *somewhat important*; 6% rated it as *not very important*; and, 3% rated it as *not at all important*. Respondents were also invited to elaborate on their opinions via written comments. These comments underscored the heretofore unspoken hegemonic barriers to equitable instruction for minority children that surprised and dismayed some district personnel.

One of Burke's research participants explained the position that some in the district have taken on the issue of equity and equitable instruction by saying, "They don't know what they don't know. And they're doing the best they can, there's just a lack of knowledge" (Norwood & Burke, 2013, p. 205). Without using the word, and perhaps without even knowing it, her observation beautifully described the essence and power of hegemony and hegemonic barriers. If people do not know what they do not know, who would ask the questions that could shake them out of their complacent ignorance? Therein lies the problem: "It ain't what you don't know that gets you into trouble. It's what you know for sure that just ain't so" (popularly attributed to Mark Twain).

Burke's research (Norwood & Burke, 2013) has led her to observe that entrenched organizational systems often operate in ways that resemble an old rusty vault with a missing key. One may well find immeasurable wealth inside, but there is no key to unlock it, and, even if there were a key in hand, the door's encrusted hinges resist all efforts to push it open. Yet, lured by visions of treasure, one tries and fails again and again to pry open the door. Why does one persist in using the same ineffective strategy? Because one is convinced beyond a shadow of doubt—one knows for sure—that there is no possible alternative. Such is hegemony.

Hegemony is a formidable barrier to transforming inequitable practices because it hides in plain sight. It is the aggregate of all the culturally and psychologically embedded beliefs, biases, and preconceptions that have been passed down from generation to generation for so long that no one remembers when, how, or even *that* they were created. One's notion of who one is, how one defines one's own and others' possibilities and limitations, and generally what is real and what is not, spring from this bedrock. This is where human beings feel most secure, and the notion that there might be something beyond what they know *for sure* can be frightening. People do not find successful alternatives to failing strategies because they most often look for them within their comfort zone, in the field of possibilities that they already know.

Norwood and Burke (2011, 2013) have proposed that educational coaching can help educators begin to access the rich potential within their organizations. Perhaps, as they have argued, cross-fertilization of research, theory, knowledge, and practice from diverse fields other than education can offer new possibilities to enrich and broaden coaching potential in education. As the saying goes, "Old ways won't open new doors" (author unknown). The key to unlocking the door would be to go beyond known change models to discover new ways of thinking, talking, and acting to give all educators and students the opportunity to experience education as something full of joy, excitement, and purpose. It is time to explore the wisdom that lies beyond one's field of experience. What keeps educators from doing just that?

> "No passion so effectually robs the mind of all its powers of acting
> and reasoning as fear."
> (E.A. Burke, 2009, p. 32)

The moment one proposes to enter unknown territory, a myriad of fears arise. The unknown presents a faceless, nameless threat to all that one knows. Organizational entities guard against this threat by erecting "institutionalized systemic barriers" (Bodilly et al., 2004, p. 118) as a protection against the potential disruption of organizational well-being. A mainstay of this protective system is organizational discursive practice, which consists of deeply rooted "institutional scripts" (Rusch, 2005, p. 89) that are the invisible foundations of the organization, the "language, narratives, and rituals" (Anderson, 1990, p. 45) that maintain organizational integrity in the face of change. All is well when people say and do the expected things, those things that *everyone knows*.

The district that was the focus of Burke's research was in many ways a district that was under siege by the wave of refugees who had moved into the area. Refugee families did not know what *everyone knows,* nor did they say or do the expected things. They had different traditions, expectations, and ways of being that were radically different from people in their new community. For longtime residents of the district, refugees became the intense focus of fear as they embodied the unknown, *The Other.* Inequitable practices often stem from entrenched hegemonic beliefs about the relative value and worth of *The Other:* "Othering, marginalisation, stigma and inequality are inter-related concepts, with a shared component of rewards for being 'normal' or, like 'us'; and costs for being different, deviant or, like 'them'" (Barter-Godfrey & Taket, 2009 p. 167). Othering generates fear and suspicion about groups such as the refugees discussed in Burke's research, who were identified by some respondents as an existential threat to the established community.

Othering reinforces the norms of what is expected by identifying as deviant the customs and practices of groups like the refugees in Burke's study. It therefore also functions as a source of psychological safety and well-being for those in the dominant group. Gillespie (2007) wrote that there is "a widespread tendency to differentiate in-group from out-group and Self from Other in such a way as to bolster and protect Self" (p. 580). In Burke's research (Norwood & Burke, 2013), this process of fear leading to self-enhancement and self-protection is clearly demonstrated in the subtext of the language some respondents used in their answers to questions in the Superintendent's survey of community beliefs about district initiatives to promote equitable instructional practices:

"It is ignorant to believe we are all created equal." [Subtext: *We* are more worthy than *they* are.]

"Cultural and economic circumstances must be considered when helping a student connect their education to their future success as an adult." [Subtext: We shouldn't waste resources on students who will not rise very far in life.]

"I am very disturbed by the amount of time and money spent on children (families) that are not socially or academically up to par." [Subtext: Refugee families do not meet our standards of worthiness for spending our resources.]

"With the exception of special needs students [i.e., developmentally disabled children], I feel that having special needs students [i.e., English Language Learners] in the public schools drains the school of financial and teacher resources that could be placed elsewhere." [Subtext: Funding the instructional support of refugee students wastes time and money that could benefit *our* students.]

"Although I don't like to see anyone not succeed in school, I feel that due to the huge numbers of non-English speaking students, my own children have not had the benefit of the academic instruction that they should have had, and that makes me angry and frustrated -- especially since we are property owners and taxpayers, whereas a majority of non-English speaking students are a transient, apartment dwelling population." [Subtext: There are two categories of students in our schools, those who belong (ours) and those who do not (refugee); we are first-class, and they are at best second-class.]

For these individuals, educational programs that support learning for refugee children siphon off resources to which they believe their own children are more entitled, by virtue of belonging to the white, English-speaking, and tax-paying dominant class. Refugees are not entitled to share in these resources, by virtue of their status as *Other:* Because they are viewed as contributing nothing of value to the community, they do not have the right to take anything of value from the community. In distinguishing *us* versus *them*, in saying that *they* do not deserve the same rights and privileges that *we* deserve, these respondents find comfort and strength in what they see as their inborn moral superiority. Underneath all the posturing about entitlement, however, is a deep-seated fear that *they* will steal *our* own children's rightful inheritance. Burke posits that this kind of reasoning represents the essence of hegemony, which always presents itself as taken-for-granted, God-given Truth used in the service of self-preservation.

Hegemony thrives in situations where perceived threats to the traditional order of things arouse deep survival level fears in the dominant group. In this particular school district, Burke's (Norwood & Burke, 2013) research uncovered multiple layers of fear, such as: fear of conflict; fear of exposing what one really thinks; fear of being the lone dissenting voice; fear of other people and cultures; fear of being controlled by authority; and fear of losing autonomy (p. 234). Prior to the advent of the refugee population, many district leaders and teachers had experienced years of professional success. This was a source of identity and pride for many. Radical changes in the district caused them to come face to face with the fearful prospect that they might not have the skills and knowledge to successfully teach these students while meeting the needs of their other non-refugee students as well.

Many in the district felt a deep sense of loss and fear, as one participant stated, a "longing for the good old days" where the community and student population were predominantly white, Protestant, and middle class. Burke (Norwood & Burke, 2013) designated this as the "institutional script of nostalgia" (p. 236). There was security in homogeneity and predictability. Hegemony enshrines the status quo and represents it as the only way to be. As many people in the district focused on looking backward, toward the established field of known certainties and possibilities, they could not look forward toward potentials and possibilities with any sense of positive anticipation.

As Krishnamurti (1950) said, "fear of the unknown is really fear of losing the accumulated known" (https://www.jkrishnamurti.org/content/madras-2nd-public-talk-29th-january-1950/fear). When one loses what one has always known, one feels uprooted and alienated

335

from one's self. This negative experience of fear is both the product and source of disconnection. Negatively perceived fear comes from being emotionally and spiritually disconnected from one's own self, from others in the immediate and global community, and, ultimately, from nature. People who are alienated from their own inner moral compass are more susceptible to a phenomenon known in the literature as "spontaneous hypnosis" (Beahrs, 1989, p. 173), particularly in situations of high pressure, stress, and fear. In this state, they become hyper-suggestible to the language of perceived authority figures—including the authority of communal common sense—and more compliant with hegemonic influence (Four Arrows, 2016; Four Arrows, in Norwood & Burke, 2013). There is not much discussion in non-indigenous literature on the need to restore one's intrapersonal and interpersonal connectedness in order to achieve transformational goals. Perhaps this gap is partly because Mezirow's ideas are the keystone for contemporary transformative theories, and, as DiSapio (2017) observed, "the notion [of connectedness] is entirely absent from Mezirow's theory" (p. 62).

Four Arrows (Norwood & Burke, 2013) argued that the negative experience of fear derives from a non-indigenous perspective wherein fear is a dreadful or damaging emotion that must be avoided at all costs. Ironically, this avoidance itself "becomes a self-defeating thing because the fear, then, becomes [a] trance image, and they wind up getting what they fear" (p. 153). Indigenous cultures, however, see fear as "only temporarily and quickly an emotion for an opportunity to survive," an emotion that inspires "an opportunity for practicing a virtue … an opportunity to practice this higher level of thinking" (p. 153). Indigenous perspectives on fear suggest that fear does not have to cause an automatic—and highly counterproductive—*duck and cover* response which freezes all creative activity as energy is directed toward defensive postures.

The ability to use fear as a stimulus for fresh creativity injects life into the community. Fear can be a catalyst for good, an inspiration for ongoing, life-giving beauty in service of the greater good. Fearlessness, as Four Arrows (2016) designates it, causes humans to "become fully alive in our realization of interconnectedness with all" (p. 61). The author believes that this is the highest purpose of coaching:

> If we think that coaching is 'the conferral of information' we are really missing the point. How do I go beyond my physical body in the sense that I realize that I am connected with everything? Another way of learning the essence is connection . . . and the essence of soul is connection. (Olalla, in Norwood & Burke, 2013, p, 128)

For this connection to occur, however, the coach and the coachee must each possess "a willingness to accept and embrace the unknown" (Four Arrows, 2016, p. 61). This is the creative--and sometimes terrifying--space where transformation is possible.

The ongoing conversation in the district concerning equity presented another interesting twist in institutional scripting, this time regarding a phenomenon that Morrison and Milliken (2000) called *organizational silence*. In their study they discovered that discursive standards in some organizations privilege some topics and conflicts while silencing others. They noted that managerial beliefs—"management knows best; unity is good and dissent is bad" (p. 709)—as well as managers' fears of being criticized led to the creation of organizational silence: "We define a climate of silence as one characterized by two shared beliefs: (1) speaking up about problems in the organization is not worth the effort, and (2) voicing one's opinions and concerns is dangerous" (p. 714). Topics and conflicts that do not conform to the standards of the dominant discourse therefore do not enter the conversation at all (Bachrach & Baratz, 1962, 1963, 1970; Lukes, 1974; Mumby & Stohl, 1991; Schattschneider, 1960).

In Burke's (Norwood & Burke, 2013) interviews, participants stated that the district had established the "non-negotiable" (p. 210) standard that *all children can learn*. The difficulty was that those individuals who disagreed on any basis with this dictum had gone underground with their beliefs because it had become unacceptable to openly espouse them. After all, non-negotiable *means* closed to discussion. This imposed—and self-imposed—silence precluded an open conversation between those who promoted across the board equity of instructional practice and those who resisted it. As Edmondson (2019) has argued, however, the problem is that if people hide what they know and believe rather than disclosing it, there is little opportunity to effect meaningful change. Coaching might help, but as one of Burke's participants observed,

> You've got to get teachers past the brown kids can't learn and if they would just say that that's what they believed, it would be much easier to coach them through it, but they're usually more skilled in hiding that, I believe. (p. 210)

Many participants expressed the understanding that the use of such a strong word as *non-negotiable* was meant to draw the line firmly in the sand, to emphasize that inequity in classroom practices was not going to be tolerated. This delimitation marginalized those individuals who did not agree with the official position on the relative learning ability of minority children. This policy did not necessarily change their opinions, but it did force them into silence, out of fear of ostracism and even losing their jobs. It is therefore somewhat ironic that designating equitable instruction as *non-negotiable* as a means of promoting equity also achieved the opposite purpose of moving dissenting views beyond the reach of coaches who could address and perhaps mitigate them.

One participant argued that those individuals in the district who did not agree with the official position on equitable instruction practices found themselves with few options:

If you disagree with that [the premise that all children can learn], where do you put yourself so that you don't put yourself in professional peril, but you're often at odds philosophically with what's going on. And I think because of the economic climate, there are probably people who would prefer not to be here or not to work in our district who feel like they can't leave. And so for them I feel really sad that if this is not a good fit for you and if this is not what you believe, you shouldn't be here, but I think some people feel like they have to be. (Norwood & Burke, 2013, p. 212)

This statement perfectly describes what can happen when what is hidden is not revealed, when people conceal their Shadow self, those feelings and opinions that they fear will alienate them from others.

How can such fundamental differences ever be resolved if people cannot talk about them? Most educators have not been trained to think critically about educational systems and practices (Macpherson, Brooker, Aspland, and Cuskelly, 2004). Educational coaches are uniquely positioned to serve as disruptors of the hegemonic scripts that so powerfully derail the transformation of inequitable practices in schools. Well-trained leaders and coaches can interject a level of thoughtful, and often disruptive, inquiry into interpersonal and district-level conversations. This function is essential if education is to serve its purpose of awakening the minds and souls of its students. Systems need ongoing refreshment and movement in order to be vital, life-giving organisms. Otherwise, the system atrophies, becoming a hardened shell of hegemonic beliefs and practices that serves no one.

Coaches can and should encourage educators to speak their truth so that they can either get on with the job of educating all their students, or, if they cannot do this, so they can make room for someone else who will do the job. This position may seem harsh to some, but as Darling-Hammond, Chung Wei, Andree, Richardson, and Orphanos (2009) argued, "Inequality in the provision of education is an antiquated tradition the United States can no longer afford . . . it is imperative that America close the achievement gap among its children by addressing the yawning opportunity gap that denies these fundamental rights" (p. 8). Ten years have passed since they wrote that statement, and, while some progress has been made, there is still a long way to go.

During her interview with Burke (Norwood & Burke, 2013), one coach talked about how educational coaching could help disrupt and transform the hegemonic complacency that allows otherwise well-meaning people to perpetuate inequity in the schools:

> I think, again, it's easy to say, well it worked for these 80 kids, these other 20 kids, it's not my fault; it's not my job. They belong to someone else, or they don't belong here. Now I think those are kind of natural responses at first until you really start asking different questions, which is where the coaches really are critical. (p. 200)

Coaches ask different questions. These questions are not a part of everyday discourse, and they require that one think about one's answers. One cannot easily fall back on rote answers that parrot conventional wisdom. Coaches' questions are meant to deviate from discursive norms and conventions. They serve to pause the customary flow of conversation, to provide the space for creative reflection. Coaches' questions create a sense of disorientation and disruption so that taken-for-granted patterns can be examined. As they chase the Shadow and bring it out into the light to see it for what it is, they strip away the veneer of legitimacy from the hegemonic assumptions that support inequitable educational practices so that they can be seen for what they are: racial and cultural narrow-mindedness.

Should one therefore conclude that the primary objective of educational coaching is to create a climate of confrontation that leads to division and anger? Not exactly, although disorientation and upheaval—Mezirow's (1975) "disorienting dilemma"—often constitutes the first step for perspective transformation. It seems that one needs to be shocked out of one's complacency in order to seek transformative solutions to seemingly irresolvable problems. Disruption that leads to a process of inquiry and transformation is therefore a healthy *first step*. It is, however, also a frightening and potentially destructive step into the unknown that most organizations, including and perhaps especially schools, go to extreme measures to avoid.

As discussed earlier in this chapter, avoidance is not the only possible response to the unknown, nor is it necessarily the best. As Norwood will discuss in the following chapter, the transformative work of educational coaching could be to look at the fear that lies hidden underneath racial and cultural narrow-mindedness. Coaches may learn much from Indigenous peoples who embrace fear as an emotion that can generate life and creativity in both individuals and in the community (Four Arrows, 2016; in Norwood and Burke, 2013). Johnson (2013) wrote of this experience as one of liberation:

> Delegitimizing the lonely, terrifying, self-doubting, despairing parts of our spirit delimits our capacity for fully appreciating moments of light, joy, hilarity, communion, triumph, and transcendence. Many organizations create a narrow, rigidly bounded range for acceptable expression of human experience.... The liberation of soul means extending our capacity to acknowledge the full range of human experiencing in all of its contexts—including work. (p. 193)

Moving Forward

Burke's (Norwood & Burke, 2013) research focused on the first half of the equation to produce transformational change, the need to identify and question the invisible hegemonic ties that bind educational systems to inequitable practices. The work is not easy. The point is never to blame or shame the coachee, and if a coach does so it is usually a sign of their own immaturity and ego. Disruption should serve to open minds, not close them down. Coaches must not go into coaching sessions with a wrecking ball, hoping that somehow everything will work out. They need a plan not only for how they will reveal hidden pain, but also for how they will help their coachees find the hopes and dreams that lie concealed there. Transformative coaching requires compassion, courage, maturity, clarity of focus, and the ability to deeply connect with others.

This is the point that leads into Norwood's (Norwood & Burke, 2013) research, where she goes beyond the field of education to introduce theories of coaching that have never been applied to educational coaching for transformation. In this chapter, Burke has explored the first step of transformational coaching in education, that of creating awareness of hegemonic barriers. Norwood's work illuminates how coaches can move this work to new dimensions, bringing it from chaos to true transformation. The reader is now invited to move on to read her chapter in the following section.

About the Author

Dr. Burke earned a PhD in Medieval and 20th Century French Language and Literature from the University of Wisconsin, Madison, and she taught as Professor of French at UCLA. She earned her EdD in Educational Leadership and Change in 2013 from Fielding Graduate University. As a licensed Marriage and Family Therapist, she has worked with individuals and families struggling with addictions to drugs and alcohol, and child abuse. She counseled adolescents in court-ordered group home placement. She taught credentialing classes for foster care parents through the Antelope Valley Community College in Lancaster, California, and classes for aspiring substance abuse counselors at Pacific Oaks College in Los Angeles. Most recently she counseled returning combat veterans and their families at the Boston Vet Center. Dr. Burke specializes in helping clients look at deeply embedded subconscious beliefs and values that may hinder their best efforts. This work requires extensive knowledge of systems theory, stages of human and group development, motivation theories, and issues of cultural and linguistic diversity. Burke applies her experience as a therapist and teacher toward developing transformational coaching theory and practice that may be applied in working with individuals and organizations. Norwood and Burke co-authored: *Transformational Coaching in Education: A Collaborative Look at the Bridges and Barriers to Learning* (Dissertation); *Education in The Handbook of Knowledge-Based Coaching: From Theory to Practice,* San Francisco, CA: Jossey-Bass, 2011; and several coach training manuals, the most recent titled: *Appreciative Leadership & Coaching* and, *School Coaching: What Is It and How Do You Do It?*

References

Bachrach, P., & Baratz, M. S. (1962). The two faces of power. *American Political Science Review, 54,* 947-952. doi:10.2307/1952796

Bachrach, P., & Baratz, M. S. (1963). Decisions and nondecisions: An analytical framework. *American Political Science Review,* 57, 641-651. doi:10.2307/1952568

Bachrach, P., & Baratz, M. S. (1970). *Power and poverty: Theory and practice.* New York, NY: Oxford University Press.

Barter-Godfrey, S., and Taket, A. (2009). Othering, marginalisation and pathways to exclusion in health. *Theorising social exclusion,* 166-172. Routledge: Abingdon, England.

Beahrs, J. (1989). Spontaneous hypnosis in the forensic context. *Bulletin of the American Academy of Psychiatry Law,* 17(2), 171-181.

Bodilly, S. J., Chun, J., Ikemoto, G., & Stockly, S. (2004). *Challenges and potential of a collaborative approach to education reform.* Santa Monica, CA: RAND Corporation. Retrieved from http://www.rand.org

Burke, E.A. (2009). II: Terror. *A philosophical inquiry into the origin of our ideas of the sublime and beautiful.* Part II in Digireads.com Publishing.

Carver-Thomas, D. & Darling-Hammond, L. (2017). *Teacher turnover: Why it matters and what we can do about it.* Palo Alto, CA: Learning Policy Institute. Retrieved from:https://learningpolicyinstitute.org/product/teacher-turnover.

Darling-Hammond, L., Chung Wei, R., Andree, A., Richardson, N., & Orphanos, S. (2009). *Professional learning in the learning profession: A status report on teacher development in the United States and abroad.* Oxford, OH: National Staff Development Council.

DeSapio, J. (2017). Transformational learning: A literature review and call forward. *Journal of Transformative Learning,* 4(2), 56-63. Retrieved from https://fgul.idm.oclc.org/docview/2193150225?accountid=10868

Edmondson, A.C. (2019). *The fearless organization: Creating psychological safety in the workplace for learning, innovation, and growth.* Hoboken, New Jersey: John Wiley & Sons, Inc.

Education Week (2019). Education Statistics: Facts About American Schools. Published: January 3, 2019, Updated: July 22, 2019.

Four Arrows (2016). *Point of departure: Returning to a more authentic worldview for education and survival.* Charlotte, NC: Information Age Publishing.

Gillespie, A. (2007). Collapsing self/other positions: identification through differentiation. *British Journal of Social Psychology,*46, pp. 579-595.

Johnson, P. (2013). Transcending the polarity of light and shadow in Appreciative Inquiry: An appreciative exploration of practice. In Zandee, D. Cooperrider, D.L. and Avital, M. (Eds.) *Generative organization: Advances in Appreciative Inquiry.* Bingley, England: Emerald Publishing.

Kegan, R., & Lahey, L. (1994). *In over our heads: The mental demands of modern life.* Cambridge, MA: Harvard University Press.

Krishnamurti, J. (1950). Madras 2nd public talk, January 29, 1950. Retrieved from https://www.jkrishnamurti.org/content/madras-2nd-public-talk-29th-january-1950/fear%20of%20the%20unknown

Levin, S. & Bradley, K. (2017) *Understanding and addressing principal turnover.* Palo Alto, CA: Learning Policy Institute.

Lukes, S. (1974). *Power: A radical view.* London, UK: Macmillan.

Macpherson, I., Brooker, R., Aspland, T., & Cuskelly, E. (2004). Constructing a territory for professional practice research: Some practical considerations. *Action Research,* 2(1), 89-106. doi:10.1177/1476750304040496

Mezirow, J. (1975). *Education for perspective transformation: Women's reentry programs in community colleges.* New York, NY: Center for Adult Education, Teachers College, Columbia University.

Morrison, E. W., & Milliken, F. J. (2000). Organizational silence: A barrier to change and development in a pluralistic world. *Academy of Management Review,* 25(4), 706-725. doi:10.2307/259200

Mumby, D., & Stohl, C. (1991). Power and discourse in organization studies: Absence and the dialectic of control. *Discourse Society,* 2(3), 313-332. doi:10.1177/0957926591002003004

Norwood, K., & Burke, M. A. (2011). Education. In L. Wildflower & D. Brennan (Eds.), *The handbook of knowledge-based coaching: From theory to practice* (pp. 211-220). San Francisco, CA: Jossey-Bass.

Norwood, K., & Burke, M.A. (2013). *Transformational coaching in education: A collaborative look at the bridges and barriers to learning.* (Doctoral dissertation). ProQuest UMI No. 3601821.

Pearman, F. A., Curran, F. C., Fisher, B., & Gardella, J. (2019). Are achievement gaps related to discipline gaps? Evidence from national data. Retrieved from *AERA Open.* https://doi.org/10.1177/2332858419875440

Rusch, E. (2005). Institutional barriers to organizational learning in school systems: The power of silence. *Educational Administration Quarterly, 41*(1), 83-120. doi:10.1177/0013161X04269546

Schattschneider, E. E. (1960). *The semi-sovereign people: A realist's view of democracy in America.* New York, NY: Holt, Rinehart, & Winston.

CHAPTER 16

BEAUTIFUL FORM WATCHER: COACHING FOR EQUITY IN EDUCATION

Kathy Norwood EdD, PCC
Fielding Graduate University EBC Faculty Member;
Coaches Evolve, LLC

Abstract

How can transformational coaching be a powerful tool to help educators increase their ability to discern, disrupt, and remedy inequities in Pre-K-12 school culture and practices? This chapter presents key findings from Norwood's (Norwood & Burke, 2013) research into this question. Norwood interviewed world thought leaders of five unique visionary approaches to coaching: Julio Olalla (Ontological Coaching), Sara Orem (Appreciative Coaching), Robert Hargrove (Masterful Coaching and Triple-Loop Learning), Four Arrows (Indigenous Approaches to Deep Learning), and Art Costa, Robert Garmston, and Jane Ellison (Cognitive Coaching[SM]). Of these five, only Cognitive Coaching[SM] has been used in schools. Through these interviews, Norwood tapped into a visionary collective wisdom that uncovered new dimensions and possibilities for educational coaching that constitute a true paradigm shift in how coaching is applied in the schools.

In her companion chapter that precedes this one, Burke uses critical inquiry to investigate possible hegemonic and non-hegemonic barriers to transformational coaching. She finds that two aspects of school culture have the greatest impact on the viability of educational coaching: 1. administrators' ability and willingness to understand, support, and facilitate coaches' work, and, 2. educators' widely divergent levels of awareness of, and openness to, equitable practice. Each area is fertile ground for well-trained coaches.

Norwood and Burke's (2013) research leads to the emergence of a third body of knowledge. They conclude that cross-fertilization of research, theory, knowledge, and practice from fields other than education hold possibilities to enrich and broaden coaching potentials for transformation in education. To illustrate how this theory might look in practice Norwood includes here a hypothetical coaching session in a case study drawn from Burke's research. As coaches cultivate mastery in an eclectic range of coaching theories and practice and learn to detect and mitigate hegemonic and non-hegemonic barriers to coaching in their schools, they will be better equipped to help educators move through their fears and doubts toward a transformed level of praxis.

Keywords: Education, Transformation, Appreciative, Cognitive, Masterful, Indigenous, Ontological, Coaching, Coach Training, Hegemony, Equity, Beliefs, Teachers

Introduction

Kaleidoscopes were invented in 1816 by a child prodigy, Sir David Brewster, a physicist in Scotland. Known as *"The Beautiful Form Watcher,"* the kaleidoscope is a metaphor for wholeness and integration. It focuses the mind in such a way that one sees into a new perceptual frontier. As one slightly shifts the lens, vibrant colors laced with dancing patterns delight the eye, holding infinite possibilities for new creations. Effective coaches are *beautiful form watchers* who, with their coachees, create a sacred space for vast potentials to emerge.

This description of what the kaleidoscope is and how it operates captures the essence of transformational coaching. Kaleidoscopic images move in the flow of an unceasing process that transforms the images before one's eyes. It is a constant cycle of deconstruction, construction, and deconstruction. Attempts to freeze given images by photographing them render them lifeless in their permanence. Their magic lies in their movement.

Likewise, transformational coaching operates according to the premise that the vitality of organizations depends upon the degree to which they can constantly reinvent themselves. Transformational coaches question the organization's hegemonic roots (see Burke, preceding chapter "Chasing the Shadow"), its "taken-for-granted frames of reference" (Mezirow, 2000, p. 4), that immobilize creativity. Kegan and Lahey (1994) defined transformational learning as learning that changes the form of one's mind, or how one knows—one's meaning systems. Transformation alters one's identity and therefore one's way of being. Burke and Norwood (2011; 2013) argue that such learning must be an ongoing, continuous process if it is to be truly transformational.

Norwood's research (Norwood & Burke, 2013) addressed the absence of appropriate theoretical and practical training of educational coaches, alternative coaching theories and approaches, including supporting empirical research, and the hegemonic barriers (Burke's research) ingrained within the system that block deep learning. Uniform coach training, practices, standards, and guidelines are missing in most K-12 coaching communities. Current educational coach preparation lacks rigor in training and monitoring of coaches and coaching programs (Brown, Stroh, Fouts, & Baker, 2005; Burkins, & Ritchie, 2007; International Reading Association, 2004; Reiss, 2007). Individuals without any type of coach training or known level of coaching competence often call themselves coaches (Brantley, 2007; Terrell & Hughes, 2008). Comparatively, educators operating in any other role such as principal, counselor, teacher and the like have gone through a rigorous educational process to become credentialed.

In the absence of grounding in well-founded theories and practice, educational coaching has been somewhat haphazard. Brown et al. (2005) found that, "The large majority of coaching programs in education appear to be a-theoretical in nature . . . it was rare that an organization presented a specific theoretical model that structured their coaching work" (p. 114). Coaches simply tend to do what they think makes sense for their schools. This unfocused approach to coaching has calcified into a system where leaders and coaches spend their time as problem solvers rather than as the true transformational change agents that they could be. This misuse of coaches' time is unacceptable at a time when educators are overwhelmed by the demands of creating an equitable and rigorous learning environment for their students.

One cannot overstate the importance of training coaches to promote the transformation of unequal and inequitable practices in the schools. High quality coaching is a necessity for schools and can be the significant relationship that educators embrace to support their ability to improve their work. How, then, might coaches' work be the impetus that unleashes educators' transformative potentials?

The next section highlights Norwood's findings that particularly pertain to equity and methodologies that hold possibilities for mitigating hegemony (explored in Burke's research). Norwood weaves a tapestry of research findings with theory and the practical application of holistic methodologies to a case study that emerged during Burke's (Norwood & Burke, 2013) interviews.

A Woven Tapestry
"Theory without practice is foolish; practice without theory is dangerous."
(Chinese proverb)

Findings, Case Study
Norwood deeply investigated nine prominent coaches, Julio Olalla (Ontological Coaching), Sara Orem (Appreciative Coaching), Robert Hargrove (Masterful Coaching and Triple-Loop Learning), Four Arrows (Indigenous Perspectives on Deep Learning), and Art Costa, Robert Garmston, and Jane Ellison (Cognitive Coaching[SM])—six of whom authored five different philosophical approaches that potentially lead to transformational learning. Each of the above coaches' transformational models arose out of the enormous passion and

universal nuggets of truth generated by their personal life experiences. Norwood longed to tap into that wisdom to better understand how it might be applied in educational settings.

Norwood used appreciative inquiry and phenomenological methods to look at the transformative potential of school coaching. Three prominent categories emerged—Holistic Methodologies, Coach, and Transformation. She tapped into a *visionary collective wisdom* that uncovered a true paradigm shift in how coaching can be applied in the schools.

Holistic Methodologies

The western educational system, while impressive in its emphasis on the development of the intellect, neglects the enhancement and development of the human heart: love, compassion and those other values that are embraced by all the cultures of the world. (Dalai Lama, 1997, p. 7)

Norwood's interviewees developed holistic approaches to their coaching methodology that address the whole person—one's spirit, soul, body, and mind. With some distinguishing features, all interviewees believed that their models encompassed a holistic approach to coaching that could potentially enhance their clients' lives on many levels. The Indigenous perspective, for example, focuses on the interrelatedness of all there is (Four Arrows, in Norwood & Burke, 2013). The goal is to balance on many levels the power of reason with other ways of knowing, where one learns to embrace the fullness of one's humanity. Each interviewee asserted that coaches must be aware of their own worldview, and how it impacts their coaching. Norwood observed that all her interviewees embody their espoused theories for coaching in their *way of being*. There is no longer a separation between who they are and what they teach.

Coach

These prominent coaches discussed the role of coach, the attributes of a masterful coach, and the belief a coach holds in the resourcefulness of the coachee. A long list of competencies emerged that better defined masterful coaching. Discussed most often was a coach's level and use of emotional intelligence, coupled with the ability to build trusting relationships. One area most fascinating to Norwood was how these renowned thought leaders discussed their use of intuition and *different ways of knowing* to facilitate their coaching conversations. To name a few, they discussed the use of dreamwork, images, floating words, and bodily sensations, offered at times to the coachee in a spirit of curiosity. By operating from the heart, coaches tap into a deeper level of wisdom in their work.

Transformation

Evidence of transformation emerged as they shared their coaching stories. Each model offers strategies, that, if understood well, enhance the potential for deep change in others. For example, the Ontological model emphasizes exploring the client's way of being in the world, the force that drives one's behavior and communication. A coach fosters shifts in several domains—*language* (how one expresses through language reflects who one is); *moods and emotions* (one's moods can either enhance or obstruct desired results); *body* (embodied physiological processes of what one feels, thinks, and acts); and *spirit* (one's ability to be present, centered, and learn to live life with gratitude). The goal is to make a shift in all four areas to ensure a deep and profound change—transformation, in other words.

As coachees become more resilient, as well as mentally and emotionally aware, they develop a deeper capacity to connect more fully to their own and others' lives. Appreciative Coaching, for instance, focuses on strengths, passion, and positive potential in designing and manifesting the dreams of the individual. Its core principles are designed to show the client how to tap into a childlike sense of wonder

351

about present life and future possibilities. Newly empowered to access deeper levels of wisdom within themselves, coachees learn to live life with gratitude. Deeper shifts occur as the focus shifts to changing how people think and not on what they do, allowing a generative metaphor to emerge.

Four Arrows (1998, writing as D.T. Jacobs), developed the mnemonic called CAT-FAWN as a way to describe Indigenous perspectives on transformational processes of change and to help clients remember how to work toward their highest potentials. CAT stands for Concentrated, Activated, Transformation which recognizes that all transformation ultimately happens when the *aha* comes, when one comes to believe in an image so strongly that that belief in the image becomes an automatic behavior. Hypnosis (and self-hypnosis) is a natural process that can produce this result. People who do guided imagery while in a light trance state use a form of self-hypnosis to implant a desired image deep into the subconscious (Jacobs, 1988). The other half of Four Arrows' mnemonic, FAWN—Fear, Authority, Words, and Nature—rounds out the transformative process, describing the four influences that determine whether the trance state leads individuals to their highest potential. Fear presents the opportunity to practice the virtue of fearlessness (Four Arrows, 2016; see Burke, previous chapter). Fear induces enhanced states of awareness, akin to trance states, that compel transformation. One then assumes the mantle of one's own authority and initiates a deeper connection with all beings and nature.

Costa and Garmston's interview outlined the desired outcome of Cognitive Coaching™ wherein one becomes self-directed by strengthening the Five States of Mind—efficacy, flexibility, craftsmanship, consciousness, and interdependence. These internal resources enlighten one's awareness, unifying the expression of wholeness, providing the impetus that moves one's intellectual, emotional, physical, and spiritual capacities toward higher levels of performance.

In the same fashion, this approach fosters the conceptual development of teachers:

> Cognitive coaching enhances the intellectual capacity of teachers, which in turn produces greater intellectual achievement in students . . . teachers at higher stages of intellectual functioning demonstrate more flexibility, toleration for stress, and adaptability. They take multiple perspectives, use a variety of coping behaviors, and draw from a broader repertoire of teaching models. (Costa & Garmston, 1994, p. 6)

Developing one's ability to function at higher conceptual levels holds transformative possibilities for teachers and their students. Teachers are better equipped to diagnose "instructional problems more effectively, think of more ideas when planning, project the consequences of their actions, use a variety of teaching approaches, and have higher quality communication with their students" (Brown et al., 2005, p. 24). Teachers can better understand the students' perspective and frame of reference, and therefore link their planning, instruction, and evaluation to deeper student learning (Hunt & Joyce, 1967).

Hargrove designed Masterful Coaching to be a challenge to clients to achieve extraordinary, seemingly impossible, results. He applied his theory of triple-loop learning to coaching as follows: "triple-loop—altering people's way of being; double-loop—altering people's mental models and thereby their thinking and actions; and single-loop—tips and techniques" (Hargrove, 2003, p. 89). Triple-loop learning describes transformation of self, and is what Hargrove defined as the desired outcome of transformational coaching.

Norwood's (Norwood & Burke, 2013) findings illuminated the need for highly trained and developed coaches who are adept at applying holistic methodologies that achieve deep transformation of educators' hearts and minds, educational policies, and instructional practices. Students and educators deserve no less.

Students dream of creating a life rich with experience and opportunities. They envision careers that match their talents and passion. *The Opportunity Myth* (TNTP, 2018), a recent national study, focused on students' voices by exploring their learning experiences in K-12 settings. TNTP's study unearthed deeply entrenched beliefs and practices prominent in educational systems (in this author's words, hegemony). The findings were troubling. Students in this study lacked ongoing access to important resources: "grade-appropriate assignments, strong instruction, deep engagement, and teachers who hold high expectations" (Summary, pg. 4). Students of color, English language learners, those with disabilities, and students from low-income households had even less access to essential resources. While 82% of teachers expressed support for state standards for college readiness, only 44% believed their students could attain grade level mastery. Students graduating from high school (many with As and Bs), were unprepared for college (40% of college students needed at least 1 remedial course, including 66% of Black college students and 53% Latinx college students). Those who took remedial courses were 74% more likely to drop out. Graduates who chose to enter the workforce in a coveted job found they lacked the skill set needed to be competent in their work.

Teachers' wavering belief in students' capacities mirrored similar comments by respondents in Burke's (Norwood & Burke, 2013) research; for example: "So do I think that most staff think that all kids can learn? I think that most staff would say yes, but I don't think they do" (p. 203). Students thrive when teachers hold high expectations and, to the contrary, fall behind when expectations are low. Educators' belief systems and the choices adults make on all levels of the educational system impact students' ability to realize their aspirations and dreams.

How does one now apply these insights toward a concrete and practical coaching process? The first question a coach must ask is, who do I need to be in order to guide deep levels of learning within others?

Preparing Self: Coach Know-How

Equity coaching takes tremendous courage and requires that educational coaches become skillful practitioners of professional coaching theories and competencies. They must acquire the information, knowledge, and skills to do the work well:

> Coaching in the hands of an unskilled coach is dangerous, mainly because they don't know how to give feedback that is non-judgmental. They may not know how to establish trust, and without trust, no learning is going to take place. And so training and skill building is, we think, absolutely essential. (Costa, in Norwood & Burke, 2013, p.163)

Norwood's findings revealed that one's emotional intelligence and the ability to build relationships were mentioned together most frequently (2013, p. 176). Having high levels of emotional intelligence and knowing how to build trusting relationships appears to be key for transformative coaching. Norwood's recommendations are:

1. Become steeped in transformational coaching theories that can best address issues of equity.

2. Receive training in detecting hegemonic influences in oneself and others.

3. Learn how to disrupt discriminatory practices by creating self-awareness.

4. Know one's limitations as an internal coach: Since those who work and live within the system often have the same mindsets, it may be difficult to discern and disrupt shared hegemonic beliefs. There may be a need to bring in an external coach, particularly for leaders and coaches. (Olalla, in Norwood & Burke, 2013).

Preparing Self: Coach Beingness

"What you are stands over you the while, and thunders so that I cannot hear what you say to the contrary" (Emerson, 1875, p. 80).

Important as knowledge and skills are, however, the internal attributes of the coach, levels of maturity, and fundamental coaching skills are critical to effective transformational coaching. Equity work and the exploration of hegemony requires coaches to embody the internal, intellectual, emotional, behavioral, and spiritual capacities necessary to cultivate deep learning within another.

For thousands of years, other cultures, traditions, and spiritual communities have taught learners the necessity to embody the essence and spirit of the discipline, as well as to master the techniques and skills. The Japanese word, "kokoro has to do with perfecting one's inner nature—one must master both the technique (of coaching) but also perfect the *way of being* that is consistent with the discipline" (Hargrove, 2003, p. 44). One's internal development is of primary importance if one is to coach for transformation, contrary to the common practice today in Western society that separates the "process of developing a way of being from the process of learning" (p. 45). It is about whom one is (Bloom, Castagna, Moir, & Warren, 2005), the concept of "self as an instrument of change" (Curran, Seashore, and Welp,1995, p. 1).

Coaches who aspire to usher in deep change must, first and foremost, reinvent themselves through ongoing internal work, to investigate personal assumptions and potential self-deception. Coachees learn as much from the coach's quality of being as from the coach's technical knowledge and skill: "Although many teachers consciously focus on what they are teaching, the evolution and structure of the brain suggests that who they are may be far more important to their students' learning" (Cozolino and Sprokay, 2006, p. 11).

The coach who has an ongoing commitment to working on self is now ready to coach the teacher in the following case study, drawn from Burke's (Norwood & Burke, 2013) research. Here are the details of the case study: During her interview with Burke, a coach vented her frustration about teachers' defeatist attitudes toward refugee students' ability to learn grade level material. As an example, the coach related how a teacher she was coaching told her that she gave passing grades to refugee students simply because they were trying to learn. She chose to promote the students up to the next grade level knowing that they had not mastered the previous level. The coach thought this teacher's decisions stemmed in part from the latter's hegemonic belief—shared by some of her colleagues—that refugee children were inherently not capable of learning to the same extent as other students. Fueling the teacher's beliefs may have been her fear of failure, as her inability to bring these students up to grade level called into question her own competence and value as their teacher. While she no doubt had convinced herself that she was being kind or fair to these children by at least rewarding their intention to learn, her choice to abandon any effort to bring them up to grade level was nothing short of a betrayal of these children's hopes and dreams.

Coaching begins: Doing the work

Now the coach becomes the *Beautiful Form Watcher*, gradually turning the kaleidoscopic lens bit by bit on this teacher's story. As the picture shifts and reconfigures, the coach accompanies the teacher through the emotional peaks and valleys as the latter experiences the moments of painful awareness and release common to transformational equity coaching. The coach remains grounded in the trust that all is in perfect order as the system reveals itself and belief systems come to the forefront. Experience has taught the coach that once the blinders have been removed, the coachee has choice, and choice creates hope and new directions in the coachee's heart and mind.

Johnson (2013) proposed that the Appreciative coaching process might be enriched if we "invite and work with resistance and shadow in a way that releases energy for positive movement" (p. 191). She suggested how one might go about addressing negative emotions that arise out of the work appreciatively, without engaging in confrontation or problem solving:

"It will require a generative synthesis of four ways of being: we must bring the mind of the social scientist, the heart of a lover, the eye of the artist, and the soul of a shaman to the work. The mind of the social scientist gives us perspective on the causes of human behavior and social/organizational arrangements that can be designed to support positive potential in systems. The heart of the lover gives us the capacity to recognize, affirm, and cherish what is most beautiful or desirable in the person or system we are exploring. The eye of the artist releases the creative spirit within systems as we help people liberate the images or metaphors of their own poetry" (p. 192).

Finally, Johnson asserts that Appreciative Inquiry "is very much about helping individuals and organizations come into contact with their soul—it is emancipatory, shamanic work" (p. 193).

What follows is the author's suggestion for how a coach might apply the above ideas in working with this teacher. Although this dialogue between the coach and teacher is imaginary, it is patterned on over 25 years of experience coaching in situations just like this one. Italicized statements in brackets describe the coach's internal processing as they do the work.

Detective Coach

The coach first considers: How ready is this teacher to be coached at a deep level? Norwood and Burke (2011) observed that "teachers, administrators, and coaches may be unaware of the most pervasive cultural patterns in their school" (p. 217). Is this teacher willing to undergo the kind of self-scrutiny and sometimes painful awareness that equity coaching demands? Hegemony presents a challenge for transformational coaches because it operates below the threshold of people's awareness (see Burke, previous chapter). It is comprised of one's "systems and structures of beliefs, values, norms and practices of everyday life which unconsciously legitimate the order of things" (Holub, 1992, p. 45). Leaders and coaches must become detectives by learning to investigate what is hidden.

Awakener Coach

[*Coach Considerations:* Create a safe space for exploration. Psychological safety and confidentiality are vital. This necessitates a deep trust in the coach. The coach now aims to the soul of the teacher with the intention of helping the teacher connect head to heart. The italicized words below refer to scripts, narratives, emotions, and hidden beliefs that are being unearthed. Listen for what is not being said. Observe body language, eye movements, energy shifts and emotional grounding. Open by creating a moment to connect emotionally with one another and then launch into the session].

Teacher: Thanks for creating time for me today. There are several things I want to think through. I am glad the year is almost over. I have been entering grades and decided to *pass our new refugee students.* They have worked hard and love coming to school. *I haven't known how to teach them* nor have my colleagues. Some of the students *have severe emotional needs.* I want them to feel proud of themselves and included in our school. One of our *district's non-negotiables,* that as teachers we try to follow, is that *all students can learn.* I am wondering how that fits in with our current set up and the continuous influx of new refugees. I would like to have time to explore this.

Coach: Sounds clear. In exploring *non-negotiable expectations* and how that relates to our new influx of refugee children, what's your desired outcome for our session?

Teacher: My hope is that I will be clearer in how to plan for next year. I am just feeling a little unsettled inside and don't know why.

Coach: OK, so gaining clarity on your emotional state and on initial planning for next year. Let's explore.

Teacher: Well, I am thinking about what the *district expects of us.* It seems like it isn't attainable. I mean, yes, all students can learn, I think, but what if there are numerous barriers to that learning?

Coach: Sounds like this holds deep meaning for you. As we opened, you mentioned that you simply pass your students. Let's pause there for a moment. [*Create a silent space.*] What's coming up for you?

Teacher: Hum! Well, it has been such an overwhelming year. I have felt very frustrated because *their children were clumped in with our children* and they all have such different needs. As a veteran teacher, I have always felt competent and successful in my career. But it seems everything is *changing quickly.* Sometimes I *long for the good old days* when I had *only our students* in the classrooms. It was just easier to teach.

Coach: Sounds very overwhelming. [*silence*] *"Their children clumped in with our children"* . . . What does that mean to you?

Teacher: Well, you know, the refugees. I mean, we have 37 languages spoken in our district. Many new students are coming in with deep levels of emotional trauma. Many haven't attended school in quite some time. *They don't speak our language.* And *their schools,* if they went at all, were so much different from *ours.* We are having to teach them about *our culture* and *how to behave* in school. It just doesn't fit with how they were raised. They are so *different from our kids.*

[*Coach Considerations*: At this point the detective coach is becoming aware of language: district beliefs, their children vs. our children, longing for the good old days, etcetera. The teacher is telling herself a story that limits her choices and impacts her sense of efficacy and ultimately impacts her students negatively. The coach notices the teacher's tone of voice and body language. The coach is beginning to get a headache—which at times can signal for the coach that there might be repressed anger within the teacher. The coach knows that equity issues and the impact on students can't be addressed until the teacher is connected back to a coherent self. It is time to move into the "emotional soup" (Olalla, in Norwood & Burke, 2013, p. 134). The coach now becomes **Shaman Coach** to explore with deep compassion the loss and fear of the shadow side—and then to discover virtues and eventually soothe to bring relief. This shift will begin the healing process with Self].

Shaman Coach

That sounds difficult. You mentioned that as a teacher you have always felt competent. How have your current experiences impacted you as a professional?

Teacher: Oh boy, I don't think I want to talk about this. So many emotions are coming up. This all just makes me mad! I have always had such a strong sense of efficacy. Now I *feel incompetent.* I don't know how to teach them, which is *embarrassing.* I don't feel the district even wants us to share our concerns. I don't want my colleagues thinking I am not competent. I don't want my students thinking I don't like them, but it is just hard. Recently we have been reading the findings from the Opportunity Myth (TNTP, 2018). Several aspects impacted me, like the fact that we should have all our students in grade level materials and hold high expectations for every student. I SAY I believe this, but do I? Brother—I can't seem to do that. *I don't know how.* My students were in materials two years below grade level this year. I find myself questioning my own beliefs and that scares me. I thought I believed that all students could learn but I honestly don't think so. I mean, how could they? I am *saddened to think this way.* How can I help myself believe that they are capable? I feel *scared* and *angry* and *stuck.* I wonder if I want to continue teaching. My colleagues have always seen me as the one in the forefront ready to try new things. But *I am tired* and deep down I am *feeling such a sense of loss.* What if *teaching never returns* to what it used to be? I now often say, I used to like people, but they ruined it for me. *[laughter to ease the tension]* I question how much I care now. I used to be so loving with my students. I am not liking me and that feels bad.

[*Coach Considerations*: With deep empathy, the coach continues to pick up on scripts, language, and body tension. The teacher is now revealing where she is living—in a whirlpool of emotion. There must be a shift in the emotional body before there can be a transformative change. During this phase, several theories come into play. The teacher is deeply grieving a loss of what was. Bridges' (2003) change model defines this stage as "the ending or letting go." Change and transition, two different aspects of the same process, are both at play here. Transition involves the psychological experience of change and can be extremely painful. The teacher is experiencing low levels of self-efficacy and craftsmanship (Costa & Garmston, in Norwood & Burke, 2013). She is compartmentalizing to make sense of her world and create safety for herself i.e., their children vs. our children. Under her biases are fear, anger, loss, and a disconnection from Self and others (Four Arrows, in Norwood & Burke, 2013). There needs to be a deep shift in coherence and a connection back to Self where she begins to find alignment with her core values (Olalla, in Norwood & Burke, 2013). This is the phase where assumptions and beliefs can be assessed to see how well they are serving the teacher and her students. The coach is now aware that time must be spent, possibly several sessions, to work through what was uncovered. Once this phase is complete, the coach can move toward an Appreciative Coaching model. However, before this session is over, the coach helps the teacher shift toward passion and strengths (Orem, in Norwood & Burke, 2013).]

Coach: I know what a great teacher you are, and I know staff deeply respects you. What brought you into teaching?

Teacher: Well, this is what is causing me to feel so sad lately. I LOVE KIDS! All ages. I love them. I know they have incredible potential, and I know it is up to us to help them access that potential. That's why I teach. I want to regain that feeling!

Coach: That is such a beautiful and loving quality within you.

Thank you for sharing. It's there. It's still there! [*pause and create space*] What gifts have you noticed in our new students?

Teacher: Oh, so much! I notice elements of deep appreciation for what we can provide them. And funny, oh my gosh, their sense of humor is wonderful. They are trusting and loving. They make friends quickly. And they are so smart, they are really smart. *I want to capture that.* They are smart in different ways and I want to learn from them so I can build on that. They have knowledge of the world that the rest of us don't have. Oh my, I think I am realizing what a disservice I have done this year in passing them based on effort. [*begins to cry*] I need more coaching from you. Let's set up several sessions. I want to figure this out. I want them to know how much I respect them, and I want to learn better how to teach them. They certainly are teaching us.

Coach: Sounds like they are teaching all of us. What are you learning about yourself?

Teacher: They are ALL my students, not them vs. us! Where have I been? Thank you! I am going to journal and work through my emotional baggage this week. Let's meet again so that I can begin to envision a new way of doing things. I now feel like I have choices.

Muse Coach

[*Coach Considerations*: Transformation is beginning to take place now that there have been deep shifts within the teacher. She is ready to dream, design, and generate a new metaphor for teaching. The coach is deep into a subsequent session with the teacher].

Teacher: Now that I am in a better frame of mind, I am more aware that we are doing some good things in the district. We have had some great trainings on responsive instruction and different approaches that support students' ability to construct meaning for themselves. There are rumblings that the district might provide some additional training to help us to better support children with PTSD (post-traumatic stress disorder). We are in a curriculum adoption year so I know we will be looking at new materials. Maybe I can ask to be on that committee. [*She's beginning to see new possibilities*]. As a district, we are promoting greater community engagement. There is a tremendous effort to invite all families. I want to lead the charge for my grade level on creating a new vision of excellence. But I need to do it first for myself.

Coach: Great! You started our session today with your mantra, every student can learn! Let's use the magic wand. If you could paint the perfect picture of what's possible for every student and every teacher, what would that look like?

Teacher: Fun! Let's do this! My vision of excellence would look like this. We fully embrace every child as our children, our students. We create a culture of learning where we all learn from each other. As teachers, we walk side by side with them, accessing their genius, supporting their learning. We hold each other accountable to maintain high expectations and stay the course. We continue to remain current with research, curriculum changes, and our data. But we add much more. We listen deeply to student and parent voices. We listen to their stories and their experiences. We listen for their aspirations and, as adult decision-makers, we agree to make the right choices in our district that create infinite opportunities for every student. We scrutinize our approaches and policies and detect when old beliefs are surfacing. We disrupt those biases. When fear and loss arise—and they will—we embrace them and choose to discover the virtues.

Coach: Sounds like you are reconnecting to your core values. You have restored your belief in students. Great work! Are you open to our playing with this for a moment?

Teacher: Sure

[*Coach Considerations*: Now that the teacher has regained her sense of self and personal power, the coach helps her deepen her support and connection with her students. This is where the biases and discriminatory practices can more fully be released, and new creative thought can emerge.]

Coach: You have the start of a beautiful vision. You desire to move in this direction so that . . .

Teacher: So that teachers know better what they can do to support students.

Coach: So that . . .

Teacher: We learn to teach all our students effectively.

Coach: So that . . .

Teacher: We hear their voices and aspirations.

Coach: So that . . .

Teacher: We can create access and infinite possibilities for all our students.

Coach: So that . . .

Teacher: I feel like I have done the best I can for them.

Coach: So that . . .

Teacher: I can feel satisfied and purpose driven in my work again. [*tears*]

Coach: So that . . .

Teacher: I know I make a difference and that I can be in my best self—because that is when I honor what's best for my students and do my best work!

Coach: Wow! How does that feel?

Teacher: Good—oh my! I feel connected again. I feel strong and powerful. I feel such love for all my students. I feel appreciation for the hard work we are doing.

Coach: Hold onto that feeling—let's now come back to the present moment. How can you ground that feeling—you in your best self?

[*Coach Considerations*: The teacher now brings the emotion of the future vision into the present moment where that core feeling can be anchored in the body. The teacher practices letting go of her vision so that it has opportunities to emerge freely. Manipulating or controlling a vision will diminish it quickly. As the teacher learns to hold onto the feeling of her best self, creative action steps will emerge along the path toward the fulfillment of her dream (Cooperrider & Whitney, 2005; Csikszentmihalyi, 1990; Seligman, 2002; Wheatley, 1999).]

365

The above dialogue represents the kind of coaching that is possible in a real-world situation. While the conversation has been streamlined for the purpose of brevity, the author believes that well-trained educational coaches working one-on-one with their coachees could likewise help them to achieve similar insights and revelations.

Conclusion

Coaches and leaders must keep in motion the district's kaleidoscopic movement. They can learn to listen for the scripts, the narratives, the complaints, and the generative metaphors prevalent in organizations that keep the status quo in place (for more on this, see Norwood & Burke, 2013, p. 65). If they listen closely, however, they will also hear the unfulfilled hopes, dreams, and desires of educators that provide directions for the way forward. Most districts have in place structures that can support some of this work for groups, such as PLCs (professional learning communities), data teams, and professional development workshops, to name a few. The author provides one word of caution: Creating group awareness is the first step, but if left there, deep transformative change will not take place. Deep shifts in the minds and hearts of educators happens individually and *requires one-on-one coaching*. Consider the following:

Are fundamental revolutions brought about by the mass, or are they started by the few who see and who, by their talk and energy, influence very many people? That is how revolutions are brought about. Is it not a mistake to think that, as individuals, we cannot do anything? .... If we have this attitude of mind, we will not think for ourselves, but will respond automatically. Is action always of the mass? Does it not spring essentially from the individual, and then spread from individual to individual? There is really no such thing as the mass. After all, the mass is an entity formed of people who are caught, hypnotized by words, by certain ideas. The moment we are not hypnotized by words, we are outside that

366

stream…. Should we not remain outside the stream… in order to affect the stream? Is it not important that there should be a fundamental transformation in the individual first, that you and I should radically change first, without waiting for the whole world to change? (Krishnamurti, 1950)

Current educational coaching practices, transactional at best, are insufficient when it comes to addressing hegemonic practices embedded deep within the institution where inequity lives. Coaches and educators must first learn how to detect hegemony within themselves and others. They must then learn how to address embedded core beliefs that support inequitable practices. The work requires a coach who is compassionate, wise, and fearless enough to gently help the coachee face their shadow self, to access the enormous transformative energy that resides there. Transformational coaching challenges the roots of current practices, for the purpose of achieving a more equitable education for all students. This work requires a deep shift in the hearts and minds of educators.

In this chapter, the author has presented a case study, including an imaginary dialogue between a coach and teacher, to illustrate how transformational theory might be applied to practice. The reader should not construe this dialogue as a formula to slavishly imitate. Rather, the intention is to show the graceful dance between coach and coachee, as the former uses skillful competencies to help the latter arrive at her own 'aha' moment. The goal, as always, is to help repair one's disconnection from self and community, prompting a return to one's whole-some-ness. This is how, one by one, educators can reclaim the soul of education.

About the Author

Kathy Norwood, EdD, PCC is a Pre-K-12 national educational consultant, trainer, professional coach and co-founder of Coaches Evolve. She has worked in the field of Education for over 35 years. Norwood earned her doctorate in Educational Leadership and Change and holds a Master of Education in Professional Development, with emphasis on English Learners (EL) and Administration. She holds credentials in: Early Childhood Education, K-8 Elementary Education, Pre-12 Special Education, K-12 Physical Education. Since 1996, Norwood has helped school districts nationwide develop and implement customized comprehensive coaching and literacy programs. She teaches for Fielding Graduate University in their Evidence-Based Coaching Program, provides Leadership Coaching for TNTP, and continues to train and coach administrators and coaches throughout the nation. Norwood and Burke co-authored: *Transformational Coaching in Education: A Collaborative Look at the Bridges and Barriers to Learning* (Dissertation); Education in *The Handbook of Knowledge-Based Coaching: From Theory to Practice,* San Francisco, CA: Jossey-Bass, 2011; and several coach training manuals, the most recent titled: *Appreciative Leadership & Coaching* and, *School Coaching: What Is It and How Do You Do It?* Through their organization, Coaches Evolve, LLC, they train educational leaders and coaches who will ignite educators' passion to teach from their heart and soul.

References

Bloom, G., Castagna, C., Moir, E., & Warren, B. (2005). *Blended coaching.* Newbury Park, CA: Corwin Sage.

Brantley, M.E. (2007). *Executive coaching and deep learning.* (Doctoral Dissertation). Dissertations and Theses Database. (UMI No. 3255517)

Brown, C., Stroh, H., Fouts, J., & Baker, D. (2005). *Learning to change: School coaching for systemic reform.* Mill Creek, WA: Fouts & Associates, LLC.

Burkins, J. M., & Ritchie, S. (2007). Coaches coaching coaches. *Journal of Language and Literacy Education,* 3(1), 32-47. Retrieved from http://www.coe.uga.edu/jolle/2007_1/coaches.pdf

Cooperrider, D., L., & Whitney, D. (2005). *Appreciative inquiry: A positive revolution in change.* San Francisco, CA: Berrett-Koehler Publishers, Inc.

Costa, A., & Garmston, R. (1994). *Cognitive Coaching*SM: *A foundation for renaissance schools.* Norwood, MA: Christopher-Gordon.

Costa, A., & Garmston, R. (2002). *Cognitive Coaching*SM: *A foundation for renaissance schools* (2nd ed.). Norwood, MA: Christopher-Gordon.

Cozolino, L., & Sprokay, S. (2006). Neuroscience and adult learning. In S. Johnson & K. Taylor (Eds.), *The neuroscience of adult learning* (pp. 11-19). San Francisco, CA: Jossey-Bass.

Csikszentmihalyi, M. (1990) Flow: *The psychology of optimal experience.* New York: Harper Perennial Modern Classics. ISBN-13: 978-0061339202

Curran, K. M., Seashore, C. N., & Welp, M. G. (1995). *Use of self as an instrument of change.* Paper presented at the ODN National Conference. Retrieved from http://www.equalvoice.com/use_of_self.pdf

Dalai Lama (1997). Education and the human heart. *Holistic Education Revue*, 10(3).

Emerson, R. W. (1875). *Letters and social aims.* Boston, MA: James R. Osgood.

Four Arrows (2016). *Point of departure: Returning to a more authentic worldview for education and survival.* Charlotte, NC: Information Age Publishing.

Hargrove, R. (2003). *Masterful coaching: Extraordinary results by impacting people and the way they think and work together* (revised ed.). San Francisco, CA: Jossey-Bass/Pfeiffer.

Holub, R. (1992). *Antonio Gramsci: Beyond Marxism and postmodernism.* New York, NY: Routledge.

Hunt, D., & Joyce, B. (1967). Teacher trainee personality and initial teaching style. *American Educational Research Journal*, 4, 253-259.

International Reading Association. (2004). *The role and qualification of the reading coach in theUnited States: A position statement of the International Reading Association.* Newark, DE: International Reading Association.

Jacobs, D. T., & Jacobs-Spencer, J. (2001). *Teaching virtues: Building character across the curriculum.* Lanham, MD: Scarecrow Press.

Johnson, P. (2013). Transcending the polarity of light and shadow in Appreciative Inquiry: An appreciative exploration of practice. In Zandee, D. Cooperrider, D.L. and Avital, M. (Eds.) *Generative organization: Advances in Appreciative Inquiry.* Bingley, England: Emerald Publishing.

Kegan, R., & Lahey, L. (1994). *In over our heads: The mental demands of modern life.* Cambridge, MA: Harvard University Press.

Krishnamurti, J. (1950). Madras 2nd public talk, January 29, 1950. Retrieved from https://www.jkrishnamurti.org/content/madras-2nd-public-talk-29th-january-1950/fear%20of%20the%20unknown

Mezirow, J. (2000). Learning to think like an adult: Core concepts of transformation theory. In J. Norwood, K., & Burke, M. A. (2011). Education. In L. Wildflower & D. Brennan (Eds.), *The handbook of knowledge-based coaching: From theory to practice* (pp. 211-220). San Francisco, CA: Jossey-Bass.

Norwood, K., & Burke, M.A. (2013). *Transformational coaching in education: A collaborative look at the bridges and barriers to learning*. (Doctoral dissertation). Available from ProQuest Dissertations & Theses database (UMI No. 3601821)

Reiss, K. (2007). *Leadership coaching for educators*. Thousand Oaks, CA: Corwin Press. Seligman, M. (2002). *Authentic happiness: Using the new positive psychology to realize your potential for lasting fulfilment*. NY: Simon and Schuster.

Terrell, J. and Hughes, M. (2008). *A coach's guide to emotional intelligence: Strategies for developing successful leaders*. San Francisco, CA: Pfeiffer.

TNTP (2018). *The opportunity myth*. Retrieved from: https://tntp.org/assets/documents/TNTP_TheOpportunity-Myth_Web.pdf

Wheatley, M. (1999). *Leadership and the new science: discovering order in a chaotic world*. San Francisco: Berrett-Koehler Publishers Inc.

CHAPTER 17

BECOMING A COACH: MAKING SENSE OF COACHING STUDENTS' TRANSFORMATIVE EXPERIENCES

Penny Potter, PhD

Abstract

Leadership coaches continue to explore ways to move clients toward more complex ways of seeing, thinking about, and responding to the complexities in their environments. One overlooked area is the process of becoming a coach. Many coaches report their coach training as transformational regardless of the program they attended. What is the nature of these transformations? New coaching students are often surprised that something as simple as a coaching conversation is so challenging to execute artfully. This article describes research that substantiates these claims of transformation and proposes a Coaching Dialectics Model to illuminate the complexities that coaching students face as they train to become coaches. The model helps educators understand in a more complete way what coaching students grapple with. Understanding these dialectics helps coaches understand the complexity of their work. Finally, the model and research design assists organizations in their efforts to develop coaching leaders and coaching cultures.

Keywords: Coaching, coach training, coaching education, adult learning, adult development, cognitive complexity, transformation, transformative learning, experiential learning, learning dialectics.

Introduction

We often hear that the world is becoming more complex than our abilities to manage the complexity (Bartunek, Gordon, & Weathersby, 1983; Kegan, 1994; Roux, in press; Torbert & Livne-Tarandach, 2009; Weick, 1979). Some research supports the idea that leaders at more complex levels of development are more effective (Brown, 2012; Day & Lance, 2004). Kegan (1994) has been at the forefront of advocating for integrative development to bridge the widening gap between complexity and our ability to manage it. Integrative development is also referred to as adult, vertical, cognitive, hierarchical, and structural development by various scholars, however the term integrative development appears to be more accessible for clients in organizations.

As used here, integrative development refers to levels of increasingly complex, nuanced, and flexible ways of thinking and making meaning of one's experiences and behaving. Integrative development generally occurs when one's current way of operating is no longer sufficient. For instance, when single contributors are promoted to a frontline manager position, they often feel overwhelmed and confused as to how to manage multiple people and their tasks. They can have a number of reactions including retreating to their expertise and taking on tasks that can be delegated to their teams. This results in being overwhelmed with work tasks. Another example is when senior managers move to executive positions. Over time they learn they must let go of day-to-day managing, in order to take on the kind of strategic decision making required at that level.

To address this issue, practitioners and educators have increasingly looked to integrative development theory to design programs that help leaders build their capacity to manage complexity. Some have proposed that coaching may facilitate leaders' abilities to manage this increasing complexity (Fitzgerald & Garvey-Berger, 2002; Garvey-Berger, 2006; Laske, 1999a, 2004). In fact, Inglis and Steele (2005) go so far as to suggest coaches serve as "developmental midwives" (p. 36). However, McCauley, Drath, Palus, O'Connor, and Baker (2006) note a lack of research that examines *how* training and coaching impact the integrative development of their participants. An interesting and largely overlooked place to explore this question is coach training.

Coaching is a relatively new field of practice that took hold in the 1990s and has exploded in the last decades. To illustrate how quickly the field has taken hold, a decade ago, organizations still asked, "What is coaching?" Today they are savvy shoppers and ask for specific credentials. In addition, the net income for the International Coaching Federation (ICF), which accredits coach training programs and credentials coaches, grew from $5.2 million in 2011 to $13.5 million in 2016 – a 250% increase in profits.

While the practice of coaching and has become mainstream, coaching theory and research is only now beginning to catch up. This has left most coaching education programs to rely on popular literature and practitioner expertise to build curricula and pedagogy. This is also true for some coaching governance organizations -- such as the International Coaching Federation (ICF), the European Mentoring and Coaching Council (EMCC), and the International Association of Coaching (IAC) -- in the development of coach credential competencies. As more universities integrate coaching into graduate and accredited certificate programs, there is more emphasis on both hands-on practice and research and theory. Since 2004, the Graduate School Alliance for Educators in Coaching (GSAEC) has advocated to establish research-based standards for coaching as an academic discipline.

As a relatively new field coaching has borrowed theory from other fields, primarily psychology, education, and management. Many suggest Adult learning theory is foundational to coaching (Cox, Bachkirova, & Clutterbuck, 2014; Cox & Jackson, 2014; Gray, 2006), and some say that a firm grounding in adult/integrative development is essential for coaches in their client work (Fitzgerald & Garvey-Berger, 2002; Garvey-Berger, 2006; Laske, 1999a, 1999b, 2004). Interestingly, despite the experiential nature of coaching and coach training, experiential learning theory is largely overlooked and has not been linked to coaching students' development. The exception to this is Cox (2013) who combines transformative and experiential learning to explain how coaching works. Only a few studies have explored how these theories apply to coaching students themselves – those who are becoming coaches.

The remainder of this chapter provides a general overview of coaching research and applies transformative and experiential learning theories to coaching. The coaching dialectics model is presented to visually depict the complexity of what a coach must learn to master in a single coaching conversation. Finally, an overview of the handful of studies of coaching students is presented, as well as a more detailed description of one study that asked whether participating in coach training affects students' integrative developmental levels.

Coaching

As stated in the introduction, research on coaching is relatively new and has primarily focused on the outcomes of coaching. Generally, studies have concluded coaching is beneficial, although it is unclear why or how. Most studies have relied on practitioner research and self-reports from coaches and their clients, which when taken alone, are an unreliable measure (Ely et al., 2010). A recent meta-analysis of coaching research indicates that little has changed in the last decade (Sonesh et al., 2015).

While the field of coaching is shaping its identity as a profession, it is interesting that there has been little research on coaches (Bono, Purvanova, Towler, & Peterson, 2009). Over time, coaches learn to cultivate a curious and open receptivity in each coaching experience. These "ways of being' are correlated to emotional complexity, wisdom, and maturity across differing situations (Staudinger & Kessler, 2009). The precursors to these ways of being for coaching students and recent graduates are the ability to maintain full presence, empathy, boundary awareness, somatic awareness, and the ability to challenge one's client while offering support. Learning to coordinate these simultaneous actions requires reflexivity, critical thinking, discernment, and decision-making (Campone, 2014).

Consider the complexity that a coach manages within a single coaching conversation:

"In a single coaching session with a client, an artful coach coordinates a complex set of skills that come together in an improvisational conversational dance with the client. While listening closely, a coach must also simultaneously observe multiple data points beyond the conversational content. She must observe subtle shifts in energy and emotion in both her client and herself. She holds the client's agenda while staying open to what unfolds and makes decisions about which response will have the most impact for the client. The coach connects multiple themes and ideas from both present and past conversations. She seeks her client's perspectives without making judgments, while observing and lightly holding her own perspectives. All this is done while being in-the-moment and fully present to her client, as well as her own thoughts, feelings, somatic reactions. How does one come to embody this complex choreography?" (Potter, 2017, p. 15).

Little is known about the impact of learning these complex moves or if learning to coordinate this "complex choreography" contributes to the coach's integrative development. What most coaching instructors come to expect, however, is that integrating these complex skills tends to be challenging for new students. They often express confusion and in the beginning struggle to listen deeply and ask open curious questions. This often is true, no matter a student's age or leadership level.

For instance, one coaching student was a 64-year old senior military leader nearing retirement. With a lifetime of leadership training, he signed up for a university coaching certification program knowing he would sail through the program. However, he found the program challenging in many ways, both from a skills standpoint and emotionally. He had built his career on telling others what to do. Now he had to learn to listen and become curious. Near the end of the program, he experienced several breakthroughs that, in his words, "Changed my life." After graduation, his superiors noted that he had become a new, more effective leader and offered him a position he had always strived to attain. He turned it down in favor of retiring and becoming a full-time coach.

Another coaching student, who is an IT professional in his thirties, experienced a disorienting moment in his coaching program that shook him to his core and opened him to an entirely new way of seeing the world. This happened from one brief observation by an instructor. This may not have not rocked another student's world, but from a developmental perspective, it was the right comment at the right time. Previously in the program, he struggled in his practice coaching, but once his perspective shifted, he suddenly understood coaching in a more holistic way. His coaching skills improved dramatically after that. Interestingly, his coaching program mentioned in passing the connection between coaching and transformative learning theory. Since then he has dived into the theory to make better sense of his experience.

These two snapshots demonstrate what coaching educators see repeatedly in their programs. Students come in excited. They experience the challenge and struggle and often become confused and defensive. About halfway through the program, however, the lightbulbs go off and they begin to integrate their learning. How might coaching educators better understand this pattern and assist coaching students to better understand their experiences?

Call for a Theoretical Foundation

As mentioned in the introduction, coaching has borrowed theory and models from other professions such as psychology, leadership and management, and education. This has led to debate whether theoretical diversity adds value to coaching (Bachkirova & Kauffman, 2008), or continues to blur rather than define its unique identity (Drake, 2008; Gray, 2006). In addition, when accrediting coach training programs, accrediting bodies tend to focus mainly on coaching skills-building and competencies. The decision whether an accredited coach training program includes theory in its curriculum rests with the program developers. One would think that university coach certification programs would offer students a theoretical foundation, however it is not a given. For instance, Fielding's coaching program does, yet other universities do not, especially if the certification is not part of a degree program. Programs run by private for-profit companies may be even less inclined.

Coaching overlaps with counseling in that it is client-centered and nondirective, which leads some psychologists to argue that coaches must have a background in psychology. However, a survey of 428 coaches (256 non-psychologists; 172 psychologists) indicated there were as many differences among psychologists as non-psychologist coaches (Bono et al., 2009). For instance, counseling psychologists generally lack knowledge of business and organizational systems, while industrial/organizational psychologists may lack interpersonal skills. However, the authors found small differences between psychologists and non-psychologists in who they coach and what assessments are used but did not find significant differences in overall effectiveness and outcomes. One important difference they did find, however, was that coaches without a background in psychology, "were *more likely* to use behavior modification, neurolinguistic programming, and psychoanalytic or psychodynamic techniques" (p. 371) than coaches with a counseling background. It appears that without a deeper understanding of theory, non-psychologist coaches do not realize when they've crossed the blurry boundaries between coaching and counseling. This should give coaching educators and accrediting organizations pause.

What does this leave for coaches who do not have a counseling or psychology background and for the programs that train and certify them? Many suggest that since client learning is at the heart of coaching, adult learning theories are the theoretical foundation of coaching (Cox, 2015; Grant, 2005; Skiffington & Zeus, 2003). Transformative and experiential learning theories are most often cited as useful theories for coaches and studies looking at the intersection of experiential learning and coaching are beginning to build (Bonrath, Dedy, Gordon, & Grantcharov, 2015; Jones, Woods, & Guillaume, 2015; Swart & Harcup, 2013). The next section describes how these theories may assist coaching educators to understand the transformations that students undergo.

Adult Learning Theory and Coaching Dialectics

Transformative learning theory was originally developed by Mezirow to explain the transitions between stages of integrative development. He primarily focused on changes in perspectives and meaning making (Mezirow, 1978, 1985) and offered the term "disorienting dilemma" to describe the state that often occurs when one is faced with a dilemma that requires new meaning perspectives. Coaches provide a supportive space for clients to reflect on the limits of their perspectives, and at times gently challenge their clients' thinking or offer other perspective to facilitate new ways of understanding.

Sammut (2014) conducted a qualitative study with eight coaches and found that the coaches actively utilized six of Mezirow's ten core elements of transformative learning: individual experience, critical reflection, dialogue, holistic orientation, awareness of context, and authentic relationships. Sammut states these coaches used these core elements, "even though they may not have been overtly aware that they were doing so" (p. 52). This underscores for educators previous findings stated earlier that coaches often are not consciously aware of the choices they make in working with their clients.

While transformative learning describes *what* changes as a result of reflecting on experiences, experiential learning theory describes dialectics as the mechanisms that incite learning. Dialectics, often referred to as polarities, are tensions between interdependent pairs – one without the other is incomplete, like single-bladed scissors (James, 1977). A simple example is breathing – which is better, breathing in or breathing out? Of course, the answer is neither. One is not better than the other. They function as an interdependent pair. Mezirow (1991) contends that learning is a dialectical process when learners interact with their environments. Elbow (1986) asserts that managing dialectics increases one's ability to see and think. However, with the exception of Basseches (1984), dialectics has been largely overlooked in developmental literature. Glassman (2000) says that this is because it occurs in the realm of ideas and concepts, as opposed to empirical evidence. Yet, Lewin's (1943) maxim, "There is nothing as practical as a good theory," persists to this day.

Kolb (1981, 1984) integrated Williams James' dialectic of experience and conceptualization with Freire's dialectic of reflection and action to develop the adult experiential learning cycle, illustrated in the inner circle, Figure 1. He suggests that complete, deep learning involves the whole person in recursive interaction and tension between these two dialectics, across all four modes: experience and conceptualization, reflection and action. While some have criticized Kolb's theory for being focused on past experiences, when one reviews his early work, he clearly references subjective experience in the present.

Intentionally and recursively navigating these learning dialectics increases one's metacognitive abilities -- an increased ability to be consciously aware, monitor, and regulate one's cognitive, affective, and somatic processes (Fischer & Bidell, 2006; Tarricone, 2011). Development of one's metacognitive abilities is key for coaches to develop and refine throughout their careers. Testing this, Zull (2011), conducted brain scan studies and found that each mode of the experiential learning cycle lights up each of four major parts of the brain. From a neuro-physiological perspective, Zull concludes that combining all four modes develops metacognition.

Interestingly, a typical coaching conversation will include all four modes. The coach will inquire about the client's direct experience in relation to the client's coaching topic and ask questions that cause the client to reflect on their reactions, feelings, and thoughts. As a result of the client's reflections, the client often conceptualizes their experience in new ways. At this point a coach may offer models or other concepts to further conceptualize and deepen the client's new understanding. While this description implies a straight-forward linear process, coaching conversations often move back and forth between these three modes. The coaching conversation typically ends with client and coach co-creating *actions* the client will take, often in the form of small behavioral experiments. This repeats in the next coaching conversation, resulting in what Kolb (2014) has described as a learning spiral that results in deep learning and development.

While Kolb's original theory explains how a coach might move her client through the experiential learning cycle, it does not fully describe the complexity that the coach *herself* navigates. For instance, while facilitating her client's experiential learning, she simultaneously moves through her own experiential learning cycle (Figure 1, outer circle) -- while staying fully present in the conversation. This type of conversational acrobatics suggests why coaching students might struggle as they practice and learn these new skills.

Coaching occurs in conversation. Interestingly, Mezirow (2003) suggested critical discourse as a way to transform perspectives. However, mirroring experiential learning dialectics, Taylor (2009), suggests dialogue as a more useful concept "...where experience is reflected on, assumptions and beliefs are questioned, and habits of mind are ultimately transformed" (p. 9). Gunnlaugson's (2006) description of generative dialogue comes even closer to what occurs in a coaching conversation: "a comprehensive and integrated practice of conversation that cultivates ways of knowing and ways of being that serve the development of new knowledge and transformation of adult learners" (p. 3). Mirroring the previous description of a single coaching conversation, Gergen, Gergen, and Barrett (2004) liken generative dialogue to "the fluid and synchronized movements of dancers" (p. 50). Like most artful performances, this description belies the complexity that coaches learn to manage in each coaching conversation.

Conversational learning builds upon Kolb's theory and describes a theoretical framework for learning with others in conversation. In developing this framework Baker, Jensen, and Kolb (2002, 2005) have drawn from rich and varied works and theories and added three additional dialectics to Kolb's two. In doing so, the authors move us closer to the complexity of a coaching conversation. In addition to Kolb's two dialects, the three additional conversational learning dialectics are described below in the context of coaching (Figure 1, middle circle).

Epistemological discourse and ontological recourse (doing and being) describes the tension between linear, forward movement (epistemological/doing) and deepening understanding through questioning and inquiry. One moves the conversation along; the other slows the conversation to provide space for new meanings and understandings to emerge. Yet, to be successful coaches must ensure that their clients progress towards their coaching goals. Therefore, managing this dialectic is foundational to successful coaching.

Individuality and relationality refer to the ability to hold and consider one another's perspectives without sacrificing one's own. Managing this tension is a key competency coaches begin to learn in their training. While a coach will typically facilitate a client exploring his own perspectives, occasionally the coach offers her own perspectives, which gives the client opportunity to consider alternative ways of seeing a situation. This recursive interaction contributes to learning for both the client and coach. The ability to hold and coordinate different perspectives is a capacity described in some transformative learning and integrative development literature (Dawson-Tunik & Stein, 2004; Fuhs, 2015a, 2015b; Kegan, 1994; Taylor & Elias, 2012).

Balancing status and solidarity (positioning and linking) is particularly important in coaching conversations, especially at the beginning. If the coach is obsequious or intimidated and assumes a lower status, the client may talk endlessly without reaching the intended goal. More often, especially in the beginning of the engagement, the client defers to the coach as "the expert" and blindly accept the coach's perspective. Neither facilitates the client's self-directed learning. On the other hand, if together they engage in too much solidarity, ideas and assumptions go unchallenged. Artfully navigating this dialectic is a subtle skill that often takes coaches years to develop.

Potter (2017) proposed a fourth dialectic, specific to coaches: rules and performance. This dialectic was described by Polanyi, Schön's theoretical predecessor (Mintz, 2016). Coaching students often struggle to learn the rules (ethics and competencies) while attempting to integrate them into an artful performance. While Polanyi suggests that tacit knowledge lies between rules and performance, for helping relationships, Mintz suggests that uncertainty lies in the center. This fits with coaching, since coaches never know what their clients will bring to the conversation or what their responses will be from one moment to the next. Learning to become more curious and embrace the uncertainty is the improvisational nature of coaching conversations. It is what Mintz refers to productive uncertainty -- "tolerating the difficulty of not knowing, can ultimately lead to a better, more nuanced, more flexible understanding of the human other across from you" (p. 292).

These dialects, when assembled together in one image (Figure 1), provide a visual image of the complexity that a coach must learn and artfully manage in every coaching conversation. Understanding these coaching dialectics may provide coaching educators insight into consistent reports of transformation and help students make better sense of their experiences. The next section describes the handful of studies that have examined the personal impact of becoming a coach.

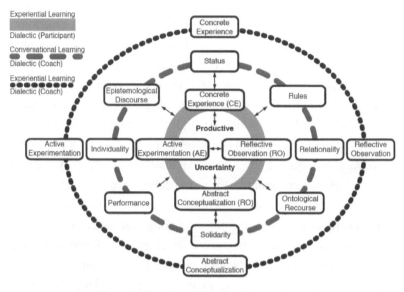

Figure 1. Coaching Dialectics[1] (Potter, in press).

Research on Becoming a Coach

There have been only five studies on the impact of coach training on new coaches. These studies were of different programs in India, South Africa, and the United States that show strikingly similar findings that support anecdotal claims of transformations. Two studies indicate program graduates demonstrated greater self-awareness, new perspectives, better interpersonal skills, and improved relationships (Beets & Goodman, 2012; Mukherjee, 2012). Another study noted reflective learning and better decision-making in complex situations (Campone, 2014). In her dissertation study, Kennedy (2012) looked at the integrative development of students in a program that utilizes Wilber's (2008) integral theory for coaching students' development. Study participants self-reported their increased integrative development using Wilber's AQUAL model, as well as empowerment, embodied presence, and empathic connection.

These studies suggest that coaching students do not simply learn coaching skills. They embody new ways of being. Although it relied on students' self-reporting, the Kennedy (2012) study suggests that these transformations may equate to integrative development. The question this raises is whether coaching students demonstrate measurable integrative development at the end of their program.

Up until recently, measuring integrative development changes in programs of less than a year has been a challenge. Scoring systems have measured at whole levels, which generally take two to three years of intentional focus to move from one level to another (Commons, 2016). They have also required time-intensive analysis by expertly trained scorers, which is not scalable to assess larger groups participating in developmental programs. Fortunately, progress has been made recently. Lectica, an educational non-profit organization, has developed assessments that measure integrative development to one-fifth of a level using a computer algorithm to analyze text. Automated scoring at smaller increments makes assessing integrative development in programs as short as three months scalable and affordable.

The next section describes in greater detail the fifth study, which explored whether students demonstrate changes in their integrative development.

The Study

In a mixed methods exploratory study, Potter (2017) researched the integrative development and self-reported changes of ten participants who completed a six-month coach training program at Georgetown University. The Leadership Decision Making Assessment (LDMA) was selected to measure changes in integrative development because it is the most robustly tested and reliable of the Lectica assessments, consistently demonstrating a .95 level of reliability against expert human raters. Participant narratives were gathered via an open text online survey question: "Thinking about your Georgetown coaching experience, please describe any changes in how you think, feel, and/ or behave."

Ten volunteer participants were recruited from one cohort of the six-month coaching certificate program. One participant held a bachelor's degree, the remaining nine held graduate degrees. Age ranges were from 24 to 64. Since the researcher is an alumna of the coaching program, interaction was limited to email invitations and instructions for completing the assessments to minimize potential researcher influence and bias. In addition, participants selected pseudonyms. During data analysis, pseudonyms were converted to random numbers and re-matched afterwards for reporting purposes.

Ten volunteers completed the LDMA assessment before attending their first class and completed it again within two weeks of completing their final class. After they completed the post-program LDMA, the researcher sent each participant a link to the online question and instructed them to use their pseudonyms to match their narratives with their LDMA scores. A thematic analysis of the narratives was conducted using a six-phase process recommended by Braun and Clarke (2006).

Findings

Overall, participant LDMA scores increased after completing their coach training program (Table 1). For perspective, based upon Lectica's unpublished ongoing research, the mean change in scores in this six-month study was twice that of undergraduate students who complete an entire year of college (Dawson, 2016). This overall increase also includes two scores that decreased. Decreases in scores may be a result of any number of factors that affect performance. For instance, a decrease may be reflective of stress -- despite having completed their final class, students were still in the throes of completing a final paper and a coaching session recording that would determine whether they passed the program requirements. Decreases may also be indicative of the typical "spurts and dips" in performances that occur during dynamic skills/integrative development (Fischer, 1980; Fischer & Bidell, 2006).

Table 1: Integrative Levels

Participant Pseudonym	Age Range	Zone of Development	Pre-Test	Post-Test	Change
Sue	24 to 34	Early Systems	11.26	11.34	0.08
Melanie	35 to 44	Advanced Systems	11.54	11.58	0.04
Ryane	35 to 44	Early Systems => Advanced	11.42	11.50	0.08
Peter	35 to 44	Early Systems	11.38	11.46	0.08
Velma	35 to 44	Early Systems	11.00	11.42	0.42
Annette	45 to 54	Early Systems	11.36	11.34	-0.02
Vivian	45 to 54	Early Systems	11.36	11.46	0.10
Jake	45 to 54	Advanced Systems	11.56	11.58	0.02
Ruby Grace	45 to 54	Advanced Systems	11.56	11.62	0.06
Diane	55 to 64	Early Systems	11.40	11.36	-0.04
		Mean	11.38	11.47	0.08
		Median	11.39	11.46	0.07

$n=10$ Adult levels typically perform between 10.5 and 11.9

While the quantitative data point to integrative development, the qualitative themes suggest the nature of the changes and distinctions inherent in the dynamic process of becoming a coach. Taken as a whole, the themes point to increased mindfulness, reflexivity, and metacognition. All research participants reported deep personal growth, including new self- and other-awareness, and increased openness. The following are a small sample of comments from participants that illustrate the profound personal impact of becoming coaches:

I am more easily able to recognize and hold multiple perspectives, as well as observe myself in action and notice what's going on for me in different domains.

...the greatest change in my way of thinking is that I am a

386

more integrative thinker and I lead with greater awareness and curiosity.

I am both more fluid and more integrated in my being. I am attending holistically to others humanity integrating thinking, emotions, sensations (body), and spirit while being a freer, more alive person...

Based upon nuances in the narrative data, Potter (2017) proposed a distinction between openness described in transformative learning – being open to others' perspectives – and pre-presencing openness. Pre-presencing openness is the novice's version of, and precursor to, presencing. While presencing refers to knowledge that is sensed but not yet embodied (Scharmer, 2000), pre-presencing openness is full-body sensing to learn from the moment. Pre-presencing openness may also be a precursor to new awareness. New awareness is defined as *intentional* and *purposeful* foregrounding that results in novelty (Potter, 2017). One must be open to new information and perspectives in order for new awareness to occur; positive experiences with new awareness reinforce openness. These themes also link to descriptions of reflection-in-action (Mintz, 2016; Schön, 1983) and increased metacognition.

These findings support coach educators and also assist coaching students, recent graduates, and experienced coaches to fully comprehend the complexity of their craft. They also suggest areas for future coaching research, including phenomenological and longitudinal studies, comparisons across coaching programs, and comparisons between coaching and other developmental programs. The study design may also be used in other programs designed to promote integrative development.

Limitations

This study was exploratory with two lines of inquiry: whether coaching students demonstrate changes in their integrative development, and whether there is a scalable method to measure integrative development at microlevels in programs of less than one year. While successful as an exploratory study, there were several limitations. The number of participants is insufficient for statistical significance. In addition, participants were selected from one cohort in one coaching program. Since groups differ in dynamics, it will be interesting in a larger study to see the similarities and differences across groups and across different programs. Another limitation is that when the participants completed the post-assessment, they were not finished with their program and therefore were in the most stressful time of their program. It is possible that their post-program scores were inhibited by their stress levels.

One recommendation for future studies is to assess one to two months after participants have successfully completed the program requirements when they have less stress and perhaps have a broader perspective on their experience. Another is to study multiple cohorts across multiple coaching programs.

Conclusion

Recent graduates of coaching educational programs consistently remark on their transformations as a result of becoming a coach. Exploring this phenomenon, this article presented three connected threads. One was an overview of coaching research and theory and a call for a common theoretical foundation for coaching students who are not trained counseling psychologists. Two adult learning theories, transformative learning and experiential learning theory, were reviewed to explain what and how transformation may occur for both coaching students and their clients. Six learning dialectics were described in the context of coaching, and a coaching dialectics model was presented to demonstrate the complexity of a single coaching conversation. Simultaneous management of the six coaching dialectics was proposed as one possibility for consistent reports of transformation.

The second thread was a discussion of five studies on changes new coaches experience from their coach training. This included a detailed description of one exploratory research study with coaching students who completed a six-month coach training program. While the study was exploratory, results indicate increased integrative development, as well as new awareness and ways of being, and suggest this may be a rich area of exploration. The study also offers a scalable research design to determine changes in integrative development for any type of developmental program.

More broadly, practitioners and educators continue to grapple with how to facilitate the integrative development among leaders and students so they may better manage the increasing complexity of their environment. When designing programs for this purpose, it is useful to have a clear understanding of the underlying cognitive and meaning making structures, as well as the dialectical mechanisms that help individuals stretch in ways that create more complex and flexible ways of thinking and being. Integrating into these programs the complex and dynamic skills that coaching students learn may be another way to accelerate participant's integrative development.

Endnote

[1] Derived from Experiential Learning (Kolb, 2014), Conversational Learning (Baker, Jensen, & Kolb, 2002), and Rules and Performance (Polyani, 1958), and Productive Uncertainty (Mintz, 2016).

About the Author

Penny Potter, PhD, is a coach, educator, author, and researcher. In her private coaching and consulting practice, Penny works with leaders at all levels and specializes in coaching leaders in transition. She also teaches coaching skills for leaders and assists organizations with the process of developing a coaching culture. In addition, Penny is adjunct faculty in George Mason University's Organizational Development and Knowledge Management masters program, where she teaches foundation coaching skills for organizational development practitioners. Penny's doctorate is in human and organizational systems from Fielding Graduate University. Her other degrees are in organizational development and knowledge management (M.S.), and psychology (B.S.). She received her coach training at Georgetown University and her PCC coaching credential from the International Coaching Federation.

References

Bachkirova, T., & Kauffman, C. (2008). Many ways of knowing: How to make sense of different research perspectives in studies of coaching. *Coaching: An International Journal of Theory, Research and Practice,* 1(2), 107-113. doi:10.1080/17521880802328186

Baker, A. C., Jensen, P. J., & Kolb, D. A. (2002). *Conversational learning: An experiential approach to knowledge creation.* Westport, CT: Quorum Books.

Baker, A. C., Jensen, P. J., & Kolb, D. A. (2005). Conversation as experiential learning. *Management Learning,* 36(4), 411-427.

Bartunek, J. M., Gordon, J. R., & Weathersby, R. P. (1983). Developing "complicated" understanding in administrators. *The Academy of Management Review,* 8(2), 273.

Beets, K., & Goodman, S. (2012). Evaluating a training programme for executive coaches. *SA Journal of Human Resource Management,* 10(3), 1-10. doi:http://dx.doi.org/10.4102/sajhrm.v10i3.425

Bono, J. E., Purvanova, R. K., Towler, A. J., & Peterson, D. B. (2009). A survey of executive coaching practices. *Personnel Psychology,* 62(2), 361-404.

Bonrath, E. M., Dedy, N. J., Gordon, L. E., & Grantcharov, T. P. (2015). Comprehensive surgical coaching enhances surgical skill in the operating room: A randomized controlled trial. *Annals of surgery,* 262(2), 205-212.

Braun, V., & Clarke, V. (2006). Using thematic analysis in psychology. *Qualitative Research in Psychology,* 3(2), 77-101. doi:http://dx.doi.org/10.1191/1478088706qp063oa

Brown, B. C. (2012). *Conscious leadership for sustainability: How leaders with a late-stage action logic design and engage in sustainability initiatives* (Doctoral dissertation). Fielding Graduate University database.

Campone, F. (2014). Thinking like a professional: The impact of graduate coach education. *Journal of Psychological Issues in Organizational Culture,* 5(2),

16-30. doi:10.1002/jpoc.21142

Commons, M. L. (2016). What are the relationships between the four notions of stage change. *Journal of Adult Development*, (Draft Special Issue). Retrieved from http://adultdevelopment.org/Commons2012a.pdf

Cox, E. (2013). *Coaching understood: A pragmatic inquiry into the coaching process.* UK: Sage Publications Ltd.

Cox, E. (2015). Coaching and adult learning: Theory and practice. *New Directions for Adult and Continuing Education,* 2015(148), 27-38. doi:10.1002/ace.20149

Cox, E., Bachkirova, T., & Clutterbuck, D. A. (2014). *The complete handbook of coaching* (2nd ed.). Thousand Oaks, CA: SAGE Publications.

Cox, E., & Jackson, P. (2014). Developmental coaching. In E. Cox, T. Bachkirova, & D. A. Clutterbuck (Eds.), *The complete handbook of coaching* (2nd ed., pp. 215-227). Thousand Oaks, CA: Sage Publications.

Day, D. V., & Lance, C. E. (2004). Understanding the development of leadership complexity through latent growth modeling. In D. V. Day, S. J. Zaccaro, & S. M. Halpin (Eds.), *Leader development for transforming organizations: Growing leaders for tomorrow* (pp. 41-69). Mahwah, NJ: Lawrence Erlbaum Associates.

Drake, D. B. (2008). Finding our way home: Coaching's search for identity in a new era. *Coaching: An International Journal of Theory, Research and Practice,* 1(1), 16-27. doi:10.1080/17521880801906099

Ely, K., Boyce, L. A., Nelson, J. K., Zaccaro, S. J., Hernez-Broome, G., & Whyman, W. (2010). Evaluating leadership coaching: A review and integrated framework. *The Leadership Quarterly,* 21(4), 585-599. doi:10.1016/j.leaqua.2010.06.003

Fischer, K. W., & Bidell, T. R. (2006). Dynamic development of action and thought. In R. M. Lerner (Ed.), *Handbook of child psychology* (6 ed., Vol. 1). Hoboken, NJ: Wiley.

Fitzgerald, C., & Garvey-Berger, J. (2002). Executive coaching. In C. Fitzgerald & J. G. Berger (Eds.), *Executive coaching: Practices and perspectives* (pp. 27–58). Palo Alto, CA: Davis-Black.

Garvey-Berger, J. (2006). Adult development theory and executive coaching practice. In A. M. Grant & D. R. Stober (Eds.), *Evidence based coaching handbook: Putting best practices to work for your clients* (pp. 77-102). Hoboken, NJ: John Wiley & Sons.

Gergen, K. J., Gergen, M. M., & Barrett, F. J. (2004). Dialogue: Life and death of the organization. In D. Grant, C. Hardy, C. Oswick, N. Philips, & L. Putnam

(Eds.), *The Sage handbook of organizational discourse* (pp. 39-59). London, UK: Sage.

Glassman, M. (2000). Negation through history: Dialectics and human development. *New Ideas in Psychology*, 18(1), 1-22. doi:https://doi.org/10.1016/S0732-118X(99)00034-3

Grant, A. M. (2005). What is evidence-based executive, workplace and life coaching. In M. Cavanagh, A. M. Grant, & T. Kemp (Eds.), *Evidence-based coaching* (Vol. 1, pp. 1-12). Bowen Hills, Australia: Australian Academic Press.

Gray, D. E. (2006). Executive coaching: Towards a dynamic alliance of psychotherapy and transformative learning processes. *Management Learning*, 37(4), 475-497. doi:10.1177/1350507606070221

Gunnlaugson, O. (2006). Generative dialogue as a transformative learning practice in adult and higher education settings. *Journal of Adult and Continuing Education*, 12(1), 2-19.

Jones, R. J., Woods, S. A., & Guillaume, Y. R. F. (2015). The effectiveness of workplace coaching: A meta-analysis of learning and performance outcomes from coaching. *Journal of Occupational and Organizational Psychology*, 1-29. doi:10.1111/joop.12119

Kegan, R. (1994). *In over our heads: The mental demands of modern life*. Cambridge, MA: Harvard University Press.

Kennedy, D. L. (2012). *The impact of development on coaches' use of self as instrument*. (Doctoral dissertation). ProQuest Dissertations and Theses database.

Kolb, D. A. (1981). *Learning from experience*. San Francisco, CA: Jossey-Bass.

Kolb, D. A. (1984). *Experiential learning: Experience as the source of learning and development*. Upper Saddle River, NJ: Prentice-Hall.

Kolb, D. A. (2014). *Experiential learning: Experience as the source of learning and development*. Englewood Cliffs, NJ: Prentice Hall.

Laske, O. (1999a). An integrated model of developmental coaching. *Consulting Psychology Journal: Practice and Research*, 51(3), 139-159. doi:10.1037/1061-4087.51.3.139

Laske, O. (1999b). *Transformative effects of coaching on executives' professional agenda*. (PsyD dissertation). ProQuest Dissertations & Theses Global database.

Laske, O. (2004). Can evidence-based coaching increase ROI. *International Journal of Evidence Based Coaching and Mentoring*, 2(2), 41-53.

Lewin, K. (1943). Psychology and the process of group living. *Journal of Social Psychology*, 17, 113–131.

McCauley, C. D., Drath, W. H., Palus, C. J., O'Connor, P. M., & Baker, B. A. (2006). The use of constructive-developmental theory to advance the understanding of leadership. *The Leadership Quarterly*, 17(6), 634-653. doi:10.1016/j. leaqua.2006.10.006

Mezirow, J. (1978). Perspective transformation. *Adult Education Quarterly*, 28(2), 100-110. doi:10.1177/074171367802800202

Mezirow, J. (1985). A critical theory of self-directed learning. *New Directions for Adult and Continuing Education*, 1985(25), 17-30.

Mezirow, J. (2003). Transformative learning as discourse. *Journal of Transformative Education*, 1(1), 58-63. doi:10.1177/1541344603252172

Mintz, J. (2016). Bion and Schön: Psychoanalytic perspectives on reflection in action. *British Journal of Educational Studies*, 64(3), 277-293. doi:10.1080/0007100 5.2015.1136404

Mukherjee, S. (2012). Does coaching transform coaches? A case study of internal coaching. *International Journal of Evidence Based Coaching & Mentoring*, 10(2), 76-87.

Polanyi, M. (1958) The Study of Man (Chicago, University of Chicago Press).

Potter, P. M. (2017). *Becoming a coach: Transformative learning and hierarchical complexity of coaching students* (Doctoral dissertation). ProQuest Dissertations & Theses Global.

Potter, P. M. (in press). The complex choreography of Becoming a Coach. In J. Reams (Ed.), *Maturing Leadership* (pp. 168-196): Emerald Group Publishers.

Roux, M. (in press). Leadership 4.0. In J. Reams (Ed.), *Maturing Leadership* (pp. 10-51): Emerald Group Publishers.

Sammut, K. (2014). Transformative learning theory and coaching: Application in practice. *International Journal of Evidence Based Coaching and Mentoring*, Special Issue No.8, 39-53.

Scharmer, C. O. (2000, May). *Presencing: Learning from the future as it emerges*. Paper presented at the Conference on Knowledge and Innovation, Helsinki, Finland.

Schön, D. A. (1983). *The Reflective Practitioner: How Professionals Think in Action*. New York, NY: Basic Books, Inc.

Skiffington, S., & Zeus, P. (2003). *Behavioral coaching: How to build sustainable personal and organizational strength*. New York, NY: McGraw-Hill.

Sonesh, S. C., Coultas, C. W., Lacerenza, C. N., Marlow, S. L., Benishek, L. E., & Salas, E. (2015). The power of coaching: a meta-analytic investigation. *Coaching: An International Journal of Theory, Research and Practice*, 8(2), 73-95. doi:10.1080/17521882.2015.1071418

Swart, J., & Harcup, J. (2013). 'If I learn do we learn?': The link between executive coaching and organizational learning. *Management Learning*, 44(4), 337.

Tarricone, P. (2011). *The taxonomy of metacognition*. New York, NY: Psychology Press.

Taylor, E. W. (2009). Fostering transformative learning. In J. Mezirow, E. W. Taylor (Eds.), *Transformative learning in practice: Insights from community, workplace, and higher education* (pp. 3-17). San Francisco, CA: Jossey-Bass.

Torbert, W. R., & Livne-Tarandach, R. (2009). Reliability and validity tests of the Harthill Leadership Development Profile in the context of developmental action inquiry theory, practice and method. *Integral Review*, 5(2), 133-152.

Weick, K. E. (1979). *The social psychology of organizing*. Reading, MA: Addison-Wesley.

Zull, J. E. (2011). *From brain to mind: Using neuroscience to guide change in education*. Sterling, VA: Stylus.

CHAPTER 18

COACHING SUPERVISION

Kimcee McAnally, PhD, PCC
Lilian Abrams, PhD, MBA, MCC
Mary Jo Asmus, PCC
Terry H. Hildebrandt, PhD, MCC, MCEC
CoachingSupervisionResearch.org

Abstract

Coach supervision [1] is becoming an important practice for continuing professional development for coaches. Coach supervision is already established as an accepted practice in Europe and the United Kingdom (UK) and is growing in popularity in the rest of the world. The authors define coach supervision and discuss its origins, history, purpose, and value. They provide a brief explanation of how coach supervision works. The authors discuss selected results of their recent global survey on coach supervision, relative to its value and benefits, as well as the issues and challenges that supervisees bring to coach supervision sessions. The authors conclude with a discussion of the future of coach supervision and next steps for additional research.

Keywords: Coach Supervision, Coaching Supervision, Coach Supervisor, Continuing Professional Development, Seven-Eyed Model, Reflective Practice.

What is Coach Supervision?

Coach supervision is a valuable developmental process for every coach, regardless of whether or not they are just getting started in their practice or are long-experienced, or if they are in an internal or an external role. Coaches are encouraged to reflect on their coaching practice and client work during supervision, for the benefit of both themselves and their clients.

One widely accepted definition of coaching supervision, developed by the European Mentoring and Coaching Council (EMCC) (2018), states:

"Supervision is the interaction that occurs when a mentor or coach brings their coaching or mentoring work experiences to a supervisor in order to be supported and to engage in reflective dialogue and collaborative learning for the development and benefit of the mentor or coach, their clients and their organisations."

Another definition, which focused on process, is presented by Julie Hay (2007), who describes supervision as "helping you to step back, metaphorically, from your work so that you can take a meta-perspective, or broader view, of your practice" (pp. 4-5).

Generally, there are three formats for coaching supervision: individual, group, and peer sessions. There are benefits and disadvantages to each type of supervision.

Individual supervision relies on a partnership, in a one-on-one format, between the coach and their chosen coach supervisor. These private sessions generally run 60 minutes in length, and focus on the coach's specific practice or agenda. Important learning in the sessions takes place when the coach brings their most important issues to the discussion, so that in each session, the coach's most important needs are addressed. These sessions are therefore time-efficient for the coach. Because of the individual focus, individual supervision tends to be more expensive than group work, and it relies on the skill and deep honesty of both the coach and supervisor for productive sessions.

With group supervision, the coach supervisor conducts sessions with multiple coaches (e.g., optimally, 6 to 8 coaches) attending simultaneously. The coach supervisor facilitates discussion among the group, including selecting topics from a variety of possible contributions and dynamically soliciting input from all group members. Coaches are able to learn from one another's experiences and sessions are less expensive per hour, since the cost is spread across the multiple coaches. Group sessions are typically longer than individual sessions, usually lasting 2 hours or more. Because of the number of coaches attending, usually not every individual coach's issues may be addressed. A coach may therefore not always get resolution to a specific issue they would have liked to discuss, during their group supervision sessions.

Peer supervision is similar to group supervision except it lacks a consistent facilitator. Instead, in this format, each member of the group serves as both a supervisor and supervisee at different times during the sessions (Carrol & Gilbert, 2005-2015). There may be an exchange of services, and therefore this format typically incurs no cost for participants. However, the success of the sessions is fully dependent on the skill, honesty, and trust levels of all participants at all times, and if any of these are lacking, this format may not be as beneficial as desired for participants. As with group supervision, a coach may or may not have his/her individual issue addressed.

History of Supervision

Coach supervision is often said to have its roots in clinical psychology and counselling. Ian Fleming and Linda Sheen (2004) offered that "the goals of clinical supervision are to encourage reflection, understanding and self-awareness in the supervisee, and to enable problem-solving. Principally, the aim is to enhance clinical practice, and its effectiveness, in the best interests of the client" (p. xii). This clinical supervision definition bears a striking resemblance to the EMCC coaching supervision definition described above, given that both definitions focus on reflection and resulting benefits for both the supervisee and their clients. More recently, Lise Lewis (2013) proposed that supervision broadly draws on adult learning theory, systems theory, the art of reflection, mindfulness, relational psychology, neuroscience, and other disciplines (p. xix). In all its manifestations, however, the purpose is to provide the practitioner with the result of greater self-insight and improved practice. Coach supervision serves this same function for practicing coaches.

What is the Purpose of Supervision?
The purpose of coaching supervision is to provide a safe, reflective space for a coach, with a partner who helps the coach/supervisee work through their own specific client situations as well as their general and/or personal "triggers", questions, celebrations, and other areas related to their practice and client situations. One useful model of the functions of supervision, based on Proctor's work, summarizes the purpose of supervision into three functions: Normative, Formative, and Restorative (Hay, 2007, p. 5).

Figure 1

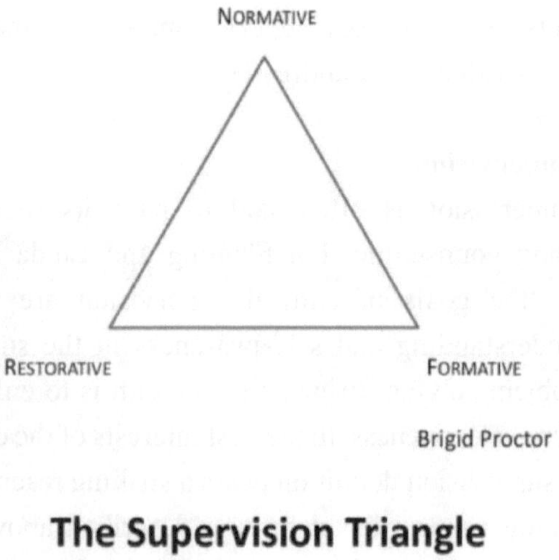

NORMATIVE

RESTORATIVE   FORMATIVE

Brigid Proctor

The Supervision Triangle

The Three Functions of Supervision

In this model, the *Normative* element focuses on standards, problem-solving, ethics, and ensuring the quality of practice for the coach in their client interactions. The *Formative* aspect is about developing the coach's skills, including learning, improving and/or practicing new skills, acquiring new knowledge, and increasing their self-awareness. Finally, the focus of the *Restorative* function is to support the coach in feeling personally acknowledged and valued for their work and increasingly greater development as a coach; reducing their internal conflicts and/or stresses as they perform their coaching work; and increasing the coach's satisfaction and "recharging" for the coach.

These three functions illustrate the contents of coach supervision session conversations, as well as outcomes. Similarly, it may be useful to delineate the service and function of coach supervision, in contrast to other processes like coaching and mentoring.

What are the differences between coaching, mentoring, and supervision?

While there are some similarities, there are also specific and definite differences between coaching, mentoring, and supervision, in terms of the skills, purpose, and intent of each practice. Similarities between these practices include that they are usually conversational in nature, build self-awareness, and may happen with an internal or external source. Differences include the focus and terms of the conversations, the nature of the relationship between the parties and the effect of the expectations about how each parties' "expertise" plays a role in the dynamics.

The purpose of **coaching** is to support the client (coachee) in *achieving their goals,* which includes creating actions in alignment with those goals and holding the client accountable for their own improvement. The client may identify a focus area tied to their personal life or their work role as a leader; in the latter case, the client goals may be tied to their own leadership development plan or their work objectives. For example, a client who desires to improve their executive presence in order to be able to achieve a future promotion might work with an executive coach to learn new techniques, practice new behaviors, and role-play applications of insights and new behaviors to their work situations, to prepare for or review actual situations as they arise during the coaching engagement.

The focus of **mentoring**, on the other hand, is to *transfer knowledge* from the mentor, who has particular expertise or experience in a certain area, to the client (mentee). Examples would be mentoring learning how to be a Chief Financial Officer (CFO) from someone who has been one or learning how to work with an age group such as Millennials from an expert in that field.

In contrast, **coaching supervision** is about *providing a safe, reflective space* for the coach, in which they can address their own issues, and challenges around their client cases, as well as reflect on situations related to themselves as coaches. Examples of client situations might be reflecting on a session that did not go well or exploring what the coach could perhaps have surfaced to better support the client situation.

While these three areas share similarities among the types of participants and the importance of listening and sharing conversations as their means to an end, the above definitions illustrate that there are core differences in their purpose as well as their conduct.

Why is coaching supervision important?

Supervision is an important support system for coaches, in terms of their personal development, ethics, and maintaining a healthy outlook and disposition as a coach. Bachkirova, Jackson, and Clutterbuck (2011) proposed that supervision is important due to the complexity of serving multiple stakeholders in each coaching engagement. They also say that coaches may be less prepared to identify their own personal processes, given that personal development work is not mandatory for a coaching practice on a global basis.

In some areas, such as Europe, professional coaching associations, often require coaches to receive supervision throughout the year. These associations include European Mentoring and Coaching Council (EMCC, 2018), Association for Coaching® (AC), and the Association for Professional Executive Coaching & Supervision (APECS) who value its use as demonstrated by requiring its members to work with a supervisor (Hildebrandt, 2019).

A recent research study by the authors (McAnally, Abrams, Asmus, & Hildebrandt, 2020) of over 1200 global respondents found that coaching supervision is widely utilized. In Europe/Africa, 93% of participants said that they had worked with an individual coach supervisor at some point, and 74% reported having worked with a group supervisor. In contrast, 85% of coaches from Asia-Pacific (APAC) region and 83% in the Americas have worked with an individual supervisor. Group supervision was less utilized, with 55% of APAC coaches and 54% in the Americas having worked in group sessions. This dispersion illustrates the worldwide representation of coach supervision.

While globally, coaching supervision has still to reach a level of perceived criticality, supervision has definitively grown and continues to gain popularity both in and beyond Europe. The authors propose that supervision is a critical practice for successful coaches, in order to continue to develop personally and professionally, as well as be optimally positioned to handle the challenges of their practice.

How Does Supervision Work?

Four steps will be described about the process of supervision: 1) Selecting a coach supervisor; 2) Contracting between the coach and their coach supervisor; 2) Models and information about conducting supervision sessions; and 4) Providing mutual feedback for the coach and the coach supervisor.

1. Selection of a Coach Supervisor

As our research (McAnally, Abrams, Asmus, & Hildebrandt, 2020) indicates, coaches most often select their coach supervisor based on the coach's personal contact or exposure to that person, in a way that builds familiarity and, presumably, an initial level of trust and comfort. When asked how they found their supervisor, responses from over 1200 coaches revealed that the most popular response was "having had prior experience with them." These responses were followed by "through a professional association," by "referral," and via "word of mouth." These responses indicate the critical importance and necessity of building prior familiarity and an initial feeling of trust between a coach and their coach supervisor.

These responses indicate a core aspect of the coach-supervisor relationship. To be effective, supervision must remain a safe space for the coach, so that the coach can reflect fully and openly upon their own inner experience, as well as the outward manifestations and outcomes of this experience in their work with their clients. To be effective, coaches therefore must feel comfortable with their supervisors, so that they can openly discuss any topic that comes to mind during supervision sessions regarding their coaching work. It makes sense, then, that the coach's direct, personal, prior experiences provide them with useful information about a potential supervisor. Similarly, a referral from a trusted source can also help a coach decide if they indeed might be able to trust and work effectively with a particular coach supervisor.

Coach populations that are relatively experienced with the practice of coach supervision, such as in those in the U.K., also know to ask prospective supervisor's about their specific training to serve as a coach supervisor, and their supervisory experience. Accreditation as a coach supervisor, such as that offered by professional associations such as the EMCC, APECS, Association for Coaching, and others, is also desirable, because it both confirms a coach supervisor's training as well as their own continuing professional development in coach supervision. Accreditation ensures that the coach supervisor meets a respected level of professional competency, specifically as a coach supervisor. Formal coach supervisor training and accreditation are yet further distinguishing points of difference for coach supervisors, as opposed to those practicing peer supervision, mentoring, and other forms of coach self-development.

2. Contracting

Once a supervisor is chosen, good coach supervision continues with good contracting. Open discussions of what the coach and supervisor would like and expect around confidentiality, mutual respect, logistics (e.g., payment details, cancellation policies, methods of meetings, etc.), management of conflicts and ethics, and other aspects of effective work together, are explicitly discussed and recorded for both. Some coach supervisors may send an initial questionnaire to their new supervisee, to speed up their acquisition of basic facts and initial preferences about their new supervisee, which can be discussed in their first meeting. Often, a coach's first session with a new supervisor includes review and explication of each party's desires, needs, and expectations around this particular supervision relationship.

3. Conducting Sessions

After describing the most popular coach supervision models, Hildebrandt (2017) describes the most popular coaching supervision model in the following way:

"Probably the most popular model is the Seven-Eyed Model created by Hawkins and Shohet (1989). This model examines the client-coach-supervisor system from seven different perspectives. These include: (1) the client's context, (2) the coach's interventions, (3) the relationship between the coach and the client, (4) the coach's self-awareness, (5) the relationship between the coach and supervisor including parallel processes, (6) supervisor's reactions and reflections, and (7) the wider context and system. Using the Seven-Eyed Model, the supervisor and supervisee engage in rich dialogue and reflection resulting in insights that can expose blind spots, deepen self-awareness, and open possibilities for new client interventions. (p. 39)"

This model provides a varied framework of perspectives (the seven "Eyes") that the supervisor can help the coach take, during their supervision session, to explore their own work as a coach. While the supervisor can assist the coach by bringing these various lenses to the supervisee's topic, it is up to the coach supervisee to choose the topics for focus during each session. Sample topics include particular client situations or challenges, ethical questions, desired skill development areas, and others.

Material to be covered in supervision sessions is almost always up to the supervisee. Another pre-supervision practice might be for a supervisee to prepare thoughtfully around what they would like to focus on during their upcoming session. While not extensive, some literature exists to assist supervisees on preparing to maximize their supervision sessions, such as *On Being a Supervisee: Creating Learning Partnerships* (Carrol & Gilbert, 2005-2015). Some supervisees obtain explicit permission from their clients both immediately before and after coaching sessions to record those client sessions; the purpose of this is so that the supervisor can themselves bring examples of their supervision work to their own supervisor, for coach supervision, to explore and use for improvement as a supervisor.

During a supervision session, a sample opening question that a supervisor might ask their coach/supervisee is, "What are you bringing to supervision today?" Most typically, the supervisee brings one or more topic(s) that are "top-of-mind" for them. For supervision, the coach/supervisee usually brings material to explore that comes specifically from their own coaching work and/or their experience as a coach while practicing coaching. The topics brought to supervision are often ones around which the supervisee has a troubling lack of personal clarity, around which they would like greater understanding and options for addressing – this aspect of supervision is quite similar to coaching. However, with a trained, experienced supervisor providing consistent support, mutual trust, and an ongoing relationship that maintains reflection, the coach supervisee usually feels uniquely able to "go deeper" in exploring their own personal assumptions, beliefs, feelings, reactions, and other inner experience aspects that arise as they coach. A coach might discuss a wide variety of topics, from challenges they have with a client (similar to a case study; this is probably the most common topic discussed in supervision, and potentially the most impactful for one's coaching;) ethical concerns and questions; systemic issues that the coach or their client must face, such as with their manager, direct reports, peers, organizations, community, home life, etc.; and others.

The supervisor also watches for relevant interpersonal dynamics between themselves and the coach/supervisee, such as parallel process and transference, and raises those as explicit topics of discussion, when they judge it to be of potential benefit to the supervisee. Concluding the session might be a mutual question such as "How would you like to close our time today?", or a question around what the supervisee is taking away from their session.

Ideally, a coach supervision session is both interactive and self-reflective. As such, it can lead the coach to powerful insights about themselves as a coach, which in itself can suffice as a meaningful and useful outcome for the session. Although practical actions are often sought and decided upon by the supervisee during the session, actions are not necessarily the goal of all supervision sessions, depending on the chosen topic. Rather, the uniquely safe, reflective space that supervision provides allows coaches to grow in ways that manifest broadly across the coach's practice, rather than a consideration of success as solely the next actions to take with a particular client situation. This broader view of session success is another difference

405

between coaching and coach supervision.

4. Providing Feedback

Because the supervision relationship is one of service by the supervisor to the coach/supervisee, best practices include regular solicitation of feedback from the supervisee to their supervisor, on how well the supervisor's practices and the relationship is serving them. During contracting, supervisors will often explicitly include mention of the expectation that they are open to feedback on their own performance at any time. At the same time, supervisors will typically ask their supervisees to agree to provide feedback to them, be it constructive or reinforcing, when asked by the supervisor, or whenever it seems appropriate or needed by the supervisee. Asking for input can be planned or unplanned, and can happen either during a session or periodically, at set points during the supervision engagement. The importance of this practice is underscored by the fact that the EMCC, one of the key accrediting professional associations for coach supervisors, requires evidence of obtained feedback from applicants to their coach supervisor accreditation.

The Value and Benefits of Coaching Supervision

The four aspects of coach supervision above describe the process, by which the value and benefits of supervision are realized. Of course, the immediate beneficiary of supervision is the coach, who can use what they have learned in coaching supervision to the benefit of the client, their organization, and other wider communities and situations that they serve. Until now, there have been some underlying assumptions about the specifics of the value and benefit that a coach might experience, but without data to back them up. In their book, *Coaching and Supervision: Growth and Learning in Professional Practice*, Hilary Cochrane and Trudi Newton (2018) state that, "Supervision is becoming the most effective way of sustaining the development of the client and the coach, the wider system in which they operate, as well as the supervisor and the coaching profession" (p. 13). Similarly, the International Coach Federation (ICF, 2020a) lists the following potential benefits to the coach when they receive coaching supervision: increased self-awareness, greater confidence, increased objectivity, heightened sense of belonging, reduced feelings of isolation and increased resourcefulness. The authors have recently acquired global information that can help define the value and benefits of coaching supervision for the coach.

Research on the Value of Coaching Supervision

A recent global survey (McAnally, Abrams, Asmus & Hildebrandt, 2020) sheds light on this topic of the value of working with a coaching supervisor. This study's analyses included data from 1280 global participants, including external leadership/executive coaches (60% of total), life and wellness coaches (15%), certified coaching supervisors (13% of total, internal leadership/executive coaches (8%), and clinicians who had received supervision (4%).

The survey approached the question of assessing the value of supervision from the different points of view of coaches who had experienced individual or group coaching, or both. The questions asked were "In your words, please describe what you value or appreciate about your individual supervision experience?" and "In your words, please describe what you value or appreciate about your group supervision experience?" Because the questions and responses were different, we will look at each of these results separately.

Responses from Those Who Have Had Individual Supervision. There was a total of 1263 respondents to the survey who indicated they have received individual supervision, and 586 coaches responded to an open-ended question about what they value and appreciate in their individual supervision experience. The top five values that were cited: the new perspectives, insights, and approaches I learned (listed 170 times); the opportunity to develop myself (listed 150 times); the time and space to reflect (listed 73 times); the support I received (listed 68 times); and the reassurance I felt about my coaching (listed 58 times).

Responses from Those Who Have Had Group Supervision. There was a total of 775 respondents to the survey who indicated they have received supervision, and 634 coaches responded to the open-ended question about what they value and appreciate in their individual supervision experience. The five top values that were cited: The broader insight I received (listed 167 times); the learning I received (listed 71 times); the shared experiences (listed 65 times); the support from the group (listed 56 times) and the opportunity to develop myself (listed 39 times).

Although there is some crossover in the perceived values by those who have had individual versus group supervision, it is notable that there are also some differences that are specific to the experience of working individually with a coach supervisor versus having coach-peers in the group supervision space.

Research on the Benefits of Working with a Coach Supervisor

In the same survey mentioned above, participants were asked "How have you benefitted from working with a coach Supervisor?" This question was asked of anyone who had worked with a coach supervisor either individually or in a group. Participants could select from as many of the items from the response options as were applicable to them. A total of 5,890 responses came from 982 coaches.

Over 50% of the participants who worked individually with a coach supervisor chose six of the statements out of 13 possible. The top two statements selected were key to the purpose of Coaching Supervision: Working through a client challenge (74% of participants chose this) and Space for me to gain greater clarity (73%). The figure following from the study report shows how the statement choices for this question ranked in frequency of selection for the study participants.

Benefits reported to be received from coaching supervision (McAnally, et al., 2020) span a broad spectrum, which are personal to the individual being supervised, as indicted in Figure 2. Some

Figure 2

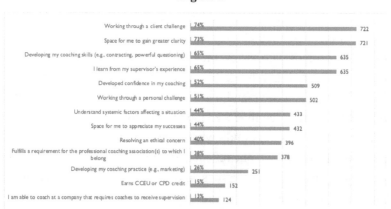

Benefits of Coaching Supervision (Reprinted with Permission). McAnally, K., Abrams, L.G., Asmus, M.J., & Hildebrandt, T.H. (2020). *Global coaching supervision: A study of the perceptions and practices around the world.*

of the benefits have cross-over with the value that coaches reported experiencing, obtained from the open-ended questions. In the end, it is clear that for many/most coaches who took this survey and have worked with supervisor, the reported value and benefits they obtained help them serve as a better coach for clients, with greater capability to help their clients achieve their goals and impact the organizations and systems in which they participate.

Issues and Challenges Brought to Coaching Supervision Sessions

Coaches who are new to supervision may initially be perplexed about the topics which they should bring to supervision sessions. For those not knowledgeable, coach supervision may be confused with numerous other methodologies (e.g., mentoring, advising, coaching, and teaching.) However, coaching supervision is unique because of its goal to help coaches build their own capacities, for themselves as well as in service to their clients. Development of the supervised coach truly takes place at the intersection of the personal and the professional.

Therefore, it is logical that the supervisor will guide a large share of supervision sessions to focus on the inner world of the coach. This is accomplished in a reflective space that invites the coach's best thinking about their practice, their clients, and the relationship with them. They also consider topics such as how they view themselves as an instrument for change; "what might be getting in their way" of their being even more effective as a coach; and many other nuances that can guide the coach's development, confidence, and transformation.

With all of this in mind, what should one bring to coaching supervision that will help one reflect and think at one's best? Coaching supervision includes those issues and dynamics that impact one's professional life and may be causing one difficulty or challenges, most especially those things that hinder one's ability to be at their best with their clients. They may also include one's own personal life challenges or difficulties that could impinge on their ability to be at their best as a coach. (It is important to note that, just as with coaching, good supervisors do not step over the boundaries into counseling or therapy, during supervision conversations and relationships.) Finally, celebrating oneself as a coach, for one's coaching work and for helping a client be successful through one's help can also create rich learning for a coach and their current or future clients.

Research on the Types of Challenges Coaches Bring to Supervision Sessions

The survey (McAnally, Abrams, Asmus, Hildebrandt, 2020) described above on the Value and Benefits of Coaching Supervision also asked participants, "What kind of challenges have you brought to your individual supervision sessions?" and "What kind of challenges have you brought to your group supervision sessions?" Survey participants were provided with a menu of responses from which to choose. Because the questions and responses included different types of supervision, we will look at each of these results separately.

Responses from Those Who Have Had Individual Supervision. Study participants were asked to describe the types of challenges they have brought to individual supervision sessions. Multiple statements were available to select from, resulting in 4,437 responses from 1058 coaches who responded.

The most common challenge that coaches brought to individual supervision was client-related issues/challenges/situations, selected 77% of the time, followed by personal-related issues/challenges/situations 60% of the time. Other responses in order of frequency included questions about my own skills and competencies as a coach (48%); developing my practice (47%); emotional reactions I have had in or about my coaching work (46%); managing my own well-being (e.g., resilience, well-being) (39%; ethical concerns, habitual patterns I wanted to change in my coaching style (37%); and appreciation of what I do well as a coach (28%).

Responses from Those Who Have Had Group Supervision: Study participants were asked to describe the types of challenges they have brought to group supervision sessions. Multiple statements were available to select from, resulting in 2738 responses from 1058 coaches who responded.

The top two most common challenges that coaches brought to group supervision mirrored those brought to individual supervision — 74% brought client-related issues/challenges/situations followed by 50% who brought personal-related issues/challenges/situations. Other responses in order of frequency included: developing my practice (43%); questions about my own skills and competencies as a coach (40%); emotional reactions I have had in or about my coaching work (35%); habitual patterns I wanted to change in my coaching style 31%); ethical concerns (31%); managing my own well-being (e.g. resilience, self-care) as a coach (26%); and appreciation of what I do well as a coach (23%).

Implications - Future of Supervision

Coach supervision is a best practice that supports coach excellence and continuing improvement in their coaching. Because the focus is

411

coach self-improvement, it is to be expected that coach supervision as a practice might follow a similar trajectory as did coaching, initially. Specifically, coaching as a field has required at least two decades to grow into a mainstream leadership development activity. Time was needed for the use of coaching to be understood, and its utilization increase and spread. As a field, however, coaching has evolved steadily and consistently until now, when it is seen as a normal practice, and even expected in some ways, worldwide. Therefore, it makes sense that the supporting practice of coach supervision would follow a similar trajectory, requiring several years lagging behind coaching until it grows and takes root as a normal, even expected practice.

Globally, coach supervision is currently utilized unevenly, but can be expected to continue to gain momentum over time, as more and more coaches establish and grow their practices, and begin to acquire the kinds of varied and challenging experiences that lead conscientious practitioners to want the types of benefits offered by coach supervision. Coaches' increased professionalism also lends itself to wanting to adopt continuous coach self-development specific to their own practices, leading to improved and refined practice for the duration of their coaching careers. It is therefore logical that there has been this time-lag between the development of coaching as an established activity and career, and the consequent continuous development practice of coaching supervision that has naturally followed – which indeed appears to be the case.

Research on the current state of supervision (McAnally et al., 2020) indicates that worldwide, the above is indeed the case. Coach supervision is certainly a growing practice, lagging behind the spread of coaching in most countries or regions. In areas where coaching has been well-established for at least a couple of decades, such as the UK, supervision is likewise well-established and in fact expected of coaches by local accrediting bodies and professional associations as well. In areas where coaching is still being established as a profession, the same time-lag is occurring in coach supervision. McAnally et al.

(2020) also support this proposition: Globally, coach supervision is more routinely practiced and expected in the geographic areas in which coaching, as such, has been taking place the longest. The largest and most prestigious European coaching professional associations such as EMCC, APECS, Association for Coaching, and others require member coaches to undertake regular supervision, and coach supervisor training programs, long established in the UK, are beginning to develop in the US and elsewhere.

A significant indication of the growing global awareness, practice and benefits of coach supervision are indicated by the recently-published new set of global coach core competencies by the International Coach Federation (ICF, 2020a), the world's largest coaching association. Published in October 2019 and based on over 1,300 coaches' input, the ICF describes its new competency model as including the importance of a coaching mindset and ongoing reflective practice [and three other elements]. Reflective practice, which coach supervision is a key example, is listed under their first "Foundation(al)" competency section, in that a competent coach who "Embodies a Coaching Mindset." among other things, "develops an ongoing reflective practice to enhance one's coaching" as a key component of their second foundational competency" (ICF, 2020b).

Future Research

Research on the field of coach supervision is in its infancy, which allows for a wide scope of research questions to be researched. We would strongly urge both academics and practitioners to include well-designed, rigorous, empirical quantitative as well as qualitative research, that specifically confirms or disconfirms theory, as well as theoretical work. Certainly, theory and research literature from allied fields might be a useful place to start.

There are many unknown but important factors around coach supervision that would be very useful to understand, as a result of rigorous, data-based, systematic, objective, unbiased investigation.

These include: Aspects of the coach/supervisor/systems relationship, as per the various coaching models; characteristics of the supervisee, supervisor, or their relationships, that contribute more or less to effective supervision, including the supervisory interaction; indexes and analyses of different types of supervision session content, process, interactions and outcomes (both short- and long-term); the types of ethical and/or developmental/skill-based issues raised in supervision, the variety of ways different supervisors manage these, and their ultimate resolution; the relevant factors, similarities and differences in the process and outcomes of coaching, mentoring, peer supervision, and coach supervision; and greater depth on the factors contributing to perceived supervisor and coach/supervisee effectiveness, and how that relates back to coach client process and outcomes. Well-validated information would also be useful for coaches and supervisors both, in terms of: Choosing a supervisor; switching supervisors; identifying and ensuring implementation of best practices in beginning and ending supervision engagements; factors contributing to valuing supervision, including monetarily, and other areas around the logistics of supervision. It would be greatly desirable to have solid knowledge about if and how the specific processes of supervisor training, credentialing, and accreditation contribute to the effectiveness of supervision outcomes. Simply knowing more about the different possible and likely outcomes of supervision, as well as more specific information about the most valued (as opposed to effective) perceived elements of supervision, would be very valuable.

In summary, the nascent research literature on coach supervision leaves a broad field of inquiry still to be investigated. Our hope is that well-designed research investigations accompany the growth of the practice of coach supervision, so that practicing coaches can maximize the benefits of supervision at all points in their coaching careers.

Conclusions

Coaching supervision is a powerful reflective practice for

continuing professional development for coaches. Coach supervision has already taken hold as an accepted best practice in Europe and the UK and is growing globally. Coaches in our global study reported many benefits of supervision including personal and client related outcomes. Both individual and group supervision are options for coaches to consider. Since coaching supervision is relatively new practice, many opportunities for future research await scholar-practitioners.

End Note

[1] "Coach supervision" is synonymous with what elsewhere is called "coaching supervision. The choice at times to use "coach supervision" herein is to emphasize our reference to the coach's whole being, as well as the coaching practice for which they are receiving supervision, rather than simply referring to their coaching work alone.

About the Authors

Kimcee McAnally, PhD, PCC is an organizational psychologist, researcher, and author with 20+ years working with businesses in the areas of executive coaching, leadership development, change management, and organizational development. Kimcee holds a PhD and M.S. degree in Organizational Psychology, and B.A. in Psychology. She is recognized as a PCC (Professional Certified Coach) with ICF and is a certified Coach Supervisor. Kimcee is passionate about research and writing about coaching and coaching supervision, also presenting at conferences around the world. She coauthored the book, "Executive Coaching for Results: the Definitive Guide for Developing Organizational Leaders" (Berrett-Koehler publishers). She also serves as the Chief Coaching Officer (CCO) for CoachSource, LLC.

Lilian Abrams, PhD, MBA, MCC is an organizational psychologist and executive coach with 20+ years consulting to global and US organizations. She earned a PhD in Organizational Behavior (Psychology) and an MBA. Dr. Abrams is accredited as an executive coach by the ICF (MCC) and by

APECS in Europe, and is a trained, certified Coach Supervisor. Her executive coaching and supervision include special focus on cultural matters as well as technical and/or women leaders. Executive coaching, and now supervision, are primary passions, and build upon her years of OD and applied research work. Dr. Abrams is also passionate about advancing the executive coaching field through research, publishing, webinars and presentations.

Mary Jo Asmus, PC is a speaker, writer, facilitator, executive and leadership coach, team and group coach, mediator, coaching supervisor, and coaching skills trainer to executives. She has coached hundreds of individuals to get ready for their next level of leadership particularly in the arenas of influence, impact, communication, relationships and executive presence. She is the author of a globally popular award-winning leadership blog and has written in it regularly for over a decade, as well as contributing articles on leadership to SmartBrief on Leadership and other publications. Prior to starting her business in 2003, she worked as bench scientist and in other administrative and executive roles at a Fortune 100 pharmaceutical company.

Terry H. Hildebrandt, PhD, MCC, MCEC is a certified executive coach, organization development consultant, coach educator, coach supervisor, and author. He is the Founder and CEO of Terry Hildebrandt and Associates, LLC and has served as the Director of the Evidence Based Coaching ACTP program at Fielding Graduate University. Prior to starting his own business in 2008, Terry worked at HP for 22 years in management and engineering roles. He is an expert in the principles of evidence-based coaching, using the best existing theoretical and researched knowledge, in combination with his personal coaching skills and client knowledge, to deliver effective coaching. Terry is a Master Certified Coach (MCC) with the International Coaching Federation (ICF), a certified Master Corporate Executive Coach (MCEC) with the MEECO Leadership Institute, and a member of the Association of Corporate Executive Coaches (ACEC). He is also a Certified Coaching Supervisor from The Goldvarg Consulting Group, Inc. Terry earned his PhD in Human and Organizational Systems from the Fielding Graduate

University. He can be reached at terry@terryhildebrandt.com.

References

Bachkirova, T., Jackson, P., & Clutterbuck, D. (2011). *Coaching and mentoring supervision: Theory and practice.* Open University Press.

Carroll, M., & Gilbert, M.C. (2005, 2011, 2015). *On being a supervisee: Creating learning partnerships* (2nd ed.). London: Vukani Press.

Cochrane, H., & Newton, T. (2018). *Supervision and coaching: Growth and learning in professional practice.* Routledge.

European Mentoring Coaching Council. (2018). *Supervision.* https://www.emccouncil.org/quality/supervision/.

Fleming, I., & Sheen, L. (Eds.). (2004). *Supervision and clinical psychology: Theory, practice, and perspectives.* New York, NY: Routledge Publishers.

Hawkins, P., & Shohet, R. (1989). *Supervision in the helping professions.* Open University Press.

Hay, J. (2007). *Reflective practice and supervision for coaches.* New York, NY: Open University Press.

Hildebrandt, T.H. (2017). The niche of coaching supervision: Creating a reflective safe space for coaches. *Choice,* 15(20), 38-40.

Hildebrandt, T. H. (2019). The next big trend: Coaching supervision for corporate coaches. *Choice,* 17(3), 40-42.

ICF. (2020a). *Coaching supervision: ICF research on coaching supervision.* https://coachfederation.org/coaching-supervision.

ICF. (2020b). *Updated ICF competency model: November 2019: Updated model.* https://coachfederation.org/core-competencies

McAnally, K., Abrams, L.G., Asmus, M.J., & Hildebrandt, T.H. (2020). *Global coaching supervision: A study of the perceptions and practices around the world.* https://coachingsupervisionresearch.org/wp-content/uploads/2020/02/Global_Coaching_Supervision_Report_FINAL.pdf

Lewis, L. (2013). Foreward. In E. Murdoch & J. Arnold (Eds.), *Full spectrum supervision: Who you are is how you supervise.* (pp. xvii – xx). Panoma Press.

Passmore, J. (Ed.). (2011). *Supervision in coaching: Supervision, ethics and continuous professional development.* London, England: Kogan.

CHAPTER 19

COACHING IN WONDERLAND

Francine Campone, EdD, MCC

Abstract

The growing research and literature in the field of coaching continues to document the increasing complexity of organizations and contexts in which coaches work. I liken this environment- volatile, uncertain, complex and ambiguous- to Lewis Carroll's Wonderland, an environment in which the unexpected becomes the norm and strict rules of rationality do not apply. In this concluding chapter, I summarize the post-modern perspectives offered by the authors of the preceding chapters with respect to implications of their work and findings for the field of coaching, coaching-related research and the education and development of coaching professionals. Taken together, these chapters offer a vision of twenty-first century coaching that may be characterized as relational, experiential, reflexive and dynamic.

Keywords: complexity, post-modern coaching, phenomenology, coach development, coaching research

> "Let every student of nature take this as his rule that
> whatever the mind seizes upon with particular satisfaction is
> to be held in suspicion."
> Francis Bacon, *Novum Organum* 1620

The skeptic, Bacon, offers useful counsel against complacency in knowing what we know. Research and consideration of evidence provide a counterbalance to certainty of knowing. I would, however, add a phrase to Bacon, suggesting that what the mind seizes upon should be held with gentle suspicion and examined with bold curiosity. Curiosity is at the heart of all good coaching: curiosity about the client, curiosity about the self as coach, curiosity about the situation, curiosity about the processes and practice itself.

When Alice tumbles down the rabbit hole into Wonderland, she finds herself growing very tall, expanding like a telescope. Her reaction to this odd and unexpected experience is to cry out "Curiouser and curiouser!" (Carroll, 1865). As thinking professionals, we have all sometimes found ourselves-like Alice- tumbling down a rabbit hole and landing in a place where our head stretches far above our feet. And, like Alice, the best possible response is inquiry. The papers in this monograph examine the people and events taking place in the wonderland of coaching in the twenty-first century, a time and place characterized by volatility, uncertainty, complexity and ambiguity. Using evidence from theory and research, the chapters offer a ground for the work of head and heart that is coaching.

Coaching, as Wildflower (this work) notes, is a relatively young field of practice. The original concept was put forward at the First Evidence-Based Coaching Conference in 2003, describing "executive, personal and life coaching that goes beyond adaptation of the popular self-help or personal development genre, is purposefully grounded in the behavioral and social sciences, and is unequivocally based on up-to-date scientific knowledge" (Cavanagh, 2005, p. v). The authors whose papers appear in this monograph act in the spirit of the original concept and offer a substantive set of examples of scholarship married to practice. Collectively, these papers provide a glimpse of a next-generation, post-modern consideration of coaching as a professional field. As the field and as practitioners have evolved and matured, coaching practice has moved beyond operationalizing a single theoretical or proprietary model to encompass integrative, multi-theoretical, evidence-based approaches in coaching practice. Research approaches, too, have expanded from descriptive case studies or positivist quantitative measures to include qualitative, post-modern methods, consistent with an increasing emphasis on phenomenological considerations of both client and coach experiences.

In operationalizing the evidence bases of theory and practice, the authors examine coaching using System 2 thinking: "attention to the effortful activities...including complex computations. The operations of System 2 are often associated with the subjective experience of agency, choice and concentration" (Kahneman, 2011, p. 5). In this chapter, I offer a perspective on what these papers suggest for the evolution of coaching practice; implications for coaches and the education and development of coaches; and the potential of theory-based coaching and phenomenological research to enrich and contribute to the development of the field.

Evolving Perspectives on Coaching: Systemic and Complex

One current prevalent in the coaching literature points to the increasing complexity of the world in general and, more specifically, the world in which coaches and their clients operate. Hellborn (2018, p. 113) states "more speed, more complexity, more interdependency- the world around our organizations is changing in radical and unprecedented ways." Kovacs and Corrie (2017) underscore the non-linear nature of the work and coaching environment and the need for coaching practitioners to have models, principles and abilities to think and respond systemically. In addition to the complexity of organizational contexts, the coaching literature is also recognizing the complexity of each individual client as suggested in second wave positive psychology and coaching the shadow (Gourov, D. & Lomas, T., 2019), and the dynamic tension between head and heart. (Viorela Pop, G. & van Nieuwerburgh, C., 2019)

Harrison, Burke and Batool's chapters all implicitly or explicitly acknowledge the influence of increasingly complex organizational environments and each offers principles and practices which can influence change. The chapters by Ostrowski and McAlpine examine the interplay of individual and group characteristics to increase coach's awareness of the synergies and psychodynamics in play within group settings.

Harrison brings to the foreground how the complexities of context and personality foster abrasive leadership behaviors. Her study of the causes of abrasive leadership behaviors, factors that precipitated abrasive events and factors that contributed to shifts in leaders' behaviors provide a continuum graph illustrating the intersection of emotional arousal and abrasive behaviors as an abrasive leadership experience unfolds. Harrison identifies antecedents as well as contextual and personality factors which create a "perfect storm" which gives rise to abrasive behaviors. She argues that given the systemic nature of abrasive leadership, coaching should address both the individual and the organization. Effective coaching also addresses both the external behaviors and the coachee's internal processes: assumptions, fears, values, and beliefs. This represents a more holistic and contextual perspective and adds the complexity of system and individual synergies for the coach's consideration.

Systemic complexity applies to all organizations, as shown in Burke's study of school systems. In her chapter, Burke surfaces aspects of educational systems as organizations where cultural, socio-economic and demographic features maintain ineffective and deeply entrenched organizational systems and proposes a model of coaching which reinforces the synergy of theory, research, and practice as a means of systemic change. Her findings indicate that a multidisciplinary, multifaceted approach to coaching can support leaders to unlock hidden organizational potential by surfacing institutionalized systemic barriers which suppress dissent and create a culture of fear. The transformative coaching approach proposed by Burke approaches fear as "an opportunity for practicing a virtue.... higher level thinking." This latter observation, especially, introduces a new and perhaps counterintuitive position for the coach in a field which has traditionally been weighted toward facilitating problem-solving.

Batool argues that complex environments require complexity in thinking. Her chapter positions coaching as a learning experience, using the term "neuromindfulness" to describe a state of mind that results from making mental models explicit, helping to reframe boundaries, perceive and embrace both sides of a paradox and find synergies and relationships in complex systems. She argues these are essential leadership skills for a VUCA environment.

Ostrowski's chapter explores the complex dynamics of coaching groups of unaffiliated individuals, recognizing both the complexity of the individual participants and the synergy inherent in group dynamics. Ostrowski extends understanding of relational dynamics beyond coach-client dyads and approaches the "complex social processes that shape learning and change in groups' dynamics." He identifies the background conditions that set the stage for effective group learning and change. McAlpine's study of women working in a male-dominated industry exemplifies the conflicts and tensions inherent in the modern workplace. Her findings surface competing tensions between desire for an inclusive culture and behaviors guided by self-censoring and avoidance; resolving tensions involves alignment between espoused values and values in action. Robertson offers a model of coaching and set of strategies to support clients to explicitly consider the organizational norms and values, alignment with the individual's goals and values, and the potential to catalyze transformative cultural shifts.

Responding to complex environments and individuals, several chapters offer integrative, multi-disciplinary coaching models and strategies. These models explicitly address the whole person of both participants in the coaching dialogue at deeper and more integrated levels. The updated Core Competency Model recently published by the International Coaching Federation incorporates new elements which address the importance of cultural, systemic and contextual awareness. This awareness refers to both the client and the coach. Both the original and updated ICF Core Competencies (Core Competencies, 2019) specifically set an expectation for exploration of the whole person. An addition in the updated version also includes standards for the coach's embodiment of "a coaching mindset", evidenced by awareness of context and culture on self and others, use of intuition and emotional self-regulation.

Implicitly, this emphasis on the coach's embodiment requires evidence of coach-client interactions that are grounded in theories and models which specifically encompass coach-client dynamics, coach presence and self-awareness and depth of engagement. The basis and principles of embodiment are considered through a multi-disciplinary lens in the chapters by Eunkeong, Marlatt and Bentz, Norwood, Nelson, and Potter.

Eunkeong Yu brings together elements of neuroscience, emotional and social intelligence and research on resonance, to offer a model of intersubjectivity which fosters deeper alignment and resonance between coach and client. Yu links intersubjectivity and intercultural competence and describes the experiences of intersubjectivity and positions as a conscious choice on the part of the coach. In making this link between intersubjectivity and intercultural competence, Yu also offers a path consistent with the updated core competency model which specifies the coach's sensitivity "to client's identity, environment, experiences, values and beliefs" and "aware of and open to the influence of context and culture on self and others" (Core Competencies, 2019). Additionally, Yu Identifies the elements in creating intersubjectivity: foundations which included embracing uncertainty, course, trust in self, other, and process and bridging which includes intention and attention.

Similarly, Marlatt and Bentz integrate somatic psychology, lifeworld phenomenology, neuroscience and insights from yoga and Vedanta to offer a model that engages and integrates body, mind and spirit. The "being" of coach and client becomes the instrument of change. "Coaching from a somatic and phenomenological foundation acknowledges being as the primary instrument of change..." Their interdisciplinary model utilizes specific techniques of bracketing (holding theory, practice and prejudices aside); horizontalization (equalizing elements of a situation to view from a distance perspective); imaginative variation. The qualities and abilities of a phenomenological coach include the ability to transcend the everyday reality of lived experience, seek common understanding, connect body, mind and soul. These coaches must be able to embrace embodied consciousness, authenticity and wonderment; look beyond the taken for granted, construct lifeworlds through patterns of communication. The authors offer a framework for the when and how of coach interventions emerging from the in the moment experience- a practice aligned with Schon's (1983) concept of "reflection-in-action."

Somatics appears again in the chapter by Nelson et al., Their model incorporates the embodiment of four evidence based coaching techniques-metaphors and somatic resonance, metaphor and movement, life story, and archetypal imagery- fosters more divergent thinking. In particular, Nelson argues, "metaphor and somatic resonance prompts a coach to create an environment free of the coach's preconceived notions of what might be best for the client," creating space for clients to visualize feelings in their own body.

Norwood, complementing Burke's chapter, cites a Chinese proverb-"theory without practice is foolish; practice without theory is dangerous." Based on interviews, Norwood proposes that a coach is an embodiment of her philosophy and theory of change, what Norwood defines as "their way of being" that is consistent with the discipline of coaching. This encompasses a coach's way of knowing and multiple ways of empowering coachees to access their own deeper wisdom. Norwood's concepts are resonant with Yu's concepts of intersubjectivity and intercultural sensitivity. By developing their ability to function at higher conceptual levels, coaches and coachees "hold transformative possibilities". Positioning the coach as a shape-shifter, Norwood identifies several ways of being which can be instruments of client transformation: detective coach, awakener coach, shaman coach, muse coach.

Potter's study of coach transformation brings an educator's eye to the transformative potential of learning to become a coach with an eye to integrative development-"increasingly complex, nuanced and flexible ways of thinking and meaning making." Her study is informed by theories of adult learning, adult development, cognitive complexity, transformative and experiential learning and learning dialectics and combined to form a model of coach preparation in coaching dialectics. Specifically, her chapter offers insight into the learning structures and processes which foster integrative development of coaches, educating coaching professionals better equipped to engage in the complex choreography of coaching.

Beyond the personal and interpersonal, complex coaching requires more complex models and theoretical underpinnings to support appropriate coaching responses to multi-faceted and multi-dimensional situations and individuals. In addition to specifically addressing coaching in VUCA environments, several chapters offer models of coaching which integrate theories and principles from diverse disciplines. The environments described in the chapters noted above are non-linear; therefore, the coach must have a significant base of knowledge and a high degree of cognitive complexity in order to make informed judgements.

Bridging models of theory and interpersonal dynamics, Clancy and Binkert's model draws on Appreciative Inquiry and existential beliefs to demonstrate how theory influences who coaches, thereby influencing how they coach. The authors' exploration of the "who" of the coach suggests how beliefs affect perspective and choice in three areas: how one defines "self"; how one defines "life in motion"; how one understands "the movement of meaning-making". The chapter offers a Quantum Based Coaching Concept of Self, encompassing complexity of thinking and perspective. The authors reinforce the relevance and importance of coaches engaging in self-work and they present nine clusters, in three groups, which open "new existential beliefs about human change".

In addressing the distinctions in relationships and relational dynamics in working with an unaffiliated group, as differing from a team Ostrowski positions coaching with an unaffiliated group as a collaborative learning process." His dynamic systemic approach incorporates understanding and elements of group counseling, group psychotherapy, and group analytic theory. Coaches facilitating entrepreneurial learning need to be able to create the background conditions essential to successful group work with respect to the social environment of the group and the social processes at work. Social environment encompasses cohesiveness and commonality; social processes incorporate social support, exchange, and accountability.

Minski utilizes five theory-based strategies for enhancing self-efficacy drawn from appreciative inquiry, adaptive leadership, social cognitive theory, adult learning theory and change theory. She identifies specific strategies associated with each of the five theories integrated into her model. In addition to demonstrating the value of increased self-efficacy on client goals and attainment, Minksi notes the influence of coach's self-efficacy, placing increased self-efficacy at the "threshold of change" and concomitantly implying a need to understand the continuum of readiness for change.

Harking back to the coaching ancestors profiled in Wildflower's chapter, it is useful to note that these theories, models, philosophies and practices remain relevant. However, these foundational models developed primarily as a means of cultivating and developing individuals in one to one relationships. There is significant emphasis on self-realization, self-actualization, wholeness and the centrality of a supportive relationship. As all of these chapters make clear, in non-linear systems, it is essential for coaches to have interdisciplinary models and perspectives as well as the ability to hold both systemic and individual dynamics in the space of the coaching conversation. The greater implications for the field of coaching include the recognition that more complex models of coaching are needed as coaching objectives expand to address both individual and systemic transformations.

These chapters together offer a vision of twenty-first century coaching that may be characterized as relational, experiential, reflexive and dynamic. The updated competencies of the International Coaching Federation, while characterizing competencies as coach behaviors, indirectly set expectations for a degree of maturity and cognitive complexity that serve as the basis for the coach's ability to responsively apply knowledge and utilize skills. The competency standards of the European Mentoring and Coaching Council more explicitly differentiates levels of coach competency with consideration of coach's familiarity with and use of theory, diverse models and on-going professional development that includes supervision and reflection (European Mentoring and Coaching Council, 2015). The evolution of the coaching discipline invites evolution in the education and on-going development of coaching practitioners.

Implications for Coaches and the Education and Development of Coaches

It is worthwhile to note that the chapters in this monograph were written well in advance of the release of the Updated ICF Core Competencies. I would argue that the authors' academic and scholarly engagement with coaching theory, coupled with practice and research, places them in the forefront of the next wave of coaching as a professional discipline. Next generation coaches require next generation abilities to complement theoretical and technical knowledge. Beyond such knowledge, however, lies the development of ethical maturity and the capacity for professional judgement. Ethical maturity is essential if coaches are to work effectively in complex environments. Such maturity requires the ability to reflect and learn from experiences; use logic and reason to weigh information; and be aware of the impact of our own emotions and feelings (Carroll, M. & Shaw, E., 2013).

As Lane (2017) observed, there is continuing debate in the coaching literature about competence and capability in coach education. The current standard in most coach education is competence based, with

427

a focus on the cultivation of coach behaviors consistent with the ICF competencies or competency standards of similar certification agencies. The ability to skillfully engage with a client intersubjectively, to explore somatically, to coach from one's own "way of being" cannot be cultivated solely through a structured, didactic form of learning. The state of embodying one's own values, philosophy and theory of change may seem accessible to understanding but it is, in fact, exceedingly difficult to enter and maintain.

The recommendations of many of the authors in this book, however, point to a greater consideration of coach capabilities as the core focus of coach preparation and on-going development. A capability framework would take a more holistic perspective and would encourage diverse coaching styles rather than alignment with a prescribed process; cultivate coach in alignment with coach's values and identities; and provide a more contextual and multidimensional view on quality of practice (Bachkirova, T. & Lawton Smith, C.M., 2015). The recommendations by the authors of these chapters point toward a capability approach to foundational and on-going development of coaches.

Clancy and Binkert propose that, from a quantum perspective, *Self as Instrument* is holographic: i.e. the coach has influence and is influenced in "a shared, intimate embodied presence with their clients." The coach's values and existential beliefs about human change influence their behaviors. Within this framework, the authors outline nine clusters which may be viewed as "way of being" competencies: values cluster, affiliative/emotional cluster, character cluster, cognitive cluster, skills cluster, courage cluster, self-work cluster, self-management cluster, continuous growth cluster. Unlike the more familiar competency standards, these clusters merge the coach's inner qualities and outer behaviors as indicators of coach maturity.

Yu's findings identify specific capacities essential to intersubjective experience: embracing uncertainty, courage, trust in self, other and processes; complete investment and intentional attention on the

428

interaction in the moment. It is a state of deep presence that transcends self and other. Nelson's "wise mind-body" model activates the physical and emotional bodies in a creative and responsive flow that liberates the client's life narrative.

Coaches in Norwood's study coached with body, mind and spirit, integrating somatic, cognitive and emotional elements and principles in a relationship bound by deep trust in the coachee's abilities and capacities. Norwood advises that "coaches who aspire to usher in deep change must, first and foremost, reinvent themselves through on-going internal work, to investigate personal assumptions and potential self-deception.

Potter issues a call for a theoretical foundation of knowledge as an integral aspect of coach education, coupled with experiential learning cycles that incorporate attention to experience, conceptualization, reflection and action. Theory, practice, and reflective learning are essential as synergistic elements of coach development. While coach may move a client through the client's experiential learning cycle, it is equally essential for the coach to move herself through her own experiential learning cycle. Coach preparation programs would do well to consider how best to incorporate six key elements of transformative learning: individual experience, critical reflection, dialogue, holistic orientation, awareness of context and authentic relationships.

Minski's study strengthens the case for an evidence-based approach to coaching and affirms that "coach training schools that provide strategies and tools consistently aligned with theory will provide the best practices in executive coaching." Minski also recommends that ICF accreditation highlight theory-based strategies.

As Potter notes in her chapter, studies on coach education and development are rare. The few that exist point to the relevance of an integrative developmental perspective in advancing coaches' integrative own development. Findings from studies show increased mindfulness, reflexivity, metacognition, self-awareness, reflective learning, improved decision making. Given those findings, the chapters in this book have implications not only for the content of coach education but for the design and delivery of the learning experience. As coaching models become more multi-disciplinary, coach education will need to extend beyond foundational theories to incorporate work from a number of related disciplines such as adult learning and development, somatics, neuroscience, and systems theory. Didactic training formats do little to engage coaches in training as developing professionals. A well-formed coach education should be designed to support the learner through iterative cycles of reflective and experiential learning and encourage learners to design and carry out their own work in cultivating body and spirit along with mind.

Beyond formal coach education, coaches must commit to a rigorous and sustained practice of reflective learning, both self-directed and in consultation with other professionals. The European Mentoring and Coaching Council considers participation in supervision with a credentialed coaching supervisor as essential for designation as a Senior or Master Practitioner. Coaching supervision provides a safe and reflective space for practitioners to consider and learn from their experiences, a place where coaches can step back from the VUCA environment and untangle the knots of complex engagements. A qualified coaching supervisor can support a coach in becoming aware of his own unconscious influences, mental models and relational patterns. (Birch, 2019) Supervision also offers coaches a space in which to experiment and play with new ideas and creative approaches to their coaching work. McAnally et al. in particular, cite studies demonstrating the impact of supervision. Among the 1280 respondents to their global study, 44% indicated that supervision was instrumental in helping the coaches understand systemic factors affecting a situation. Forty percent of respondents indicated that supervision was helpful in addressing ethical concerns. Their study also explored the range of situations that coaches bring to supervision, encompassing both client/ organizational situations and personal issues affecting their abilities to coach or respond effectively.

To support a post-modern practice of coach education and development organizations which set standards for the certification of coaches and coach education programs need to identify and articulate competencies which reflect the necessary knowledge of systems and system dynamics, as well as appropriate indicators of the maturity of cognitive and emotional development necessary for coaches to effectively work in complex and ambiguous environments.

Implications for Coaching Research

Coaching related research has come a long way from the earliest publications which documented the impact of sales training, manager training and psychological interventions with executives. Within the 93 articles, empirical studies and dissertations on coaching that were published between 1937 and 1999, there remained a heavy emphasis on training, management development and coaching for behavioral change. Of the 156 outcome studies published since 1980 were 104 case studies, 36 within-subject studies and 16 between-subject studies (Grant, 2009). These earliest publications were carried out following the norms and standards for research reporting set out by the American Psychological Association (APA).

In 2018, the APA released a document described as a "historical moment-the first inclusion of qualitative research in APA Style" (Levitt, H.M., Creswell, J.W., Josselson, R., Bamberg, M., Frost, D.M., Suarez-Orozco, C., 2018) The research approaches reflected in this book bring rigorous, post-positivist methods to the fore in deepening our understanding of coaches and coaching. All seven of the chapters documenting coaching research, applied narrative, phenomenological methods to explore the experiences of participants in schools, corporations and personal contexts. There is a persistent theme of transformative learning throughout the chapters and this may be reflected in the methodological orientations of each author. These researchers opened inquiry with an eye toward learning more deeply, transforming current knowledge and real-world experience through the alchemy of dialogue and story. Returning to our friend Alice at the start of this chapter, I see these forms of inquiry as a curiosity of head and heart, firmly grounded in theory and method.

One of the chapters where this connection is most evident is McAlpine's exploration of women in the construction industry. The coach-researcher is not standing apart from the experience. By positioning herself in the framework of an Integral Activist Research Epistemology- i.e. researcher as activist- she uses an integral lens interconnecting four domains: the individual's subjective and objective experiences and group's intersubjective and interobjective worlds. McAlpine's use of narrative methods of data collection and a grounded theory approach to data analysis to improve understanding of women's experiences in construction industry, surfacing structural and behavioral boundaries to women's thriving. Numbers alone could not tell this story as McAlpine and her participants have done.

Norwood and Burke brought in the dimensions of collaboration and complementarity in their approach to studying school transformation at systemic and individual levels. These two chapters may be read as fractals: each containing all of the information of the other, yet viewed in differing degrees of magnification of perspective (whole and part). Fractals are found throughout nature and using this concept as a framework for research opens the door to multiplying the potential usefulness of a single study.

Transformative learning is also at the heart of the studies presented by Ostrowski, Yu, and Potter. Yu's phenomenological approach, incorporating iterative data gathering and participant validation, is consistent with his core concept of intersubjectivity and provides a framework for identifying core elements of an abstraction relevant to the issue of coach and client's way of being. I am intrigued by his linking intersubjectivity and intercultural competence. Given the clarity of his findings on the causes and conditions of intersubjective states, it suggests to me that intersubjectivity may be appropriate as an advanced coaching competence. Ostrowski chose a narrative approach as a means of generating knowledge about the specific phenomenon of coaching with unaffiliated groups. Potter's concluding remarks specifically recommend phenomenological and longitudinal studies of coach education. Given the paucity of extant studies on this matter, the process of coach transformation and the journey from novice to mastery is an area in dire need of exploration.

In preparing to write this section of the current chapter, I had recourse to a much earlier article on the topic of coaching-related research (Campone, Riding the waves: A quantum framework for coaching-related research, 2005). In that paper, I cited the physicist Werner Heisenberg who, with his peers, introduced the Uncertainty Principle and upended the paradigm of Newtonian science. The Uncertainty Principle sets up a relationship between observer and observed by introducing the element of the observer's choice of where and how to focus attention. Heisenberg demonstrated that the act of observation changes what's being observed, thereby effecting a significant shift in the practice of science. Centuries of foundational research in physics preceded the Uncertainty Principle and related quantum principles. The nature of physics itself is such that it lends itself to abstract representation using equations. This human endeavor known as coaching has its own Uncertainty Principle. Human beings are complex and each of us is unique. In the course of a coaching engagement, multiple constellations are in motion: the coach's being and all that entails, the client's being and all that entails and the situations and contexts within and surrounding the conversations. While theories and research may guide us in choosing what we wish to observe and the position we assume in observing it, it is essential that we recognize the limitations in doing so. Scholarly practitioners in coaching are still surfacing and exploring all of the constituent particles of this field and practice. Using narrative and phenomenological methods allows the explorer to stand in a place of not knowing, of uncertainty, and to engage in observing with the faculties of mind, heart and body.

I once compared the experience of writing about coaching research

433

with trying to describe the color blue: "everyone agrees it exists but each person experiences it somewhat differently" (Campone, 2008). If violet represents where light is first visible on the spectrum, blue, being next to violet, has a slightly longer wavelength, moving toward the heat of red. The earliest generations of coaching related research may be considered the violet phase. The studies and articles offered in this monograph are in the blue trending toward red spectrum as the complexities of coaches and coaching are made more evident. Studies such as these are aligned with the humanistic roots of coaching. It strikes me that applying Kahneman's System 2 is inherent in phenomenological research and appropriate to the continuing evolution of coaching's knowledge base.

About the Author

Francine Campone, EdD, MCC, coaches mature professionals making mid-life and mid-career transitions, including leaders in the corporate, education and nonprofit sectors. She is a PCC and MCC assessor for the ICF and an approved ICF Mentor for those certifications. Francine holds a Diploma in Coaching Supervision and offers supervision for coaches seeking to deepen their learning and skills. Dr. Campone's decades of work in coach education and development include serving as Director of Fielding University's Evidence-Based Coaching certificate program for twelve years and as a founding faculty member of the coaching program at the University of Texas at Dallas. Her recent publications include a case study on the coaching/psychotherapy boundary; the impact of life events on coaches and their coaching; relational flow; and book chapters on adult learning theories in coaching, reflective learning for coaches, coaching in the adult workplace and trends in coaching related research. Dr. Campone co-chaired the review process and co-edited the Proceedings of the ICF Research Symposium in 2004, 2005 and 2006. She hosted the ICF Research Special Interest Group for four years and was chair of the ICF Research Committee. She is reached at francine@reinventinglife.net.

References

Bachkirova, T. & Lawton Smith, C.M. (2015). From competencies to capabilities in the assessment and accreditation of coaches. *International Journal of Evidence-Based Coaching and Mentoring*, 13(2), 123-138.

Birch, J. &. (Ed.). (2019). *Coaching Supervision: Advancing practice, changing landscapes*. New York, NY: Routledge.

Campone, F. (2005). Riding the waves: A quantum framework for coaching-related research. *Proceedings of the Third International Coach Federation Coaching Research Symposium* (pp. 152-160). The International Coach Federation.

Campone, F. (2008). Connecting the Dots: Coaching Research-Past, Present and Future. In D. B. David Drake (Ed.), *The Philosophy and Practice of Coaching* (pp. 91-105). Chichester, UK: John Wiley & Sons.

Carroll, L. (1865). *Alice's Adventures in Wonderland*.

Carroll, M. & Shaw, E. (2013). *Ethical Maturity in the Helping Professions*. London: Jessica Kingsley.

Cavanagh, M. G. (Ed.). (2005). Evidence-Based Coaching: Theory, research and practice from the behavioral sciences. *Evidence-Based Coaching: Theory, research and practice from the behavioral sciences*. 1, p. v. Bowen Hills Qld Australia: Australian Academic Press.

Core Competencies. (2019). Retrieved February 4, 2020 from International Coach Federation: https://coachfederation.org/core-competencies

European Mentoring and Coaching Council. (2015). Retrieved January, 2020 from https://www.emccouncil.org/quality/supervision/competences/

Gourov, D. & Lomas, T. (2019). It's about wholeness. I love my awesomeness and I love my flawsomeness. *The Coaching Psychologist*, 21(2), 11-21.

Grant, A. (2009). Grant, A.M. (2009) *Workplace, Executive and Life Coaching: An Annotated Bibliography from the Behavioural Science and Business Literature (May 2009), Coaching Psychology Unit, University of Sydney, Australia*. University of Sydney, Coaching Psychology , Sydney.

Hellborn, K. (2018). Organizational Coaching- the New Frontline of Coaching. *EMCC Mentoring, Coaching and Supervision Research Conference* (pp. 113-124). Chester: European Mentoring and Coaching Council.

Kahneman, D. (2011). *Thinking Fast and Slow* (digital ed.). Farrar, Strauss and Giroux.

Kovacs, L.C. & Corrie, S. (2017). Executive Coaching in an era of complexity. *International Coaching Psychology Review*, 12(2), 74-100.

Lane, D. (2017). Trends in Development of Coaches (Education and Training): Is it

Valid, Is it Rigorous and Is it Relevant. In T. S. Bachkirova (Ed.), *The SAGE Handbook of Coaching* (pp. 647-661). Thousand Oaks, CA: SAGE.

Levitt, H.M., Creswell, J.W., Josselson, R., Bamberg, M., Frost, D.M., Suarez-Orozco, C. (2018). Journal Article Reporting Standards for Qualitative Primary, Qualitative Meta-Analytic, and Mix Methods Research in Psychology: The APA Publications and Communications Board Task Force Report. *American Psychologist,* 73(1), 26-46.

Viorela Pop, G. & van Nieuwerburgh, C. (2019). Listening to your heart or head? An Interpretive Phenomenological analysis of how people experienced making good career decisions. *International Coaching Psychology Review,* 14(2), 84-96.

About Fielding Graduate University

Fielding Graduate University, headquartered in Santa Barbara, CA, was founded in 1974, and celebrated its 45th anniversary in 2019. Fielding is an accredited, nonprofit leader in blended graduate education, combining face-to-face and online learning. Its curriculum offers quality master's and doctoral degrees for professionals and academics around the world. Fielding's faculty members represent a wide spectrum of scholarship and practice in the fields of educational leadership, human and organizational development, and clinical and media psychology. Fielding's faculty serves as mentors and guides to self-directed students who use their skills and professional experience to become powerful, socially responsible leaders in their communities, workplaces, and society. For more information, please visit Fielding online at www.fielding.edu.

Made in United States
Troutdale, OR
01/26/2024

17181534R00268